PRIMARY TEACHER SOLU1

This timely book offers a raw critique of the current educational issues and debates, alongside 'teacher hacks' to provide teachers, trainee teachers and educators with a plethora of stimulating material to ignite curiosity, maintain passion and culture creativity in the classroom.

Made in partnership with academics and primary school teachers working on the frontline from around the globe, this book is threaded with honest practitioner voices as the big educational issues are boiled down and explored. Chapters cover day-to-day organisation such as planning, subject knowledge, setting homework and behaviour management strategies, right through to considering how we can best support children's mental health and staff well-being. As well as including critical questions to encourage reflection throughout, the book offers insights into meaningful experiences such as:

- Teaching overseas
- Taking on responsibility roles in schools
- Considering how teachers can become educational researchers for transformative change
- Engaging with parents and carers
- Deploying teaching assistants

Whether trainee teachers, early career teachers or established practitioners, this book provides insight into trialled tips and techniques for shaping pedagogy in the classroom. A modern, well-resourced guide as we emerge from the global COVID-19 pandemic.

Poppy Gibson is a senior lecturer in education and currently leads both the three-year BA (Hons) Primary Education Studies degree and the innovative Blended Accelerated BA (Hons) Primary Education Studies degree at Anglia Ruskin University (Essex). Poppy's key research interests focus on supporting well-being and mental health.

Robert Morgan is a member of the National Association of Primary Education (NAPE). He is the editor of its journal 'Primary First'. He is also a senior lecturer at University of Greenwich in primary 'Initial Teacher Training'. Robert's key research interests concern the purpose of education and the deployment of teaching assistants.

Ashley Brett is a senior lecturer at University of Greenwich in primary 'Initial Teacher Training'. Ashley's key research interests focus on how schools adapted their strategies to support learning in the home during the COVID-19 pandemic, and teachers engaging with action research.

PRIMARY TEACHER SOLUTIONS

Ready Pedagogy and Inspirational Ideas

Poppy Gibson, Robert Morgan and Ashley Brett

LONDON AND NEW YORK

Designed cover image: © Getty Images

First published 2024
by Routledge
4 Park Square, Milton Park, Abingdon, Oxon OX14 4RN

and by Routledge
605 Third Avenue, New York, NY 10158

Routledge is an imprint of the Taylor & Francis Group, an informa business

© 2024 Poppy Gibson, Robert Morgan and Ashley Brett

The right of Poppy Gibson, Robert Morgan and Ashley Brett to be identified as authors of this work has been asserted in accordance with sections 77 and 78 of the Copyright, Designs and Patents Act 1988.

All rights reserved. No part of this book may be reprinted or reproduced or utilised in any form or by any electronic, mechanical, or other means, now known or hereafter invented, including photocopying and recording, or in any information storage or retrieval system, without permission in writing from the publishers.

Trademark notice: Product or corporate names may be trademarks or registered trademarks, and are used only for identification and explanation without intent to infringe.

British Library Cataloguing-in-Publication Data
A catalogue record for this book is available from the British Library

ISBN: 978-1-032-11027-1 (hbk)
ISBN: 978-1-032-11028-8 (pbk)
ISBN: 978-1-003-21809-8 (ebk)

DOI: 10.4324/9781003218098

Typeset in Interstate
by KnowledgeWorks Global Ltd.

*In memory of Henry Aylett who inspired so many.
As Henry himself told us:*

'Find out about people: take an interest in their lives; lift them up through encouragement and celebration of success; help and support them when you have the capacity to do so.'

You can read Henry's full contribution in Chapter 17.

This book is dedicated to all the teachers past, present and future who are inspiring change and making a difference.

Poppy, Robert and Ashley

CONTENTS

Contributors   ix

1 Introduction   1
2 Classroom organisation   3
3 Behaviour management   13
4 Planning   29
5 Subject knowledge and pedagogy   54
6 Maths anxiety in the classroom   81
7 Formative assessment   89
8 Engaging with parents and carers: Promoting the home-school partnership   111
9 Teaching assistants   122
10 Fundamental British values: What is British about them?   134
11 The wider curriculum   151
12 Career progression and further study   168
13 The power of actioning action research: Becoming an education researcher   192
14 Teaching overseas   221
15 Developing parent partnerships after COVID-19 lockdowns: Giving a positive spin to the effects of the pandemic   245

16	**Supporting pupils' well-being**	260
17	**Self-care and well-being for staff**	276
18	**Homework**	293

| | *Index* | 307 |

CONTRIBUTORS

Oksana Agamova
PhD Student
London, England

Leeza Ahmed
Early Career Teacher
Colchester, England

Sara Alston
Consultant and Trainer: SEA Inclusion & Safeguarding
Surrey, UK

Amanda Araceli Alejandre
M.Ed., 8th Grade Science Teacher
Morris Middle School
Houston, Texas

Kelly Austen
Teacher
Isle of Sheppey, Scotland

Henry Aylett
Key Stage 2 Leader
Worcester Park, England

Chris Ball
Headteacher
Rangefield Primary School
London, England

Chris Barnes
Prep schoolteacher
Manchester, England

Elizah Barnes
Qualified Primary Teacher and Trainee Educational Psychologist
West Midlands, UK

Alex Baxendale
PhD Student and Psychology Tutor
Bangor University
Bangor, Wales

Vidya Bellur
Dip Hyp, GQHP, CNHC; Therapeutic Coach and Mentor; Anxiety and Stress Expert: Vivid Outcomes
Redhill/Reigate, England

Belinda Benatar-Kotler
SEN Teacher
Zevulun, Israel

Joanne Bowser-Angermann
Associate Professor of Applied Teaching and Learning
Anglia Ruskin University
Chelmsford, England

Ashley Brett
Senior Lecturer in primary Initial Teacher Education
University of Greenwich
London, England

Contributors

Paul Brown
Head Teacher
Bransgore Church of England
 Primary School
Christchurch, England

Amber Browne
MSc Psychology student
London, England

Claire Browning
Nursery Manager
Purple Lion Day Nursey
Benfleet, Essex, UK

John Bullen
New Close Primary, Warminster
Wiltshire, UK

Nathan Burns
Head of Maths
Derbyshire Secondary School
Derby, England

Sally Burns
Director
The Values and Visions Foundation
(Registered charity (CIO) number 1180605)
London, England

Amy Burrows
Primary Education studies graduate
Anglia Ruskin University
Essex, England

Olly Cakebread
Primary Teacher
Bexleyheath, England

Sven Carrington
Headteacher
BISR Tabuk Campus
Tabuk, Saudi Arabia

Jayne Carter
School Effectiveness Advisor
Lincoln Anglican Academy Trust
Lincoln, England

Mark Carter-Tufnell
Headteacher
St Osyth CoE Primary School
and
Mistley Norman CoE Primary School
Manningtree, England

Ella Catley
Student Teacher
The Cathedral School
Chelmsford, Essex, England

Craig Chaplin
Assistant Head and Maths Lead
Primary Special School for Pupils with
 SEMH Needs
Lincoln, England

Katherine Childs
Head of English
Wey Valley Academy
Weymouth, England

Rebecca Clarkson
Senior Lecturer in Primary Education
Anglia Ruskin University
Chelmsford, England

Laura Colam
Primary School Teacher
Dogsthorpe Academy
Peterborough, UK

Robert Coyle
EAL Adviser and Former Primary
Teacher
Norfolk, UK

Mark Cratchley
English Teacher
Cheltenham Bournside School
Cheltenham, England

Sam Crome
Deputy Headteacher and
 Executive Coach
London, England

Ami Crowther
Researcher
Anglia Ruskin University
Manchester, England

Jessica Crumlish
Teacher
Windsor-Essex Catholic District School Board
Ontario, Canada

Sarah Cummins
Lecturer in School of Education
Leeds Trinity University
Leeds, West Yorkshire, UK

Kate Coulson
National Teaching Fellow, Head of Learning and Teaching Enhancement
University of Northampton
Northampton, England

Maddie Coulson
Secondary school pupil

Hayley Danter
Representative for the Showmen Community
Future 4 Fairgrounds
Hunstanton, Norfolk, UK

Sue Davidowitz
SEN Teacher
Zevulun, Israel

Daniel Davies
Assistant Headteacher
Woodland Academy Trust
London, England

Kate Davies
Headteacher
The Pines School
Bracknell, England

Charlotte Day
Year 3 Teacher
Swanley, Kent, UK

Suzie Dick
Lecturer in Education
Queen Margaret University
Edinburgh, Scotland

Graham Dickie
Headteacher
Kilchrenan Primary School
Taynuilt, Scotland

Leah Downie
Primary School Teacher
Cardiff, Wales

Sam Durrant
Online Private English Tutor
Chester, England

Becky Ellery
Mathematics Lead
Hook Lane Primary School
London, England

Gemma Fitzsimons
Qualified Teacher
Broxbourne, England

Andrew Flowerdew
Technology Strategist
L.E.A.D IT Services
Derby, England

Matthew Flynn
History Leader, Chartered Teacher of History
Ryders Hayes School
Walsall, England

Harry Garland
Early Career Teacher
Maidstone, England

Terri Gibson-License
Primary Education studies graduate
Anglia Ruskin University
Essex, England

Thomas Godfrey-Faussett
Research Assistant and DPhil Candidate
University of Oxford
Oxford, England

xii *Contributors*

David Goodwin
Assistant Principal
Author and Illustrator of Educational Ideas
Grimsby, England

Jess Gosling
International Early Years Teacher
Warsaw, Poland

Clare Greene
Headteacher
St. Michael's Junior Church School
Bath, NE Somerset, UK

Simone Hackett
Senior Lecturer and Researcher
Department of Physical Education Teacher Training
The Hague University of Applied Sciences
The Netherlands

Paul Hamilton
Teaching Fellow in History Education
Edinburgh University
Glasgow, Scotland

Evo Hannan
Founder
Innovation X
London, England

Suus-Anna Harskamp
Doctoral student
The Ossigeno,
London, UK

Andrew Hartshorn
Head of Food Preparation & Nutrition, Product Design and Engineering
Finham Park 2
Coventry, England

Lee Hill
Headteacher
Howden Junior School
Howden, East Yorkshire, UK

Nicola Hill
Representative of the Showmen Community
Future 4 Fairgrounds
Hunstanton, Norfolk, UK

Steve Hoey
PhD candidate researching school exclusion
University of Hull
Hull, England

Lynsey Hunter
Senior Lecturer
Sheffield Hallam University
Sheffield, England

Stephanie Hunter
Class Teacher
Springfield Primary School
Chelmsford, UK

Vikki Hurst
Primary School Teacher
Greater Manchester, UK

Andrew Jack
Probationer/Student Regent
PTC Science
St. Kentigern's Academy
Blackburn, Scotland

Madeeha Kashif
Early Career Teacher
Colchester, England

Jasmine Kay-Moyle
Assistant Headteacher and School of Sanctuary Leader
Suffolk
Suffolk, England

Rachel Kerridge
Teacher
Wentworth Primary School (Academy)
Kent, England

Agnes Kosek
Lecturer for BA Hons in Child and Educational Psychology
Maidstone, England

Jessie Krefting
Educator
Spruce Grove, Alberta, Canada

Georgeanne Lamont
The Values and Visions Foundation
London, England

Stella De Larrabeiti
Mentor Lead
Redbridge Primary School
London, England

Gerard Lavelle
Head of Innovation and Computing
Victory Heights Primary School
Dubai

Mary Leighton
Educational Psychologist
Doncaster, England

Andrew Lloyd
Copywriter
Liverpool John Moores University
Manchester, England

Emma Longley
Programme Lead PGCert SENCo
University of Greenwich
London, England

Debbie Marlow
English Lead
Thundersley Primary School
Benfleet, Essex, UK

Stephanie Martin
Primary School Teacher
Pinchbeck East Primary Academy
Spalding, England

Steve Martin
Assistant Headteacher
Valley Invicta Primary School
Maidstone, England

Maritza Masiello
Podcaster, Writer and Business Owner
London, UK

Rebecca Massheder-Stuart
Teacher
London, UK

Jake Matthews
Primary Headteacher
Somerset, UK

Jay Maxwell
Coordinator and Learning Support Lead
Assumption College English Program School
Samut Sakhon City, Thailand

Miss May
Primary Teacher
England

Mike McGrother
Teacher and Community Engineer
Stockton on Tees
Durham, England

Karen McNerney
Headteacher
Merchant Taylors Prep School
Rickmansworth, England

Philip Van Mellaerts
PGCE student
Chelmsford, England

Susannah Miles
Nursery Manager
Purple Lion Day Nursery
Essex, UK

Jo Montgomery
Primary Science Specialist
Science Solutions
Cambridge, UK

Ashley Morgan
Masculinities Scholar
Cardiff Metropolitan University
Cardiff, Wales

xiv Contributors

Robert Morgan
Senior Lecturer in Initial Teacher Education
University of Greenwich
London, England

Lou Mycroft
Nomad
Yorkshire, England

Natasha Nechat-Murphy
Teaching Assistant and Primary Education student
Anglia Ruskin University
London, England

Philip Nicholson
Lecturer in Primary Education Studies
University of Suffolk
Suffolk, UK

Charlotte Nohavicka
Teacher Trainee
Colchester, England

Narvenka Noyce
Representative of Showmen Community
Future 4 Fairgrounds
Hunstanton, Norfolk, UK

Annelies Paris
Primary Teacher and YouTube Content Creator as 'Petite Primary'
Dorset, England

John Parkin
Senior Lecturer Practitioner
School of Education and Social Care
Anglia Ruskin University
Chelmsford, UK

Joannie Peak
Representative of Showmen Community
Future 4 Fairgrounds
Hunstanton, Norfolk, UK

Jack Phillips
Primary School Teacher
Rothley CofE Primary Academy
Leicestershire, UK

Oscar Pimlett
Primary Teacher
John Ball Primary School
Lewisham, London, UK

Ian Pugh
Principal
Al Ain Academy
Al Ain, Abu Dhabi

Elise Ramadan
NTP Tutor
Dartford, Kent, UK

Scott Read
Year 1 Specialist Teacher, PSHE/Wellbeing Curriculum Leader--Foundation
Amnuay Silpa School
Bangkok, Thailand

Michael Redmond
Deputy Headteacher (Pastoral)
Bedford Modern Junior School
Bedfordshire, England

Katherine Richardson
Academic Development Consultant
University of Leeds
Leeds, England

Rhiannon Rigby
MA Graduate
Staffordshire University
Stoke on Trent, England

Colleen Roper
Future 4 Fairgrounds
Hunstanton, Norfolk, UK

Joe Rose
Further Education Curriculum Team Leader, Lead IQA and Lecturer
The Sheffield College
Sheffield, England

Saira Saeed
Secondary Leader (SENCO and DSL)
SafeSENCOSaeed
Birmingham, UK

Ted Samaras
Instructional Technology Coach
Franklin Township Public Schools
Somerset, New Jersey

Andrie Savva
Researcher
University of Cambridge
Cambridge, England

Mike Scott
EdD Researcher in Neurodivergence
University of Bournemouth
Dorset, UK

Nyree Scott
Educationalist
Canterbury Christ Church University
Canterbury, Kent, UK

Seraphina Simmons-Bah
Senior Teaching Fellow in Primary Education
University of Greenwich
London, England

Payal Sinha
PGCE Educator
India

Marc Smale
Programme Leader for PGCE Primary Education
University of Wolverhampton
Wolverhampton, England

Sara Spear
Head of School of Management
Anglia Ruskin University
Chelmsford, UK

Natalie Starkey
Pupil Voice Champion
Howden Junior School
East Yorkshire, UK

Susan Strachan
Leader of English
St. Bernadette Catholic Secondary School
Bristol, England

Kate Sturdy
Departmental Lead for Years 5 and 6, KS2 Curriculum Lead
Flintshire, Wales, UK

Stefanie Tinsley
Quality Improvement and Well-being Specialist
Culture of Excellence Ltd
Cheshire, England

Matthew Tragheim
Lecturer in Primary Education
London, England

Allen Tsui
Subject Lead for Computing
Willow Brook Primary School Academy
London, England

Nieky van Veggel
Senior Lecturer in Department of Animal Health
Writtle University College
Chelmsford, England

Cara Veitch
Teacher
Humbie Primary School
Scotland, UK

Paul Wade
SENCO
Lincolnshire, England

Bernice Wall
Representative of the Showmen Community
Future 4 Fairgrounds
Norfolk, UK

Sarah Wall
Senior Lecturer
Anglia Ruskin University
Essex, UK

Polly Ward
Teacher
Manchester, England

Contributors

Bernie Westacott
Maths Consultant – Rickmansworth
Hertfordshire, UK

Lucy Westley
Senior Lecturer in ITT Mathematics and
 PGCE 5-11 Programme Leader
University of Northampton
Northampton, England

Laura Whiteman
Early Career Teacher
Colchester, England

James D. Williams
Director of Student Experience and Senior
 Lecturer in Education
FLS FRSB CSciTeach
Brighton, England

Kate Williams
Social Work Apprentice
Anglia Ruskin University
Essex, England

Michelle Windridge
Lecturer of Education
University College of Birmingham
Birmingham, UK

Jordan Wintle
Senior Lecturer in sport and exercise
University of Gloucestershire
Gloucester, England

Dan Young
i-PEP curriculum and Coaching Manager
Complete Education Solutions
Cheshire, England

1 Introduction

Welcome to primary teacher solutions!

Teaching is one of the most rewarding, exhausting, creative, challenging, and satisfying professions in the world. Sometimes, we all need a little inspiration to continue to develop our teacher toolkit or to consider other angles to our practice.

Whilst the majority of this book's content is written by the three co-authors, all of whom were primary school teachers and now lecturers in primary education, what makes this book so valuable are the voices scattered throughout the chapters. This book offers in-house expertise from over one hundred enthusiastic educators; it's about togetherness, a sense of communal learning and support. This book shares several solutions and lived experiences from practitioners to support other primary educators in their daily practice, offering inspirational ideas to trial in the classroom and beyond.

This book contains 18 chapters, covering day-to-day organisation such as planning, subject knowledge, setting homework and behaviour management strategies, right through to considering how we can support children's mental health and staff well-being. Sections offer insight into experiences such as teaching overseas in a range of countries, taking on responsibility roles in schools and considering how teachers can become educational researchers for transformative change. Engaging with parents and carers and deploying teaching assistants are also covered, offering advice on how to build positive relationships across the board. Schools' responses to COVID-19 are also shared as we continue to teach and learn in our post-pandemic landscape.

Each chapter presents key words, poses critical questions, and contemplates theory in the light of contemporary practice.

This book addresses national issues related to primary education and makes reference to the most current documentation to enable students and practitioners to have access to relevant and recent literature in order to inform their practice.

With the global COVID-19 pandemic, there has been a serious effect on the delivery of teacher training, with most lectures and seminars moving to online, remote learning. With this shift, those lunchtime conversations over coffee, or chats before the lecture begins as students unpick the course material, have been lost. This book, therefore, is more relevant than ever in providing spaces for the reader to digest some of the big educational issues.

DOI: 10.4324/9781003218098-1

Introduction

Whether you are a trainee teacher, an early career teacher or an established practitioner, this book provides insight into trialled tips and techniques for shaping our pedagogy in the classroom. The culmination of many voices from educators all around the globe helps to bring inspiration to our daily practice, offering the opportunity to look at our teaching and learning in fresh ways through the eyes of others. The need for this book is NOW, as trainee teachers and recent primary education graduates grapple with the demands of teaching today.

We hope you enjoy reading this book as much as we all enjoyed writing it.
   Happy teaching!

Poppy, Robert and Ashley

2 Classroom organisation

KEY WORDS
Classroom, organisation, resources, displays, layout, grouping

Contributors within this chapter:
1. Debbie Marlow
2. Ella Catley
3. Gemma Fitzsimons
4. Steve Martin
5. Payal Sinha

Introduction

If the eyes are the window to the soul, perhaps the primary school classroom is the window to the teacher's ethos, values and pedagogical style. Watson (2012) encourages us to question, what does a classroom tell us? An effective teacher is much more than just someone with a good subject knowledge; teachers need a wide and diverse range of tools in their skill set to best engage and support the learners who come into their spaces, learners who all bring with them different interests and learn in different ways. One way that an educator can help their class access the curriculum is through careful consideration not only of the information they need to teach but also through organising the learning environment in such a way that children can have adequate space, appropriate time and relevant resources to facilitate that learning (Dean, 2013).

To avoid burnout and insurmountable workload lists, teacher organisation is key. Primary teachers, although working within the boundaries and policies of the school system, have to be their own manager. Teachers have to set goals and target for each pupil, manage the class, organise the class and provide all resources needed (Handy and Aitken, 2002).

In this chapter, we explore a range of areas linked to class organisation, including management of resources, the use of interactive displays as part of your organisation, pupil grouping and the layout of your room. When your classroom is organised well, it helps to facilitate child-led learning and promotes a positive learning environment. We begin by asking what

DOI: 10.4324/9781003218098-2

4 Classroom organisation

the key elements of classroom organisation involve and go on to find out more about what these elements look like on a practical level in the primary classroom.

The chapter ends with an evaluation of how classroom organisation enables you to balance workload and keep on top of day-to-day teaching in a manageable way.

Classroom organisation

> **Critical question**
>
> What are the key areas to organise in a classroom to foster an inclusive, engaging space?

Many researchers and educators over the years have explored variables in teaching and learning practice that may relate to learner outcomes (Wilks, 1996). The way that a teacher organises the learning environment can be key in fostering a safe and productive space to heighten productivity and engagement; classroom organisation is key. Classroom organisation refers to a wide range of strategies, techniques and areas of the primary classroom and structure. As you read through this chapter, hopefully you will see that the main advice is to get to know your learners and their needs; consider the layout of your room and the management of your resources as a response to these needs. Remember that the personal experiences shared here from educators as well as the author are strategies that have worked in particular microcosms of schools; not all strategies work in every school, and this is where knowing your class is vital.

The handover

Don't underestimate the role of the handover, namely learning from the class's previous teacher (unless your learners are starting school for the first time). Find out which organisation strategies worked well in their previous academic year and don't be afraid to replicate them, or trial your own! Teaching is fluid, and your pedagogy should reflect our own passions and ethos. It is also important to remember how learners respond different to different teachers; think back to when you were at school – which teachers can you remember enjoying lessons with and why? How were your favourites and who were those teachers you found more difficult to relate to? Remember that this may be the same for the children coming into your class; they may respond different to your way of teaching than their past teacher, so also be willing to learn about their educational background, but also give them a new chance to find their feet as they begin a new academic year with you.

Equally, remember the power of the handover as you come towards the end of your academic year with your class. Which information is it essential you make the next teacher aware of, or which parts may be something only relevant to this academic year and are not necessary to pass on? What are the most valuable things about your pupils that you can share with their next teacher to help foster the feelings of community and caring and help their positive relationships to develop?

Seating and groups

Seating is always an interesting question. Some teachers are bound by school policy or rules on seating, whilst others can choose between pairs, rows, groups or the 'horseshoe' seating patterns. Organising seating is important. Tables and chairs are not always easy to move, so thinking about the best seating patterns that work in most lessons is a good idea to reduce furniture-moving on a daily basis. Classroom layout may vary, from a more teacher-initiated learning space (children all facing forward, in rows) or child initiated (children facing each other in groups, and this seating can lend itself to the style of tasks used, i.e. teacher led or child led (Martlew et al., 2011).

But don't just think where the pupils will be sat; what does this seating pattern mean for your flow as a teacher? Can you easily move around the room to access all pupils and speak to them or view their work? How does the seating pattern affect pupils' access to resources in your classroom?

Displays in your classroom

Once the important task of seating is decided, take a look around your room. How much display space do you have? This may be display space on walls or laid out along cupboards or worktops. Imagine you were one of the learners in your class; what is the **classroom** telling you? (Watson, 2012). Good examples of child-centred display spaces include having a clipboard for all children (if you have space!) so they all have a piece of work displayed at any time. Also, a smaller board with perhaps three or four clipboards could be used to pin up and show best practice over a few subjects.

Pupil ability grouping

> ### Critical question
> How should I group the pupils in my class?

One conversation that often has educators on both side of the fences is that of whether we should group our pupils into same ability groups and tables or have the pupils put into mixed ability groupings.

McGillicuddy (2021) warns grouping by ability encourages social and academic hierarchies in primary school. Those in favour of ability groups state that ability-homogeneous classrooms increase the attainment of high-ability pupils without detriment to the attainment of pupils judged to be of lower ability (Boliver and Capsada-Munsech, 2021). Educators against ability groups claim that these groups lead to low-ability pupils doing significantly worse; this ties in with McGillicuddy's findings (2021) above that grouping may lead to 'labelling' and a self-fulfilling prophecy of poorer attainment. Overall, findings suggest that ability grouping in primary schools does more harm than good, at least in relation to pupils' enjoyment of maths (Boliver and Capsada-Munsech, 2021).

Do you rotate the adults working with different groups or is there a set pattern of adults, such as the teaching assistant (if you have one!) working with a particular group? Adult presence is associated with control of knowledge and behaviour, and different types of adults are associated with the support of groupings at different levels of ability (Kutnick et al., 2002). It is important, therefore, that the 'social pedagogy' behind grouping is considered when groups are employed.

In addition to groups, consider how you may wish to organise your class in terms of pupil responsibility roles. Whilst your school may have set roles of 'form captain', for example, can you help your class to stay organised by having pupils in charge of different aspects of the room, such as line monitor, cloakroom monitor, laptop monitor … encourage pupils to take responsibility for age-appropriate roles in the classroom can improve their levels of satisfaction and well-being as they have daily purpose aside of their academic learning, but will also help your day-to-day organisation run more smoothly.

How technology has changed classroom organisation

Technology is a key aspect of teaching that has changed in recent decades. Of course the electronic equipment available in each school may be different, from tablets to laptops to virtual reality headsets for climbing up a virtual Everest, but it is undeniable that use of any tech equipment changes your classroom organisation and can have benefits for class productivity and engagement.

Critical question

How has edtech shaped organisation in the classroom?

After reflecting on their experience, primary school teachers were able to observe that the organisation of the classroom space has changed since they use technology. The integration of educational technology (edtech) in our schools requires a redefinition of teaching practices and teaching-learning processes (Fernandez et al, 2021). Research suggests that edtech can help learning to be more accessible (Fernandez et al., 2021).

Technology can also help our learning to be more creative, offering ways for pupils to engage, collaborate and present work in digital spaces like never before.

Creativity and possible thinking

When you are organising your spaces, consider your position in the room. Ensure your classroom is a curious space, where seating plan and teacher position encourage communication and collaboration and foster a culture of questioning.

What will be on your walls? How accessible are your resources? Do pupils feel they can take ownership of their classroom and use manipulatives how they want and when they want, or is there an element of teacher control?

Cremin et al.'s seminal work (2006) highlights the role of the teacher in the classroom, including the practice of 'standing back', profiling learner agency and creating time and space. Particular strategies were employed by each of the teachers. These approaches appeared to foster possibility thinking in young learners. In addition, the paper considers the development of the teachers' thinking through the phases of the research process and presents a model for conceptualising a pedagogy of possibility thinking (Cremin et al., 2006).

The Role of the Book Corner and Stories

By Debbie Marlow, English Lead at Thundersley Primary School, Thundersley, England

Do not underestimate the power of reading stories regularly to your class. It is a great way of developing children's vocabularies, comprehension and their interest in books. You can read stories that might be beyond the children's independent reading ability and that perhaps they cannot access by themselves. Your use of intonation, expression and different voices enhances their understanding and, of course, their enjoyment. You can explain new vocabulary, ask and answer a range of questions to develop their understanding and also create cliff-hangers and show how excited you are to find out what happens next. You can expose children to authors and genres that they might not have considered. So many times, when I have read stories to my class, the children have chosen to re-read these stories (and others by the same author) at home with their families. It can be a real challenge to find time for story reading when our days and the curriculum are so packed, but it really is worth making story reading a part of your daily routine. I find that if I leave story-time until the end of the morning or afternoon, it rarely happens as the day runs away from me. So, because it is a real priority for me, I timetable it for after morning break time. Instantly, the children become calm and focussed as they listen attentively. I recently interviewed a number of children at my school about their reading experiences, and when I asked if they enjoy it when their teacher reads to them, without fail, every single child's face immediately lit up and they responded with an emphatic 'Yes'. One child told me that she enjoyed it because no one reads to her at home. So many parents stop reading to their children once they can read independently, which is such a shame. Some of the best readers I have encountered in Year 6 were still regularly listening to stories read to them by adults. Another child explained that listening to stories took him to new, imaginary worlds, and all the children I spoke to said that they had greater understanding of stories read to them by an adult. You are, after all, the best reader in the room so shows your children how it's done, open their minds to new worlds, genres and authors, and I guarantee you will enjoy it too. For me, it's one of my favourite parts of the day.

Classroom Organisation

By Ella Catley, Student Teacher at The Cathedral School, Chelmsford, Essex, England

The key to a happy classroom is an organised environment. The children in your class will learn best when they can understand and access the classroom, just as you have organised it. Ensuring your classroom is organised into learning areas is a fundamental property of allowing children to access the learning activities, through a variety of

(Continued)

learning styles. The organisation of your classroom will be dependent on the age and ability of your children; however, the idea that you should ensure each area has a pure purpose is paramount.

This is evident in my current Key Stage 1 classroom which demonstrates accessibility for all through the use of a creation station, maths zone, role play area, investigation station, small world station, construction area and writing area. The children are introduced to each area at the beginning of the year and understand that the resources associated to that area are found in the surrounding drawers. During each lesson, the children are then presented with a selection of activities; these activities are planned to meet the lesson objectives, but also allow the children to complete the learning through a learning style which encourages them to learn best. The children then have access to these activities throughout the week, whilst new content is being taught; they are encouraged to challenge themselves and attempt all the activities within the classroom by the end of the week. The main content of this lesson can then be taught using 'carpet space'; the children have the freedom to move around the classrooms' different learning areas, instead of having a seat at a table which conflicts the idea that children learn best through play.

Within your classroom you should ensure that your space is utilised effectively; every idea you put into practice should be actively contributing to the outcomes for the children. Ensuring that your wall displays are linked to the children's current learning and that they can use these display walls to aid their understanding of a topic is critical. Introducing vocabulary walls is an excellent learning tool; this continuously reminds the children of the key vocabulary for each subject but also allows them to use the vocabulary accurately within their learning. They are able to go over to the display and use the vocabulary wall to remind them of main vocabulary and use it within their work. This enables the display board to be an active reminder for the children, making the most of the opportunity to have an extra learning tool.

Teaching is rewarding yet challenging profession. Creating an organised environment for you and the children to work in is the key to allowing the children to be the best learners they can be, but also allows you as a teacher to educate in a calm and organised manner.

Organising your Learning Environment

By Gemma Fitzsimons, Qualified Teacher at Broxbourne, England

When I first began teaching in 2008, primary school classrooms, particularly those in Key Stage 1, were bright and colourful – at times almost garish – with every wall surface covered in laminated numbers, letters and key words.

Children's work was mounted on brightly coloured paper on an equally bright backing board, which often meant that their work – their achievements – was lost, hidden amongst the riot of colour and other stimuli.

(Continued)

My own classrooms and practice followed this design until I visited a school in Potters Bar, Middlesex, several years ago now, where their Early Years team were trialling the use of natural materials and a sparser learning environment. The children also played a huge role in setting up their classroom, truly making the learning environment their own.

I will admit that at first this new and somewhat empty looking environment shocked me, but after talking to the staff there and their reasons for following such a scheme, I realised I could not dismiss its potential for supporting the learning in my own classroom. It made sense that classrooms which were overly full of stimuli were not going to help create an environment that aided learning, particularly for those children who struggle to maintain their attention and concentration.

The following summer holiday I redesigned my Year 1 classroom. All the boards were backed with hessian with a simple black paper mount around their edges. Learning from my school visit, I hoped that the use of hessian to back the board would better absorb sound than the usual backing paper, helping to make the classroom less echoey and loud. Board headings were also printed in a simple black font. The simplicity ensured that learning resources or the children's work would stand out, making it easy for the children and staff to use as a reference point.

The boards were not the only part of the classroom that got a makeover. Brightly coloured plastic boxes were replaced by woven and wicker baskets made from natural materials (these can be expensive so check charity shops or ask parents in advance if they have anything suitable that they would like to donate). Using baskets not only helped the children find and tidy away resources easily, as they tend to be shallower and less bulky, but they also – like the hessian's natural fibres – help to absorb noise.

The carpets in the reading corner were also replaced by furry, soft rugs in natural shades of beige, grey and sage. A larger, fluffy carpet soon found its way to the main carpet area as we noticed the children loved running their fingers through the soft threads, the action helping with their focus and attention.

Our learning environment was now more natural, more peaceful. It had a depth and texture that was calming and more tactile for the adults and children. The boards and their learning props were no longer competing for dominance. It was a classroom that truly supported learning and emotional well-being.

Establishing a Classroom Culture

By Steve Martin, Assistant Head at Valley Invicta Primary School at Kings Hill, Maidstone, England

As a new member of the profession, this can be an area where you get very little guidance. This is for a very good reason, as this is not really an element of the job that can be 'taught'. It comes with experience and by you bringing your personality to the classroom.

(Continued)

Setting boundaries early is essential, and all children then know where these are. This can be more challenging for some children, and the age and stage of the child will define some elements of the boundary setting. Each school will have a set of non-negotiables when it comes to rewards and consequences, and these will need to feed into your classroom culture. These will be more firmly established in older children and will be less established if you are teaching in the Early Years or Key Stage 1. It is the layer above this that you as a teacher must establish with your class. It is this, which is at the heart of your teaching. Get this stage right, and you will reap the rewards over the year.

I remember, as a new teacher, being told not to smile until Christmas and then they will respect you. At the time I was dubious; nearly 20 years in, I know this to be utter rubbish. The children need to know you are there as a partner; they are not to be 'done to' but to be part of an amazing team. I have always tried to quickly establish an ethic of not wanting to let anyone else in the team down. This is especially key when outside of the classroom. Getting the children to buy into this has been the bedrock of my classroom culture. Not wanting to be the person caught talking in assembly or running in the building or misbehaving on the playground has a power that can be used to your advantage throughout the year.

Classroom cultures do not establish themselves over night and, even once established, will need revisiting. This can often be after one of the key elements that have been breached, but I try to also revisit these at other times as well. New members of the class joining start terms, before going on a trip as this helps to reinforce them.

Ultimately, you want happy children because happy children are the reason we all do the job. Happy children are better learners, of course, but also, they will become happy adults. If you can establish a culture where being happy, relaxed and fun is had, you are 80% of the way to having a successful classroom, and when those children eat out of the palm of your hand, it is so much easier to do the other 20%!

Inclusion in the Classroom

Payal Sinha, PGCE Educator, India

I taught in the UK as a substitute teacher, a teaching assistant when my primary teaching qualifications were from India. I went on to do my PGCE and then returned to India to teach in the most prestigious international school in Mumbai, India. My PGCE had an overlying umbrella of equality, inclusion and citizenship. There was certainly a lot of talk around it. But how was it in practice? I remember substituting in a private school and during lunchtime hearing teachers asking the students to not use their hands to eat. As if there was something not proper about it. And I thought, we eat using our hands all the time. On the one hand, we say we are practising inclusivity by having the so-called curry on the menu, and on the other hand, we won't let our diverse student population use their choice to eat the way they want to?

(Continued)

> The question is how much is being done to include the entire student population and give them a sense of real belonging beyond colouring the sheets of Lord Ram and Sita every Diwali?
>
> **What can be done?**
>
> Spend time learning about your students: their family background, festivals and celebrations. Actively include books of as many cultures as possible in your classroom. Parents are the best source for this as they suggest good-quality books. Let it not be a checklist exercise.
>
> Include displays in other languages. Not just the generic welcome poster but personalise to the diversity in your class. It could be names written in different scripts or basic vocabulary in the languages spoken in your classroom. I remember one year our diversity department made us basic ring cards that had words in Japanese, Korean, French, etc., for water, food, and toilet. This was a good start, but we also later added words for don't worry, mummy will be back soon, well done and many more.
>
> Keep in mind that not everyone who is Asian looking feels they come from there. It could be a second-generation family where the children are born in the UK and that is their identity. A world map helps. I once had a four-year-old American girl put a pin on Brazil as she was born there and had never actually lived in the USA even though her passport was American.
>
> Above all, as teachers, let's not make inclusivity a token exercise. Genuinely be interested in learning. Celebrate Christmas and Easter but Diwali and Eid too. It takes time to include these in the DNA, but it is almost our responsibility to embrace out diversity. In India we celebrate many religions. Eid, Diwali, Easter, Christmas, and Budh Purnima are all holidays. But then we would rather have those than generic Bank Holidays!
>
> It's uncomfortable reading, but I genuinely believe we want to be inclusive. We just don't know how.

Chapter summary

- Classroom organisation refers to a wide range of strategies, techniques and areas of the primary classroom and structure.
- The main advice is to get to know your learners and their needs; consider the layout of your room and the management of your resources as a response to these needs.
- Offer responsibility roles to pupils to encourage them to share in the classroom organisation as well as build their self-efficacy and self-concept.

References

Boliver, V., and Capsada-Munsech, Q. (2021). Does ability grouping affect UK primary school pupils' enjoyment of Maths and English? *Research in Social Stratification and Mobility*, 76, p. 100629. Available at: https://www.sciencedirect.com/science/article/pii/S0276562421000494?casa_token=5nowy-uhrt4AAAAA:VlgNF-vXgdOoa3rQ7bGzk4Sa7oo_C-gZoeEHQ8Kdn-yNUI7IefFO7nMdBu_BRaXodhKxEx952Q4 [Accessed 3 May 2022].

Cremin, T., Burnard, P., and Craft, A. (2006). Pedagogy and possibility thinking in the early years. *Thinking Skills and Creativity*, 1(2), pp. 108-119.

Dean, J. (2013). *Organising Learning in the Primary School Classroom*. London: Routledge.

Fernández, I.M.G., Lorente, L.M., and Regalado, M.E.A. (2021). Primary educational strategies in times of digital curriculum. *Digital Education Review*, 40, pp. 66-81. Available at: https://revistes.ub.edu/index.php/der/article/view/32837 [Accessed 3 May 2022].

Handy, C., and Aitken, R. (2002). 'The organisation of the primary school'. In *Teaching and Learning in the Primary School* (pp. 249-259). London: Routledge.

Kutnick, P., Blatchford, P., and Baines, E. (2002). Pupil groupings in primary school classrooms: Sites for learning and social pedagogy? *British Educational Research Journal*, 28(2), pp. 187-206. Available at: https://bera-journals.onlinelibrary.wiley.com/doi/abs/10.1080/01411920120122149?casa_token=y8L1bDGPUdQAAAAA:0EI5-7eQdu5EUd-at9c93hOtwZdauYuWtwpRMsUpC7VWhZeRWCyw-yZyE4VarJ2PPCZV1gIRY9IrCwU0w [Accessed 3 May 2022].

Martlew, J., Stephen, C., and Ellis, J. (2011). Play in the primary school classroom? The experience of teachers supporting children's learning through a new pedagogy. *Early Years*, 31(1), pp. 71-83. Available at: https://www.tandfonline.com/doi/full/10.1080/09575146.2010.529425?casa_token=mB2EJOv47VQAAAAA%3AoKdpqCDsfy1WsXzRYXsdE4JzchDzja0tibXe_vuRWOXhOLHb_wNunBSYQw-2MWSgQSNVqCdiChyIX7A [Accessed 3 May 2022].

McGillicuddy, D. (2021). "They would make you feel stupid"-Ability grouping, Children's friendships and psychosocial wellbeing in Irish primary school. *Learning and Instruction*, 75, p. 101492. Available at: https://www.sciencedirect.com/science/article/pii/S0959475221000517 [Accessed 3 May 2022].

Watson, F. (2012). Classroom layouts. *Primary Teacher Update*, 2012(11), pp. 53-54.

Wilks, R. (1996). Classroom management in primary schools: A review of the literature. *Behaviour Change*, 13(1), pp. 20-32. Available at: https://www.cambridge.org/core/journals/behaviour-change/article/abs/classroom-management-in-primary-schools-a-review-of-the-literature/E43F8114F9D40E5969095DF61D2CD7C2 [Accessed 3 May 2022].

3 Behaviour management

KEY WORDS
Behaviour, power, balance/imbalance, reward, sanction

> **Contributors within this chapter:**
> 1. Suus-Anna Harskamp
> 2. Sue Davidowitz
> 3. Sarah Wall
> 4. Cara Veitch
> 5. Jessie Krefting

Introduction

Out of all the Teachers' Standards, and now the Core Content Framework descriptors, it is my experience that suggests that it is behaviour management – TS 7 'manage behaviour effectively to ensure a good and safe learning environment' and CCF 3 Standard 1 'set high expectations' – that causes the greatest trepidation of all the major facets of teacher training. Behaviour management is a skill that requires developing, but not one that should cause undue duress or alarm. This chapter explores what behaviour management is, the key dynamic that underpins behaviour, its policy, its rewards and its sanctions. It explores key perspectives from leading behavioural experts in the professional field before exploring in analytical detail a behaviour policy and what the messages are that lie behind it.

Understanding behaviour is a complex human interaction, and it is therefore unsurprising why trainee teachers and early career teachers (ECTs) may feel apprehensive about it. This chapter argues that being comfortable with behaviour management rests with knowing oneself in the power dynamic, interpreting the ethos of a school in setting a behaviour policy, seeing the remit of schools under wider government policy and being assured that incidents of major misbehaviour are extremely rare.

DOI: 10.4324/9781003218098-3

What is meant by behaviour management and who decides what is bad behaviour?

The Department for Education (DfE, 2016) in its *Behaviour and Discipline in Schools* guide does not define 'behaviour management' as such but describes what an effective behaviour policy should aim to do:

- Promote good behaviour, self-discipline and respect (for authority)
- Prevent bullying
- Ensure that pupils complete assigned work (reasonably assigned to them in their education) and which
- Regulate[s] the conduct of pupils (to be acceptable)

The 'management of behaviour' is the regulation, adjusting and controlling of something so that it operates correctly; 'promoting behaviour' is the encouraging of progress; 'respect' is an attitude of deference so that something occurs that is recognisable and welcomed or that something does not occur that is unwanted. Such verbs in themselves are controlling and suggest that a power dynamic in favour of the policymaker is established and that the observed (be it pupil or even the school) is monitored. The 1989 *Discipline in Schools* report (otherwise known as the Elton report) stated that their recommendations

> ... relate to a wide range of discipline problems, particularly persistent disruption. We find that most schools are on the whole well ordered. But even in well run schools minor disruption appears to be a problem and that the most effective schools seem to be those that have created a positive atmosphere based on a community and shared values.

This puts behaviour management on an immediate spectrum (see Figure 3.1) – the management of desired conduct between no control, negotiation and direct imposition, which you, as a teacher, will find yourself according to the design of your school's behaviour policy.

It is within this dynamic that the rest of the chapter presents itself. What is minor disruption? How is persistent disruption measured? How much respect is enough respect for authority? The answer, quite simply, is that it is an arbitrary measure, and this is where you can consider your positioning on this spectrum by questioning your right to power and what to do with it. What one teacher may allow, another will tolerate, while another would ban it; a behaviour policy is designed to be consistent, but what is it about that consistency? Who applies it? Where does that come from? What does it look like in practice? And is it fair?

Behaviour, or the conduct that is being judged, is basically the observer agreeing to a standard that needs to be upheld, whereas bad behaviour, or misbehaviour, is the observer agreeing that a standard has not been reached or that there is a deficit in expectation. The

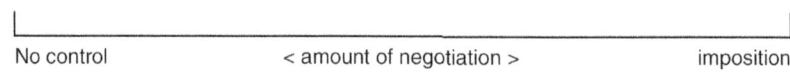

Figure 3.1 Spectrum of behaviour management

DfE (2016, pp. 4-5) is clear in that the responsibility of determining a standard of behaviour is met by the headteacher. The headteacher will be responsible for devising a set of rules to articulate this before issuing rewards and sanctions to maintain the standard of acceptable behaviour.

Therefore, the values that have shaped the headteacher will shape the behaviour policy of a given school.

The school and its power dynamics

A school is an institution where learning occurs but one in which influence is a powerful abstracted force. The Core Content Framework, under its first standard, states that

> teachers have the ability to affect and improve the wellbeing, motivation and behaviour of their pupils; and that teachers are key role models, who can influence the attitudes, values, and behaviours of their pupils.

This is a directive that needs examination for you as a trainee or as an ECT, a concept of identity – who are you? And what do you believe in?

Your identity is fashioned by your upbringing, your education, your social network and, in this case, your pedagogical values. Before accepting a behaviour policy, a good idea would be to consider the values you believe should operate in the classroom. This is not a critique of your preferred teaching style, but it is something that would help in dealing with the vicissitudes of daily classroom practice. If you believe that children should ask many questions, be sceptical and autonomous, you will judge and respond to children's behaviour accordingly. If you believe that children should listen to and accept instruction, then likewise. Let us consider the example of carpet time which is a prevalent scenario in today's primary schools.

Carpet time is an oddity because it can appear illogical if you are seriously reflective about it. The class is invited to sit away from chairs on the hardest space left in the room. The teacher, meanwhile, is sat on a chair at the front; why is that? Do you as a teacher believe in a hierarchy; do you need to be sitting on a chair to see everyone? If you see yourself as more egalitarian, would you sit on the floor as well? Is there a need for carpet time? Some teachers may argue that having the children sit on the floor allows for more controlled formative assessment – others may say that pedagogy can be replicated with the children seated at their desks. Would you insist on children sitting bolt upright and putting their hands up to speak (or answer your questions) or would you allow them to slouch a bit and discuss freely? How would you control this environment – would you reward good posture and correct answers, or would you reward the child who interrupts you with a critical observation? Then what happens after twenty minutes or so – do the children become restless, and how do you respond to that? More rewards for good posture and the introduction of sanctions for those who fidget or ask permission to go to the toilet? Can you relate to such distractedness if you are in a comfortable chair while the children are on a hard mat? Such an example will allow you to explore the balance of power in your teaching!

How you reply to the above scenarios of the carpet time session may determine the values you hold and then allow you to consider why you hold them in the first place. It also introduces you to the concept that is important within this chapter of behaviour management and that is the power imbalance within the school environment – who holds the power and what do they want to do with it? This chapter is not going to suggest that you refuse the adoption and implementation of your school's behaviour policy because that is an unrealistic expectation. It can, however, prepare you and inform your policy when you become middle leaders and senior leaders.

You, the teacher and the children

The obvious starting point is the relationship between you and the children. Articulate to your class the behavioural values you believe in and want to encourage. This could be from the drawing up of the classroom rules (simple guidance is to have no more than five and to frame them as 'do' rather than 'don'ts' – or as I used to have in my classroom as the only rule, 'If you think it is wrong, then it probably is') and the modelling of expected behaviour. For example, if you advocate autonomy and risk, then children can leave their seats to retrieve resources without asking permission to and can speak without raising hands – although this will take some practice. You are not their friend but the children's teacher; whether you are approachable or bound by obvious markers of respect, then that is for you to decide. Smile for the first time after Christmas to your new class or smile on day one; it is your decision because behaviour management must be your interpretation of consistently applied methods. That is key advice.

Decide for yourself what is worth intervening for and what is worth ignoring. It may be worth thinking of possible classroom situations ranging from the most trivial (where the 1989 *Discipline in Schools* report maintained was the most common form of misbehaviour – and I see no evidence of that having changed since) to the moderate and to the extreme. I am not suggesting that the trivial, for example fussing with pens, should be ignored, but you should consider your imagined response to it. Either it will be in the 'does it matter?' camp or in the 'yes it does matter' camp. It may be that, depending on whatever is happening in the class, these two different imagined responses can change.

You may wish to approach the behavioural concerns of your class by considering how you would approach children with special educational needs (SEN). If you think you require more patience, more time and more understanding (and training) to deal with complex needs for inclusive practice in terms of behaviour management, then that is the underpinning ethos you could adopt for all children. The social model of inclusion works for all and it is a philosophy that all children soon accept. Praise is important; learn to praise but not to praise too effusively, or children will see through it and, if overused, become ineffective. Your school's behaviour policy may indicate the type of reward on offer, be it intrinsic (praise as words) or extrinsic (praise as tangible rewards), and this will be your choice in deciding whether you are in favour of praise that encourages through kind words or whether you are in favour of rewards that are distributed, such as merit points or 'dojos'. Research as to what you think your class prefers.

Janet Moyles (1992, p. 108) made a valid point that a teacher's adult perception of right and wrong will not be the same as a child's – this is one obvious way of the observer (the teacher) judging an incident and ascribing a value to it (either accepted and rewarded or dismissed and sanctioned). As a teacher you have a behaviour policy to apply, but her advice is

Behaviour management   17

that *'it is the behaviour which is unacceptable- NOT the child'*. Such advice will allow you not to be 'annoyed' at a child and to use any negative bias to creep into your relationship with that child; for example, how would you mark their learning later in the day? Children need forgiveness and a trust in you that they will be able to resume their learning and place in the class without a worry of being labelled.

Learn your ABC, not the alphabet, but the ABC of behaviour intervention. Skinner (1938) developed his theory of antecedent, behaviour and consequence. The antecedent (A) is a 'signal' that something has happened prior to a behaviour (B) occurring. For example, a child may not have a pencil and take a pencil from another child's pencil case. The consequence (C) could be that the child who has had a pencil taken from her without consent has become angry and snatched it back off the offending child and issued a threat not to repeat the action. Depending on where you enter this scenario, based on experience, or use of good behaviour management (such as scanning techniques), you may catch the consequence and apply a sanction to the child who was relieved of the pencil because she was caught snatching it back and heard to be unkind. Experience will allow you to reflect on the situation and to search for the antecedent as you either ask questions about what happened (short term) or ensure that all children are adequately resourced (long term).

Bullying is always unacceptable and needs to be dealt with in the first instance, at the expense of learning time, and there needs to be no further guidance on this.

As a teacher, it is important to consider your well-being. Teaching, as you already know, is frenetic, rewarding, exciting and frustrating; in other words, it tests the range of human emotions, let alone professional skill. Children will test you, but most will want to please you and most children will want to please you all the time. The reason is that you will have constructed (and keep developing) a working relationship with your class. They will attune to your values (it is your choice whether to impose them or co-construct them), your mannerisms and your accent, but overall, it is important they believe in you as their teacher.

> **Critical question**
>
> How can I identify my pedagogical identity?

Your pedagogical identity through effective behaviour management can be recognised through the acronym PRESSED as you teach:

PRESSED

P - Planning

Planning is detailed within Chapter 4 of this book, but although 'failing to pan is planning to fail', it is an indication that the children are not buying into the impression they have of you as an organised and dedicated teacher who has their learning interests at heart. A plan should not be rigidly adhered; it is acceptable to change a plan when matters are not going well or when children's interests need to be sustained. Likewise, should external influences occur, for example a sudden snowfall, you will know that a plan should be shelved as the behaviour of the children in anticipation of an exciting weather pattern now becomes a more pressing concern. Contingency plans are also needed. They should not be detailed but would cover the basic requirements of a failed IT platform or device or a change from dry to wet weather in PE.

R – Resources

Resources should be timetabled for your use, fully working and all component parts available and enough to be distributed so that access is conducive to learning. In other words, it does not matter if something is shared in pairs or trios if children can see it or use it without access to it being diminished. Three examples would be that dry marker pens all work, that any electronic devices are charged for the duration of the lesson or that all PE equipment is safe and appropriate to use in advance of the lesson, so that there are no unpleasant surprises when the store cupboard is opened.

E – Environment

Consider what it must feel like to be a child in your learning environment. Sit for twenty minutes on the carpet area to experience the sensation of such a surface or sit under the projector for the interactive whiteboard to see whether that is a disturbing feature. Line up in the space where you want the children to line up as they enter and exit the classroom; is there enough space, or are there any pieces of furniture that protrude? Will you insist on 'no talking' as the children line up and then proceed to walk? Do you talk to colleagues when you meet them in the corridor and walk along? It may cause you to reflect why some teachers insist on silence rather than low conversation voices. Children will get naturally more excited as they leave the classroom for a music lesson in the hall or for PE in the sports field; how will you allow that sudden rise of interest to be expressed in a different behaviour?

S – Subject knowledge

This, as the vernacular goes, is a 'no-brainer'! Although you still need your brain to hold all the knowledge, skills and information that make up this necessary feature of your teaching, you cannot 'wing it'. Children will see through you, and your credibility will diminish and children's behaviour will demonstrate a lack of respect for you. There is, however, a difference in not knowing something either genuinely (but rarely) or to use it as a teaching point; for example, 'well, what do you think an answer could be?', which is more authentic. You must read, research and evidence this in your teaching; having errors pointed out by children is one thing, but it can be discomforting when adults do so.

S – Solo

One of the earliest things you would note on your plan is whether you have an additional adult with you. Before we look at this, let us look whether you are really on your own in the classroom. You may feel daunted by the prospect that you are alone with up to thirty children before you; however, that is not the case. Most children, as has been written above, will want to learn and will want to conform to the expectations of the classroom. That means a trust has been cultivated; the children are 'on your side' so if you are taking a class for the first time, you need to rely on the expectation that the children will behave, that they will listen to you and that they want to be taught by you. You will develop the ability to be comfortable in a class using Kounin's (1970) theory of 'with-it-ness' and 'overlapping' from 'discipline and management in classrooms' (cited in Pollard 2002). With-it-ness is the 'eyes in the back of your head' technique of conveying the message that you know what is going on. The trick is to guess that you know what is going on when you are not entirely sure. For example, when writing on the board, you may say, 'I can hear you', or a more mischievous trick is to say to a group of children, 'try not to do that again', to demonstrate that although you are not sure, you can guess but that that doubt in the group's mind that they know that you may know!

'Overlapping' is dealing with two matters of behaviour simultaneously and developing the ability to prioritise. It is important to deal with incidents of misbehaviour as soon as you set the scale for when an intervention is necessary. Some advice may be to ignore something or to act, but I think you may want your own system of deciding when to intervene on your own 'sliding scale' because you will get to know the children quickly and how they operate as a class dynamic. One example, which will arguably occur on a frequent basis, is the ability to listen to a child give an answer while 'scanning' the rest of the class, albeit for formative assessment practice (i.e. to see who can support or contradict that answer) or to see who is actively engaged and probably listening. You may want to consider how some children may appear not to be listening and appear to be looking elsewhere, when really, they are paying acute attention.

Although you may be the only adult in a room, the children are your allies. They can act as monitors for you in the distribution of resources, for necessary errands. They are sometimes the source of information that could be useful in finding out what is happening or about to happen. It is not necessarily a case of 'telling tales', but it can be useful. For older children, you may need a 'trusted' child who can get assistance when required; that child could leave the classroom, be able to deliver a message or seek another adult if there is a serious incident that demands attention, when you cannot leave the classroom (unless you have a sanctioned form of communication in the classroom).

Should there be a teaching assistant at your disposal, this is where you would involve her in the role of supporting behaviour management. A good idea is to make it clear to the class that they cannot 'play one adult against another' and that the teaching assistant would be deployed to promote positive behaviour and to sanction misbehaviour at her discretion. You may wish to split the classroom into two zones, where each adult acts on the behaviour as observed in that zone, especially if your assistant is working some distance away from you. Teaching assistants are an invaluable source of information and may be able to supply information to you about a child and previous history, but be careful not to let bias affect your judgement.

E – Exits (transitions)

You will need to give some thought as to how children leave one activity and enter another. There are many 'exits' in a classroom from exiting the playground and entering the classroom in the morning, to exiting a carpet space, to exiting the classroom for collective worship, to exiting the classroom for lunch, and so forth. Ensure the walkways and spaces are designed for the whole class to move with minimal fuss and maximum efficiency. When the children are entering, first thing ensure you greet them, and they know where all their belongings go and how they can find them. Ensure anything of value is stored with you; some schools allow mobile phones. Practice all the exits and transitions in the first two weeks; it will save you time later. You can be almost like a drill sergeant here with how you organise it and at a tempo of choice. Will you line them boy/girl/boy girl? If so, why? Will it be according to who gets their first? Will you reward quickly cleared desk? If so, why? Is there a need to reward those who are first, or does this disadvantage those with difficulties or who wish to take pride in a clean area? Or is there anything wrong with untidiness? These questions are merely designed to make you think about why you might say things when such practices are occurring.

D - Difficult

Sometimes being a teacher is hard. Sometimes the children's tensions boil over; sometimes a fight breaks out. Perhaps the weather (usually wind) upsets the concentration of the class; perhaps the class has received some bad news. Perhaps you are tired and the children sense this. When 'difficult' times arise, it is important to not think you are at fault, assuming the previous points above are followed. Children are still developing so will not be able to necessarily control their emotions or thoughts but will still need to be cared for even if their behaviour is erratic or dangerous.

You will probably experience that class's tensions rising, and that is when you may intervene with strategies to cool matters. Sending a child to another class or to the headteacher is one option; suspending the learning for an impromptu circle time to discuss the issue is another. Moving the children around is another; it does not matter what you do if you feel comfortable in the situation and the children know that you have control. Never shout; save shouting for very serious occasions which may necessitate danger to life. Suppose a fight breaks out; you will already know whether your school advocates the use of restraint control (or the use of the minimum force necessary to physically intervene). Raising the voice and moving quickly and with discovery is what is required; you will need to protect the protagonists from increasing injury and any bystanders from being injured as well as protecting property. If you cannot move the fighting children, move the rest of the class. Send a trusted child to get help while you are either physically intervening and separating the fighters or using a serious enough raised voice with explicit commands; for example, 'stop'. It is more likely the children will tire quickly, but emotionally they will still be carrying strong, negative feelings, which may take up to thirty minutes to fade. Only then will you be able to talk to the children involved, but it will give you time to reassure the other children, tidy the mess caused and write a report while the incident is fresh.

The incident may be over, but it will need to be dealt with; this is where you may involve a learning mentor, for example as part of a restorative justice programme, but usually it will be to reflect on why it happened and to think about approaching the topic with all the class. That is a quick thing. Other difficult issues may be slower. Racism, anti-Semitism, Islamophobia, misogyny, homophobia and poverty shaming, for example, need dealing with; it does not evaporate once you have initially intervened - it takes time to address why it happened, how to educate the perpetrators of the abuse and how to ensure the victims are supported. For this, you would need to seek advice from experienced colleagues and may involve counselling sessions and wider teaching sessions. For children who are defiant or who refuse instruction, this will take time. It is not you who should be defeated here, but see it as an opportunity to develop a longer term strategy with the support of others.

For all difficult incidents, you will need to embark on self-care. Something that was unpleasant to witness may have been a shock, and although you correctly followed procedure, you would need to think about your own well-being. Emotion burns energy; perhaps you did not think children could act in such a way; perhaps you feel that you were at fault (which is incorrect!) or that you engage in endless re-runs of the incident and consider alternative things you could have said and done. That will not be helpful, and the only advice to offer is to talk your line manager about what happened. Your line manager would be able to put you in the right direction for support and even put preventative measures in place to eliminate or reduce difficult situations from arising again.

Taking a Relational Approach

By Suus-Anna Harskamp at The Ossigeno, London, UK

Almost 20 years ago, a very wise psychologist said to me, 'if a child isn't learning, ask them if they like their teacher'. This has sat with me since then.

What has this got to do with behaviour you might wonder? So, I ask, have you ever been somewhere where you don't feel emotionally safe, or that perhaps the person running a meeting or training session isn't 'on it', or that perhaps the person in charge doesn't like you? What impact does this have on you, your engagement and your willingness to try, get involved or be compliant even? Now take those memories or experiences and just sit with them and reflect. This feeling is exactly what we can do and create within the classroom. Or we can do the opposite and we can create a climate of safety. And the difference would not go unnoticed when it comes to how children 'behave'.

You will hear it often, but relationships are key. They underpin so much of the work we do. I don't talk about behaviour management, and I never use the phrase 'challenging behaviour'; in fact I switch off when I hear it. Perhaps that is a challenging behaviour! This is because it attaches a label to what is happening rather than being curious as to why it is happening.

Many children will work with you and do what is asked by you as an adult because they have had the experiences that allow them to do this. But some children will have been let down by adults, hurt by adults, and the expectation that they act like the rest of their class can be unrealistic and unfair.

The very nature of behaviour is that it communicates something. Do I stare out the window because I'm bored and not listening or because I'm tired and worried? Do I keep my hood up because I am defiant or because I feel it is a protection, do I not listen

(Continued)

to you because I want to be a pain or because I am wary of people I don't know, or am I snappy because I don't like you or because I am hungry and tired? We don't always know. We can't always know. But we do know that behaviour communicates something! And we cannot help a child to 'manage' their behaviour unless we try to understand it.

We need to take time to notice our children, know them, understand them, understand their experiences and the way they communicate, and listen to them. Are they demonstrating something by how they communicate? And more importantly are we responding in a way that meets the need? Just as we want our friends, peers, family and bosses to do with us. We are less likely to respond negatively if we feel understood, liked, heard, valued and supported.

So the 'don't smile till Christmas' approach won't work. Yes, set boundaries, yes have routines and yes have high expectations but remain non-judgemental, curious, open, reflective and always check yourself too. Are you ok? Creating a safe environment will allow us all to thrive.

Behaviour from an SEN Perspective

By Sue Davidowitz, SEN Teacher, Zevulun, Israel

All teachers, especially special education teachers, need to take note and meet their pupils' needs socially, physically, emotionally and intellectually. Reality, however, says that for each pupil in the same class, there are various degrees of distraction, frustration and boredom blocking the learning process. Usually, when a pupil falls into one of these categories, behaviour management becomes a serious issue.

As a special education needs teacher who teaches English abroad, my first rule of behaviour management is to give respect and receive it by creating a strong and trustworthy relationship with my pupils. Get to know your pupils, their strengths and passions. Include this information in your teaching. Teachers can turn classes into a harmonious group that will make it easier for behavioural management.

It is important to meet and greet your pupils by name and with a smile. Behaviour needs to be monitored but in a relaxed, friendly atmosphere. Place a poster on a wall and point to it as a reminder of the rules. Make sure to use pictures, as well as simple phrases that can be easily understood. Use genuine praise as often as possible. Praise is so much more beneficial than punishment. If there is a late straggler, welcome him into the class with a smile.

Make sure you do your homework and be prepared for anything and everything. Some pupils might test you by not bringing school supplies. They may assume they will be sent out of the room. Having backup like pencils, paper and sitting with a friend to follow the text will avoid interruptions and also show the pupil you want him to be a part of the class and learn. Teachers need to make sure pupils know what you expect of them, but also they need to know what to expect from you.

(Continued)

Easy access is important. I suggest a giant 'U-shape' if there is enough room in the class. This way the teacher can be seen and heard easily, but most importantly, reach any child who needs the heads-up for positive reinforcement, answer a question, lend a hand or a pencil or add any other comment that needs to be made. Flexibility to move chairs around for group projects or games will avoid behavioural problems.

When a pupil just cannot stay still, offer an alternative task. I have arranged a task for a pupil that sends him to a designated person to return a book to the library or a note to the secretary that needs to be answered. This timeout with honour calms the pupil and helps them to come back into the class. In addition, including pupils as helpers like handing out papers, erasing the board or taking off objects that were put on the board can make a child feel focused.

Developing Effective Relationships

By Sarah Wall, Senior Lecturer at Anglia Ruskin University, Chelmsford, Essex, UK

As a SENCo in the early 2000s, one book changed the way I taught forever: it was entitled 'Punished by Rewards: The Trouble with Gold Stars, Incentive Plans, A's, Praise, and Other Bribes' (Kohn, 1993). Kohn has been described as an 'outspoken critic' of educational practices and, controversially, in a climate that endorses behaviourist strategies – which includes rewards, sanctions, exclusion and even reasonable restraint – like Kohn, I believe that extrinsic motivators and deterrents do little to support many children, especially when their primary need is social, emotional and mental health. Without effective support, these children have poor outcomes in terms of achievement at school, employment, their health and relationships: some may become involved in crime.

Throughout my career, I have witnessed children embark upon many behaviours – spitting; kicking; absconding; flooding the toilets; setting fires; tearing down displays; and climbing the walls – and I mean literally, not metaphorically! Yes, I could have persuaded them to behave differently with a marble, or a sticker, or a house point. Similarly, I could have excluded them on a sliding scale of officiality; even 'inclusion' rooms, in my opinion, are 'unofficial' exclusions; after all the child is not in the room where they should be. However, the behaviours listed above are manifestations of an underlying, unmet need, and many of these children have experienced trauma. When we use behaviourist techniques, we only seek to change the behaviour, not understand it, and, as a result, the change may be temporary. The observable behaviours are likely only to have been the tip of the iceberg.

I am lucky to have worked in, and supported, many primary school settings. A few stand out. Their behaviour policies were not founded upon behaviourist strategies, but attunement. In child development, attunement describes optimum levels of interaction between a caregiver and an infant (Stern, 1985). With children whose caregivers have not

(Continued)

been responsive to their needs, insecure attachments may form, and outward presenting behaviours may challenge staff. The schools I refer to above had a family feel and their mantra was inclusive. They never excluded children, believing that doing so only reinforced the negative views the individuals already had. The children were attached to the setting. Consequently, they achieved academically, emotionally, socially and behaviourally. The difficulty with this approach is that it is less tangible than behaviourism and it takes time. There is no 'quick fix', or a 'sticking plaster', that we can apply.

In an 'Attuned School' (Wall, 2017), the strategies I outline below mimic those of an available and responsive caregiver, who develops effective relationships and a secure, safe base for children. To achieve this attunement, schools need to address key areas. These are as follows:

- Developing whole-school approaches (e.g. sending the inclusive message 'We want you here. You belong')
- Using key adults (this is someone in addition to the teacher – this person should not be working with others, but be available and responsive when needed)
- Teaching children to regulate their emotions (through modelling, or validating their feelings)
- Putting structures in place (all children respond to boundaries)
- Using 'therapeutic' techniques (e.g. colouring, sorting or construction)
- Having a 'Nurture Group' – or nurturing environment. Nurture Groups are run by two members of staff for up to twelve children. They aim to replace missing early experiences through developing relationships between teachers, teaching assistants and peers, and they follow the six principles of nurture (Nurtureuk, 2021)
- Seeing the child as part of a family (thus responding to wider needs)
- Working in partnership with all stakeholders (both the child's and the family's)

I am not suggesting that behaviourist strategies do not work entirely; for some they might, but it depends upon the individual's sense of self, their values and their goals. It is our job as educators to recognise that each child is unique, and their diverse needs should be responded to as such. Some of the above strategies have helped many children.

Autism and Sensory Profiles

By Cara Veitch, Humbie Primary School, East Lothian, Scotland, UK

Have you ever seen a child and wondered why they are flapping their arms, constantly tapping their feet, spinning around without stopping, humming or moving their body repeatedly in a certain way? This is probably stimming behaviour and is very common amongst individuals with autistic spectrum condition (ASC). It is a very important tool in allowing them to self-regulate and is usually fulfilling a deep intrinsic and sensory

(Continued)

need. Stimming rituals help ASC individuals feel grounded, and for staff that work with them, it can be very informative in realising their sensory preferences.

There are five main senses, touch, taste, smell, hearing and sight, but there are also three more 'abstract' senses that aren't as well known. However, to a person with ASC, these senses can be very pertinent depending on their sensory make-up. 'Interception' is the sense of reading your own body signals, for example knowing if you are thirsty, hungry, feeling hot or cold or in pain. 'Exteroception' is your outward body sense, for example knowing when someone has touched you or feeling your clothes on your skin, and it also encompasses spatial awareness. 'Proprioception' is a combination of the two and involves mainly the awareness of your own body movement. A lovely example of this is when you see babies fascinated by their hands as they wave them in front of their faces as they have yet to make the connection that their hands are part of their body, and in this way they are exploring this 'proprioception' sense.

ASC individuals can be over- or undersensitive to any of these eight aforementioned senses. If they are undersensitive, they will seek out stimulation via that sense as it brings them enjoyment and helps them to self-regulate. If they are oversensitive to a particular sense, they may avoid that sense as in some cases it can cause them extreme pain. For example, a child undersensitive to movement, exteroception or proprioception sense may find it problematic to sit still for any length of time instead preferring to constantly be moving such as spinning their body, climbing or fidgeting as this may help them to feel more grounded in their own body. If a child is oversensitive to noise, the sound of the school bell or a noisy classroom may make them feel very anxious and stressed. Knowing your child's sensory profiles is key to supporting them in accessing the curriculum and helping them to feel happy, safe and supported at school and in your classroom.

So how can you better support children's sensory profiles in the classroom?

If a child is oversensitive to any of the senses:

- Beneficial to avoid (if possible)
- If it can't be avoided, lots of warnings before it happens/followed by or paired with a social story
- Adult support to manage activities involving this sense
- Resources to support such as change in timetable, ear defenders, calming aids, etc.

If a child is undersensitive to any of the senses:

- Have set times or try to build learning into the senses they are understimulated in as these activities will be extremely motivating for them and they will be most engaged when using this sense
- Plenty of warnings for sensory task finishing time
- Adult support to stop task
- Learning breaks that incorporate the sense they are drawn to such as movement breaks, quiet time, etc.

(Continued)

Here are some more specific sensory examples and of little adjustments that could make a big difference:

- Oversensitive to touch – own space in class/carpet, can pack bag at quieter times to avoid busy times or choose a space they feel comfortable in within the line
- Oversensitive to noise, ear defenders, being aware of bell times and ensuring pupil is in a quieter area of the school during those times, quiet space to work
- Undersensitive to movement – movement breaks, fidget toys and adult support to sit at certain times
- Undersensitive to touch – deep pressure, weighted blankets and shoulder weights, stress balls and fidget toys

It is so important to always bear in mind that a reaction to over stimulus in ASC learners is never a bad behaviour. It is a stress response caused by sensory overload and is not dissimilar to a panic attack. All behaviour is communication, and knowing their sensory profiles will mean you can provide them relevant and motivating support that will help them to be able to self-regulate more quickly.

A Canadian Perspective

By Jessie Krefting (Educator – 18 Years), Spruce Grove, Alberta, Canada

I attended Concordia University College of Alberta (now known as Concordia University of Edmonton) in Edmonton, Alberta, Canada. This two-year after-degree in education program only accepted seventy students each year, and every applicant had to hold another degree, pass an interview and demonstrate that they had experience working with children whether it was in childcare or the like. The graduates of this program were, and continue to be, amongst the most sought-after teacher candidates in the province. Part of the reason for this, I believe, is a result of the structure of the program itself. In the first year of the program, prior to doing their first field experience or practicum, students go into the classroom where they will be completing their practicum each Friday for the ten weeks prior to starting their placement in the winter semester. This allows the students to become acquainted with the students and their cooperating teacher. In the second year, prior to beginning the second field experience or practicum, students can choose to go into their cooperating teacher's classroom for the first two weeks of the school year. The first week (at the end of August) is to work elbow to elbow with their cooperating teacher setting up the classroom and attending the start-up meetings. The second week (at the start of September) is to meet the students and see how the cooperating teacher sets expectations and establishes classroom routines. At the end of the

(Continued)

second week, students return to the university until mid-October where they work on developing their unit and lesson plans for their upcoming practicum and receive feedback from their professors related to these plans. Finally, at the end of the university year in April, students have the option to participate in an additional field experience or practicum for 4 weeks of full days or 8 weeks of half days in May and/or June. The students are responsible for setting up this field experience for themselves, and the university provides participating students with about $1500 Canadian from their tuition as a stipend. These experiences were invaluable to me as a first-year teacher. I was better prepared for what was going to be expected of me in those first few days and weeks of my first teaching position.

Summary

This chapter has explored how a successful behaviour policy and its implementation as 'management' are designed to promote good behaviour, regulate conduct behaviour and prevent bullying. It has asked you to reflect on how the ethos within behaviour management is an arbitrary concept that is advanced by the headteacher (and the governors), and where you sit with this frame.

It may be obvious that as a teacher you must agree with the behaviour management policy of your school, but there could be scope for you to consider your identity in how much you are willing to share your power with the children because of your inherent assumptions about control and autonomy.

Most misbehaviour will be low-level actions that are deemed to be deficient in a teacher's expectations, and that is where you will have a choice of what rewards or sanctions to issue (if you issue a detention, you will have to be present!); what words you will say and what post-behaviour strategies you will create. There is a room for choice – a sliding scale of your professional decision-making.

Be confident, know the routines to apply in likely-to-happen situations, and remember that it is not you the children are acting against but situations; you represent the person that happens to be there at that moment in time. You can deal with it and will have the strategies at your disposal to keep the children learning.

References

Department for Education (DfE). (2016). *Behaviour and discipline in schools*. [Online]. Available at: https://www.gov.uk/government/publications/behaviour-and-discipline-in-schools

Department of Education and Science and the Welsh Office. (1989). *Discipline in schools*. [Online]. Available at: http://www.educationengland.org.uk/documents/elton/elton1989.html

Kohn, A. (1993). *Punished by Rewards. The Trouble with Gold Stars, Incentive Plans, A's, Praise, and Other Bribes*. Boston, MA: Houghton Mifflin.

Kounin, J. (1970). Discipline and group management in classrooms. In A. Pollard (Ed.), (2002) *Readings for Reflective Practice* (pp. 223-228). London: Continuum.

Moyles, J. (1992). *Organizing for Learning in the Primary Classroom*. Buckingham: Open University Press.
Nurtureuk (2021). *What is nurture?* [Online]. Available at: https://www.nurtureuk.org/what-is-nurture/ [Accessed 29 November 2021].
Skinner, B. (1938). *The Behavior of Organisms: An Experimental Analysis*. New York, NY: Appleton-Century-Crofts.
Stern, D. (1985). *The Interpersonal World of the Infant: A View from Psychoanalysis and Developmental Psychology*. Abingdon: Routledge.
Wall, S. (2017). *The Attuned School: The Effect, and Effectiveness, of Developing Relationships Between Pupils with Attachment Difficulties and Significant Adults*. (Unpublished PhD) University of Birmingham.

4 Planning

KEY WORDS
Pedagogy, data, learning objective, empathy, transitions

Contributors within this chapter:

1. Jake Matthews
2. Ian Pugh
3. Bernice Wall, Narvenka Noyce, Hayley Danter, Nicola Hill, Joannie Peak, and Colleen Roper
4. Robert Coyle
5. Clare Greene
6. Kate Sturdy
7. Michelle Windridge
8. Steve Martin
9. Mike Scott
10. Philip Nicholson
11. Claire Browning and Sue Miles
12. Saira Saeed

Introduction

Planning and assessment are probably the two most important forms of paperwork that provide a daily or weekly record as to the formative guide of showcasing children's progress. You will be familiar with the 'plan, teach and assess' cycle from your teacher training and how the cycle is kept relevant according to the quality of the information that comes from supplying it. Planning, although seen by schools to be essential, should not be formulaic; it must therefore represent the teaching that is required from it. In this chapter it is argued that planning is only as effective as the background pedagogy, knowledge, awareness, data and risk that informs it. These, therefore, should be the factors that inform the planning session under your Planning, Preparation and Assessment (PPA) time. Do ensure you are given adequate

DOI: 10.4324/9781003218098-4

PPA time, and once allocated, ensure you are using it efficiently; there will be other times for photocopier discussions and coffee chats. The planning document is important and is a sign of your pedagogical quality; it will guide you in a lesson, but also you should have the freedom not to be constrained by it. It is a working document that serves an intended purpose, a record of what should be aimed for underpinned by previous assessment data, knowledge of your class and the ethos of the school.

Pedagogy informed planning

> **Critical question**
>
> What is the true purpose of planning, and what does good planning look like?

The chapter will begin by exploring the pedagogy that should underpin and inform every planning decision. You may think that the key purpose of planning is for children's learning and to demonstrate how progress should be achieved. That is still an important consideration, but it will be enhanced if you, as a reflective teacher, bring forth the pedagogy, your way of teaching, organising and preferred learning methods. This is not something that can be done for every weekly or daily plan (this chapter is not focussing on the frequency of planning required because that will be determined by the school), because you will not have the time. It is reckoned that your pedagogy will gradually become a subconscious act over time, in that you will be aware of what you do but not necessarily be aware of why you do it. This is where this exercise, probably every half-term, will be useful. For example, if you are a behaviourist, you will plan for behaviourist teaching and that is how the children will learn; if you are a social constructivist, that is how you will plan and, therefore, that is how you will teach and how the children will learn.

Begin your planning reflection with the chosen pedagogy in mind; look at organising the classroom, its furniture, the position of the interactive whiteboard (whether, even, that will be a feature of your teaching) and how you will ensure the children are taught how to discuss or to listen. I am not advocating any particular pedagogy; I am arguing that you should recognise what style you favour so that it will translate into effective practice. You are likely to be influenced by the ethos of the school in this aspect of your teaching, and the school should have written policies that explain how the favoured pedagogy can be enacted in the classroom.

Where does planning originate?

Planning ultimately is derived from schools' interpretation of the national curriculum, which means that most (community) schools that follow it have what is known as a school curriculum. This is then disseminated and organised through long-term plans (which cover subjects and brief outlines of learning intentions), then medium-term plans (although this varies) and then to short-term or daily plans, which is where you are more likely to be involved. Some schools may buy in planning provisions in the form of published schemes, or that external providers who visit schools for certain subjects will have their own planning scheme. If a school opts for a published scheme, your role is to adapt that to the needs of your class, bearing in mind that such schemes are written for an average class that does not exist and would not be cognisant of any particular special learning need. The better plan is one that has been crafted with care and attention to the needs of the class based on a teacher who knows them well.

Resources

The amount and condition of resources available to any school will partially determine the school's ethos and attitude to the expectation in planning. One obvious example is that if the school has a lot of woodland in or nearby its premises, then outdoor and experiential learning will feature on planning.

To be aware of what is included within the school, surrounding the school and at a reasonable travelling distance calls for you to conduct an audit, unless that has already been compiled by an efficient school. Go through the school curriculum and see not only what is available, but when it is timetabled for your year or class; this is where as an early career teacher (ECT) you will be stockpiling your own resources and knowledge bank. One tip is to always check that whatever you require is timetabled or booked for your class's use, that you have the requisite quantity and, importantly, that it all works. Observe what is available to you and the school in the immediate catchment area, the local library, museum or place of worship. What human resources are there? Can you build up a network of contacts that can offer help with particular subjects, such as RE or IT? If you are in a large town or city, this is somewhat easier; if you are in a rural location, perhaps you can reach out to neighbouring schools and discover what is available through their networks.

Assessment data and information

Data, like money and love, makes the modern world go round. A plan is only as strong as the data that informs it (which as you have guessed seems to be a recurring theme so far). Your data of previous assessment and observations is the starting point for adaptive teaching (what was known as differentiation).

The data will be in two forms: recorded and tacit. Your recorded data is the one in which you will need to make adaptations based on ability groupings or on stretching children's learning, or focussing on a group, or deciding where to put a teaching assistant (TA). Ensure the recorded data is reliable and valid. Does it measure what you want it to, and is it an accurate measure? For example, in mathematics are you systematically measuring what the children can achieve and what they cannot? Is there a decent enough sample so that all children are covered? From the data, you can then interrogate and ask questions, such as who is missing out, what methods are working and what methods are not working? It is important that when reading the data, you are able to translate it into planning themes and activities.

Tacit data is the information only you carry in your head. These are all the important pieces of information that show how well you know your class. You will know who works well with whom, which children respond to using their initiative and which child needs that encouragement. You know when you are building your tacit data when you can recognise the children's handwriting without their names on it or just develop that sense of thinking that a given activity or line of questioning will just suit a particular child. Plan your lessons with this type of feeling as well.

How long should planning take?

This is a question that is likely to concern you as an ECT. The answer is that it should not take too long because of your precious work/life balance. Training, advice and support will be offered to you after you have qualified as a teacher, but you will need to protect the PPA time available. PPA time is not to be squandered but to be spent efficiently; it is not for you to be distracted and if you can use a smart phone for nothing else than planning searches that would be a good discipline to acquire. Enter the PPA time with the tools you require, namely a laptop, planning proforma, assessment data and the school's curriculum and medium-/long-term planning documents. Aim to leave the PPA allocated time with up to 75% of the planning completed; the rest can be done in other after-school sessions. It is not unreasonable that you would be expected to spend a ratio of 1:2 planning to teaching. In other words, if a lesson is planned to last for 60 minutes, you should spend no more than 30 minutes planning it and, over time, reduce that ratio to your favour.

That said, planning is not designed to take an unhealthy proportion of your school-based time, let alone your time spent outside of school. If you are having difficulty in understanding planning or are spending too long on planning, then do consider your well-being and get help from school colleagues. Although planning is important, huge detail should not be required. The basics need to be in place, but a good plan allows you to teach as someone who already is confident in subject knowledge, behaviour management, assessment, knowledge of children's learning and knowledge of resources. In other words, a plan is only a tool to aid a good pedagogy; so too much time should not be spent in producing a finely detailed document. Look to develop your own shorthand, acronyms and similar devices that save time. If you are in a multiple-entry school, have some plans written for you; if you are in a single-entry school, you may want someone to assist you with planning; there will be someone to help you. A good teacher is not a tired teacher (see our well-being chapter).

The centrality of the lesson objective

Once you are ready to plan, unless you are planning sequentially, you are likely to focus on planning for discrete subjects, otherwise known as daily subject plans. The focus on this sub-section is the importance of the learning objective (LO). The credit for the inspiration of this advice goes to the excellent work of Shirley Clarke (2001) in her insightful work on formative assessment, but here, I am elaborating on the importance (as well as the distinction with the success criteria) of the LO (also known as the learning intention or 'WALT' – We are Learning To).

The LO in any form is the key to understanding planning. Learning is an active use of time. Therefore, you must determine what that active time is spent being achieved within a given LO. That active time can be characterised by an active verb, usually written as an imperative verb. For example, we are learning to 'write', to 'catch', to 'swim', to 'analyse', to 'count', to 'add' and so forth.

In setting a LO or writing it on a lesson plan, you should isolate the active verb and plan everything from that point on. There will be various questions one needs to ask in this process. So, for example, if you consider the following statement as a learning objective, 'We are learning to write an introduction to a story', then **'to write'** is your starting point. You can be reflective in the application of 'to write' when planning, and these can be the ten questions asked:

LO: I can *write* an introduction to a story.

1. *Where is the best place to conduct the teaching/learning for 'to write'? Does it have to be indoors or outdoors? If indoors, will I need carpet time, books, tables or a pen?* Many trainee teachers and ECTs will automatically decide that any lesson should take place indoors. That way of thinking is usually broken when it comes to taking the children outside the classroom to the hall or sports field for PE. Apply that same thinking for any lesson, something which colleagues in the Early Years recognise daily. There is nothing wrong in having the classroom as a default starting point for many lessons, but the point here is to question and reflect on key aspects of your planning process.

2. *Who will I have to help me with 'to write'?* If you have a TA, use her. Therefore, include the TA on the plan in terms of what is expected for her to complete in the given time. You may need to give the TA a separate plan with the bare outlines of the lesson content (from a teaching perspective) as well as space for her to record the assessment details from teaching an individual child or a small group. Be clear in what you want the TA to do; writing 'sit with yellow group and help' is directionless. Consider what vocabulary is to be used, what question should be asked, how long the session will last for, whether the TA can use her own discretion for early finishers or to go back and recapitulate an earlier teaching point. In effect, the plan for the TA is also a plan for yourself.

3. *How will I assess 'to write'? What questions will I ask? How will I record the learning for 'to write'?* It can be a difficult task to think of questions to ask when a lesson is planned up to a week before teaching it. The lesson itself may venture down an unexpected but considered path that necessitates the asking of different questions that could not be previously considered. Therefore, start with one or two questions that need to be asked, but plan for the option of asking questions that you determine should be asked and that therefore do not need to be recorded on the planning proforma. Ensure that the question(s) asked relate to the need to assess how the children's progress in 'writing' can be measured. It may be an obvious statement to declare that the children's writing should be recorded in their writing (or English/literacy books), but this could allow you to fall into the default trap that was described in question 1. It may be that most writing will be recorded in an exercise book, but that should not preclude you from allowing children to record their writing on any medium that you find works best for them. Children could write on planning paper, hand-held white boards, on electronic platforms, on a working wall or on a table. It could be that you allow children to record their thoughts into an automatic speech-to-write application that can be downloaded as a record of their learning.

4 *What resources will I need to teach 'to write'?* Check that the resources work beforehand and that there is enough required. If you need electronic equipment, does it work, is it charged and is it timetabled to you? If you want to teach writing outdoors, will the learning environment be comfortable for the children to sit/stand or roam, be free of risk, can you carry the resources to the setting and will the TA know where you will be located?

5 *How much time will I devote to the learning of 'to write'?* Many trainee teachers will assume that there is such a thing as a tripartite lesson with a starter, a 'main' and a plenary. Yet pedagogically speaking, no such guidance needs to exist. What you favour as a pedagogy should determine the incremental parts of the lesson. It is feasible to have no starter (input) and allow the children to navigate their learning from the start. This not only fosters autonomy but also gives more of a freedom to the lesson. Similarly, there is no precedent set in introducing the learning objective and success criteria at the start of the lesson. This could be revealed at the middle of the allotted time, or even at the end, where you ask the children what they decide they have been learning. In the same fashion there is no guidance that suggests there must be a carpet session (starter), table/desk session (main learning) and a return to the carpet (plenary); this can all be decided and planned by a teacher who questions 'why' practices occur. That said, however, if you are wanting some guidance on how to structure a 45-minute lesson, you use this format (which again is only a suggestion):

A total of 45 minutes is divided into three parts: 15 minutes for an introduction, 20 minutes for a main activity (where the bulk of the children's learning can be recorded on a format of choice) and 10 minutes for a plenary session.

The introduction could cover referring to previous learning, displaying today's learning objective and associated success criteria and modelling of 'to write' an introduction, talk opportunities and any questions.

The main lesson content could cover which group of children you are spending the session with, who the TA is with and who needs help after ten minutes, with a reminder to display the success criteria.

The plenary (more later this) would cover reminding the children of the learning objective and checking their progress against the success criteria.

6 *How will I differentiate my teaching and the children's learning for 'to write'?* Adaptive teaching must be set against the verb 'to write'. Therefore, all children must, according to their ability and understanding, be writing, because otherwise they would not all be accessing the same learning and curriculum objectives. They may 'write' in different ways and with different methods, but you need to ensure that the whole class makes progress with writing.

7 *What language or subject knowledge do I need to prepare for 'to write'?* Let us take language first. With children who have English as an additional language (EAL), this becomes an obvious question to consider. Unless the lesson is specifically 'English' (literacy), the end product may be in English, but during the process, can it be that instruction or guidance, or support, can be in the child's own language? Now that there are software and applications available that have an immediate translation service, for example having key phrases or teaching points written in the child's first language, if the lesson is not English, but say, a humanities lesson, can the product (that is the

visible record of the learning) be captured in the child's first language? In the case of subject knowledge, that is more straightforward; there is no substitute for good and accurate subject knowledge. You will need to be prepared. There can be circumstances when you defer that knowledge to another, for example the teaching assistant in art and design, or a visiting teacher or agency in PE or RE, but you will need to revise if unconfident. Prepare for the child who will likely ask that difficulty question and have an answer for it. Ensure you can spell and pronounce key vocabulary and ask the teaching assistant, if applicable, for feedback on the clarity of your subject knowledge when you have a debrief.

8. *Will I set homework from 'to write'?* As most parents will remind you, homework has to have a purpose and a focus. Set homework that reflects the key lessons in the week and focuses on the learning objective. Set homework that develops the learning rather than merely repeats what was accomplished in the classroom and set it during the plenary.

9. *How will the teaching of today's 'to write' affect the next time I teach this concept or subject?* This will not be on the plan much unless you are planning sequentially; however, it does allow you the opportunity to reflect on the assessment of the learning and to alter subsequent plans. Of course, it does enable you as a teacher not to be rigid in the teaching of sequential plans and to reflect on where issues need to be reinforced or where concepts can be quickly addressed and moved on.

10. *Will the children and any observers soon realise that I am teaching 'to write'?* In many schools, learning walks or observational practice are a regular feature of quality assurance and monitoring procedure. Should a member of the leadership team enter your classroom, you will instantly know why they will go to a child and ask what it is that she is learning. The prepared teacher will not have to worry here because the child will be able to tell the questioner not only that they are learning to 'write an introduction to a story' but be able, hopefully, to provide a short statement on what the previous lessons on writing were, and possibly what the future lesson(s) on writing will be. The observer would be able to see at a glance the resources, use of displays and whiteboard evidence that there is no doubt what the learning is; that is how secure a lesson should be when planned tightly with a focus on the LO.

When you prepare for a daily subject, you plan, teach, resource, deploy and assess against the key verb within the LO. The LO does not need to be addressed at the beginning; it can be revealed at the end – 'what do you think we have been learning about today?' could be a question to commence the plenary session. Do note that the success criterion (singular) or criteria (plural) cannot be the same as the LOs. Success criteria are designed to show the children the steps needed to achieve the learning and are usually examples of previous learning, or even learning objectives!

The plenary

The plenary can be the most dynamic part of the lesson (assuming you are still subscribing to the tripartite approach) but can be rushed for time and executed poorly. You need to devote adequate time to the plenary, and as suggested above, this can be 15 minutes out of a 45-minute session; so ideally, a third of the time. The word 'plenary' is derived from the Latin 'plenus' meaning full, so it is the concept of the lesson being filled or finished, a sense of completeness.

If you are running out of time, it is better advised not to have a plenary session for a lesson. The plenary needs careful construction. That said, a whole lesson can be a plenary, based on the preceding sequence of lessons; just as a starter/input format can be a whole lesson.

A plenary could be comprised of a recapitulation that needs to focus on the learning objective and the children's assessed progress in achieving it. This is where the success criteria are useful. Ask questions to determine how the children have understood their learning and the progress made – you can sample the class for this. Do not repeat an activity from the main part of the lesson for the plenary because such repetition is time-consuming and ineffective. You may plan for some children to evidence their progress against the main activity, or design an extension activity (or even the need to go back a step in the conceptual understanding). Finally, the plenary should have time for the future learning signpost. What do the children think they could be learning tomorrow? How could they prepare for it? It is also the opportunity to set homework that is based on the learning. This means the homework will be relevant and fresh in the children's minds, and, with parents in mind, it will be the time for you to explain what is required and the deadline for returning it.

You may wish to plan for a 'mid-main activity' plenary, when the children have been learning during their main activity after ten minutes or so, or even have a series of short plenaries throughout a lesson rather than rely on one at the end of a lesson. This will be your pedagogic choice based on your feeling for how learning is progressing. One tip is that you should not dismiss the children from the starter phase of a lesson until you are sure, through a good sampling of questioning, that you and the children have a confidence in the next steps.

Considering adaptation

There is no fast rule for how to adapt (differentiate) your teaching; some teachers think there is a need to plan 'for the middle' and adapt below that and above that. You are likely to be guided by the assessment policy of the school or by advice from a phase lead/assessment lead. You will know your children, what they can do, what they struggle with and, for some children, their individual need that requires a specific intervention. Adaptation is not fitting an intervention to a child with need; it can be seeing how many, if not all, children can benefit from that same need. For example, can all children benefit from larger print, coloured overlays and listening to the text being read?

In the planning stage, envisage all the children in the class by physically sitting in their seats as you plan one lesson. You cannot do this every week, but doing it every half-term may get you to think of how that child could feel and their perspective in the classroom. For example, if a child sits at the back of the class, can she see your writing on the interactive whiteboard, or if a child sits by a window, is she distracted by passing traffic? Or if a child's vision is distracted by passing children in the doorway that leads to the corridor?

Plan as if you were a child at times; what do children like to do?

Freedom to change from a plan

If you are on a long car journey and have the misfortune of being stationary in a traffic jam, a good satnav system will automatically redirect you onto another route. It may not be the quickest route, but at least you are moving and making progress on the originally planned journey. So, it must be with a planned lesson. A plan that is not working when being taught is ineffective, and you will need to have the confidence to make a bold decision at any point. Think about when the fire alarm goes off during a lesson; you automatically abandon the teaching and ensure the children are escorted to the assembly point quickly. The same thought process needs to apply if children, or most children, are unable to access the lesson. This may be tough at first, especially if you are being observed as part of your performance management or your ECT moderation, but it is the preferable option to staying with it.

A teacher makes many decisions during a lesson, and deciding whether to abandon it or proceed with the next day's lesson, because the children have grasped the learning so quickly, is an indication of a confident teacher. Such decision-making adds to the strengthening identity of a teacher – you will be able to feel how the needs of the children can be met 'in the moment', and the children, and indeed the observers, will recognise this as a strength of your pedagogy. You will then be able to reflect at a later point on why certain things happened, why you reacted and what you would do next time. Build in time within the school day (if possible) to include the reflections of the TA and other aspects of how the plan was taught in the day's or week's lessons. The teaching assistant can draw on her knowledge and experience of teaching and learning within that school and will have a different perspective, especially when she has been directed to work with a small group of children or an individual child. Encourage the teaching assistant's feedback so that it will inform future planning. If you are brave and democratic in your pedagogy, invite the children to critique your planning and how the lesson went.

Planning for Impact

By Jake Matthews, Primary Headteacher, Somerset, UK

Planning has always been a tricky one for me; of course there is great importance placed on the topic, and it is essential to plan effective lessons in order to achieve good progress. It can be, however, all-consuming and ultimately take over the thoughts of any teacher. Often I hear stories of teachers who complain about a huge workload which hinders their time in the classroom and prevents them from building effective relationships with their pupils; creating large planning documents can often add to this stress and worry.

I always remain of the same mind; all we do must have a positive impact on the children we teach. It is completely pointless for a teacher to be spending hours and hours planning a single lesson. All that time and effort could be put directly into working with children, building relationships and getting to know what makes them tick. Often, as a new teacher, planning can be the safety net that we need to ensure our

(Continued)

lessons progress in the way we intend and that the dreaded learning objective is met. On numerous occasions, I have seen even a thoroughly planned lesson with numerous resources derailed in the first few minutes by an argument at break time spilling into the classroom, a child losing a tooth or a perfectly timed fire drill by senior management. Thanks!

So, I pose this question to anyone reading this, what is your priority for *your* children? Spend time really getting to know your class, build the relationship, find the little nuggets that make your classes tick and use this to truly inform your planning. Find a planning format that works for you, be efficient and don't spend every evening and holiday on in-depth plans.

Give yourself permission to occasionally embrace the chaos. Be brave and step away from the planning sheet. Of course, have your eye on the long-term goal, but if you meander and move off course along the way, don't panic, trust yourself and enjoy being derailed. You have a unique opportunity to shape the lives of the children you work with each day. Look up and see them.

Planning

By Ian Pugh, Principal at Al Ain Academy, Al Ain, Abu Dhabi

When I qualified as a teacher, I remember my mother telling me not to turn into 'one of those' teachers. She had been a PA to the SLT in a local secondary school for many years. Upon asking her what she meant, she informed me that during her time in schools, she came across some teachers who had grown disaffected by the role and had forgotten why they started teaching in the first place.

Immediately, I vowed to myself that I would not be that teacher. Nor did I come across many, and now, as a principal myself, I can honestly say that times have changed, and I have encountered very few teachers I would ever place in this bracket. But at the time, as a Newly Qualified Teacher (NQT), I set out to make as many lessons as possible WOW for pupils. I wanted to inspire every day. So planning was important to me. Seeking ways to include elements of pupils' passions, an array of toys, footballers and movie stars would regularly make their way into my lesson plans in a bid to 'hook' the children with their passions.

Years passed, and my skills improved as my career voyaged into new schools, some graded as outstanding. Excellent practitioners and leaders taught me that differentiation is so much more diverse than simply three well-thought-out activities. With increasing focus, I began to place individual kids/pairs of children onto my planning, literally naming them on the plan and how the activity would be tailored to their needs, varying from top end of the class to low end and some More Able (MA) along the way. Sometimes this would still include personalised activities based on their hobbies.

(Continued)

However, as one's career progresses in teaching, quite naturally we make that transition to Middle Leader/Subject Lead/Year Leader (insert school's terminology of choice). Time becomes the most precious resource at this stage. Almost all middle leaders have a teaching timetable, with many remaining full time in the classroom still. Suddenly, I found myself planning lessons, whilst monitoring books, providing feedback, lesson observations, attending more meetings, parent concerns…. We all know the list is endless. I still remember one Sunday afternoon writing a lesson plan. The plan was complete, and I was about to rejoice in that moment of closing the laptop and enjoying what remained of my weekend. After a pause of reflection, I noticed there was no mention of anything inspiring for the kids, no mention of any individual pupil's name. Most concerning for me, I read over the plan and it didn't inspire ME. It didn't make me excited to go into school and teach those lessons.

All of a sudden I felt precariously close to becoming one of those teachers my mother warned me of. After all, I am sure all of those teachers were not disaffected by TEACHING, but by all of the other above-mentioned tasks that come with it.

So on that day, I vowed to myself a few things. And today, as you read this, I will share with you the simple advice I would give to anyone who wants to create a good plan. If you get to the end of a week's core lesson plan and you don't have:

- At least one or two days on the plan that give you genuine excitement to teach the lesson and intrigue as to how the pupils will enjoy or achieve within the lesson
- One or two pupils individually named on the plan for areas of the lesson tailored to their ability or their passions

Then it is probably time to do some heavy editing or start the plan again.

Planning for Inclusion: Supporting Children of Showmen

By Bernice Wall, Narvenka Noyce, Hayley Danter, Nicola Hill, Joannie Peak, and Colleen Roper at Future 4 Fairgrounds, Hunstanton, Norfolk, UK

Future4fairgrounds are a group of six lady Showmen who came together in September 2020 because of our joint concerns surrounding the issues Showmen were facing due to the impact of the pandemic. Our initial focus was to highlight the fairs that were unable to open during 2020 and create a better understanding of the amount of Showman families that were affected because of this. During 2020 we attended many locations that would have usually held fairgrounds on an annual basis. Our #f4f banners were used to highlight the loss of the fair. They also displayed our aims as a community group – to celebrate our past, raise awareness for the present and protect our future. We raised our profile on social media, contacted our own MPs and became an additional voice for our community establishing ourselves alongside the number of trade

(Continued)

body representatives that speak for our industry. We realised from the interest in F4F that there was a very real need for a community group such as ours, and we were very proud to be mentioned in a Westminster debate in December of 2020, just 3 months after we had established Future4Fairgrounds.

https://hansard.parliament.uk/commons/2020-12-17/debates/3B335883-D800-426D-ACAD-2204734ED4F7/FairsAndShowgrounds

In 2021 our work continued, and there are many highlights that spring to mind including the census work that we got involved with; where we produced information postcards to make sure our community knew that they could identify as a Showman for the first time on the census using their background. Almost 4000 postcards were delivered to Showmen up and down the country, pointing out the importance of the census and why everyone should fill it in including Showmen. We hope the data collected by the Office for National Statistics (ONS) will be used in a way that helps our community to be better recognised in all areas.

We would say one of our biggest personal successes was that we'd managed to remain as a proactive group for a full year, and our group F4F celebrated being one year old on 24th September 2021.

This anniversary took place during World Fun Fair Month (WFFM); an initiative we came up with to help raise further awareness of our community and join together with other Showmen on a global scale; World Fun Fair Month (future4fairgrounds.com).

There has never been anything to celebrate our community before. We were overwhelmed by the number of Showmen that got involved with our project. A video was made to launch the idea.

https://m.youtube.com/watch?v=bNeUbCy7qI4

'I Am A Showman' was declared by Showmen of all ages, genders and nationalities and highlighted a community coming together united in their pride for who we are as a people. It was a perfect start to a month-long celebration. The WFFM logo was also flown at fairgrounds in the UK, Europe and around the world, making its way to Australia, New Zealand and even Times Square New York! WFFM was being shared by so many enthusiasts and supporters that it became much bigger than we ever expected. The project evolved organically, and we were overwhelmed at the success of the event.

One of the main aspects of WFFM involved the newly published independent reading book *The Show Must Go On*.

https://www.pearson.com/uk/educators/schools/news/schools-blog/2021/06/the-show-must-go-on-the-writers-representing-fairground-culture.html

Having been contacted by co-author Michelle Russell early on in F4F's conception, it was wonderful to finally hear about this book being published and the positive representation of the Showmen family at its heart. We need to make clear we did not have any input in the book's creation, but it perfectly fit in with our ethos and we could see the huge impact this little book could have. We wanted to make sure this groundbreaking book was available to as many schools as possible. We know that funding for new

(Continued)

books is not always a top priority for schools, and we were concerned this book would not be on many schools' reading lists. So, we felt we had to do what we could do to make it more accessible. With Michelle's help, we were able to speak to the publisher, Pearson, to discuss the concept of the book project. The books cost £5.80 each; we had raised some money from selling our WFFM flags and F4F merchandise as well as kind donations. We were able to place an initial order with Pearson and buy 1000 copies. They were sent out to tie in with the launch of WFFM. We gave five copies each to schools that had fairgrounds linked to their towns during the month of September.

This amazing little book is so much more than a just reading book. We believe it can be used as a tool to spark a thought, start a conversation, raise awareness of our community and with the help of WFFM help make further links to the towns the Showmen visit annually. Many schools have been in touch with us because of our project. They are aware that there is a lack of understanding and knowledge about Showmen. They understand the need for positive representation of our community in their school and in the education system as a whole. Since September, our 'book project' has gained momentum, and we have purchased a further 1000 books! They were posted out in January, and this time at the request of parents, they were given to schools that already have Showman children attending. Imagine being a child in school and not one book relates to who you are. This is just one of the issues our children face in school. Word has spread about the project, and we have now had many personal requests from teachers to be included in our next distribution. With the continued support from fairground enthusiasts and Showmen, we are in a position to place our 3rd order – another 1000 copies. We are hopeful this distribution will coincide with World Book Day. In the future we would like to be able to see copies of The Show Must Go On in every primary school in the UK, but this is reliant on our funds.

Our aims for 2022 remain the same as those we first set out in 2020, 'Celebrating Our Past, Raising Awareness For The Present, Protecting Our Future'. One of our focus points will remain with raising awareness of Showmen in education. This has been extended from our initial look at primary schools and what they are doing into every stage of learning and teaching. We are hoping we can make changes in early years right through to higher education. Showman children's attainment in education is at an all-time high. This is evident with more Showmen than ever before staying on in school, achieving fantastic exam results and following their academic career into university. Yet the truth is there are no statistics to back this fact up as our community is still invisible in education. Currently we cannot identify as a Showman on any enrolment form at any stage of school life.

We think education is key to raising awareness. If we can help stop misconceptions and prejudice by offering an authentic voice and sharing positive, accurate information with teachers in schools and universities to share with their students, we can create a better understanding of who Showmen are, from the ground up. We hope that we can encourage all educational settings to identify the Showmen that they do have in attendance in an official way on enrolment forms. At the moment, our community is invisible on most official forms.

(Continued)

We are raising the issue in many ways. With our collaboration with other associations and our contribution on the GTRSB pledge into higher education, we are hopeful that we can make a difference in how Showmen are seen in education and bring about a change for the better.

We continue to speak to various significant people, groups and associations about our community to achieve our aims. We have made many friends and allies to our cause, and the truth is we wouldn't be anything without all of them. We are so grateful for all the people that have helped us along the way and taken an interest in our group. We are most definitely stronger together.

We hope that that support will continue as we continue to build on the work that we have done in our first year. F4F is certainly here to stay as a community voice, and we look forward to celebrating WFFM with everyone again each September!

Planning for Bilingual Learners

By Robert Coyle, EAL Adviser and Former Primary Teacher, Norfolk, UK

When planning for learners with EAL, consideration needs to be given to the breadth of vocabulary the learner may have in English but also the opportunities afforded by their first language. It is important to remember that these are not learners with special educational needs, and they may be highly knowledgeable and skilled when given the language support to show what they can do.

It is essential that you identify any vocabulary that may not be familiar to the learners. This may not simply be the Tier 3 words but also Tier 2 words that will be familiar to native speakers. They may describe a material as 'hard' but may not recognise 'durable' or 'rigid'. Identifying these words and pre-teaching vocabulary to bilingual learners is essential to ensure they can access the lesson material. Word mats and vocabulary cards with visuals will give learners something to refer through throughout the lesson. It is also important to consider cultural considerations. A lesson about the English Civil War is likely to require more pre-lesson input than one about the Solar System as much of the material will not have been previously encountered in their first language.

Bilingual learners should be given opportunities to orally compose, discuss and clarify answers before tackling writing tasks. This is a beneficial activity for all learners as it allows them to sequence, order and justify their ideas whilst hearing modelled language from other learners. Activities that focus on the meaning of the text are particularly important for EAL learners as they will often have good decoding skills but weaker comprehension skills.

Scaffolding and structured writing support should keep the cognitive challenge high. Sentence frames, cloze exercises and substitution tables all support the learner to use their current level of language ability to answer questions to the same level as their peers. They also provide a valuable model of correct language structure.

(Continued)

One of the most underused resources when teaching bilingual learners is the students' first language (L1). Learners' critical thinking and problem-solving skills are likely to be higher in their L1. Allowing pupils to make notes or plan writing in L1 can help them to arrange their ideas and plan more coherently. Younger students might use L1 words in their writing when they don't know the equivalent word in English (this is an example of translanguaging). The words can then be checked afterwards using bilingual dictionaries or translation apps. Teaching learners to use these apps independently allows them to edit their work to replace L1 words. These strategies also value the learner's first language and show the learner and the class that you acknowledge its value and importance.

Assessment is key to ensuring the success of these planning strategies. Ensuring that you have accurate information about the learner's educational experience and their first language ability will allow you to tailor the support to their particular individual needs. Tracking their progress using a framework such as the one developed by the Bell Foundation will ensure that you are aware of appropriate language goals for your bilingual learners.

When planning for bilingual learners, value their full linguistic repertoire, give them constant speaking opportunities and always challenge them to expand their vocabulary!

Planning is not about the Proforma you Use

By Clare Greene, Headteacher at St. Michael's Junior Church School, Bath, NE Somerset, UK

It's in Teacher Standard 4 which states 'plan and teach well-structured lessons'. Simple. Yet the subsequent bullet points don't actually address the process of planning in order that teachers can 'impart knowledge and develop understanding'. Not so simple. Effective teaching needs effective planning (or quality first or great or whichever term you prefer), but that doesn't mean the completion of a template, usually designed by someone else. Experienced teachers will tell you anecdotally that some of their best sessions were unplanned or my personal favourite 'on the back of a fag packet'. I'm not sure that's entirely true, more that they didn't spend hours completing someone else's proforma, which was deemed to be an effective plan. Maybe it was more that they spent that time thinking and making decisions about content, order and method of delivery. Maybe they even rehearsed in their head a script of how they were going to chunk the content into small, logically ordered steps or spent some time finding a resource to support pupils who might find the concept challenging. Maybe what they needed to record required little paper because it was for them, just notes and prompts on the direction and links to resources. All feasibly would fit on the back of a fag packet or beer mat!

So planning isn't just as simple as what they will learn and in what order, although that is addressed in the teacher standard (contributing to curriculum). Effective planning is thinking about how your pupils will learn. Therefore, understanding their needs

(Continued)

is essential for them to progress through the planned learning. And that's not forgetting their social, emotional or mental health needs too. EEF guidance suggests strategies that can be particularly useful for pupils with SEND:

- Flexible grouping
- Cognitive and metacognitive strategies
- Explicit instruction
- Using technology
- Scaffolding

And if it works for SEND pupils, trust me it will be beneficial for all. This is what planning should focus on to enable high-quality teaching. Teachers historically have spent an undue amount of time planning and resourcing lessons (Eliminating unnecessary workload around planning and teaching resources 2016). Daily planning and completing unnecessarily detailed proformas are poor proxies for effective planning. A proforma with prompts may be helpful, and some schools direct a particular lesson structure; however, it is still for the teacher to plan within those parameters. So, keep in mind who is your planning for? Ofsted don't require a specific format; SLT cannot ask you for it. It should be for you, to help you meet your pupils' needs. Discussing it with colleagues is helpful, sharing resources too, whereas planning too far ahead is less so. The more time you spend planning (particularly if this involves a lengthy format), the less likely you are to embrace adaptive teaching during your sessions, and the temptation is to plough on through your planned content, in the way you planned it, regardless. That is a waste of everyone's time – yours and your pupils. And for the SLT box ticking you've completed your planning! This is equally true when you're checking for understanding. If they've got it, great. Move on! Right there and then, take them to the next step and challenge them – they can do it! Don't be bound to what you've planned; celebrate in their achievement.

Plan for the *current* needs of your pupils, prepare to be adaptive and share the load. The best planning happens in your head and not on a proforma. And remember knowing where you want them to end up is important, but the real craft of planning is how you get there.

'If you Fail to Plan, you Plan to Fail'

By Kate Sturdy, Departmental Lead for Years 5 and 6, KS2 Curriculum Lead, Flintshire, Wales, UK

Gone are the days of long-term plans accompanied by detailed medium-term planning; folders that could be pulled out with all resources lesson by lesson. I would know exactly what was to be planned and taught each day of each week of each month or each term of each academic year – boring!

(Continued)

Looking back, the advantages were that it was all done for you – it was easy. Now when I reminisce, I question the supposedly good practices of the past:

- Where was the creativity for both the practitioner and more importantly the learner?
- Were the topics and lessons centred around what the learners actually had an interest in? Were the topics relevant to my learners year on year? We all know how cohorts can vary drastically from one year to another and even class to class if teaching in a larger school with more than one form entry.
- Did the topics represent the history and diversity of communities, in particular the stories of Black, Asian and minority ethnic people within our societies locally and further afield?
- Was there a huge opportunity to adapt lesson on lesson from teacher observations or learners' needs for individual progression to occur?
- Was there enough flexibility to deviate away from the detailed plans?
- Would I have been allowed to carry on with mathematics, for instance, all morning if I felt this was best for my learners that day? No!
- Were we too focussed on teaching facts, and more should have been focussed on the skills needed to find the answers to such facts independently?
- Was this type of planning failing learners to be equipped with the skills needed to be lifelong learners in the twenty-first century?

Having reflected on my experiences as a teacher over the years, I now wonder if *planning too much actually sets you up to fail as a facilitator of learning and crucially fail our learners with the experiences and skills now needed in today's society.*

Planning is about quality not quantity. Planning if done properly is for each individual learner in order to progress and achieve at their pace. It is the driving force for excellence and equity for all. It is not about instructing the teacher what to teach every step of the way, basically forcing all learners to say and do in a specific way and timescale. We as practitioners are now facilitators of learning, providing rich learning experiences that encourage learners to question for themselves, develop the skills needed to find answers independently, present their work in the way they feel is best for them and have the ability to use sources of information to make their own well-balanced beliefs and decisions that may impact on themselves and others now and in the future.

In Wales, practitioners have been preparing for a new curriculum since 2017. At the heart of all planning, no matter what key stage/phase, the main vision is equity and excellence for all through universal access to experiences, knowledge and skills needed for employment, lifelong learning and active citizenship in the twenty-first century.

Whilst planning or making any key decisions that will impact on teaching and learning, the Four Purposes must be at the forefront.

The aim of any school's curriculum in Wales is to support its learners to become

- Ambitious, capable learners, ready to learn throughout their lives
- Enterprising, creative contributors, ready to play a full part in life and work
- Ethical, informed citizens of Wales and the world
- Healthy, confident individuals, ready to lead fulfilling lives as valued members of society

Children at the Heart of Planning

By Michelle Windridge, Lecturer of Education at University College Birmingham, Birmingham, UK

Children must be at the heart of the planning process; after all, it is them that we are planning for. It can sometimes feel like our planning is to please Ofsted or to demonstrate to SLT how we have mapped out a sure-fire way of ensuring that our children meet their 'next steps'; however, the 30 individuals within our class deserve better than this. Those 30 little people deserve the very best; they deserve a teacher who will take what needs to be covered from the curriculum and present it in a way that meets the individual needs of the children in their class.

Research tells us that children learn best through play, and we know that children play more successfully if they feel safe and secure; relationships within a classroom are the make-or-break factor in allowing children to feel safe enough to take risks in their play, and this must be present for learning to happen. High-quality relationships between the adults in a classroom and the children must be where the planning process starts. There is nothing that excites me more than rolling my sleeves up and getting down on the floor to play. The planning process begins here. What does the child already demonstrate that he knows whilst he is engaged in play? What are his interests? How does he interact with the environment around him? It is from this point that the teacher can then step away and plan purposeful next steps.

Having qualified almost 25 years ago, downloadable lesson plans were non-existent, and so getting to know the children in a class was the basic foundation of the planning process after all; how else would we find out what our children could do? Yes, we had curriculum guidance, but the endless downloadable plans, lists of expectations and next steps did not exist. The children in our class had no alternative but to be the amazing individuals that they were, and it was our job to mould the curriculum around their needs and interests.

Planning must consider the needs of the children in the class; children are not programmed robots that all develop at the same rate; they need an individualised plan that meets their needs and interests, which is taught by a teacher who is excited to see what they do next. This relationship is what makes the planning process successful, and it is not available for download.

Planning and Teaching of Writing

By Steve Martin, Assistant Headteacher at Valley Invicta Primary School at Kings Hill, West Malling, Kent, UK

The teaching of writing to primary-aged children is one of the greatest pleasures in teaching but is a path littered with potholes and obstacles to trip you (and the children) up. The analogy of driving a car always comes to mind, when first learning nothing seems

(Continued)

automatic. It feels like you will never get master it, but given time and plenty of practice, you build confidence, and the next thing you know, you have driven to work and not even really thought about how. This is exactly how a young writer feels when first trying to write. Handwriting, content, spelling, punctuation and vocabulary are just a few elements which need to be mastered during the writing process. Children need to be given time to master these in an age-appropriate way independently, before trying to combine them to produce pieces of written work. Of course, phonics being taught explicitly will begin to teach the building blocks around spelling, but ensuring that the other elements are well sequenced, appropriate and structured in a way which is accessible to the children is essential.

Children love a piece of technical vocabulary, a 'big word' which they can go home and show off about. Teaching a Year 2 child to describe where an adverb can go in a sentence or to use the word clauses when discussing the use of subordinating conjunctions can seem very complex, but by allowing the children to really understand and talk about their learning builds the foundations on which KS2 and 3 colleagues can continue the build. When planning explicit spelling, punctuation or grammar lessons, it is vital the children have the opportunity to investigate, play with and use what they have learnt, there and then, and then apply this in subsequent lessons. The 'penny dropping' moment will never lose its excitement, when a child puts what they have learnt into practice and are successful. This could be writing a CVC word within the early years to explaining word choice in a Year 6 biography.

Shared and modelled writing are two essential elements for me when teaching children to write. I look back and wonder how I managed it before these had become tools of my trade.

Shared writing is when the teacher and student work as one. Quite often, the teacher being the hand and the children being the givers of content. This gives the teacher chance to use the ideas generated by the children, without them having to worry about the technicalities of handwriting, spelling and punctuation. In my room, children have whiteboards in front of them if they want to write ideas, but speaking and listening come to the fore.

When modelling writing, the teacher takes the role of the complete writer, but verbalises every step in the process, modelling for the children that the writing process is a process full of decisions and quandaries. By using rhetorical questions aloud, the children see and hear the small steps which build and develop into a final piece. Which as I say to every class is only a great start and then the editing process starts!

Planning for Neurodiversity: An Alternative Way

By Mike Scott, EdD Researcher in Neurodivergence at University of Bournemouth, Dorset, UK

As a child growing up in the North East of England, I found myself at odds with the educational system in terms of teaching styles and approaches to their students. I was often in the middle set of classes for most subjects, and this meant I would go 'under the radar' for needing help or support.

(Continued)

Often my school reports would say 'bright but shy student, needs to interact more in group discussions', and this would go on verbatim till I left education at seventeen. What the schools and educators did not realise was that I was autistic. Autistic as described as higher functioning at the cost of energy due to 'masking or scripting' my behaviour in order to fit in with other expectations, be it with other students or the educators.

My own diagnosis did not come about till I was in my thirties, studying, as a mature student. As a mature student at a university, I was struggling to disseminate texts – I later found out I was dyslexic and had a memory, processing delay that meant I needed more time to read and understand information being given. In retrospect, I was always late in finishing work, be it the teacher writing on the board or moving on to the next page in an English class. I now wish I had been given that bit more time to process and, therefore, to understand the content and get better grades at school.

Another example of where I could have been given support was being shown alternative strategies, such as in maths, for example. I could never understand the way in which to do long division or multiplication till in secondary school a teacher said try this box method (Figure 4.1). This alternative allowed me to move up a set in maths as I could do the calculations and I felt a sense of relief that I wasn't being stupid.

However, these patterns of not getting it and then trying to find alternative strategies are something I have now been able to do on my own. At university, whilst I was initial to support, I would not often get it in the way I needed to, such as PowerPoints 48 hours in advance. Most lecturers found this bothersome and often would leave me catching up to my peers as I had to process the information after class and then do all the work I needed to.

My autistic traits and behaviours are what made me so resilient, but I did wonder if it wasn't for this, I probably would have achieved as much as I did. I am now doing my doctorate in education; my passion is for learning and passing on the knowledge I have learned. As educators we need to think about students as individuals and their individualistic needs. Taking that bit more time in the beginning to know your students will pay off dividends in the future.

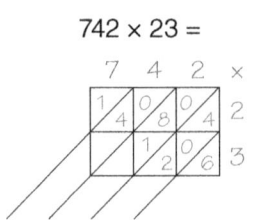

742 × 23 =

Figure 4.1 The box method of multiplication

Planning for Transitions

By Philip Nicholson, Lecturer in Primary Education Studies at University of Suffolk, Ipswich, Suffolk, UK

The transition from Reception to Year 1 is an important time for children, parents, carers and teachers. Although both Reception and Year 1 are located within the primary school, the transition between these year groups should not be viewed simply as a move to the next classroom down the corridor. Instead, it is a time and space where different – and often conflicting – ideas, beliefs and policies relating to children, learning and teaching confront one another. These differences are, to a great extent, reflected in the curriculum frameworks that inform Reception and Year 1. Reception teachers are required to follow the Early Years Foundation Stage (EYFS) (Department for Education [DfE], 2021) which is based on four 'overarching principles': the unique child; positive relationships; enabling environments with teaching and support from responsive adults; and children develop and learn at different rates (p. 6). Year 1 teachers, by contrast, are required to follow the National Curriculum (DfE, 2013) which is described as providing 'pupils with an introduction to the essential knowledge that they need to be educated citizens' (p. 6). The shift in emphasis within these curriculum frameworks is significant and often contributes to Reception and Year 1 implementing different pedagogical approaches. This can pose both challenges and opportunities for children and families, depending on the level of support provided by schools and teachers.

I have recently completed a PhD that explored the pedagogies enacted in Reception and Year 1 in two different schools. It considered how children and their parents experienced and perceived these pedagogies as well as the transition between them. My research identified that the actions of, and interactions between, Reception and Year 1 teachers and senior leaders are critical to supporting and empowering children and families to negotiate the changes involved in the transition. The following considerations can support teachers to develop transition practices that result in enjoyable and positive experiences for all involved:

- Create a space for ongoing reflection where Reception, Year 1 teachers and senior leaders can come together to engage in conversation, share expertise and negotiate understandings of appropriate educational practice across the transition.
- Seek, listen and act on the experiences and perceptions of children and provide opportunities for them to exercise agency over their learning across the transition.
- View the transition from Reception to Year 1 as a process rather than an event. It is not just the first day in Year 1.
- The transition from Reception to Year 1 is subjective and will be experienced in different ways by different people in different contexts.

(Continued)

- The transition from Reception to Year 1 is also significant for families. Consider how reciprocal, responsive and respectful partnerships can be established and developed across the transition. Well-informed and actively engaged parents and carers are able to support their child's transition more effectively.
- Children expect, anticipate and look forward to experiencing change at times of transition, but too much change, if not appropriately supported, can be overwhelming and difficult to negotiate. Try to establish a balance between continuity and change and consider these concepts as existing along a continuum, rather than binaries.

Planning for Transition from Nursery into Reception

By Claire Browning and Susannah Miles, Nursery Managers at Purple Lion Day Nursey, Benfleet, Essex, UK

Transition is easier to say than do, especially if you are talking about a child leaving an Early Years setting and moving to 'big school'.

We are a PVI setting. Children start with us around the age of 9 months and stay with us until it is time to go to school, so for them it is a huge physical and emotional development. We have supported parents and children for up to 4 years, sharing many 'first' milestones along the way. From the children's perspective suddenly, everyone is talking about leaving nursery, their comfort zone and going to this thing called 'big school'! Early Years settings strive to be as home-like as possible. We follow a child's interests and do not have a particularly rigid structure to the day. Children are encouraged to self-choose toys and activities. Learning is very much through play. When many parents talk about school, recollections are often based on their later experiences – sitting at a desk all day and learning from textbooks.

Particularly noticeable in our 2021 cohort, we find that parents conceal the anxieties they feel over their children going to school. The stresses and strains of coronavirus changed the structure of normal family life. The children of COVID-19 find it hard to self-regulate and are also lacking in the social and communication skills that we normally see in our children transitioning to school. The parents' concerns were around how their child would cope in a bigger group of children with unfamiliar adults.

As a small setting, we have the time to discuss the specific concerns that families have when their children approach starting school. Our knowledge of local schools and what they do helps us to reassure parents that the majority of their fears are not unusual or out of the ordinary. We share helpful and simple information packs that we have put together. The pack includes books to read with the children, a short 'tips to prepare your child for school' leaflet and a child-centred 'getting ready for school' checklist.

(Continued)

We feel that a strong connection with the schools in our local community benefits the transition period for the family as a whole. Our nearest partner primary school has helped us to understand, translate to parents in a 'user friendly' way and embed our 'school readiness' ethos. Teaching staff have said that coming into our setting to visit the children gives them a better understanding of the children's development and needs, compared to those children who just have a home visit. The information gathered from us is of a professional prospective, enabling EYFS staff to 'start off, where we finished'. Our children are excited to see meet new people and seem confident to talk to their new teacher because their surroundings are comfortable and familiar to them with their key person nearby. Teachers can talk to them about similarities of our setting to school, such as toys available to access, where the children hang their belongings, etc.

In the second half of the summer term, we add school uniform in our role play areas. This is so that the children develop their self-help skills further by dressing and undressing, and this allows them to independently explore their thoughts and feelings around going to 'big school'. Through our strong relationships with the schools in our community, we receive information from them such as class and teachers' names, photos of the school, classroom, dining hall and playground, etc. This has been particularly important during the last 2 years as schools have restricted the amount of prior access for families. We share these photos and other information given to us, at key parts of our day, such as circle times, to familiarise those children with their new setting.

Planning the Transition from Primary to Secondary

By Saira Saeed, Secondary Leader (SENCO and DSL) @SafeSENCOSaeed, Birmingham, UK

'I'm worried about remembering all of my different teachers and the school is huge'. (Year 6 student)

'She's so shy and I'm scared she'll get bullied in the playground'. (Year 6 father)

The quotes above are paraphrased but stated by numerous students and parents alike, as the transition to 'big school' is equally daunting for both. It isn't any less so for the Year 6 teachers letting go of their class who are facing the imminent change in status from oldest to youngest year group. This change isn't without its worries: the prospect of having different lessons in multiple classrooms with different teachers, gargantuan school building/s, the fear of not having the support they had in Year 6 and more.

As the last teacher they'll have in Year 6, you are in a privileged position to positively influence this process in the following ways:

(Continued)

SEND

Ensuring the transition process is as smooth and pleasant as possible is key for all Year 6 students. It is paramount; however, this is the case for any students with SEND, as their needs may well present with considerable barriers that will need to be overcome. Collaboration is key here: you know your SEND students best; hence you should be involved in conversations with their secondary SENCO (or at least your own SENCO who will relay information from you to the necessary secondary colleagues.) Furthermore, as best as capacity allows, you should accompany your SEND students to any transition visits (and yes, there should be more than one in order to help them acclimatise to their new surroundings) because your presence will make that process far less overwhelming.

Safeguarding

You may not be your school's DSL, but as class teacher you should still have been informed of any safeguarding matters affecting your students, as you see them more than most. This knowledge will in turn enable you to have gained a thorough understanding of what further support these respective students require in secondary school (for instance, subtle signs to look out for that may be bespoke to specific students and not commonly associated with key forms of abuse). It is important that you share this knowledge with either the secondary DSL directly or via your own DSL.

Student Welfare

Knowing the secondary destinations of all of your students is given, but it is particularly important to have planned for the 'lone ranger' (the student who is the only one from your school joining a particular secondary school and doesn't know anyone else there.) Ideally, a familiar adult will need to accompany them on any transition visits and also seek to get them connected to any other 'lone rangers' from different schools so that they can share their mutual experiences.

Coming from the perspective of an experienced secondary specialist, the following is contentious but also usually true. In short, Year 6 parents trust you – the primary teacher – more than secondary staff; especially until they have faith that their child is safe and in good hands at secondary school. As a result, reassure them (parents and students) that the transition is an exciting and positive process via coffee mornings; have class discussions around any worries students might have and what they can do in the face of any particularly common scenarios (getting lost and struggling to make friends); and also focus on what they can look forward to.

The transition to secondary school is an exciting journey that offers students an abundance of opportunities, and it is inarguable that primary staff play a pivotal role in the beginning of this.

Summary

This chapter has argued that an informed and prepared teacher will have a plan that gives her the confidence to be an effective and efficient teacher. Begin by reflecting on your identity as a teacher in terms of favoured pedagogy; what you believe is the best way children learn is how your plans will be written. If you take risks, the children will take risks; if you think discussion is an optimum way of learning, the children will learn by discussing freely. It has been argued that planning to get the learning objective right will be key to a good plan.

Be confident, know your children, know the setting of the learning objective, know what resources are available and rely on the quality of your pedagogical understanding. If it works, learn why it worked; if it did not work, learn why it did not. A good plan may not automatically result in a good lesson, but at least you have prepared for one. Preparation and careful thought are what are required in the planning stage. What happens in the classroom when teaching the children is the time that may be planned for and be expected but should also be seen as a time when things become unexpected, and the plan may not cover that. This is when you have the freedom to adapt the plan, abandon it and trust your pedagogical instinct. What you learn during those times will ultimately inform your future planning.

References

Clarke, S. (2001). *Unlocking Formative Assessment*. London: Hodder & Stoughton.

Department for Education (DfE). (2013). The national curriculum in England: Key stages 1 and 2 framework document. Available at: https://assets.publishing.service.gov.uk/government/uploads/system/uploads/attachment_data/file/425601/PRIMARY_national_curriculum.pdf

Department for Education (DfE). (2021). Statutory framework for the early years foundation stage. Setting the standards for learning, development and care for children from birth to five. Available at: https://assets.publishing.service.gov.uk/government/uploads/system/uploads/attachment_data/file/974907/EYFS_framework_-_March_2021.pdf

5 Subject knowledge and pedagogy

KEY WORDS
Knowledge, learning, knowing, curriculum, pedagogy

Contributors within this chapter:

1. John Bullen
2. Rachel Kerridge
3. Oscar Pimlett
4. Sarah Cummins
5. Jay Maxwell
6. Stephanie Hunter
7. Debbie Marlow
8. Jessica Crumlish
9. Laura Colam
10. Jack Phillips
11. Bernie Westacott
12. Jo Montgomery
13. Andrew Jack
14. Nyree Scott
15. Gerard Lavelle
16. Charlotte Day
17. Elizah Barnes
18. Elise Ramadan

Introduction

Pollard (2019, p. 288) draws the reader's attention to what he considers as the *'most influential analysis of subject knowledge in education'* as provided by Shulman (1986, cited in Pollard, 2014), who, in turn, addressed the three areas of subject knowledge under content knowledge, pedagogic content knowledge and curricular knowledge. This chapter interpolates Shulman's work with examples of subject knowledge in religious education that may be

DOI: 10.4324/9781003218098-5

useful. Subject knowledge may be perceived as 'information I already know or can access', but a skilful teacher will realise how to link it cross-curricularly, how to develop the need to maintain current subject knowledge and how to use the pedagogy to teach it effectively in the classroom. There is no shame in not knowing something, just shame in not finding out. This chapter suggests that a confident teacher is one who is equipped with sufficient, all-round knowledge, who does not fret when questioned during teaching, can model how children can develop their own subject knowledge and one who seeks to improve in the three types of knowledge explained below.

Content knowledge

> **Critical question**
>
> What is the role of knowledge in a modern classroom?

Content knowledge is what those teachers know from their own education, reading or research and can be divided into two areas (Schwab, 1978, cited in Pollard, 2019, p. 288):

Substantive subject knowledge which is the understanding of *'facts, concepts and principles of a subject'* and syntactic subject knowledge which is why *'such knowledge is deemed important and is justified'*.

In religious education there is a difference between what you should know and what you do not need to know. You would need to know the basic terms, names, faiths, festivals and key stories. These are the building blocks and the key components of subject knowledge. More nuanced subject knowledge comes from spelling names and key phrases correctly and pronouncing them accurately. A simple way to develop your subject knowledge is the creation of a subject knowledge sheet which can be filled in prior to the timetabling of a subject (see Table 5.1). This sheet acts as an audit of what you know and what is left for you to know. It breaks down the subject of religious education into the six world major faiths (with a column spare for another faith or belief that you may feel is relevant to your class, for example humanism).

As you fill in your audits of subject knowledge or read the curriculum requirements, it will be obvious to you what there is to know in order to teach that subject for the best interests of the children; that is, of course, different from knowing everything there is to know about a particular subject. The memory is only so productive (as cognitive load theory suggests) so you need to rely on relevant literature. In religious education, for example, this would be a key teaching resource such as Derek Bastide's (2007) *Teaching Religious Education* 4-11 or, for in-depth knowledge, Ninian Smart's (1998) *The World's Religions*, or the contemporary work of Lat Blaylock in RE Today (2022).

Syntactic subject knowledge is why 'knowledge is important and justified'. This gives rise to understanding 'why' knowledge is so, who has given knowledge its validity and why a piece of knowledge should be taught rather than something else. In other words, what you know within a subject has been selected from a trusted source, or from accredited continuing

Table 5.1 A simple audit sheet for subject knowledge in Religious Education, with Judaism as an example filled in

Basic subject knowledge requirements	Buddhism	Christianity	Hinduism	Islam	Judaism	Sikhism	+1
Names of deities/ key people					God or YHWH		
Name of the sacred text/holy book					Torah		
Name of a key festival and the basic knowledge					Hanukah – the Jewish Festival of Lights. 'Hanukkah' means 'Dedication' in Hebrew. It celebrates a miracle that happened in Jerusalem over 2,000 years ago.		
Name of the centre of that faith					Synagogue		
Basic knowledge of a key story					Moses and the ten commandments in Exodus 20:1-15		
Describe one key artefact					Sukkot – the Seder plate consists of a lamb bone, a roasted egg, a green vegetable, bitter herbs, charoset and romaine lettuce		
Website					https://www.bbc.co.uk/bitesize/topics/zvp8f4j		

+1 could be a significant faith or belief relevant to your class, e.g. humanism.

professional development, or gained from membership of a subject-based association (see Table 5.2 for some examples).

Within content knowledge, it is important to perhaps frame it as contemporary knowledge. It is not a surprise that knowledge is always changing, but that knowledge is taught as if it is current. One example is that prior to 2006 Pluto was the ninth planet of the solar system and taught as such; now it is related as a 'dwarf planet'. Vincent (2022) explained how the history of measurement is similar. He describes how the original metre and kilogram were created out of platinum and fixed to be the unit of length (as a fraction of the Earth's meridian) and weight (1,000 cubic centimetres of water) but are now defined by the speed of light per second and Planck's constant. In history he also stated that the barleycorn may be perceived as an obsolete measure, at one-third of an inch, but is in fact still

Subject knowledge and pedagogy 57

Table 5.2 Religious education resources

NASACRE
http://www.nasacre.org.uk/

An example of a SACRE (Royal Borough of Greenwich)-agreed syllabus
http://www.royalgreenwich.gov.uk/info/32/school_curriculum/1152/teaching_religious_education_re_in_our_schools

NATRE
http://www.natre.org.uk/

AREIAC
http://www.areiac.org.uk/

RE Council
http://religiouseducationcouncil.org.uk/

RE Online
http://www.reonline.org.uk/

Report of the Commission on Religion and Belief in British Public Life
https://corablivingwithdifference.files.wordpress.com/2015/12/living-with-difference-online.pdf

The Shap Working Party on Education in World Religions
http://www.shapworkingparty.org.uk/

The Inter Faith Network for the UK
http://www.interfaith.org.uk/

Ofsted publishes research review on religious education
https://www.gov.uk/government/news/ofsted-publishes-research-review-on-religious-education

recognised as the unit of shoe size in the UK; some knowledge changes and other knowledge needs to be rediscovered.

It does pose the more philosophical question, what is there that I do not know? Not quite the famous Donald Rumsfeld 'known known' speech but in the subject of religious education it brings to attention those difficult questions which have no answers at hand. For instance, 'why do we feel sad when someone dies?' or 'where is heaven?' or 'why is nature beautiful and awe-inspiring?' Subject knowledge may not be useful here, but drawing on the skills of questioning, asking the child to develop her own thoughts and perspectives on the matter and allowing children time to think and ponder on the mysterious aspect of the subject (applicable to all subjects!) is one approach. This will enable you to field such questions in a confident manner and not be fazed by simply not knowing (which is acceptable here) but providing an alternate method to develop children's learning.

Pedagogical content knowledge

Knowing stuff may matter, but teaching it is entirely different. It is defined as *'the ways of representing and formulating the subject that make it comprehensible to others'* (Shulman,

58 Subject knowledge and pedagogy

1986, cited in Pollard, 2014, p. 234). It is the difference between knowing a lot and being a boring and uninspiring teacher and an entertaining teacher with gimmicks from whom the children learn little.

Pedagogy is the *'art, science and skill of teaching'* (Pollard, 2019, p. 342), and you have been trained or educated in the application of subject knowledge to children's learning, but the distinction here is knowing how and when to represent the knowledge, to overcome (and avoid) misconceptions and what resources to use. It is therefore to be supported by the pedagogical theory; knowing how children develop cognitively, knowing about various theories (of behaviour management, planning and assessment which are already covered in this book) and theorists who are important and knowing who the new theorists are, or the ones who have not been brought to your attention. For example, you may be teaching with a need to teach something with vibrancy or poignancy because of the new socio-economic or political events that have determined the design of new plans and a new interpretation of teaching a subject as bell hooks (1994, p. 140) warns,

I know so many professors who are progressive in their politics, who have been willing to change their curriculum, but who in fact have resolutely refused to change the nature of their pedagogical practice.

> **Critical question**
>
> How do I decide on the pedagogy I want to use in my lessons?

If you are going to base your pedagogy on theory, a warning is to revise the theory at periodic intervals in your teaching career. Ensure you fully understand, for example, Vygotsky's concept of the more knowledgeable other, Rosenshine's principles and Sweller's cognitive load theory, and interpret it to your own working application of pedagogical content knowledge.

In religious education knowing how to teach a particular festival or story can be planned and taught using a flowchart (Figure 5.1). The example deals with the festival of Hanukah (but the template is flexible for any topic) and calls for an immediate revision of content knowledge, before prompting you as the teacher with how you are going to teach it. Each stage requires an answer, and that is how you will utilise your existing pedagogical knowledge to be comfortable with the teaching. For example, how will you make the Jewish festival of Hanukkah relevant to a 'contemporary class'? This will involve you knowing your class, what they will be familiar with, how they best cope with being read a story, or whether they prefer more kinaesthetic-based activities, or what the useful contemporary device/film/event at hand is. It will demand that you consider 'adaptive teaching' the pace of the lesson and where the lesson will be taught. In other words, the flowchart is a reminder to base the lesson to be taught to the needs and stages of learning of the children. If you require extra-pedagogical content knowledge support, then there is the assistance of the subject lead/co-ordinator or experts from the subject associations; if you require extra content knowledge, you can rely on those within faith communities to help, for example a visit to a place of worship or a talk by a guest (see Table 5.2).

Subject knowledge and pedagogy 59

Flowchart for teaching RE
(Name of festival or story, e.g. Hanukkah*)

⬇

What is the key theme here?

⬇

How can I apply this to a contemporary class?

⬇

Have I considered Attainment targets 1 and 2?
Have I considered children of faith and no faith?

⬇

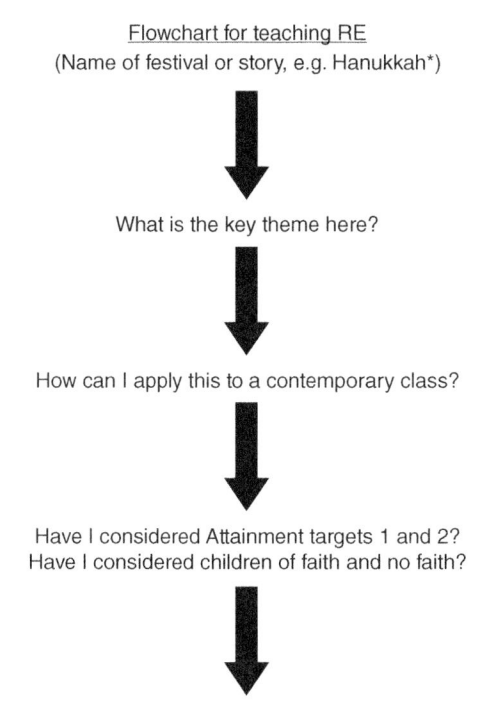

How shall the learnig activity come alive? (wider curriculum and creativity)

Figure 5.1 A flowchart to aid the teaching of festivals or story

Curricular knowledge

The final part of Shulman's (1986, cited in Pollard, 2014, p. 291) work centres on all the *'programmes of study, syllabi, schemes of work, resources, technologies and instructional material'* that allow lessons to be planned, taught and assessed; in other words, where it originates and what you choose. Ultimately it derives from interpretations of the national curriculum, through long-/medium-term plans, which is where you will be able to judge your content knowledge and consider your pedagogical content knowledge.

Religious education is not a national curriculum subject, so the origin of curriculum knowledge will usually be from the local authority's appointed Standing Advisory Council on Religious Education (SACRE), from external providers or in faith-based schools from the local diocese or faith centre. SACRE-agreed syllabi are comprehensive, informative, outline points to be aware of (sensitivities), the key functions of Attainment targets (which, when realised, allow the subject content to be covered in a purposeful and relevant way) and, important of all, the learning objectives to be taught.

It is useful to consider external bodies that monitor subjects; of course, this means, for instance, Ofsted, who are now focused on 'deep dive' subject inspections, as well as subject-focussed organisations who provide reports that detail new ways of thinking. Examples include Ofsted's recent subject inspection (2021a) and the CORE report (Commission on Religious Education 2018). Being aware of such trends and accountability will only improve your all-round subject knowledge and ultimately relevance in teaching the subject.

To finish this section, it is worth reminding you that curricular knowledge should not be necessarily discrete; there is the opportunity to blend various subjects' curricular knowledge so that you can teach in a cross-curricular fashion. The argument for such an approach is that through blending 'disciplines' of study (Barnes, 2015), children can learn in an efficient, deep and meaningful way that promotes creativity. This would, in turn, affect your pedagogical content knowledge and probably streamline your content knowledge, but it is something to be considered.

The Curriculum - Definitions, Beliefs and you

By John Bullen at New Close Primary, Warminster, Wiltshire, UK

With so much work in schools surrounding building effective curricula, it can be a struggle for practitioners, who are always in the classroom, to find time to unpick what schools are trying to achieve through their curriculum. Alexander (2010, p. 203) states, *'the curriculum is not just a political and profession battleground; it is a conceptual minefield'*. This suggests that there are many ideas related to the definition of a curriculum and its design, all of which are contentious. So, let's consider what a curriculum is.

Tanner and Tanner (1980, p. 13) define a curriculum to be as follows:

> The planned and guided learning experiences and intended outcomes, formulated through the systematic reconstruction of knowledge and experiences under the auspices of the school.

There are common features in these definitions which you will see in school. They consider intended learning outcomes and suggest that curricula contain tasks and experiences that help achieve that outcome. These definitions, however, only consider the role of a syllabus and do not go far enough in describing the complexities of what a curriculum is and what schools are trying to achieve.

Hass (1987) suggests that a curriculum includes experiences that individual learners have in a programme where the purpose is to achieve broad goals which are related to specific objectives, planned in terms of a framework of theory, research and practice of the subject. This is also supported by the General Teaching Council for England (GTCE) (2011), who suggest that any curriculum should be seen in terms of content and pedagogy together and should provide an understanding about the important interrelationship between the two.

So, what is a curriculum? Essentially, and academically, it is the ideological documentation outlining the values and content of education with a pedagogical indication of how both the values and content of a subject are to be disseminated to learners. So, why discuss the curriculum here and now? Well, if you talk to the teachers and leaders that are designing their curricula, they will say it is the heartbeat of the school and the subjects they teach. Therefore, understanding it is imperative.

Subject Knowledge and Pedagogy

By Rachel Kerridge at Wentworth Primary (Academy), Dartford, Kent, UK

Subject knowledge and pedagogy underpin planning, learning and teaching. With so much subject knowledge encompassing the curriculum and ways of delivery to pupils, it is important for teachers to see themselves as lifelong learners. This is an exhausting mission for teachers, who can feel overwhelmed with the daily requirements of teaching and planning. This article unpicks the qualities and skills needed to embrace seeing oneself as a learner to facilitate learning about subject knowledge and pedagogy.

It is essential as an education professional to have an understanding of the key theories of learning in order to appreciate the journey pupils go on each lesson, day, term and scholastic year. What better way to understand this more deeply than to experience it yourself? As a teacher, when you are in the classroom you are by in large the most knowledgeable person in the room, and it is easy to forget just what it means and feels like to be the learner. Engaging in a course of learning yourself, whether directly or indirectly related to work, helps to support this understanding of the learning journey. Many councils have adult education centres with a wide variety of courses on offer. I have enjoyed short courses with the Open University. Many are free and can take as little as two hours to complete.

Despite the large workload, I try hard to ensure that I 'give myself permission' to stop work and focus on something that allows 'me time'. One of the things that I enjoyed post-COVID-19 was learning to bell ring by joining a bell-ringing group in my local community. It is an activity that doesn't require too much commitment, provides low impact exercise and stimulates the brain. As a complete novice, it provides me with the chance to be a beginner: navigating through new vocabulary; following instructions; exploring and learning techniques. It also involves using skills to navigate a role within a group of people from different backgrounds and with different abilities and challenges – much like the classroom environment. We work collaboratively to successfully achieve, both individually and as a group.

The Importance of Play

By Oscar Pimlett at John Ball Primary School, Lewisham, London, UK

Play as a concept is indefinable; the esteemed writer, poet and lecturer Michael Rosen subscribes to the broadest rationale of play and would be giddy with joy at this exchange of 'adult play' now, where you the reader and me as the writer are exchanging thoughts and playing with the malleable definitions of words to create meaning and understanding from simply ink and paper. In more ways than one, Rosen's broad definition of play holds importance to us adults who usually might not play, as when we argue that we haven't

(Continued)

got the time, the money, the space or even the facilities to play, his interpretation of play tells us that we play every day in the way we think about things and interpret the world around us. Whether we doodle on a newspaper when we're on the train, act out imagined situations in our heads or even play air guitar in the privacy of our bedrooms as we get dressed, we are playing and exploring the boundaries of our imagination whilst creating – and having – fun. These small exchanges of self-consciousness for enjoyment are fun (it only takes a quick dabble into air guitar to prove this), and beyond this they are hugely important to our well-being; they keep our imagination ticking over and keep the often-disregarded creative section of our brains alive and well, suppressing and satisfying our urges to do something we haven't been instructed to do and giving us means to express ourselves. In short, play gives us the opportunity to be our truest self for an undefined period of time and work our creative muscles in ways that are not regulated or assessed like many other aspects of our lives, which poses huge emotional benefits for us all.

Play by any means is incredibly important and pertinent to children, so if we are thinking about inspirational ideas for the classroom, the most accessible and beneficial of these has to be free play. If we make play an integral part of our teaching, whether through continuous provision in Early Years or play-orientated lessons higher up the school, we unlock the part of our children that ignores societal norms and allows them to become their truest selves, whilst exposing them to a world of mental and physical benefits. Embodying Michael Rosen again then for my final word, I ask and recommend that you look for these transient instances of play in your teaching that you seek them out, plan them in (whilst enjoying them alongside your class) and, if you can, make explicit time for them with your class, because, ultimately, school can be challenging for staff and students alike, but I'm still yet to hear of some good old play ever making a situation worse.

Incorporating Montessori Pedagogy into your Classroom

By Sarah Cummins, Lecturer in School of Education at Leeds Trinity University, Leeds, West Yorkshire, UK

Montessori theory is based on scientific observation of children. She believed that education began at birth and children go through sensitive periods of learning. Montessori believed that the environments for children should be designed and prepared to meet the needs of the child and to offer freedom within limits for the child, such as freedom to move and freedom to make choices in their learning. The environment we prepare for children should offer the child uninterrupted periods of concentration, and Montessori believed that it is through this carefully prepared environment that children can become self-disciplined.

If we consider the child when they are born, they are born without the ability to speak or to take care of themselves but within those first three years of their life,

(Continued)

using their senses, they gather the information they need to develop and construct themselves. They gather this information naturally, without thinking. Montessori refers to the capacity of the mind to take in information of the world that surrounds them as 'The Absorbent Mind'. Basically, the child's mind soaks up all that is around them.

The child between 0 and 6 years may go through a variety of sensitive periods (such as language, movement and order), and it is our role as the adult to prepare the environment to meet the child's needs during that time. When preparing the environment for the child, we need to be conscious of not only their sensitive periods but also their development of concentration and their internal drive for independence. This will support the whole child and also support their development of growth mindset and self-confidence. Considering the most natural way to build self-confidence and self-awareness within oneself is to do tasks for themselves; we as educators do need to value the reflective time to consider how we may be the barrier by interfering too much.

The learning environment allows children to move freely, and Montessori recognised that movement enhances learning. Montessori based her method of education on the premise that learning is linked to movement. All areas in a Montessori environment offers movement, but this is easily developed in a mainstream environment. The areas within the environment should have a clear purpose. For example, the practical life area supports a child's development to independence, coordination and refinement of movement, hand and eye coordination, left to right sequencing, concentration and focus as well as culture awareness. What Montessori called the practical life area is where there is a range of real-life activities that have multiple purposes and one being life skills.

There may be challenges to overcome when incorporating Montessori into your traditional environment but none that cannot be overcome. It is important to understand the link between the Montessori curriculum and the national curriculum. It is also important to note that you do not have to adopt the whole approach. You can attend workshops to understand the philosophy better and then adapt the ideas to the needs of your learning community.

EAL at the Crossroads

By Jay Maxwell, Coordinator and Learning Support Lead at Assumption College English Program School, Samut Sakhon City, Thailand

Over the last two decades, a crisis has been brewing in English as an additional language (EAL). A total of 20.9% of pupils in England now use EAL (Bell Foundation, 2022), and as numbers increase, research and guidance have waned. Whilst much good work has been done pre-2010, significant challenges remain, particularly in EAL components of initial teacher education (ITE) programmes. Only a few studies scrutinise how ITE students are prepared to support EAL pupils, fewer still examine the pedagogical

(Continued)

foundations of EAL courses (Foley et al., 2018), and there is almost no research where student teachers evaluate EAL courses' effectiveness over time (Anderson et al. cited in Foley et al., 2018). These issues are amplified for international and bilingual school teachers who work in classrooms of up to 90% EAL pupils. Whilst EAL is mentioned in the national curriculum framework, it lacks a comprehensive guidance of its own. These issues have culminated as a significant challenge that is also an exciting generational opportunity. EAL stands at a crossroads.

All children should have the opportunity to fulfil their potential via accessing the curriculum. Research demonstrates the importance of proficiency in English as an indicator of educational outcomes (Bell Foundation, 2022). Ensuring pupils' access to a high-quality curriculum means schools need to ensure pupils at risk get the support they need. In the view of someone who has become passionate about EAL through my role as a learning support lead at a bilingual school in Thailand, the only feasible long-term solutions for EAL are more funding for research, funding for EAL organisations (The Bell Foundation and NALDIC), more robust yet reflective EAL ITE and the recognition and provision for EAL in a similarly comprehensive way as is done for SEND in the SEND Code of Practice.

In the meantime, there are helpful resources, active researchers, amazing EAL organisations and adapted solutions to consider when seeking how to best meet the needs of EAL pupils. Resource wise, before 2010 the Department for Education (DfE) produced quality guidance and materials on EAL – although outdated they still contain a lot of useful information. These resources work well when combined with effective lesson planning based on sound EAL pedagogy. This centres on six areas: multilingualism being an advantage, proficiency in English linked to academic success, accessing prior learning, provision of context, encouraging independence and extension of vocabulary (Bell Foundation, 2022). Assessment of this must give EAL pupils an opportunity to demonstrate what they know. I recommend Assessment Tracker 1.2 from the Bell Foundation's Primary EAL Assessment Framework: a classroom-friendly, curriculum-language-integrated approach with rating scales and materials for informal and summative assessment. To stay current, follow some of the active researchers in the area that remain.

EAL needs are unique. NALDIC puts it succinctly when it states, EAL pupils '... *have distinct and different needs from other pupils by virtue of the fact that they are learning in and through an additional language, whilst also learning that language. In addition, they come from cultural backgrounds and communities with different understandings and expectations of education, language and learning*'. (NALDIC, 2022). Whilst western-centric research-based strategies remain somewhat successful despite different cultures, tailoring approaches to local or individual pupil needs can significantly improve this. Global research-based EAL practices require careful adaptation to local contexts to form a 'glocal' approach. If successful EAL practice is to be adapted to other cultural contexts, and those *from* other cultural contexts, inclusive schools must ensure that local or first culture norms are not overlooked.

Jay is the Year 1 coordinator and learning support lead at Assumption College English Program school. He has been teaching in Thai bilingual schools for 22 years and has a keen interest in EAL.

A Literacy Lesson with a Bang!

By Stephanie Hunter, Class Teacher at Springfield Primary School, Chelmsford, Essex, UK

There is so much you can do in a literacy lesson to spark the children's imagination. My favourite way is to start the lesson with a bang! by doing something unexpected. I like to do this using an interactive hook that reels the children in, getting them excited and engaged in stories.

An example of this was, before I began my literacy topic on 'Where the Wild Things Are' by Maurice Sendak, when I used an old cereal box as a template and cut out some big footprint shapes with pointy toes. Whilst the children were out of the classroom (doing the daily mile), I sieved some flour through the template, making footprints on the floor leading into the classroom and to the class cupboard.

As the children came back into the class, I had to put on my best acting face and pretended I was just as surprised and confused myself, by the footprints that were on the floor. I allowed the children time to come in and investigate the prints that had been left. I had a few sceptics at first who were adamant that an adult had done it. However, as soon as they got a closer look at the prints and into the cupboard, our discussion was full of excited children sharing their ideas of who had left them.

The next day the headteacher came into the classroom; she told the children she needed help to find the 'Wild Things' as they had broken into her office and stolen her secret stash of sweets. This led to the children carrying out their own investigation and leaving some sweets out overnight. When they came back into the classroom in the morning, they discovered they had all been eaten, except the yellow ones. This led to the children producing fantastic character descriptions, drama performances and quality letter writing to Max's character, asking for help on how to catch a 'Wild Thing'! This has now helped me to understand the purpose and importance of drama. I find I now enjoy coming up with new interactive ideas and constantly challenging my teaching by pushing myself to further use drama in my lessons.

Reading Fluency

By Debbie Marlow, English Lead at Thundersley Primary School, Benfleet, Essex, UK

After spending a number of years teaching years 5 and 6, I moved into Year 2 where I noticed that a significant number of children were not able to read fluently. A majority of the children had good phonics knowledge and could decode well, but their reading tended to be slow and stilted with poor prosody. It was also clear that many of the children did not understand what they were reading and consequently were probably

(Continued)

not enjoying reading very much either! This is hardly surprising since all their cognitive abilities were absorbed by decoding the words, with little cognitive capacity for understanding and therefore enjoyment.

I decided that the children should change their reading books less frequently and should re-read their books two or three times before selecting a new one. I also encouraged children to re-read individual sentences or pages after decoding to develop their fluency. This approach had some impact, but I was then fortunate enough to take part in some research and training into improving reading comprehension at Lyons Hall School in Braintree. As a result, I introduced reading fluency homework to my class, before rolling it out across the whole school. This weekly homework comprises a short text, poem or extract from a longer text. We display the text on the board and then the teacher reads it to the class, pointing at the words whilst reading. Teachers model reading fluently with appropriate prosody. We discuss the vocabulary within the text; then the adult reads it again, a line at a time, with the children repeating the line after the adult. We call this echo reading. Immediately, the children begin to imitate the intonation and expression modelled by the teacher. We then re-read the whole text all together – choral reading. The children take a copy of the text home, and the idea is that they read it as many times as possible to develop their fluency. By fluency, I mean that they can read it accurately, at conversation pace and with appropriate prosody. We encourage children to read it to anybody they can, even over FaceTime to grandparents or to pets. Each week we select a small number of children to read the text to the class after they have practised it at home; even children who generally find reading difficult can participate if they have practised.

You can see their confidence grow as they feel like confident readers. Some children may be relying on memory and initial letters as prompts, but it teaches them what fluent reading should sound like and shows them what they're aiming for when they read new texts independently. This very simple strategy has had a significant impact on developing the children's ability to read fluently. We do not differentiate the text as we want all children to have the same opportunity to access high-quality texts and challenging vocabulary.

Reading

By Jessica Crumlish, Teacher at Windsor-Essex Catholic District School Board, Ontario, Canada

Recently, more and more schools have done away with guided reading carousels and taken on a whole-class reading approach. When planning a unit of work, many teachers search for a core text with which to make cross-curricular links. This is wonderful, as of course, we want to share quality texts with our pupils. But finding a text which really fits the theme can be difficult. How do you choose one perfect book with which you can plan engaging lessons across a half-term or term? Which one core text can we use to support a unit on the Stone Age, or electricity, or space?

(Continued)

The answer is this: no one text can do it all.

Use each new unit of work as an opportunity to introduce the children to as many books as possible! Sure, you can still have one really wonderful novel which you read alongside your topic work, which inspires the children's writing and keeps them on the edges of their seats. But do this in conjunction with a variety of other texts: non-fiction, poetry, picture books, magazines and newspaper articles. You want to be able to say to your class, 'Look at how much there is to explore. Look how many authors and illustrators are going to help us with our learning'. You don't have to commit to reading all the texts. Pick out extracts to share with your class in various lessons, or read aloud any shorter selections like picture books, poetry or magazine articles.

By carefully curating a collection of texts which link to your topic, you can cultivate a community of readers who will have so many exciting facts and recommendations to share with one another. They'll be able to make links within and across texts, broadening their knowledge and deepening their understanding of the topic you've been teaching. Do they want to find out more about Vikings? Point them towards your non-fiction selections. Are they eager to hear what happens to Hiccup and Toothless next? Stock the next few books in the series. Will some children struggle to access texts at their age level? Sprinkle in a selection of picture books or Hi/Lo texts.

Most importantly, consider representation. Have you included books with diverse and inclusive casts of characters? Are you recommending books by Black, Asian and minority ethnic authors and illustrators? Can your children see themselves represented on your bookshelf? For your library to really have an impact, spend some time drawing attention to your choices. I always allocate a box or a shelf in my classroom to my 'Recommended Reads'. Tell the children which books you've chosen to read with them this term and why. Make the links to your topic clear so the children can see the value in reading to support our learning across the curriculum.

Vocabulary: The Importance of Words

By Laura Colam at Dogsthorpe Academy, Peterborough, UK

Words are amazing and form the foundation of everything we teach. From English to science and PE to history, it is important that children are exposed to a wide range of words across the curriculum. Lots of research show that vocabulary can be split into three tiers.

- Tier 1 – Everyday words that are used in communication. These words rarely need direct teaching and are learned through conversation.

(Continued)

- Tier 2 – High frequency words that need some amount of teaching across the curriculum
- Tier 3 – Subject-specific words that need explicit teaching and only appear in specific topic areas

Over the last five years I have become passionate about finding interesting, exciting and innovative ways to embed the teaching and exposure of vocabulary across my school setting. It is important that children are allowed to actively explore and engage with words regularly, whether that is through student-led practical exploration or direct teaching of the vocabulary.

My top vocabulary activities/resources

The recipe book

Issue children with a vocabulary book (a small exercise book) at the start of the year which they can use to record all vocabulary that they meet across the curriculum. It will take time and practice, but over time the children should start using the words they collect within their writing.

Topic vocabulary organisers

It is important to ensure that vocabulary is prevalent across the curriculum not only in core but also through foundation subjects. When you consider how many foundation subjects there are, the thought of teaching new vocabulary for each one may seem like a daunting task, but it doesn't need to be. Something that we have implemented in my school is a Topic Vocabulary Organiser, an A4 page detailing all the vocabulary that could be taught or encountered throughout the foundation subjects being taught within the topic.

Zone of relevance

Children love to find alternatives for modelled vocabulary; however, they do not always understand how to choose the most relevant word to fit within their writing. This activity can really help them begin to build that understanding. Children are given a bank of vocabulary relevant to what is being studied and are asked to sort within a target, usually split into red, amber and green sections, with red being the least relevant and green being the most.

'Post-it note' game or 'heads up'

It is a versatile game that can also be used to ensure vocabulary knowledge has been embedded. Children work in pairs choosing a new word they have learnt that week, either Word of the Day, Topic or Core vocabulary. Pairs choose each other's words, and they can either ask yes or no questions to work out the answer or their partner can describe the word to them. This can be used as a quick time filler activity, starter task or morning activity.

A Love Letter to Vocabulary

By Jack Phillips, Primary School Teacher at Rothley C of E Primary Academy, Leicestershire, UK

Having patrolled the streets as a police officer, and stood in front of hundreds of children over innumerable lessons, I possess a unique view on the subject of this piece – words. I have seen them used to talk people down from bridges and coax children from under tables. I have seen them used to support a victim of domestic abuse and calm children struggling with home or school issues. I have seen them used to tell a father that officers have located their missing daughter and to tell a child how proud they should be of their learning. Words are, in essence, our most inimitable source of communication.

Words are mesmerising. The shape and sound of them; the way they are formed in the brain, throat, tongue, teeth, wrists and fingers before their expulsion in whatever way the speaker – or writer – chooses. There is a paradoxical caveat to that, however. Sometimes, we are unable to choose how our words are spoken or written. The immense range of human emotion is sometimes difficult to manage, resulting in flippant vitriol or irrepressible joy. This only adds to their magic and places greater emphasis on the teaching of and exposure to words in a classroom or school environment.

Be attentive to the language your children are using, particularly when spoken. There is this joy I feel after hearing a child talk to their friend about snakes having potent venom, or speaking to their parents about bioluminescence in nature. If I hear children using accurate or vibrant language, I will, as they are speaking, write the word and the time on the board. This is a simple way of drawing positive attention to spoken language. There is nothing to stop you joining the fun, too. Whole-class feedback provides an opportunity to do the same with written language.

Too many children grow up in homes that are word-poor; teachers are a large part of the antidote to this. A classroom environment awash with words, books and a language-conscious teacher is a huge step in reducing the word gap. Have an unfettered enthusiasm for words!

Teaching Mathematics

By Bernie Westacott, Maths Consultant – Rickmansworth, Hertfordshire, UK

I have been involved in mathematics education for 48 years as a teacher, head of department and consultant. My experience has shown me that teachers need to have the right subject and pedagogical knowledge in mathematics. This is vital because pupil achievement in mathematics is strongly linked to teacher subject and pedagogical knowledge. International comparison studies have demonstrated that pupil achievement in mathematics in the UK is considerably lower than in some leading jurisdictions.

(Continued)

My work in a variety of schools and settings (UK, international, Early Years, primary, secondary, tertiary, state and independent) has revealed that many teachers, particularly primary and Early Years in the UK, do not feel as confident about their subject and pedagogic knowledge in mathematics compared to English. Within the UK, national policy recently has focused on raising pupil attainment in mathematics and how this must come about through improved teacher subject and pedagogic knowledge.

Your own feelings about your efficacy in teaching mathematics will vary from other teachers. I do not want to assume that teachers in the UK lack subject and pedagogic knowledge, but I have encountered many who feel that they fall into this category. No matter how you regard yourself in this respect, I urge you be reflective and evaluative about your mathematics teaching and remain open to improving your practice – I am still working at developing my subject and pedagogic knowledge. Most of you will, at some stage, encounter at least one pupil who simply does not understand any of what you are trying to teach in mathematics, and I guarantee that this will lead you to puzzle as to what you can do to rectify this situation. My advice to you is to utilise as many opportunities as you can to access professional development for Maths teaching. If that is the case for you, see if you can contact your local maths hub – all the 37 maths hubs across England offer professional development to help teachers. Finally, ensure that you know what maths concepts are taught after your year group/stage of learning so that you can gain a deep understanding of the progression of skills and concepts. Above all, observe your colleagues teach maths and keep a regular and analytic dialogue with them about maths subject and pedagogic knowledge.

A Quick Guide to Primary Science

By Jo Montgomery, Science Solutions, Cambridge, UK

Primary science is often the poor relation to the other core subjects of English and mathematics and gets bumped down the pecking order and often viewed alongside the foundation subjects, as highlighted by Wellcome's State of the Nation report in 2019. Over half of the primary school teachers say science is getting squeezed out (Confederation of British Industry, CBI, 2015). We have a STEM skills gap and need a scientifically literate population in order to engage in current worldwide issues such as climate change, technology, medicine and health and research. Research suggests that children may have made up their minds about whether science is for them by the age of ten (Archer Ker et al., 2013, Archer et al., 2020), so primary science plays a crucial role (Dunlop et al., 2021). I am here to advocate that not only is science worthy of its pedestal position but also that it is a creative, cross-curricular and joyous way to develop critical thinking, problem-solving and communication skills alongside developing subject knowledge – and to showcase some great resources to help inspire your pupils.

(Continued)

The recent Ofsted research review (Ofsted, 2021b) advocates for developing substantive (content) knowledge alongside disciplinary knowledge (working scientifically and enquiry). What does this mean in practice? Science is both a content and skill-based curriculum, with enquiry, working scientifically and subject knowledge intertwining as children have opportunities to practise and apply skills and knowledge in relevant and meaningful contexts. Subject knowledge, working scientifically and enquiry skills should not be taught separately (Turner et al., 2022), and children should be taught using a host of tools from a primary teacher's toolkit such as direct instruction, drama, exploration and enquiry, according to requirements.

Practical primary science has several purposes:

- Introduces scientific objects and phenomena to help learn substantive (content) knowledge
- Enables pupils to learn and practise disciplinary knowledge (how to do science)
- Enquiry

(OfSTED, 2021b)

- Supports teaching scientific inquiry
- To improve understanding and theory through practical experience
- To teach specific practical skills
- To motivate and engage
- To develop higher level skills

(Gatsby, 2017)

I am particularly keen on the inclusion of motivating and engaging as a purpose of practical science in the Gatsby list. Scientific investigation is at the heart of primary science: it is about being curious, wondering about the world, asking questions and finding things out.

Top websites for primary science

Organisations

- **Primary Science Teaching Trust (PSTT)** https://www.pstt.org.uk
  Resources, support from regional mentors
- **ASE** https://www.ase.org.uk
  Membership body, resources, networks and conferences
- **STEM Learning** https://www.stem.org.uk
  CPD, resources
- **Primary Science Quality Mark (PSQM)** https://www.psqm.org.uk
  CPD journey supporting science subject leaders
- **SSERC** (Scotland) https://www.sserc.org.uk
- **CLEAPSS** https://www.cleapss.org.uk
  Health and safety body, resources and advice

(Continued)

Useful resources for teaching and learning

- Teacher Assessment in Primary Science (**TAPS**) https://www.taps.pstt.org.uk
  Project from Bath Spa University and PSTT, resources to support assessment in primary science
- Pan-London Assessment Network (**PLAN**) https://www.planassessment.com
  Planning, assessment, progression and exemplar materials
- **Explorify** https://www.explorify.uk
  Resources to share with children to support thinking and discussion skills around science. Support for teachers and science subject leaders. Now supported by PSTT and STEM Learning

Social media

Follow #ASEchat Monday 8-9pm, #PrimarySTEMchat all the way from Australia for international support on Thursday mornings in the UK, and build your network.

There are a number of Facebook groups to support primary science, including the following:

- Unleash 1 KS1 Science for Infants https://www.facebook.com/groups/1040410769353006/
- Unleash 2 KS2 Science for Juniors https://www.facebook.com/groups/186117835214562/

Other resources

- **Great Science Share for Schools** https://www.greatscienceshre.org
  Annual free campaign to encourage children's scientific questioning and enquiry. Resources to support teaching and learning
- **Dr Jo Science**. I have also collated a comprehensive list of activities, resources and websites to support primary science teaching and learning at https://www.drjosciencesolutions.co.uk/resources

Reflections of a Scientist

By Andrew Jack at St. Kentigern's Academy, Blackburn, West Lothian, Scotland, UK

Within my career, I have often worked with colleagues in a primary context. Whilst as a subject specialist in the sciences, I have a background that caters to the delivery of such content; I often find or have found that some (not all) practitioners in primary settings can come across as almost being 'afraid' of the content they are expected to deliver. Now whilst I work in a secondary context, where the expectation is for practitioners who are subject specialists to deliver broader thematic areas such as literacy and numeracy in which they may lack confidence and experience, thus making consistent

(Continued)

delivery problematic (Stables et al., 2004), primary colleagues find themselves working in contrast to this often, which is challenging and daunting in equal measure.

The sciences, as a field, have their nuances from the smallest conceivable particle up to the largest conceivable objects and the universe itself. So, it's understandable that worry can creep in that maybe you don't say the right thing, or you make a mistake here and there, but that's the beauty of science; we aren't always right. No theory is infallible, and, as practitioners, please know that anything you do to capture the hearts and minds of the learners in your care is a fantastic step for them in their development.

Often, we overlook the real burning outcomes that we want the learners to gain from a science lesson, and through reflection we can get bogged down asking ourselves, 'Did we meet the outcomes? Did we cover a topic in enough depth? What would the inspectors say?'

The real questions we should ask are as follows: 'Were learners engaged? Did they ask questions? Did I deliver that to the best of my ability so that learning took place? Did they have fun?'

In essence, science isn't there to be feared or be an uncomfortable area to delve into with learners; it should be something to be enjoyed, experimented with and ultimately anything you do as a practitioner can and will have a positive impact on the natural curiosity of those you teach. Approach the sciences with a bit of enthusiasm; we are all actors in the classroom with different personas, different approaches to situations and different experiences. Bring those things together and put on a show; teaching science can be the best lesson in the world.

Primary Computing from an ITE Viewpoint

By Nyree Scott at Canterbury Christ Church University, Canterbury, Kent, UK

Little issues in computing

Ever wonder why some of you, when you think about teaching computing, appear to almost fear teaching it? Well, it really is not your fault. Despite the new computing curriculum being a statutory requirement since 2014, when I work with ITE primary students both undergraduate (UG) and postgraduate (PG) I am frequently informed that for the duration of their school placements, no computing is being taught.

Teaching a slightly unfamiliar subject

You, too, of course, may remember ICT – because you were never taught computing. And perhaps, this is where the problem starts. When I used to struggle thinking about how to teach something less familiar, I would end up teaching it how I was taught, but if you have not been taught computing, you cannot do this! What you need to do is recognise this

(Continued)

and realise you just need to gain some subject knowledge to give you enough confidence to start teaching it. But you also need to know there are reasons more than the statutory requirement that should make you want to teach it. Just please stop calling it ICT!

There are many types of computing teachers

I see there being three types of teachers when it comes to computing: those who teach the computing curriculum (do not get me wrong there are a lot of you out there), those who take PPA during computing so that someone else teaches it and those who do it when they really must but would rather not. You may see yourself as one of these, and if you are one of the latter two, you are likely to feel far less confident. Again, this is not your fault! But I want to discuss why you all should be teaching it. Two words, Computational Thinking.

Computational thinking

Putting it simply, Computational Thinking is an approach to problem-solving. More importantly for you, Computational Thinking is part of the aims of the computing national curriculum, but this approach is much more than the computing curriculum, and for many of you, these are the skills you teach without even realising it. Thinking about Computational Thinking may just be the start to helping you realise not only why you should be teaching computing but encouraging you to learn how.

Computational Thinking is not something that has a simple explanation; however, it is imperative for children to develop the skills they gain through experiencing Computational Thinking in the classroom. Consider the skills of decomposition and abstraction when it comes to solving problems.

Next steps

The good news is there are many free resources out there you can use, and many teachers and professionals including myself are there to help you develop this subject knowledge. It is really not as hard as you think it is, and once you start and see the benefits, you will wonder whatever stopped you in the first place.

Technology in the Classroom

By Gerard Lavelle, Head of Innovation and Computing at Victory Heights Primary School, Dubai

I have always had an active interest in technology in classrooms, but only recently can I say that I have a teaching mantra to live by: let the learning dictate the technology – not the technology dictate the learning. Too often, companies come calling with the ultimate software to do x, the hardware that will revolutionise y. For me, the pupil needs to be in charge. Not happy with a routine in school – what can you use to fix it? Creating a game for wet break times, choose a platform that you are happy with. The outcome is

(Continued)

way more powerful and incisive when pupils choose to use Minecraft, Nearpod, Lego or whatever the technology du jour is, rather than thrusting upon them a platform which makes both the teachers and pupils utterly miserable using it.

And remember, technology does not solve everything. Sometimes, all you need to solve a problem is some critical thinking, masking tape and cardboard. Open-ended questions and problems may use 3D CAD software to produce cutting edge designs and prototypes – but so can a pencil, a blank piece of paper and a ruler. It is the **ideas** you want to promote and celebrate from pupils – not the risk of running into a cul de sac because they cannot complete a task on a coding platform. In my experience, the greatest innovations come from dropping the technology. Agreed, this is not the showy, shiny simulation that schools want prospective stakeholders to see, but it is quite often the solution that pupils need in order to really explore their ideas. Of course, do not tell my head teacher I said that!

Last, I keep hearing that in 20 years' time, pupils will be taking jobs that haven't been invented yet, and we need to future proof them by learning about the latest and greatest technologies and software. Yet the **skills** that pupils need will not have changed. We are not creating a new subspecies of super-charged androids – they are still humans. They will need to be kind, persevere when times get tough, show creativity and work successfully in a team to complete projects and tasks. So we as professionals need to give children these opportunities when working with digital and analogue materials. We need to structure tasks and projects to incorporate so-called 'soft skills'. Perhaps these skills, above all others, are the skills our future generations need in order to make the world just that little bit better.

Teaching in Year 1

By Charlotte Day, Year 3 Teacher, Swanley, Kent, UK

Teaching in Year 1 must be the most magical of experiences. If you are lucky enough to teach Year 1, you have clearly landed the best role in the school. From helping them to finesse their fluency in phonics and reading, to helping them to express themselves in their extended writing, to watching them grow (not only in height) but emotionally, socially, and mentally. It truly is the most amazing of all the year groups.

Five-year-olds are the funniest little people you ever will meet, with their love for life and learning and their never-ending questions; you will never have a boring day in Year 1. If there are four things you need to have to be able to teach in Year 1, they would be the following:

- Post it notes (for spelling help purposes of course)
- A refined collection of picture books (for innumerable story times)
- Endless boxes of tissues (for the sniffles and occasional tears)
- And of course, a never-ending supply of patience (self-explanatory I think!)

(Continued)

Of course, there are a million and one other things you will need, but these are the most important (along with a great sense of humour and the motivation to fuel a small army of determined little people.

By far the best subject on the curriculum to teach Year 1 is computing. After spending weeks reminding them how to log in and find the computing programme within the internal drive, and of course reminding them never ever to share a password with anyone apart from trusted adult, it finally clicks and the work produced during these sessions is beyond incredible. After not really being exposed to computing in the EYFS (Early Years Foundation Stage), starting afresh with a clean slate in Year 1 provides you to have the opportunity to introduce concepts and put into practise lots of techniques. You then get the privilege of feeling super proud of them when they fly off to Year 2; with a great underlying knowledge of the computing curriculum (makes it even more special if you also happen to be the computing coordinator within the school too!)

What Contributes to being a Successful Teacher?

By Elizah Barnes, Qualified Primary Teacher and Trainee Educational Psychologist, West Midlands, UK

Teaching is a demanding job, and at times, it can feel quite isolating; therefore, it is important to build up a supportive network around you.

Below are four areas which have been the most important contributions to my success as a teacher:

Relationships

Firstly, the most important influence (I feel) is building positive rapport. It is extremely valuable when you really get to know the children, who you teach, and their families: what interests them? What motivates them? What are their values? What are their best hopes? Time is always a challenge in teaching, but if you prioritise small chunks of time getting to know your children, it can save you time in the long term. This could be a quiet one-to-one or group chat with the children, or it could be showing your face in a club, a sports match or a show which they attend. Sometimes you will need to be creative as it can take longer to earn some children's trust: don't pressure them but build up your relationship through genuine interactions. The same goes for the children's families: keep in contact with them, and consciously ensure that your contact is not always about negatives. Communication is key with creating positive relationships.

Behaviour is Communication

When children are exhibiting unexpected or inappropriate classroom behaviour, it can be draining and exhausting for teachers. To help you to support the child, it is essential to view behaviour as communication. There will be many factors which contribute, but

(Continued)

how you view and respond to it will be key to the outcome. This is when time prioritised for building rapport can help you. To assist with your expectations of children's behaviour, model what you expect to see (all the time) – yes, that involves no shouting and no running down the corridors!

When teaching some children, you will have prioritised time to build a relationship, yet they are still pushing the boundaries or behaving in an inappropriate manner. As difficult as it can be, do not take it personally, but consider what they might be trying to communicate. It is essential that you respond to children by showing that they are still valued even when they make mistakes and be clear that every day is a new day.

Creativity

Every lesson does not need to be 'all singing and dancing', but having snippets of imaginative content can support children's engagement. The manner you introduce or present a new topic to children can shape how they respond to it. It is also valuable to involve children in their learning. By encouraging learners to be involved in their learning, it can help them with understanding why, which can also develop their resilience and self-reflection.

Well-being

My final contribution is about your own well-being and aiming for a work-life balance. This was the area of teaching which I found most difficult. On reflection, these would be my top three points:

1. As noted above, draw upon experience from others and share resources. This will save you time and help inspire your creativity.
2. When reflecting on your practice, be accountable for your development but also be kind to yourself. You are human, and like the children, you may make mistakes. Learn from them and remind yourself that every day is a new day.
3. Finally, do not be afraid to say 'No!' You can't do everything! You have years to enjoy the variety of roles and opportunities which teaching brings. Do not try to do it all at once.

The Role of Self-Knowledge in the Classroom

By Elise Ramadan, NTP Tutor, Dartford, Kent, UK

Are we alright? Individually, societally, environmentally <u>and</u> politically? Because I feel like the benchmark for the next ten minutes of your engagement is based on whether we can agree that we've got some collective hurdles to jump. We need not agree on the reasons behind these challenges, merely that they exist.

The basis for proposing a rebalance of the curriculum, where emotional aspects of learning share centre stage with academia, partially comes from a need to stay

(Continued)

relevant in a changing world, but also from a need to help us untangle some of the stresses we've encountered since living out of alignment with our truest nature – the way we evolved as a species to hunt and gather. This 'new' curriculum is about assimilating the natural laws of the past with the technological advances of the present and future, so that we can tackle the underlying causes of our modern crises, each of which has a root in our sense of connection and belonging (or lack thereof). Obesity, mental illness, poverty and climate change are just a few examples.

We all possess a unique offering or gift. We all have a blueprint for our lives and the world which we're each trying to realise so we can feel at ease. We have an idea of what an ideal world looks like; we know what feels good or what goes against our values and ground rules. Teachers' vocations are our offering, but we all go about educating in our own way, based on who we are and what we feel is important. When we understand and express our uniqueness, we also feel more at ease and therefore more connected to those around us: family, colleagues and children. These are the hardwired coping strategies given to us by tribal living. Conversely, when our blueprint for the world is not met by the challenges of the day (something conflicts with what we deem most important), instead of assuming that the entire education sector is falling apart, we might understand that something we value was missing or threatened. Therefore, when we don't know who we are, or we try to be someone else, we feel less connection because we're not seen or accepted as our true selves. Perhaps we start to blame external factors.

So how do we determine, articulate and live as our truest selves?

How curious are you about the difference between your most authentic self and the person you've trained yourself to be in order to meet external expectations? Our trained selves appear frequently, often without our awareness. However, there is genuine power and connection when we find, label and communicate our authenticity. More importantly, children and young people notice this change. They sense when we're playing a part or living into the archetypal teacher we've created in our heads. They also respond differently when we're not.

As an educator, I consider that I have a responsibility to address these questions in myself and then help us address them as a community. Now that we embark on a technological revolution where content, information and experts are everywhere, our role in the classroom is shifting, yet we still carry many of the old cultures in our classrooms. I can have someone from NASA explain physics to my class through YouTube, so young people are looking to me for something more than mere pedagogy. I can show them the difference between human interaction and virtual learning and explain why different people respond in different ways. I can explain why one teacher might tolerate pupils talking when someone else in class reads their work aloud, but why this bothers me. (To answer that: I value acknowledgement and self-expression, so it feels rude when people don't give their full attention, whilst another teacher might value curiosity or independence so will be fine with multiple conversations happening at once.) By defining what's important to us, the qualities we deem essential and the skills we possess to make life seem effortless, we become a beacon of self-knowledge that is revered by our pupils.

Summary

This chapter has explored Shulman's (1986) tripartite exposition of subject knowledge. It is interesting to reflect that of the Teachers' Standards (number 3) and the newer Core Content Framework (Standard 3) both reflect the need to either 'secure' or 'demonstrate' subject or curriculum knowledge. This would infer that subject knowledge (content knowledge) is not taught; it is something you possess and keep acquiring. References to 'misconceptions' and 'collection of powerful analogies, illustrations, examples, explanations and demonstrations' reflect curricular knowledge, whereas 'observing expert colleagues' reflects pedagogical content knowledge.

Teaching is never static, neither is knowledge and the links to skills and understanding; it cannot rest on complacency. A good teacher is contemporary, well informed, widely read and able to source information and perspectives away from the dominant and narrow media platforms. Knowledge is global and thirsty. You may have, incidentally, wondered why there has not been a focus on the core subjects of English or mathematics; that is because it is not only an invitation to explore the wider (still national) curriculum, but because it is applicable to all subjects.

References

Alexander, R. (ed.). (2010). *Children their World, their Education*. Final Report and Recommendations of the Cambridge Primary Review. London: Routledge.

Archer Ker, L., DeWitt, J., Osbourne, JF., Dillon, JS., Wong, B., and Willis, B. (2013). *ASPIRES Report: Young People's Science and Career Aspirations, Age 10-14*. London: King's College. [Online]. Available at: https://kclpure.kcl.ac.uk/portal/en/publications/aspires-report(a0237ac7-cb43-473e-879a-1ea0addff0e3)/export.html

Archer, L., Moote, J., Macleod, E., Francis, B., and DeWitt, J. (2020). *ASPIRES 2: Young People's Science and Career Aspirations, Age 10-19*. UCL Institute of Education. [Online]. Available at: https://discovery.ucl.ac.uk/id/eprint/10092041/

Barnes, J. (2015). *Cross-Curricular Learning 3-14*. 3rd edn. London: Sage.

Bastide, D. (2007). *Teaching Religious Education 4-11*. 2nd edn. Abingdon: Routledge.

Bell Foundation. (2022). [Online] Available at: https://www.bell-foundation.org.uk/

bell hooks. (1994). *Teaching to Transgress*. Abingdon: Routledge.

CBI. (2015). *Tomorrow's world: inspiring primary scientists*. [Online]. Available at: https://www.cbi.org.uk/tomorrows-world/assets/%20%20download.pdf

Commission on Religious Education. (2018). *Religions and worldviews: The way forward*. [Online]. Available at: https://www.commissiononre.org.uk/wp-content/uploads/2018/09/Final-Report-of-the-Commission-on-RE.pdf

Dunlop, L., Bennett, J., Hanley, P., Reiss, M., and Turkenburg-van Diepen, M. (2021). *EEF: A review of evidence on primary science teaching*. [Online]. Available at: https://educationendowmentfoundation.org.uk/education-evidence/evidence-reviews/primary-science

Foley, Y., Anderson, C., Conteh, J., and Hancock, J. (2018), *English as an Additional Language and Initial Teacher Education*. Edinburgh: University of Edinburgh

Gatsby. (2017). *Good practical science*. [Online]. Available at: https://www.gatsby.org.uk/education/programmes/support-for-practical-science-in-schools

General Teaching Council for England. (2011). *Creating the curriculum*. [Online]. Available at: http://www.gtce.org.uk/tla/rft/creating_curriculum/ [Accessed 4 August 2011].

Hass, G. (1987). *Curriculum Planning: A New Approach*. 5th edn. Newton, MA: Allyn & Bacon Inc.

NALDIC. (2022). *EAL learners in schools*. [Online]. Available at: https://naldic.org.uk/the-eal-learner/eal-learners-uk/eal-learners-in-schools/

Ofsted. (2021a) *Research review series: Religious education*. [Online]. Available at: https://www.gov.uk/government/publications/research-review-series-religious-education

Ofsted. (2021b). *Research review series: Science*. [Online]. Available at: https://www.gov.uk/government/publications/research-review-series-science

Pollard, A. (2019). *Reflective Teaching*. 5th edn. London: Bloomsbury.

RE Today. (2022). *Meet the team*. [Online]. Available at: https://www.retoday.org.uk/

Shulman, L. (1986). 'A perspective on teacher knowledge'. In A. Pollard (Ed.), (2014) *Readings for Reflective Teaching* (pp. 233-235). London: Bloomsbury.

Smart, N. (1998). *The World's Religions*. 2nd edn. Cambridge: Cambridge University Press.

Stables, A., Martin, S., and Arnold, G. (2004). Student teachers' concepts of literacy and numeracy. *Research Papers in Education*, 19(3), pp. 345-364.

Tanner, D., and Tanner, L. (1980). *Curriculum Development: Theory into Practice*. 2nd edn. New York: Macmillan.

Turner, J., Bianchi, L., and Earle, S. (2022). *A response to Ofsted research review for science: Guidance for primary schools*. [Online]. Available at: https://www.tinyurl.com/OfstedReviewGuidance

Vincent, J. (2022). *Beyond Measure*. London: Faber & Faber Ltd.

Wellcome. (2019). Understanding the 'state of the nation' report of UK Primary science education: A baseline report for the Wellcome Trust.

6 Maths anxiety in the classroom

KEY WORDS
Anxiety, mathematics, mental block, barriers, inclusion

Contributors within this chapter:
1. Lucy Westley
2. Alex Baxendale
3. James Williams
4. Craig Chaplin
5. Kate and Maddie
6. Paul Wade

Introduction

The term 'maths anxiety' refers to a feeling of worry or fear when confronted with mathematical questions. Worrying about maths can present in a mental block when attempting to answer questions, and can present in physical symptoms, too, with a quickened heart rate, sweating, and feeling hot or nauseous. Maths anxiety can affect individuals of any age, although research shows girls and women are more commonly affected. Why is it important to consider maths anxiety when teaching? If people are fearful of maths, this can lead to them avoiding maths; in adulthood, this could mean being able to help children with homework, or avoiding jobs or training or promotions where maths may be involved, thus having a detrimental effect on someone's career pathway.

What causes maths anxiety?

Critical question
How can we recognise maths anxiety, and why does it occur?

The National Numeracy Organisation (2022) explain that the actual reasons behind an individual having maths anxiety are diverse and complex, but may have developed through situations of high pressure, such as exams, past experience of humiliation for making mistakes, and cultural bias.

In this chapter, we have six contributions from individuals who have either experienced maths anxiety personally or helped to support learners in finding strategies to deal with their maths anxiety. We hope that as you read through these reflective, personal recounts, you can consider how to best support learners who are worried about maths in your classroom.

Reducing Anxiety

By Lucy Westley, Senior Lecturer, ITT Mathematics, PGCE 5-11 Programme Leader at University of Northampton, Northampton, England

Mathematics is a controversial subject with the capacity to provoke extreme feelings and emotions. The manifestation of these feelings begins to develop in primary school and then may be further confirmed as a child goes through secondary school. There is a general consensus surrounding the term mathematics anxiety, a debilitating condition which may have a strong impact on the learner. Feelings of apprehension and discomfort alongside a negative impact on performance have been reported. Mathematics anxiety may arise when undertaking a mathematical task, suggesting that the point at which the anxiety may begin can exist before a task is introduced or that a learner may begin a task without anxiety present but may develop this as the task progresses.

A consistent link has been demonstrated between mathematical anxiety and mathematics achievement with a negative correlation being seen. Further, this research has demonstrated that mathematical anxiety may be responsible for low achievement in the subject, further proving that in the long term the self-concept and self-efficacy of the learner will be affected.

There are a number of factors that contribute to mathematics anxiety. These factors may be classed as affective in that they are closely related to the learner or they may be external, not arising from the learner but more contextual in nature. Cognitive factors such as low ability have been put forward as a cause for mathematical anxiety, which could be plausible in that those students with mathematical anxiety tend to stay away from all things mathematical, thereby learning less. If mathematical anxiety can be conceptualised as the physical manifestation of unreasonable fear towards the subject, then those stress responses will subsequently influence achievement. Reactions such as panic, tension doubt, fear and shame alongside physical indicators such as sweating palms, nausea and breathing difficulties will have an effect on the way in which mathematics is tackled by the learner.

Mathematics is a metalanguage that helps us as humans explain the world. It is crucial that teachers empower learners to think mathematically and promote the creativity of the subject. The ability to memorise procedures and rules should not become the focal point for teaching and assessment.

The Role of Memory

By Alex Baxendale, PhD Student and Psychology Tutor at Bangor University, Bangor, Wales

Once established, maths anxiety is a tricky issue to deal with once it has settled in. It brings a lifetime's worth of problems that impact society on a daily basis. It can push you away from getting that hot deal on a microwave because you cannot face working out '60% off' (Suri et al., 2013), but it can also lead to more detrimental impacts like incorrectly calculated dosages of medicine because the nurse was distracted by their anxiety (Trim, 2004). The anxiety itself influences several processes within the brain that lead to this reduced performance.

To perform maths adequately, we rely on our working memory; this is our ability to temporarily store and manipulate information both verbally and visually to rationalise problems to ourselves; this reliance is especially significant in children (Ansari et al., 2005; Libertus et al., 2009). This resource is a key aspect of maths anxiety as putting a heavy load onto it typically produces the reductions in performance that we are familiar with observing (Ashcraft and Kirk, 2001), although exceptions arise for those with low working memory capacity (Ramirez et al., 2013). This arises as maths anxiety disrupts working memory efficiency through ruminations, or negative self-talk, as it clogs up one's attention and ability to 'think straight' as we are too busy telling ourselves how much we hate the situation.

We do, however, require more than just working memory. Following the Triple Code Model (Dehaene and Cohen, 1995), we understand that the area in our brain mainly responsible for number processing develops in the spatial processing segment, mainly an area known as the intraparietal sulcus. This area is involved in subtraction and large addition problems (Piazza et al., 2007) as it requires access to our internal 'mental number line' that represents our understanding of quantities. Likewise, simple addition and multiplication are more verbal memory based and are processed in an area called the angular gyrus (Grabner et al., 2013) which stores our understanding of numerical facts, such as memorised times tables.

This balance of verbal and spatial processing is quite delicate. Within my own research, we have been interested in freeing up verbal working memory from the clutches of ruminations in order to improve performance. We found that whilst simply identifying characteristics of numbers (e.g. 'odd vs. even'), those with high maths anxiety obtained performance benefits by listening to instructions as opposed to reading them silently, as a means of 'overriding' their ruminations and directing their attention, bringing them closer to the performance of those with low maths anxiety. However, when scaled up to performing a math test with a variety of arithmetic equations, auditory instructions failed to provide any benefits and in some cases were detrimental. Ultimately a delicate balance of different processing systems is required to perform standard math tasks, and simple, quick interventions thus far have not been able to provide any benefits over more intensive ones such as math training sessions or expressive writing exercises

Play with Numbers

By James D. Williams, FLS FRSB CSciTeach, Director of Student Experience and Senior Lecturer in Education, Brighton, England

Maths anxiety is a real thing. I know I had it in primary and secondary school. I passed my maths O level, but only because of a maths tutor, Lou Evans, sadly no longer with us.

School created my maths anxiety as we had on the spot times table questions chucked at us at the beginning and end of each day. Learning the times tables is, in my view, a good thing. Being terrorised by them is not. The point is that this early anxiety over maths in primary school stuck with me into secondary. My secondary teacher, let's call him Mr Jones, continued the terror across not just arithmetic but geometry and algebra. We were all anxious when he took maths. The structure of the lesson was always the same. A problem, an on-the-board solution in chalk that sped across the board at 100 miles an hour, his hair bouncing up and down like a demented Hitler, then it was turned to page X and answer questions 1-10. He strode up and down the rows of desks and wasn't beyond tearing out a page from your exercise book if he spotted that it was not neat or had too many incorrect answers – that led to a detention and the repeating of the work in class. The end of the lesson was always the worst; pick on a child and get them to do question 11 – the most difficult – on the board.

But maths anxiety is so much more than being terrified of the maths teacher. It's a panic when you can't understand the method or when you fail to get that letters act as numbers. For a scientist, as I was hoping to be, it's a bit of a problem. What I wanted to study meant that I needed to be maths confident. Geology is not very mathematical, but there are concepts that rely heavily on maths, angles in crystals, mapping strike, dip and constructing 3d images of rock formations, etc.

So, what did Lou do to lessen my anxiety? He patiently showed me methods and took me through theorems and proofs of theorems – he didn't explode when I said 'I don't get it'; he tried another way. He taught me not to be frightened by numbers but to play with them – almost (though he never said it) become friends with them. He showed me number patterns and how things like geometry solve real-life problems.

This is where my uncle, an engineer and a Second World War bomb disposal expert, taught me how long-range missiles work and how a triangle on a curved surface has more than 180 degrees. It explained why his first calculations of where a projectile would land were always wrong – until he remembered that the Earth isn't flat.

Over the years my anxiety waned (it's still there, hidden away), but I learned to play with numbers and not be afraid. I see new maths as a challenge, not a monster waiting to devour me.

Delivering Curriculum without 'Maths Anxiety'

By Craig Chaplin, Assistant Head and Maths Lead at a Primary Special School for Pupils with SEMH Needs, Lincoln, England

The pupils within our setting have often experienced a challenging start to their education, with approximately only 2% transitioning into special education from full-time mainstream education. The rest have either attended part-time, moved from temporary pupil referral provision, had home tuition or simply been excluded from education whilst awaiting a placement. For a significant proportion of pupils (although not all), this disrupted start has impacted the way they view themselves as learners in some form or another. Learning for many is a daunting prospect, and this is as true in maths as in any other subject.

In developing our curriculum there were some fundamental questions that we needed to consider, which when viewed through the lens of maths anxiety provide useful points to reflect upon:

- Should maths be taught in blocks or spread over time? Why?
  Allowing time between lessons that follow on from one another has the potential to allow for more meaningful and targeted interventions.
- Should maths objectives be taught in fixed allocations of time? Why?
  The research and thought that go into establishing the timings of 'off the shelf' schemes should not override a teacher's professional judgement to slow the learning down to secure progress. The pace of learning can be as anxiety inducing for teachers as it is for learners, and in the grand scheme of things, doing something slower but effectively should trump doing it quickly but ineffectively.
- What makes an effective sequence of learning?
  Across all stages, a build it, draw it and write it approach can help children move from the concrete to the abstract. Spending time securing a concrete understanding will make the abstract easier to understand. There also needs to be careful thought about how procedural learning is used – an over-reliance here can foster anxiety in non-procedural contexts (specifically testing).
- Do our policies and procedures work in a connected way? How could this be better?
  Parents are often not considered here, and we need to make explicit how we are teaching maths. Homework can be a source of maths anxiety for parents, and this can then feed into the children.
- Do we really make full and effective use of assessment?
  In the literature, maths anxiety can often be equated with test anxiety. Cold calling the introverted child or testing with constraints (Looking at you Year 4 Times Table Check!) generates anxiety because of the delivery rather than the maths, but the two can quickly become entwined.
- Do we take time to reflect?
  Whilst a good worker does not blame their tools for a poor job, good teachers cannot blame their pupils if the content is just not grasped. Taking time to discuss and reflect on what we do as pedagogists so that we can simplify and make it more explicit should be a core element of our work. Are we recognising maths anxiety? Do we unwittingly create maths anxiety? What could be done differently?

Maths Anxiety: Parent and Student Viewpoint

By Coulson, National Teaching Fellow,
Head of Learning and Teaching Enhancement, University of Northampton, England

Maddie, Secondary school pupil

Maddie: Secondary Pupil

Parent view – Kate

The concept of maths anxiety never really registered with me as I found it easy, and my eldest child enjoyed maths and did well all the way through to GCSE level.

My daughter, Maddie, attended our local village primary school which is rated Good by Ofsted. Her overall experience at the school was excellent; she formed good friendship groups, was supported well by her class teachers and teacher assistants (TAs), was given extra-pastoral support when she found transition challenging. Maddie consistently engaged with her schoolwork and was working at the expected level. The maths anxiety started in about Year 1. She would get very tearful on the days she had maths or had a test; she worried she wouldn't get the answer right; she would get upset when she had maths homework, and eventually, I got a version of maths anxiety too! I tried to work with the school, but it felt like they just wanted her to do well in the test without any thought to her as a human. She was taken out of activities she loved to do extra maths and was mortified that she was singled out, which made it even worse. She was so relieved when she didn't have to take her SATs due to COVID-19. And even now she tells me 'Only 4 more years of maths and then I don't have to do it anymore' even though she does know it and excels in her set. I have lined up a maths tutor for her, but I feel guilty that I can pay for extra support – many parents can't.

Student view – Maddie, aged 12

I really love going to school and learning new things; my favourite lessons are English and Spanish. I am now in Year 8 at secondary school, and I am in set three for maths. Most of my friends are in set one or two for maths, and it makes me sad that I am not with them. I always do my homework, and I am working hard to practice and do well in my tests. I find tests for maths and science really tricky; I know the topics and can answer the questions or explain the answer to someone, but I often misread the test questions or get all flustered and upset in the test. Last week my teacher asked me to stay behind to discuss my test score; I only got 27%, but she said I knew the content. She told me we needed to work on how I do the test. I asked her if she had practice papers, but she said she wasn't sure. Mum said she will find some for me.

At primary school, I started to worry about maths in about Year 1. I would worry that my teacher would ask me a question and I wouldn't be able to answer it, so I used to cry sometimes before the lesson. I used to tell my mum before school that I didn't like the lesson and that I was really worried they would ask me. I used to practice at home, but I found it really upsetting, and sometimes mum didn't know how to help me. Sometimes I just freeze and don't know what to do when I have read the maths question. And once I do that I just

(Continued)

panic and get upset, and that makes it worse. It was really bad in Year 5 and 6, and I was so worried about my SATs. I also hated it when I had to have extra lessons at school; it was always during fun things like practising for the school play or PE. I love PE, and I was cross that I had to do extra maths. I can't wait until I am in Year 11 and can stop doing maths.

English Versus Maths

By Paul Wade, Founder of Educators Running Club, Grimsby, England

Words? Love 'em. Have done ever since I was a little boy, and I'd be told to amuse myself with a book. I would do so with pleasure. Do some little boys amuse themselves with maths problems? They probably do somewhere, but they didn't in our house.

Kids who amuse themselves with books tend to like English at school, and this was no different for me. Maths, though? Not so much. I developed a set of defence mechanisms to help shield myself from the horror I felt when the questions were about numbers not words. I was the joker, class-clowning my way through Xs and Ys that hurt my head. Then I was that irritating voice that asks their maths teacher, 'Will we ever use this in real life, though?' I'd already decided I wouldn't, of course; that I would lead a life free of anything that required a formula, or showing your working out.

Kids who like English at school tend to become English teachers, and I will happily tell my classes there was no other specialism open to me. But my life isn't free of NumberFear, not by any stretch. Marks on tests must be added up, data must be entered on spreadsheets, Progress 8 must ... well; if I'm honest I've never properly understood Progress 8. It's a thing that has a number in its name, so it is not my friend – a fate also suffered by the film 2 Fast 2 Furious and the band S Club 7. It's often my excuse for not having a six-pack too, though I am willing to accept there may be other possible explanations.

If I'm being honest, I know maths isn't the problem. I know I'm the problem. The two times I've really needed to pass a maths exam, I have. I had to resit my GCSE in college, and throughout the process I was painfully aware that my friends were out having fun whilst I was grumping my way through work I should have taken seriously a year earlier. I needed to know maths things, so I taught myself those things and got myself a C. Later, in order to become an English Teacher, I had to pass the maths skills test that's part of gaining Qualified Teacher Status (QTS). Faced with the possibility of failing at the first hurdle and being left with zero income, I took those maths things seriously again and got myself whatever the pass mark was.

There is one branch of maths I sort of enjoy. Football maths – working out how many points my team needs to be promoted, or to avoid relegation (it's the latter much more than the former; I support Huddersfield Town), is something I like doing. Kind of.

And without my maths anxiety, I wouldn't have an awareness that information on paper can make people feel deeply sad. I know words can make others feel the way numbers make me feel, and I teach English accordingly.

So thanks, numbers. Maybe it's time to give S Club 7 another chance...

Conclusion

- Maths anxiety may present at different ages and stages of a person's educational career.
- Ensure that maths learning is real-world, relevant and relatable.
- Show learners the value in maths, with the gift of numbers something to be cherished, not fearful of.

References

Ansari, D., Garcia, N., Lucas, E., Hamon, K., and Dhital, B. (2005). Neural correlates of symbolic number processing in children and adults. *Neuroreport*, 16(16), pp. 1769-1773.

Ashcraft, M.H., and Kirk, E.P. (2001). The relationships among working memory, maths anxiety, and performance. *Journal of Experimental Psychology: General*, 130(2), 224-237. doi:10.1037/0096-3445.130.2.224

Dehaene, S., and Cohen, L. (1995). Towards an anatomical and functional model of number processing. *Mathematical Cognition*, 1, 83-120.

Grabner, R.H., Ansari, D., Koschutnig, K., Reishofer, G., and Ebner, F. (2013). The function of the left angular gyrus in mental arithmetic: Evidence from the associative confusion effect. *Human Brain Mapping*, 34(5), 1013-1024. doi:10.1002/hbm.21489

Libertus, M.E., Brannon, E.M., and Pelphrey, K.A. (2009). Developmental changes in category-specific brain responses to numbers and letters in a working memory task. *Neuroimage*, 44(4), pp. 1404-1414.

National Numeracy Organisation. (2022). What is maths anxiety? Available at: https://www.nationalnumeracy.org.uk/what-issue/about-maths-anxiety [Accessed 1 October 2022].

Piazza, M., Pinel, P., Le Bihan, D., and Dehaene, S. (2007). A magnitude code common to numerosities and number symbols in human intraparietal cortex. *Neuron*, 53(2), pp. 293-305.

Ramirez, G., Gunderson, E.A., Levine, S.C., and Beilock, S.L. (2013). Maths anxiety, working memory, and math achievement in early elementary school. *Journal of Cognition and Development*, 14(2), pp. 187-202.

Suri, R., Monroe, K.B., and Koc, U. (2013). Maths anxiety and its effects on consumers' preference for price promotion formats. *Journal of the Academy of Marketing Science*, 41(3), pp. 271-282.

Trim, J. (2004). Clinical skills: A practical guide to working out drug calculations. *British Journal of Nursing*, 13(10), pp. 602-606.

7 Formative assessment

KEY WORDS
Assessment for learning, formative assessment, understanding, feedback, questioning, success criteria, peer assessment, self-assessment, engage

> **Contributors within this chapter:**
> 1. Rebecca Clarkson
> 2. Charlotte Nohavicka
> 3. Laura Whiteman
> 4. Katherine Childs

Introduction

> **Critical question**
> How might I enhance assessment for learning within my practice?

This chapter reflects on practical measures enabling formative assessment (assessment for learning) to be a tool which can be harnessed by teachers and pupils to support teaching and learning. To enable effective pupil progression, formative assessment is deployed as an effective tool by teachers. To enable this, it is critical to employ strategies which are targeted, pupil centred and involve teacher and pupils as partners. It is also important to allow pupils time to engage with formative assessment within time constraints imposed by the timetable.

The chapter begins with consideration of what formative assessment is about and how it may be used diagnostically at the beginning of a teaching and learning cycle, with a think piece from Rebecca Clarkson. Next, the principles developed from The Assessment Reform Group (2002) are detailed followed by what aspects may be formatively assessed within a lesson. The rest of the chapter unpicks Black et al.'s (2004) key themes of what contributes to effective formative assessment: questioning, teacher feedback, peer assessment and self-assessment and the use of summative assessment for formative purposes. The theme of questioning contains a contribution from an initial teacher trainee, Charlotte Nohavicka, who undertook an action research project as part of her PGCE, which reflects on the importance of questioning and the environment we create to support children engage effectively with questions. Additional themes considered within the questioning element are as follows: what sits behind effective questioning to prompt and facilitate peer talk?; reflection on closed versus open questions to support peer talk; consideration of the critical reason for questioning; some ideas as to how children may respond to questions posed within assessment for learning; and reflection about using and monitoring questioning constructively. Discussion about techniques of teacher feedback to pupils considers live versus distance marking and written versus verbal feedback, with some prompts provided to support marking and a reminder to allow children to respond to feedback. Reflection of pupil self- and peer evaluation also considers the use of success criteria and how these may be developed and generated with the children. Next, Laura Whiteman, an early career teacher, reflects on her action research project as part of her PGCE training, which looks at self- and peer assessment in a Key Stage 1 class. This is followed by Katherine Childs' consideration of a manageable whole-class formative assessment strategy, which also links to the use of success criteria and supporting summative assessment. After a very brief consideration of formative use of summative tests, the chapter concludes with a consideration of the impact of assessment for learning.

The use of formative assessment

> **Critical question**
>
> When does formative assessment come into play?

Formative assessment (assessment for learning) informs future teaching and learning, as opposed to summative assessment (assessment of learning) such as a test, which gives a snapshot of a child's ability. Nevertheless, it would be remiss to ignore the fact that summative assessment could be used formatively. For example, a teacher could use results of a formal test diagnostically to see where gaps may lie, and use this to inform future planning and teaching.

Defining and positioning assessment for learning within a cycle

> **Critical question**
>
> What exactly is assessment for learning, and how does it link to teaching, learning, planning and evaluation?

Assessment for learning 'provides information that teachers and their students can use as feedback in assessing themselves and one another and in modifying the teaching and learning activities in which they are engaged' (Black et al., 2004, p. 10). This means that formative

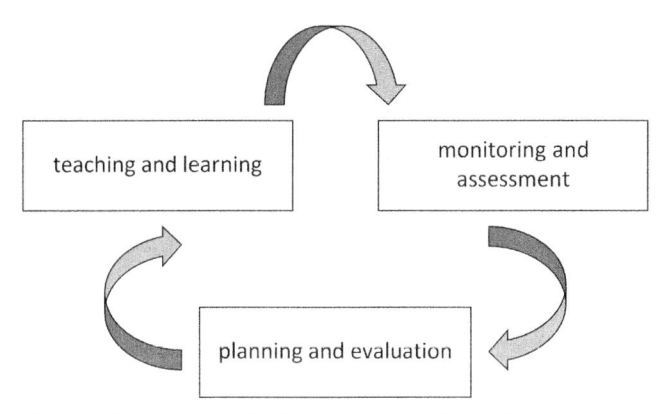

Figure 7.1 The cyclical nature of monitoring and assessing, planning and evaluation and teaching and learning

assessment enables relevant planning and teaching to occur, facilitating sharp learning by pupils (see Cambridge International Assessment Education, no date). Effective practice means that, as practitioners, we have knowledge of how to use assessment for learning to support appropriate learning challenges within lessons and between sequential lessons, recognising the cyclic nature of planning, teaching and assessment for reflective teachers. Figure 7.1 illustrates this cyclical nature. It is important that feedback to pupils is included within the 'monitoring and assessment' and 'teaching and learning' components.

The beginning of our assessment journey

Rebecca Clarkson begins our learning journey into formative assessment by considering an often overlooked element within the assessment for learning process.

Diagnostic Approaches

By Rebecca Clarkson, Senior Lecturer in Primary Education at Anglia Ruskin University, Chelmsford, England

Diagnostic approaches as a method of formative assessment are often overlooked. We have all heard about the importance of clear learning objectives and success criteria, the value of using open questions and the significance of giving good, specific and targeted feedback that moves the learner on. However, let us explore the benefits of using diagnostic approaches in the classroom. In contrast to the usual summative assessments you might have experienced, diagnostic approaches are low stakes because they do not involve giving a grade; they are used at the beginning of a lesson, topic, term or course to give a detailed analysis of an individual's strengths and weaknesses that you can then exploit as a teacher to inform next steps in learning. The main benefit of using

(Continued)

a diagnostic approach is that you get to elevate your teaching by focussing on the specific challenges your learners are facing. The information you receive allows you to tailor your whole pedagogical approach, to update and reorganise the content of your teaching. Activities can be designed to meet the needs of individuals or groups – making adaptation more straightforward. In addition, by undertaking diagnostic assessment at the beginning of your teaching, you have a ready-made baseline from which to map learning against the success criteria.

Elicitation exercises are a great way to find out how much a learner knows and identify any gaps or misconceptions before you start teaching a new topic. Elicitation is based on three core principles: 1) that your learners know a lot collectively and this can be mined and used constructively; 2) teaching is based on what your learners already know; 3) the use of questions, in different forms, is essential in the discovery of what learners know. Elicitation exercises may be done through mind mapping exercises or asking children to pose their own questions, e.g. via a question box.

Developing formative assessment

Critical question

What principles can help develop formative assessment?

The Assessment Reform Group (2002) proposed ten key principles to help practitioners develop assessment for learning (AfL):

- AfL should be part of planning effectively for learning and teaching; it is flexible in its approach and enables children to identify what they will be learning about and how they will be assessed; it also incorporates planning for how children will receive feedback, their involvement in AfL and how they will be supported to make progress.
- AfL should focus on how pupils learn with the 'how' being made explicit to the children, so that they are taken beyond the 'what'.
- AfL should be central to classroom practice, with responses to tasks and questions observed to improve learning; it involves the teacher and learner.
- AfL is an essential skill and needs engagement of continuing professional development by teachers to refine their procedures to plan assessment, make observations of learning, give feedback and support children in self-assessment.
- AfL should be dealt with sensitively, and use constructive comments because of the emotional dimension.
- AfL should acknowledge that a learner's motivation is important. It should emphasise progress and achievement [that is not to say next steps cannot be identified] as part of constructive feedback and enable autonomy as part of self-direction.

- AfL should help learners to understand the assessment criteria. This is facilitated when pupils have involvement in discussing them, with teachers providing examples of how to achieve them, and engagement in episodes of peer assessment or self-assessment.
- AfL involves learners receiving constructive information to help them improve.
- AfL enhances a learners' ability to self-assess, enabling them to become proficient with reflection and self-management.
- AfL recognises all educational achievement, enabling pupils to reach their best and have their endeavours recognised.

Assessing in lessons

> **Critical question**
>
> What aspects am I looking to assess within a specific lesson?

Alongside assessment for learning helping to identify what needs to be taught and what does not, formative assessment can help a teacher to evaluate what elements of teaching and learning have been successful or unsuccessful and provide insights into the reasons why.

It is essential to know the lesson objective – what we want the pupils to learn. The assessment method will link to either the product of learning (the learning outcome – the tangible end result of the lesson, perhaps a specific element from the national curriculum) or it might focus on the processes of learning. This latter aspect might hone in on developing children's metacognitive processes (learning how to learn), enabling children to make connections between ideas or even take risks in their learning to challenge themselves or help children to develop group skills as part of a social dimension of learning.

Teacher monitoring is integral to formative assessment and has a degree of continuity about it. For example, you might be monitoring how children are progressing in their English over time (e.g. a term), but as part of that you might undertake assessment at particular points, within a particular sequence of teaching, to gather evidence of particular elements of their learning, which then informs your practice and impacts on the children's learning. You might also be doing formal assessment over the course of an individual lesson – monitoring how child/children are getting on over the course of the whole lesson but doing snapshot assessments of particular aspects of their learning and understanding at particular points. It should be noted that it is not just teachers who can monitor children's achievement (and provide forms of feedback, as appropriate). Monitoring can be from additional adults in the room: teaching assistants, adult helpers, parent helpers, teacher trainees or those making formal/informal observations of lessons.

The Early Career Framework (Department for Education [DfE], 2019) highlights that planning effective formative assessment tasks should be 'linked to lesson objectives and thinking ahead about what would indicate understanding (e.g. by using hinge questions to pinpoint knowledge gaps)' (p. 19). It is this spotlight on effective questioning strategies that lies at the heart of formative assessment, enabling both teacher and pupil to work together and identify what has been learnt, any gaps and what should come next.

The importance of checking children's prior knowledge before teaching a learning episode is extremely important, and it is even better to check learning before the planning stage so that activities are sharp, timely, relevant and have the most impact. It may be that pre-existing misconceptions are also identified at an initial stage of pre-planning so that planning for teaching addresses them.

Effective assessment for learning is an enabling and reciprocal tool for both children and teachers. For teachers, it is a vehicle to provide children with feedback and encouragement and lead to effective live and pre-planned adaptation of teaching and learning, and for children, it can foster the development of self-evaluation skills.

Unpicking effective formative assessment

Critical question

What key elements underpin what effective formative assessment looks like?

Black et al. (2004, p. 10) highlight that teachers need a 'variety of living examples of implementation', and they present practical and authentic illustrations. Although their research is focused on secondary schools, the findings have relevance to the primary phase, under the themes of 'questioning, [teacher] feedback, peer assessment and self-assessment, and the formative use of summative tests' (p. 11). These themes interspersed with sub-themes will now be explored.

Questioning

Black et al. (2004) remind us that the response time between a teacher asking a question and receiving a response can be less than one second and focused on quick, factual memorisation, with superficial dialogue. In 2004, they proposed that a longer wait time can indicate to pupils that greater thought is required in the response. Fast-forward to the present day, and one example of this may be seen in classroom activities where meaningful talk is encouraged. An area of discussion as part of a main teaching input may be presented to the children within a question who then are asked to talk with a partner for a short period of time. Responses by the teacher may then be collected after. This method of peer discussion for a few minutes can be used effectively to develop meaningful pupil-teacher thought and discussion. This also can help teachers to gather information about children's prior knowledge and understanding, including gaps and misconceptions, to then inform appropriate next steps.

It is important to develop a supportive climate where pupils are comfortable with also responding to questions and giving answers which might be incorrect, and where the teacher will help to explore the thinking behind the strategy or answer given. The mindset of 'it is ok to make mistakes, we can learn from them' seems a suitable approach to take within this context. Charlotte Nohavicka presents a useful reflection of her action research, undertaken during her PGCE training. It considers the relevance of questioning and how important the environment is which we create to help children engage with questions in an effective way.

The Importance of Questioning and of the Environment

By Charlotte Nohavicka, Teacher Trainee, Colchester, England

As part of my PGCE course, I conducted action research looking at the impact questioning had on challenging pupils in their learning. The research was conducted with a selected group of six Year 4 pupils within a two-form entry Church of England Primary School in the East of England. The research focused on maths and included: a baseline survey of pupils' understanding of why teachers ask questions; observations of questioning techniques during an experienced teacher's maths lesson; delivery of my own maths lesson based on the previous two stages; and a group discussion with participants.

The baseline survey identified factors which influenced whether pupils would answer a question in class, which were a) their personality (whether they were confident or shy) and b) their sense of their own ability in a particular subject – they all said that they would feel happiest in volunteering an answer if they felt confident that they had got the answer right. Aguiar et al. (2010) argue that learner safety in the classroom centres around anxieties of what the peer group thinks and it is something of a tightrope walk between being 'considered stupid or a boffin' so 'pupils must feel secure before they risk' (p. 176) answering a question. Participants in my study echoed this in saying that they felt more confident in sharing ideas with a talk partner than the whole class (a smaller audience to make the mistake in front of) and felt more confident sharing their ideas with the whole class once they had received positive feedback from the teacher either individually or as a small group discussion.

It is not only about the teacher's question that is of relevance, but encouraging a questioning classroom where pupils are also empowered to ask their own questions and are rewarded for taking ownership of their learning. Creating an intellectually and emotionally safe environment, where children are willing to pose questions and take risks in their learning, and are not always focussed on getting it right, is not a new idea. Solutions to this problem of fear focus on psychological approaches such as Growth Mindset (see work by Carol Dweck, e.g. Dweck, 2006) and the Learning Pit (Nottingham, no date). Low-stakes formative assessment like Kahoot! and the use of individual whiteboards for answering questions are common. Another idea might be to have a 'mistake of the week', where a misconception that is common in the class is put up on the board, worked through and referred back to as the learning progresses during the week.

Creating a safe environment is more about the classroom culture than the tools used to measure learning. For this to be effective, pupils need to truly believe and trust that making mistakes is not a bad thing. What if we used time constructively at the beginning of the academic year for meaningful conversations with our pupils to address the fear around failure and mistakes?

Peer talk and questioning

> **Critical question**
>
> What sits behind effective questioning to prompt and facilitate peer talk?

It is important to ensure that guidance or peer discussion is kept focused upon the task in hand. This necessitates that key understanding of what peer discussion entails and does not entail is made explicit with the children. Through the teacher sharing expectations of what a good listener and a good speaker is, the pupils engaging with regular practice of peer talk and children reflecting on the process too, the use of peer talk can become embedded in teaching and learning. It should be acknowledged that how pupils are paired is important too and may differ according to the task at hand. It is also important that the teacher and any additional adults are actively involved in the peer discussion too. There is a need in teacher planning to consider the relevant types of questions that can be used in peer talk, as well as other areas of the teaching sequence, which can challenge all children and act as a hook on which to hang lessons and motivate children. An example of such practice may be exemplified through the use of the National Centre for Excellence in the Teaching of Mathematics' (NCETM, no date c) reasoning statements – these could serve as use for questioning within the main teaching input, main activity or towards the end of a lesson. The NCETM highlights the importance of reasoning as linking to the aims of the mathematics national curriculum (DfE, 2013) and the research undertaken by Nunes et al. (2009), which spotlighted 'the ability to reason mathematically as the most important factor in a pupil's success in mathematics' (NCETM, no date c). Reasoning (linked to the deeper level of questioning) also ties in with a mastery approach to teaching. Mathematical thinking is one of the key components of a mastery approach and is underpinned by the idea that 'If taught ideas are to be understood deeply, they must not merely be passively received but must be worked on by the student: thought about, reasoned with and discussed with others' (NCETM, no date a). Examples of mathematical mastery are further illustrated in the NCETM's examples of primary assessment materials (NCETM, no date b) utilising questions, tasks and activities to help assess children's degree of mastery.

It should also be acknowledged that peer talk can facilitate getting a response from children back in front of the whole class if pupils have articulated and rehearsed with a peer or adult. Moreover, an expectation that feedback will be required after the peer talk helps children to consider that there can be no freewheelers just sitting idly by and that their contribution is important and valued. Even if a child within the pair is still reticent to share feedback, then the partner (or the adult who may have listened in) can share the idea of the other, which can help to develop confidence of the reluctant speaker.

Peer talk takes us away from the hands-up approach of a closed question and that some pupils may not answer because they know someone else will. It also distances us from a situation where a child does not put their hand up, but is asked by the teacher to answer, or where a child may be anxious about being put on the spot and getting the answer wrong. This can also take us to a 'no hands up' style of teaching practice, because the expectation is that all children 'are expected to be able to answer at any time even if it is an "I don't know"' (Black et al., 2004, p. 12).

Closed versus open questions

> **Critical question**
>
> Which is better – closed or open questioning?

Alexander (2020) highlights dialogic teaching where questions may influence a pupil's learning by challenging them to think beyond what is currently written and so develop their thoughts into more thoughtful and considered perspectives. Whilst open-ended questions enable the thinking of multiple answers and probe children's thinking deeper (Boyd, 2015), it is important to point out the value of closed questioning and to not devalue them. There is a place for knowledge retrieval which will be garnered by using questions which are more closed (Boyd, 2015), and these questions can also serve as assessment for learning tools. Moreover, a closed question can also support children to respond because they can use its structure upon which to base their answer. However, in planning lessons, it can be easier to devise those closed questions and expect quick response answers as opposed to also developing more open ones (the how and the why), alongside the closed, which can support deeper levels of thinking by the children. For example, instead of asking only for an answer to a mathematical calculation, the teacher might explore the strategies to get to the answer as part of peer talk.

So, what is the critical point about questioning?

Questions can enable children to reflect on their learning strategies and to discuss these with their peers. Questioning strategies 'can become part of the interactive dynamic of the classroom and can provide an invaluable opportunity to extend students' thinking through immediate feedback on their work' (Black et al., 2004, p. 13).

Questions to prompt thinking can ask children to

- Explain how they know something to be true
- Spotlight similarities and differences around a theme
- Explain an error
- Explain why

One of the reasons for asking questions is to get children to think (Black et al., 2004). Through this, all children should be enabled to actively participate, and teachers become facilitators of children's 'exploration and development of ideas' (Black et al., 2004, p. 13).

Pupil involvement

> **Critical question**
>
> How might children respond to your questions as part of your assessment for learning?

There are several approaches which may be employed for children to respond to formative assessment. The key issue is that questions must produce productive thinking (Black et al., 2004), and Askew et al. (2015) pick up on a useful checklist for assessing a child's mastery (of understanding) in mathematics if they can do the following, which may be tweaked for other curriculum areas. Ideas could include children

- Expressing something using their own words
- Expressing ideas in lots of different ways
- Explaining something to others
- Demonstrating what they have learnt through examples (and non-examples)
- See connections between what they have learnt and other themes
- Identify and make use of what they have learnt in alternative ways and in new situations and contexts

(Askew et al., 2015)

An even greater depth of mastery may be assessed by monitoring and formatively assessing pupils' ability to

- Solve more complex problems, where the strategy is not instantly apparent, which demonstrates imaginative, creative solutions
- Approach investigates tasks independently and explain solutions and results with clarity and with a systematic approach to generalise ideas

(Askew et al., 2015)

Teachers could include activities like 'always, sometimes, never true' where children reason over a mathematical statement (see https://nrich.maths.org/12672), or debating over what might be the odd one out (e.g. the Eiffel Tower, Buckingham Palace or the pyramids) and why, or where teachers facilitate children bouncing ideas off one another as to whether or not they agree or disagree with a given answer and why. These activities enable children to explore and unpick ideas at a greater depth of understanding than simply providing simple yes or no answers.

Monitoring responses when questioning and observational monitoring

Critical question

What do we need to consider when monitoring assessment and using it constructively?

We need to discover what children know, understand and need to find out to develop their learning. Part of this will be through utilising questioning techniques. When asking questions, e.g. during the main teaching input, it is important to notice and fully take on board the response(s) you get. If, for example, you are asking all children to hold up white boards to get a response to a question asked, how are you going to respond to what you see? How are you going to make a note for your current teaching or future planned teaching? Are you going to regroup children? Are you going to spend longer with certain children before letting them go away to do a task? Do you have an additional adult who might note the responses of children who might need further input or intervention?

Observational monitoring encompasses a teacher listening to pupils describing and reasoning about their work, and noting approaches used and their interaction with others. These aspects resonate with assessing the process of learning. Since a part of an observation is the need to record, noting children's responses to questioning needs to be thoughtful and considered by the teacher, or it gets lost; it needs to be purposeful and have impact. Observation of longer segments of children engaged in activities may involve the teacher writing a narrative and freely describing what is occurring, marking against a checklist perhaps with pre-coded categories, or using a time schedule and sampling activity at pre-designated points using points of structured description.

Alongside questioning are developing responses to feedback (including marking), techniques of pupils' peer evaluation and self-evaluation and feedback, and the use of summative assessment for formative purposes. These themes are now explored.

Teacher feedback to pupils

The way in which feedback is given to pupils is important, with responses of numerical grades alongside written commentary unlikely to have much positive or constructive impact, as pupils may ignore written comments if both are presented (Black et al., 2004). The amount of feedback also has to be manageable by teachers. It is likely to be unsustainable for teachers to provide daily deep-level marking for every single subject area where hard copy work has been completed by the children. The Education Endowment Foundation (EEF, 2021) produced a report to support teacher feedback. It is targeted towards class teachers and senior leaders around all subjects and provides feedback examples. The recommendations focus upon the following: building groundwork to provide effective feedback; providing timely feedback to support progression of learning; consideration for how pupils receive and implement actions from feedback; planning for using meaningful and time-productive, written feedback, as well as using meaningful oral feedback; and producing a feedback policy that crystallises the key features of purposeful and effective feedback. The guidance acknowledges the 'opportunity cost' associated with feedback – 'limiting the time teachers can give to other tasks and often with a negative impact on their wellbeing' (EEF, 2021, p. 8). Additional documentation is available about feedback on the EEF webpage. The DfE (2018) also provided guidance around workload reduction, which also included considerations around reducing marking.

Some schools, in their marking policies, indicate sensible levels of marking, which might include the following:

- Marking two pieces of written work by a child each week in a subject area in depth
- Use of agreed signs within the margin or within a piece of work indicating areas of strengths and next steps
- Marking a specific number of books each day in depth whilst the rest might indicate more surface level of completion
- Use of pupils' self-assessment

- Use of peer assessment
- The relevance and use of live marking (responses) during the lesson, which might be written or have a verbal feedback annotation indicated on the work
- A tick list of achievement noted against success criteria (useful in PE or where no written or hard copy work is produced)
- Responses from a teaching assistant, where appropriate, though also checked by the teacher

Is live marking or distance marking better, and is written or verbal feedback better?

Live versus distance marking

Live marking refers to responding to pupils' work through verbal and/or written commentary during the lesson. The response from the teacher will be instant and enable the children to make immediate changes to what they are doing or how they are doing it, as appropriate. If a child is doing well, then it can encourage them to continue progressing and responding to the task in hand, and if they have made errors or have misconceptions, then it can serve as a useful pit stop to deal with the situation and get back on track. Live marking can also serve the purpose of the teacher being aware of what is and what is not going right in the lesson and may prompt mini breaks to focus in on elements of good practice or indeed to refocus the whole class with relevant learning points and to help re-guide them. A good rule of thumb when assessing the usefulness of live marking versus distance marking is this: if a child is going wrong with a task in a lesson for whatever reason, then the error they are making (whether because of carelessness, misconceptions, lack of clarity from the teaching or another reason) is likely to be reinforced and has to be untaught at a later stage. Distance marking (completed at a later stage of time away from the children, for example in the staff room or at home at the end of the school day after the children have left) runs the risk of not being able to pick up on issues as and when they arise and dealing with them during the lesson, whereas the response to live marking is instantaneous. That is not to demerit distance marking – both live and distance marking have their purposes. Distance marking can help a teacher to look at what the work looks like after input has occurred and to let the child demonstrate what their understanding and knowledge or skill development has been. A combination of both distance and live marking, as appropriate to the lesson, can work effectively. In some instances, a child or group of children might celebrate or demonstrate what they have achieved during the lesson, by presenting back to the class teacher and their peers at the end of the lesson. This can also serve as a useful assessment for learning opportunity for teachers and pupils.

Written versus verbal feedback

Feedback should encourage thinking and support the process of learning (Black et al., 2004). The preference for written or verbal feedback is likely to depend upon the task in hand and what subject area is being covered. For example, a response from a teacher during a P.E. lesson is unlikely to be written, though a summative record may be kept as part of a checklist or some form of written summary. Verbal feedback is likely to have an instantaneous response from the pupils and can help deal with misconceptions and errors, and boost children's confidence if they are being praised, thus supporting their learning behaviours. Verbal feedback is also likely to be employed as part of peer evaluation (see later in the chapter). Some schools have a no written marking policy (e.g. see Sealy, 2021). However, their systems will be robust and will still involve the teacher recording pupil achievement in some way; the teacher will still need to know at what level their children are working at and what their next steps are in their learning. Progress of the children over time must still be evident.

If written feedback is given to children, then it has to be meaningful and linked to the objective. For example

- Share success – the teacher identifies three pieces of achievement in the child's work, linked to the lesson objective, and highlights them.
- Indicate improvement – the teacher uses a symbol to indicate exactly where the work could be improved.
- Give improvement suggestion – the teacher writes down a specific improvement, example or explanation.
- Two stars and a wish – at the end of a piece of work, a teacher indicates two elements where the work demonstrates it has met the objectives and one area that needs developing (an area not quite met as part of the learning objective) or an area which could be extended based upon the learning objective at a deeper level of understanding.

Feedback should also focus or highlight any misconceptions rather than focusing on careless mistakes.

Improvement prompts can focus around a reminder, scaffold or example.

A reminder prompt reiterates or elaborates upon (reinforces) the learning objective.
To reiterate, use prompts such as follows:

- Remember to…
- Explain why this works.
- To elaborate, use prompts such as follows:
- Show me a different way to…
- Explain a different way how you might…

A scaffolded prompt supports and extends learning.
To scaffold, use prompts such as follows:

- Those which have a gap in a sentence structure or part of a diagram missing to be completed, or part of a calculation in mathematics missing
- Those which pose a question around the method used to explore an element in greater depth, e.g. would this method work if you used…? Why/why not?
- Focusing on a specific element, e.g. we could check this by doing … instead of…; why not combine your likes and dislikes next time in your description about yourself?
- Those questions which are more open ended, e.g. what was your most effective part of your description and why? How many different ways can you…?

An example prompt provides a choice of answers to help improvement

- Alternative methods:
  Which of the approaches below are correct, and why?
- Alternative reasons/explanations:
  Underline the explanation below which you think is correct or write your own.
  Which of these reasons is correct, and why?

(Adapted from Bexley Webfronter, no date)

Allowing time for feedback and response to feedback

Enabling children to respond to feedback is critical, and there are different ways in which teachers engage with this and schools have expectations around this. Some lessons may start with children responding to next steps' comments – whether from those posed by the teacher or from self- or peer assessment. If feedback is live, then there is a chance that children will respond in the moment too, during the lesson, and improvements are made instantly. If distance marking is used for feedback, then strategies for responses to feedback might develop around the following:

- Making improvements – the class are given time to read their improvement suggestion and respond accordingly.
- Making a response – children are able to make comments back to the teacher, thus building a dialogue. However, care needs to be taken that this does not become onerous upon the teacher's time.

It is when children are applying strategies, within and across curriculum areas, that they demonstrate competence with their knowledge. If assessment for learning is to support a child's development, it is encouraging for the child when the teacher acknowledges when any improvements made (in response to any form of feedback) are embedded to help reinforce the learning point. For example, a teacher might explicitly note this improvement at another (later) point in time within the same or a different teaching sequence, or within a different subject area, where the skills, knowledge or understanding may be applied.

Pupil self- and peer evaluation

> **Critical question**
>
> How may children become involved with assessment for learning with greater autonomy?

Pupil involvement as part of assessment for learning must inform pupils about their progress and support their next steps (The Assessment Reform Group, 1999). Most of this will emerge through teacher feedback, whether verbal or written, but some may occur through self-assessment (ibid) or peer assessment. This autonomy nurtures lifelong learning (ibid).

Pupils can only achieve a goal if they understand what they are meant to be achieving and assess what they have to do to reach that end point (Black et al., 2004). This highlights the importance and relevance of metacognition (ibid).

Peer feedback is effective when pupils have clarity about 'what they are discussing and the areas that they should (and should not) be giving feedback about' (Cambridge Assessment International Education, no date). Pupils also need to consider and understand 'how they are judging each other's work' (ibid), and the more they engage with the success criteria (guiding the lesson), the more useful is their feedback to others. Peer assessment also serves a purpose in that pupils may be more accepting of advice and criticism from their peers than their teacher; the language used will be immediately at the level of a child but delivered in a constructive way 'because students learn by taking the roles of teachers and examiners of others' (Black et al., 2004, p. 14). Also of relevance is that if children do not understand a response from their peer, they are more likely to interrupt and ask for explanation from them, than they would from their teacher (Black et al., 2004). There is a degree of autonomy ascribed to peer (and self-) assessment, and this can facilitate teacher observations to consider appropriate immediate and longer term interventions (Black et al., 2004).

Pupils need to become skilled with evaluating their own work and that of others, and modelling will often be needed to help scaffold the process at the early stages. Different strategies may be employed to help guide this, and a whole school approach can yield dividends so that by the end of Year 6, pupils have become confident in autonomous evaluation of their own and others' learning. Initial strategies may be employed in Key Stage 1, like the use of a traffic light system where children indicate their work (red, amber and green) according to their confidence of their understanding or achievement; these indications can then serve as useful discussions in peer evaluation too, as well as it being used by a teacher for intervention purposes too, by pairing or grouping those highlighting themselves as green with amber to help support one another and those with red icons can be supported further by the teacher (Black et al., 2004).

Pupils need to understand conventions underpinning self- and peer assessment, in that evaluation is not against how much they enjoyed, or did not enjoy, an activity, but against their learning achievement. Moreover, when working alongside a peer, they need to align themselves with being able to give effective, constructive feedback and being an active listener to take on advice.

One relevant source for self-assessment comes from the Learning Without Limits (no date) philosophy. It is relevant to formative assessment because children can select tasks at their own level of ability and, as such, need an understanding of where they are at and what they are going on to develop. There is co-agency with thinking about this between the teacher and the learner.

Use of success criteria

Alongside the use of traffic light icons, as detailed earlier, many teachers make use of employing success criteria to help guide a lesson and to help assessment for learning as part of self- and peer feedback. Shirley Clarke has written many publications around assessment for learning and success criteria (see https://www.shirleyclarke-education.org/publications/).

104 Formative assessment

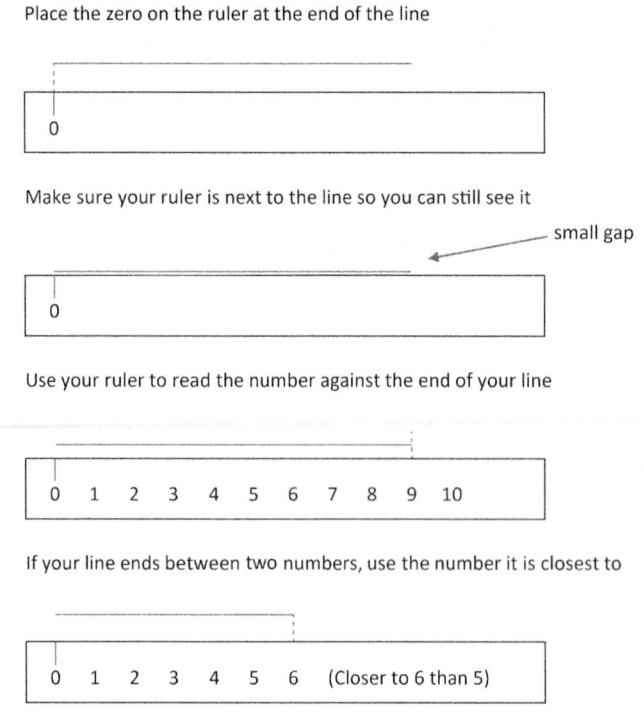

Place the zero on the ruler at the end of the line

0

Make sure your ruler is next to the line so you can still see it

— small gap

0

Use your ruler to read the number against the end of your line

0 1 2 3 4 5 6 7 8 9 10

If your line ends between two numbers, use the number it is closest to

0 1 2 3 4 5 6 (Closer to 6 than 5)

Figure 7.2 Sharing success criteria with children

Source: Trinder, no date.

The idea behind success criteria is that they help to guide children how to get to the end point of what they are setting out to do - i.e. to achieve the learning objective. The objectives must be clear to the children and rephrased from the national curriculum, if appropriate, in child speak. Success criteria can be written in child speak, and/or they can be represented in visual form via symbols or diagrams (this latter consideration can be most valuable for children in Reception and Key Stage 1) - see Figure 7.2.

Success criteria may be considered in three ways: as steps to success, as a menu from a set of possible criteria or as a learning outcome.

As steps to success

As steps to success, success criteria detail a linear order in which children may progress through to achieve the learning objective. The success criteria may be used as scaffolding and modelling for children in a teacher input and represent teacher instructions of what should be done and in what order. It can act as a prompt list for children should they become stuck and as a guide to check that they have done everything in a particular sequence to get to the answer. At the end of a lesson, children can use the success criteria to self- or peer assess against, as a tool for formative assessment. However, with step-by-step success criteria, it is important for children to fully understand what they are learning and not just using it for rote learning purposes. Moreover, with considering some elements of success criteria, we may need to break things down even more. Consider long division and the processes and knowledge needed. To do long division, knowledge of multiplication facts is needed. If a child does not know facts, then the process stops. This then necessitates the need for additional learning (and success criteria around acquisition of multiplication facts) to support the long division process.

As a menu

Success criteria can be used as a menu for when a learning sequence may not have to be in a particular order, e.g. within a mathematical investigation where there may be different approaches to reach a possible solution, or within a character description where the areas which may be included may be thought of as a menu which a child can select from and the order for the most part may not be so critical. The elements can still serve as tools for formative assessment, and the use of success criteria in this way means that they are less likely to be used for rote learning purposes.

As an outcome

Some schools detail their success criteria as learning outcomes. A leaning outcome may be considered as what the children can say they achieved as a result of their learning. It may be illustrated in an example of a child rushing out of school to say to their parents, 'Mum, dad, I can do a self-portrait'. In other words, they are acknowledging what they have been successful at (against the outcome). As an outcome for formative learning purposes, it gives a general overview for the end of a lesson, but might not be so useful for unpicking anything that went wrong, or unpicking elements that helped children to work in an efficient or correct way. Nevertheless, it distances itself from the risk of rote learning associated with step-by-step success criteria.

Generating success criteria

The way in which success criteria are shared with children can differ where the teacher

- Presents a ready-made list of success criteria – indeed, some teachers may print out lists of success criteria which they have generated for children to tick off against at the end of the lesson as they assess their work
- Asks the children to generate their own set of criteria which have enabled them to be successful during the task
- Models the activity in which the children will be engaged and ask them to come up with a set of success criteria
- Presents an example of a completed piece of work by the teacher or by one of the children and asks the class to generate a list of success criteria

Laura Whiteman reflects on a piece of action research she undertook, as part of her PGCE around self- and peer assessment. Perhaps you might decide to explore what these aspects of formative assessment look like in your class.

Use of Self- and Peer-Assessment

By Laura Whiteman, Early Career Teacher, Colchester, England

With the effects of COVID-19 still impacting upon education, Ofsted (2022) are highlighting the importance of assessment within the classroom to identify gaps in learning. Many teachers are focusing on formative assessment to tailor learning to support their pupils by using informal tests, and by providing regular feedback and more opportunities for self- and peer assessment to close gaps in attainment. As part of my PGCE, I undertook a small-scale action research project (with five pupils making up a focus group) in a vertically streamed, mixed-age group of a Key Stage 1 class, to explore how self- and peer assessment can impact upon pupils' engagement, motivation and learning.

Used as part of the learning process, research suggests that self- and peer assessment have a positive impact on learning and are most successful when time is allocated for pupils to reflect and make alterations based on the assessment (Black et al., 2004; Harris and Brown, 2018; Andrade, 2019; Double et al., 2020). Limited research has been undertaken to explore these forms of assessment in Key Stage 1.

Results from my action research found that pupils' engagement and motivation (Double et al., 2020) increased when reflecting upon and editing their own work and the work of their peers when using a checklist. Initially, pupils' self-assessments were inaccurate when compared to those made by the class teacher, supporting the findings of Harris and Brown (2018). However, as time progressed and the intervention was adapted, results suggested that pupils were able to make more accurate self-assessments with the use of a checklist, corroborating the findings of Andrade (2019). Consequently, I was able to use the pupils' self-assessment traffic light results to identify gaps in learning and therefore adapt lesson plans accordingly to support the pupils' learning and understanding.

It is important to acknowledge that although a checklist may support a pupil to self-monitor by remembering the key elements to their work, Harris and Brown (2018) argue that a checklist rarely encourages a deeper understanding of the importance of the key elements. Nevertheless, introducing strategies linked to the use of success criteria may help promote independent learning and critical reflection, if used appropriately and not as a tool akin to rote learning.

(Whiteman, 2022)

As part of the process of assessment for learning and developing children's confidence, some teachers set targets with children as part of what is termed pupil conferencing (e.g. see https://oaksprimaryacademy.org.uk/wp-content/uploads/2017/12/Conferencing-Feedback-Policy-2017-2019.pdf and https://literacyforpleasure.wordpress.com/2016/08/31/meeting-children-where-they-are-using-pupil-conferencing/). This may be around pinpointing a learning outcome, and reflecting on what steps and success (criteria) will be needed to achieve the outcome. Some schools set up designated time slots during the term around pupil conferencing, through which targets are set based upon reviews with the children; they are also shared with the parents. At the next pupil conference, achievement against the targets is noted and discussed and further targets can be generated.

Katherine Childs reflects on how we may use success criteria as part of whole class feedback, and which also links to future summative assessment, to make a manageable but purposeful way of assessing pupils' achievements and refining their skills through further practice.

Whole-Class Feedback as Formative Assessment

By Katherine Childs, Head of English at Wey Valley Academy, Weymouth, England

Using whole-class feedback is a great way to ensure that students are receiving specific feedback on their areas of strength and weakness without over-burdening teachers. It involves setting a task in which students need to use similar skills to those that will be required for the summative assessment, and then providing them with an opportunity to refine and practise those skills with expert teacher guidance. The nature of whole-class feedback means that a teacher can assess an entire class in a relatively short time, noting the areas for development on a shared sheet rather than writing comments in every child's book.

The first step in using whole-class feedback is deciding on the success criteria for the task. These should be the same criteria that students will be assessed on at the end of the unit. An important thing to note here is that the feedback needs to be focused very tightly on the success criteria. Make a note of those students who are struggling with other associated areas, but come back to this later in order to keep your feedback lesson focused on the specific skills that are being assessed.

Once the success criteria have been selected, a task needs to be set that is similar to, but not exactly the same as, the summative assessment. For example, if students are going to be analysing the presentation of a specific character in a novel, the formative assessment may be an analysis of a different character. Students then complete the task in lesson time, with appropriate scaffolding and teacher modelling so that they understand what the end product should look like.

The feedback lesson then needs to be carefully guided by the teacher. Each student receives a copy of a whole-class feedback sheet that simply states whether they have achieved the success criteria or whether they still need to work on certain aspects. They then need to complete a specific task that develops their proficiency in the skills that were being tested. These tasks do not need to resemble the final product. The key here is to devote time to this reflective work. Students need to have the time, with an expert in the room, to consolidate their skills and then apply them to either a new task or a re-draft of the previous task.

Formative use of summative tests

Teachers can use summative assessment results diagnostically to see if there are any gaps in learning which need to be addressed by individuals or groups of children, or perhaps as a subject lead across different year cohorts. For example, if an area of weakness is appearing in a Year 6 class, this may have implications for teaching priorities for younger year groups. Children can also make use of summative questions (Black et al., 2004) as an assessment for learning tool – questions can be looked at within class, answers generated by the children and discussed and evaluated and improvements made.

The impact of assessment for learning

Assessment for learning enables children to become active participants of learning, as opposed to passive recipients of teaching, enabling autonomy (Black et al. 2004) and skills to develop lifelong learning. It can support child motivation and self-esteem (ibid). Black et al. (2004) conclude their article with gentle prompts for next steps' actions by teachers. Suggestions include staring small with a small group of children as a class teacher (perhaps you might even do some action research – see Chapter 13 – around formative assessment with your class or as a subject lead in a particular curriculum area). Developments may occur through collaborations and mutual observations with other colleagues within your school, form the basis for designated meetings or staff development meetings or perhaps you may search for an online learning community focused on formative assessment. Year-long exploration can then provide within-school evidence and form the basis for changes within the whole school at a later stage. You might even go off and do some further reading or exploration before deciding on a next step action. The Chartered College of Teaching has a suite of materials around assessment for learning (see https://impact.chartered.college/?s=assessment+for+learning). These include case studies and short reflection articles, as well as its 'Impact' magazine, e.g. on Assessment and Feedback – see https://my.chartered.college/impact/issue-12/. The materials can be used as think pieces as part of continuing professional development and inform whole school discussion or self-study, which might trigger relevant next steps' actions.

I finish with a set of questions:

- What are you going to do as a result of reading this chapter?
- How are you going to do it?
- How will you evaluate its effectiveness?

Conclusion

The impact of effective assessment for learning is demonstrated through changes in pupils' attitudes about their learning, and changes in their levels of motivation, confidence and autonomy. Moreover, they will respond more thoughtfully in their answers, pose relevant questions themselves, improve their attainment and engage with the processes of setting targets, self-assessment, peer assessment and identifying their achievements. This chapter has given an overview of the key themes relating to what contributes to effective formative assessment: questioning, teacher feedback, peer assessment and self-assessment. Contributions from practitioners, suggestions for key readings and prompts for you to go off and explore what formative assessment looks like in your class will hopefully yield dividends to enhance your teaching and children's learning.

References

Aguiar, O.G., Mortimer, E., and Scott, P. (2010). Learning from and responding to students' questions: The authoritative and dialogic tension. *Journal of Research in Science Teaching*, 47(2), pp. 174-193.

Alexander, R.J. (2020). *A Dialogic Teaching Companion*. London: Routledge.

Andrade, H. (2019). A critical review of research on student self-assessment. *Frontiers in Education*, 87(4), pp. 1-13.

Askew, M., Bishop, S., Christie, C., Eaton, S., Griffin, P., and Morgan, D. (2015). *Questions, tasks and activities to support assessment Year 1*. [Online]. Available at: https://www.ncetm.org.uk/media/qjpctp24/mastery_assessment_y1.pdf [Accessed 1 October 2022]. Also see NCETM Primary assessment materials for all year groups https://www.ncetm.org.uk/classroom-resources/assessment-materials-primary/

Bexley Webfronter. (no date). *Marking*. [Online]. Available at: http://webfronter.com/bexley/primary-maths/menu/mnu1.shtml [original source no longer available].

Black, P., Harrison, C., Lee, C., Marshall, B., and Wiliam, D. (2004). Working inside the black box: Assessment for learning in the classroom. *Phi Delta Kappan*, 86(1), pp. 8-21.

Boyd, M.P. (2015). Relations between teacher questioning and student talk in one elementary ELL classroom. *Journal of Literacy Research*, 47(3), pp. 370-404.

Cambridge International Assessment Education. (no date). *Getting started with assessment for learning*. [Online]. Available at: https://cambridge-community.org.uk/professional-development/gswafl/index.html [Accessed 1 October 2022].

Department for Education (DfE). (2013). *The national curriculum in England: Key stages 1 and 2 framework document*. [Online]. Available at: https://assets.publishing.service.gov.uk/government/uploads/system/uploads/attachment_data/file/425601/PRIMARY_national_curriculum.pdf [Accessed 1 October 2022].

DfE. (2018). *School workload reduction toolkit*. [Online]. Available at: https://www.gov.uk/guidance/school-workload-reduction-toolkit [Accessed 1 October 2022].

DfE. (2019). *Early career framework*. [Online]. Available at: https://assets.publishing.service.gov.uk/government/uploads/system/uploads/attachment_data/file/978358/Early-Career_Framework_April_2021.pdf [Accessed 1 October 2022].

Double, K., McGrane, J., and Hopfenbeck, T. (2020). The impact of peer assessment on academic performance: A meta-analysis of control group studies. *Education Psychology Review*, 32, pp. 481-509.

Dweck, C.S. (2006). *Mindset: The New Psychology of Success*. New York, NY: Random House Publishing Group.

Education Endowment Foundation (EEF). (2021). *Teacher feedback to improve pupil learning: Guidance report*. [Online]. Available at: https://educationendowmentfoundation.org.uk/education-evidence/guidance-reports/feedback and https://d2tic4wvo1iusb.cloudfront.net/eef-guidance-reports/feedback/Teacher_Feedback_to_Improve_Pupil_Learning.pdf?v=1635355218 [Accessed 1 October 2022].

Harris, L., and Brown, G. (2018). *Using Self-Assessment to Improve Student Learning*. Oxon: Routledge.

Learning Without Limits. (no date). *The first LWL project: Key ideas and principles*. [Online]. Available at: https://learningwithoutlimits.educ.cam.ac.uk/about/key.html [Accessed 1 October 2022].

National Centre for Excellence in the Teaching of Mathematics (NCETM). (no date a). *Five big ideas in teaching for mastery*. [Online]. Available at: https://www.ncetm.org.uk/teaching-for-mastery/mastery-explained/five-big-ideas-in-teaching-for-mastery/ [Accessed 1 October 2022].

NCETM. (no date b). *Primary assessment materials*. [Online]. Available at: https://www.ncetm.org.uk/classroom-resources/assessment-materials-primary/ [Accessed 1 October 2022].

NCETM. (no date c) *Reasoning skills: Developing opportunities and ensuring progression in the development of reasoning skills*. [Online]. Available at: https://www.ncetm.org.uk/classroom-resources/pm-reasoning-skills/ [Accessed 1 October 2022].

Nottingham, J. (no date). *The learning pit*. [Online]. Available at: https://www.challenginglearning.com/learning-pit/ [Accessed 1 October 2022].

Nunes, T., Bryant, P., Sylva, K. & Barros, R. (2009) *Development of maths capabilities and confidence in primary school* (Research Report DCSF-RR118). [Online]. Available at: https://dera.ioe.ac.uk/11154/ [Accessed 6 March 2022].

Ofsted. (2022). *Research and analysis. Education recovery in schools: Spring 2022*. [Online]. Available at: https://www.gov.uk/government/publications/education-recovery-in-schools-spring-2022/education-recovery-in-schools-spring-2022 [Accessed 1 October 2022].

Sealy, C. (2021). *How the new no marking policy for our primary school works*. [Online]. Available at: https://thirdspacelearning.com/blog/new-no-marking-policy-confessions-primary-headteacher/ [Accessed 1 October 2022].

The Assessment Reform Group. (1999). *Assessment for learning: Beyond the black box*. University of Cambridge, School of Education. [Online]. Available at: https://www.nuffieldfoundation.org/sites/default/files/files/beyond_blackbox.pdf [Accessed 1 October 2022].

The Assessment Reform Group. (2002). *Assessment for learning: 10 principles*. [Online]. Available at: https://www.researchgate.net/publication/271849158_Assessment_for_Learning_10_Principles_Research-based_principles_to_guide_classroom_practice_Assessment_for_Learning [Accessed 1 October 2022].

Trinder, J. (no date). *Student Slides for Planning for Progression, Formative Assessment and Mathematical Questioning*. London: The University of Greenwich. Unpublished.

Whiteman, L. (2022). 'To what extent does self-assessment and peer-assessment impact upon pupils' engagement, motivation and learning within a key stage 1 classroom?' *ACAD1445: Professional Development Two: Making an Impact on Teaching and Learning*. Colchester SCITT and University of Greenwich. Unpublished essay.

8 Engaging with parents and carers

Promoting the home-school partnership

KEY WORDS

parents, carers, home partnership, homework

Contributors within this chapter:

1. Karen McNerney
2. Andrew Flowerdew
3. Steve Hoey
4. Jayne Carter
5. Paul Brown
6. Andrie Savva
7. Annelies Paris

Introduction

This chapter explores the importance of building up positive and purposeful relationships with your pupils' parents and carers. Having open channels of communication is in your pupils' best interests to support them both academically and holistically. The chapter begins discussing the contract of a 'Home School Agreement' and considers the value of such contracts between schools, parents and pupils. Strategies to help bring families into the school community are shared. Seven contributors share their insight into some practical strategies to employ to help build bonds with the parents and carers of your learners.

Engaging with parents and carers

It is easy to segregate the two domains of 'school' and 'home'. This chapter explores the value in a strong partnership between home and school as the heart of a positive education. When parents and carers are involved in their child's education, it can lead to a better understanding of their child's school life, as well as a constructive relationship with

DOI: 10.4324/9781003218098-8

the staff to facilitate communication about a child's behaviour and progress amongst other things.

> **Critical question**
>
> When should I engage with parents and carers, how often and by which means?

One top tip before proceeding further is to remember to use the channels of communication for good, not just to relay negative messages. Some schools do this through the use of strategies such as 'praise postcards' where special cards are sent home when a child does something special or achieves something notable (not just academic!).

It is important that teachers are seen to catch parents and carers at the end of the day not just to comment on poor behaviour, for example, but to share proud moments that have happened or just to pass on a pleasing comment about effort. Ensure that parents do not have a sense of foreboding when they see their child's teacher approaching them, but aim to build up a relationship where parents feel involved in their child's learning and school life and see the classroom as an extension of the home as opposed to a distant and disparate place (Goodall, 2020).

COVID-19

In 2020, the sudden and unprecedented switch to home learning due to school lockdowns as a result of the coronavirus (explored in more detail in Chapter 15 later) gave parents greater responsibility for supporting their child's education and meant that many felt more in touch with the curriculum content for their child. Having to facilitate remote learning was not easy or welcomed by all, and research by Sari et al. (2021) found that some of the main barriers and issues involved learning value, learning efficiency, mental and physical health and accessibility. This phenomena of school lockdowns, which spanned over two years, 2020-2021, prompted greater insight and consideration of home channels of communication that could be fostered between home and school and how home learning could be made accessible for parents.

Home school partnerships

Some schools create partnership agreements for parents, carers and pupils to sign.

A Home-School Agreement is a statement explaining the aims and responsibilities of both school and parents (GOV.UK, 2022). The home school agreement is a simple contract between the pupil, their parent and the school, which encourages all parties to reflect upon how proactive and positive relationships can be maintained to help support the learner as they travel through the school.

Simple strategies for a school to employ

- Coffee with the head
- Parent workshops on topics such as maths – long division
- Parent assemblies
- Volunteers for reading

Parent-teacher communication is important as research shows that sharing teaching practices and strategies through workshops encourages parents to be more proactive in their child's learning at home (Yulianti, 2022). But how do we, as teachers, learn to build effective bonds with the families of our pupils? Whilst much content of teacher training focuses on subject knowledge and pedagogical skills, learning to interact with parents is often something that we develop as we clock up years of experience in the classroom.

Engaging Parents

By Karen McNerney, Headteacher of Merchant Taylors Prep School, Rickmansworth, England

Building effective partnerships with parents was not part of my teacher training, which took place 27 years ago, and is a skill that I have developed 'on the job'. What became clear straight away is that engaging parents is a vital part of a successful education for pupils. I know many schools can struggle with parental engagement, sometimes because there are parents who feel that school takes care of education and they do not need to be involved. However, most of my experience is within the independent sector, and my challenge has been at the opposite end of the engagement spectrum. I have often worked with parents who are extremely engaged, with an understandable aspiration for their children to succeed. Some of these parents can be perceived as being very 'pushy' in their desire to ensure that their child is not only achieving or even exceeding their potential but also better than other children. This type of parent is usually the minority, but I have found that their voice can be persuasive to others who quickly become anxious that their own child might be 'left behind' if they do not follow suit. I have often been approached by concerned parents who feel that they are doing their child a disservice by not being as proactive as some parents, tutoring being a donemajor topic that causes alarm when parents think that they might be the only family not employing a tutor. I know for certain that tutoring and excessive pressure to achieve at school are not necessarily conducive to realise potential. The question was, how do I help parents to understand the kind of engagement that will most benefit their child without being unduly influenced by the views of a minority of parents? When I became a Head, 6 years ago, I decided to set up a Parents' Forum in order to have open discussions with parents about issues relating to engaging with school and how to help children to be successful. It has easily been the most useful initiative that has been introduced and has enabled us to explore and even challenge views as to whether tutoring makes children achieve more highly. Each meeting starts with a stimulus, maybe be a newspaper article or a podcast, and will focus on a particular theme, for example tutoring, homework, reading, sleep, resilience and screen time. Parents discuss the stimulus and theme in groups containing parents of older and younger children so that they can hear different perspectives. Towards the end of the meeting, the groups feedback centrally, and this gives us all a chance to establish some common ground that works for both school and home. Parents are always extremely complementary about the usefulness of these sessions and say that it helps them to gain an insight into how to best support their children in a way that works in harmony with the school and not based on the views of one of some vocal parents.

Building Parental Engagement

By Andrew Flowerdew, Technology Strategist at L.E.A.D IT Services, Derby, England

Many effective teachers have long been aware of the benefits that accrue from enabling parental involvement in the education that their children are receiving, and this is reflected in research carried out in a variety of studies that suggest involving parents as much as possible in the learning journey of their children can bring real benefits to the classroom environment.

A step up in parental engagement is a class blog. At the end of the day, an adult spends five minutes with one of the class who recounts what the class has done that day. The adult then posts this, along with some photos of the activities and perhaps some examples of outcomes, onto the class blog for parents, and perhaps other family members to view and comment upon. The class teacher moderates comments before they are published to ensure that they are appropriate. It is surprising how popular these become with both learners and their parents, especially as some family members may not, for whatever reason, be able to go to the school.

Taking this one step further, setting up individual portfolio areas for each learner so that they can share the outcomes of their own learning journey, reflect on how they could improve and share this with their family can have a powerful impact on learning outcomes. Even more so if parents are encouraged to comment on elements of their portfolio as well. Updates to this portfolio happen when the learner makes particular progress, which can be large or small and provide the opportunity to engage in significant assessment for learning conversations that involve the learner, the teacher and family members in helping the learner in their learning journey. There are several free and commercial tools that enable this kind of portfolio to be created and used effectively.

Effective schools make sure that they empower parents to engage with the learning that is happening in their classrooms. Holding regular in-school and/or online workshops about the learning and teaching that happens in their child's classroom and how they can support their child is incredibly important. Most parents are not educational experts, and helping them make a positive contribution to their child's progress involves giving them an understanding of good learning and the language to use to support their child.

However, a school chooses to encourage parental involvement as it seems to be most effective when everyone, parent, child and teacher, feels that they are working together to help the learner achieve.

Building Bridges

Steve Hoey, PhD candidate researching school exclusion, University of Hull, Hull, England

The why

All schools recognise the importance of developing effective partnerships between home and school. When parents are involved and engaged in their education, children do better academically and socially and are happier. Parental engagement is crucial because it has a positive impact on the child. It is a constant challenge, and many schools work wonders, but there is no one size fits all solution.

The way

Improving parental engagement requires a whole school strategic approach, and it needs to be part of the whole school development plan because if you don't plan it then it won't happen. Make it sustainable, and focus on the process not just on the people. It is not a quick fix, a 'bolt-on' or just for an Ofsted tickbox. It should be an essential part of the school vision and at the very heart of what you do because it is the right thing to do.

If something isn't working, change it and try something else. It requires leadership but involves everyone. Empower all your staff to share this responsibility. They may need some training to improve their confidence in engaging with parents, but it is an essential skill.

Be proactive, think differently and do not be afraid to try new things. The impact of what you do needs to be evaluated, and if it does not work, then do something else. Small changes can make a big difference.

Clear communication

Communication between home and school needs to be regular, meaningful and two ways. Make it clear what you expect from parents. The Home-School Agreement or code of conduct can help schools explain why and how parents can support them in these matters.

Use a variety of ways to gather parental voices – surveys and focus groups – but ensure that you feedback with 'you said, we did'. A big barrier to getting parents involved with school life is not being asked. Listening is sometimes the forgotten part of communication. Encourage dialogue – what can WE do?

Listening to and then acting on parent voice enables schools to meet their needs and serve them more effectively. Schools need to ensure that they reach out to the needs of all parents. Don't just listen to the engaged parents. Seek out ways to interact with those who are harder to reach. Potentially engagement with home could involve more than just parents and careers. Other family members like grandparents can be really powerful allies.

(Continued)

Making meetings flexible and accessible can also engage parents. All the recent improvements in technology can make a massive difference. Virtual parents' evenings and meetings have made things more personal and increased engagement. We now have the technology for people to attend remotely or on catch up.

The school website is a brilliant place to share what is going on. Make sure it is easy to navigate with a dedicated section for parents. The best ones have all the relevant information, direct contact details, staff photos and bios, and parent areas full of clear dates, curriculum plans and homework advice and are places to celebrate school life.

Use social media like Facebook, Twitter and Instagram to share what is going on. Keep it up to date. Remember there will be far more positive than negative comments. Photos are great to share the good work schools are doing, but people interact with short videos better.

Investing in a parent engagement app can ensure real-time connection that parents can access anytime and anywhere. For busy parents, this can be a game changer. Empower parents to opt into the way of communication that suits them.

Offering opportunities for volunteering can engage the community and break down barriers. The PTA is a fine example of this.

We have all been through some tough times recently, and change is constant. Dealing with all this can not only be difficult for children but also for adults. Developing positive relationships is key, and creating a sense of belonging to a school community that listens and responds to families' and child's needs is not easy, but it is always worth the time and effort.

Engaging with Parents and Carers

By Jayne Carter, School Effectiveness Advisor at Lincoln Anglican Academy Trust, Lincoln, England

I'd like to celebrate some of the fantastic ideas which the Lincoln Anglican Academy Trust (LAAT) schools have put in place to make sure that their families are also able to live our vision: **'SCHOOLS SERVING THEIR COMMUNITIES THROUGH EXCELLENCE, EXPLORATION AND ENCOURAGEMENT WITHIN THE LOVE OF GOD'**

- School online portal platform: many schools found that this was the key form of communication during the pandemic, not only providing clear information to continue home schooling but also acting as a virtual community. For these reasons, the use of platforms, such as tapestry, has been reignited to ensure that it is one of the places schools and families use.
- One of our schools started a reading library, originally for children, but due to its popularity their families are now including books for both children and adults to increase their reading for pleasure agenda.

(Continued)

- Now schools are opening up to more visitors; our schools are keen to start again the 'play & stay/look & learn' sessions so families can see for themselves how their children learn through play, as well as the more formal information meetings where key points are explained (such as the schools' approach to reading).
- Children centre model of engagement: for some of our schools, this means that the existing children centre uses the school as a satellite venue, and for other schools, it means that the school itself becomes the children centre providing sessions for families and children to learn together as well as being a host venue for other agencies such as health visitors and family support.
- Family learning sessions: all of our schools include these in their parental engagement with dedicated sessions happening throughout the school year. These sessions outline how their children learn, with the intention to both inform and improve confidence.
- Engaging parents further within their church community: as a church trust it is paramount that the church and the school not only work in partnership, but families recognise that this is important too. As well as the regular visitors to church and the church community visits to school; many of our schools also support each other in strategic planning and policy development.
- Working with local businesses: the parent partnership plans in pace on our schools also includes the expertise from local businesses to acknowledge the developing and changing community. For example, many of our schools have houses being built around them so they have been able to engage the building team in visiting the school to talk about their job and show children how to practically take part on their job (wall building in Early Years, for example!) as well as agreeing to gift books for the school library.
- Visitors into schools to share their interests and jobs: providing all of our children with ambition and aspiration
- Breakfast clubs and after-school clubs offer our families the opportunity to work flexibly.
- Extracurricular clubs introduce children to new adventures, possibly experiences they wouldn't be able to take part in out of school.
- Pupil premium funding is used precisely to support our children and families the most in need to ensure that they can fully engage with all aspects of school (funding uniform and other resources, for example providing additional targeted programmes, etc.).
- Home visits for those joining our schools: these visits not only are a privilege but also show that the child and their family are an important part of the school community even before the child's very first day. Some of our schools have shared a picture book on these visits to set the scene of the importance of reading too.

Engaging Parents as Vital Partners in Pupil Learning and Progress

By Paul Brown, Head Teacher at Bransgore C of E Primary School, Christchurch, England

I tell my staff that we are only ever as good as our parents say we are. Ofsted will come and go; you may have a great school doing great things, but if you do not communicate to a critical mass of parents then they will feel disconnected, distrustful and isolated from their child's educational experience and will tell each other that you aren't a great school. Be transparent and as open as you can. Be human.

As pupils arrive in school, carry out informal home visits. Not just for Early Years' pupils but all pupils new to the school. This allows for rapport to be built in a safe place, especially for parents wary or intimidated by school. Have a chat; don't make it an interview. Use the time in the home to gauge the interests of the child as well as understanding the family dynamics and such. This visit can give you lots of 'intel' to use later when building rapport with pupils, even if it is as simple as,

> How is that dog of yours?

Offer parents the chance to ask you lots too. It puts them at ease and makes them feel they are heard and you can be trusted.

Invite new starters and their parents to events prior to starting school so they 'feel' the ethos and care and can see relationships in action.

Be available informally to parents by being on the playground regularly and be open to a short chat, or if you don't have time, promise to call them and tell them when or ask them to call you, but be sure to follow this through. Know the school policy for this and honour it.

At our school we invite parents in for 'exit point' celebrations at the end of each half-term as a theme is completed. Pupils welcome parents into class for 20 minutes and share their learning with them. We also hold 'big' events such as big art, big build and big sing where parents can come along and join in with their pupils to create something. This is lovely to witness. We also ask parents to support their child in creating a home learning project which can be anything related to a theme we are about to study and provides a 'hook' to draw pupils in, and it guarantees some pre-learning has taken place. The children bake, make models, create comic strips or stop motion animations to demonstrate what they already know about a subject. We once received a fabulous Titanic sponge cake which was most welcome in the staff room!

Try to provide short and simple workshops for parents to inform them about how and why you teach phonics/maths/spelling or anything else as you do. Reassure them about mathematical methods, and maybe provide simple crib sheets to help them understand the calculations policy. We sometimes assume too much of parents, and they really appreciate workshops about topics such as managing challenging behaviour or early reading to support them to feel they are doing a good job.

(Continued)

Be brave and address the challenging parents. In my experience most challenging parents tend to not feel heard, and so invite them to help with reading, gardening or the school library. It is remarkable how often these parents shift from being your most vocal opposition to your most staunch supporters when they see you all hard at work to help pupils.

For pupils in receipt of pupil premium or who are otherwise disadvantaged, we put an HLTA in charge of the register for the odd morning on rotation and give staff 20 minutes to catch up with parents of the most vulnerable pupils in each class. This meeting is short, sharp and informal, but actions are followed through and concerns recorded. This goes down really well.

It's in the Connection ... Becoming-in-Company

By Andrie Savva, University of Cambridge, Cambridge, England

In botany, the rhizome is a plant stem with no fixed root system, rather a complex network of roots, nodes and tendrils that grows horizontally. Bamboo, ginger and grass are some rhizomes. Take for instance the weeds. They are difficult to control and contain, they grow beyond their native habitat and they expand in diverse environments. Deleuze and Guattari drew on the notion of the rhizome and suggested that the world does not consist of dispersed and isolated individuals and objects, rather forms through heterogeneous connections 'between semiotic chains, organizations of power, and circumstances relative to the arts, sciences, and social struggles' (1987, p. 7). Acknowledging that we are interconnected, part of multiplicities requires us to value complexity, fluidity and difference and avoid binary thinking such as school-world, teacher-learner, hierarchical structures, linear processes and progressive narratives, and compartmentalisation of knowledge in subjects and disciplines. Rhizomatic connections are shaped through or outside formal systems and spaces, and they can take the form of activism both in the everyday life and in organised events. In rhizomatic spaces, curriculum is not enacted as bounded knowledge or a set of instructions, a recipe to be executed. Rather, it is enacted as an area that is emergent, created and re-created and negotiated in the everyday life through connections in and with the human and more-than-human world. A rhizomic space is formed through a community engaged in curious, equitable, playful inquiry, always in motion, becoming rather than being, just like the world is in a constant state of transformation.

For this contribution, I revisit my journey as a teacher for nearly two decades. What glows for me are the connections with children, colleagues, parents, organisations, places and spaces. These are connections of care. These connections, like the rhizome, would grow new roots and shoots, between people, partners, places and

(Continued)

spaces. These connections matter in education. Alleviating inequalities has been the main focus of discussions around the world. In the area of education, discourse shifts amongst traditional and progressive education, liberatory praxis and conscientisation, and post-human pedagogies. For me, it is in the affirmative connection, in becoming-in-company. The zoom shifts in between rhizomic nodes, sending out new roots and shoots. Sometimes it is in the small acts of everyday life, sometimes in the coming together of a community and other times it is in reforming policies. Rhizomatic education emphasises relationality, complexity and emergence, and as such, connection. Connection materialises in the symbiotic, dynamic, ongoing relation and collaboration between the human and the more-than-human world, nurturing improbable kinships between bodies, materialities, things and ideas, as Donna Haraway (2016) reminds us. In these spaces, our capacity for relation and action for positive social change increases. In these spaces, we become-in-company.

Parent Communication

By Annelies Paris, Primary Teacher and Youtube Content Creator as Petite Primary, Dorset, England

Communication with parents or caregivers, at any point in your career, can be daunting. We take pride and delight in sharing positive news, achievements or updates about their child making progress academically or behaviourally. It feels rewarding and is a big reason why we teach: to see a child grow and learn. Realistically though, communication with parents will not always be positive, and this the focus of this section on parent communication.

Parents are like their children. They are all different; all have had different upbringings and backgrounds, and all have different personalities. Some have your back; some don't. Some believe you and see the same problems at home; some believe you're exaggerating 'because they're an angel at home'. When it's your first time meeting the parents (especially as not all schools do a Meet the Teacher session), or your first time speaking to a parent for a negative purpose, it can be hard to know how to approach the matter.

The thing to remember is that parents are humans. You may have had the worst day ever, their child may have caused you a lot of grief or may be a constant behaviour challenge, or they may have hurt other children or hurt yourself in either a physical or verbal manner, but the parents are **humans**. Be careful and sensitive with how you approach them with this. Don't yell it from a distance or say it loudly in front of other parents. Ask them to wait to one side and do it sensitively. Don't re-enact behaviours or mimic their voices and don't use harsh adjectives or use terms such as 'bad', or 'naughty'. In terms of behaviour, you don't know what the home situation is like.

(Continued)

> The child might behave like that at home too and the parents might feel overwhelmed and stressed, with school being a break or safe place for their child. The last thing you want to do is remind them and make them feel embarrassed, but for your sake too, you don't want them to potentially react by getting defensive, angry or blaming you.
>
> As a summary, remember that no matter how your day pans out, communication with parents is key, but any negative news must be done sensitively, politely and with purpose. Doing this, as well as acknowledging any emotional reactions to this news, is how you will develop a good relationship with parents and ultimately work together to do what's best by the child.

Conclusion

- When we take time to get to know the parents and carers of our learners, we can gain valuable insight into the motivators and beliefs behind their children's behaviours.
- Always try to find time to communicate the positives from a child's day or week, even if only a 'thumbs up' at the door at home time as you make eye contact with a parent across the playground.

References

Deleuze, G., and Guattari, F. (1987). *A Thousand Plateaus. Capitalism and Schizophrenia* (B. Massumi, Trans.). Minneapolis, MN: University of Minnesota Press.

Goodall, J. (2020). Scaffolding homework for mastery: Engaging parents. *Educational Review*, 73(6), pp. 669-689. doi:10.1080/00131911.2019.1695106

Gov.UK. (2022). *Home school agreement guidance*. Available at: https://assets.publishing.service.gov.uk/government/uploads/system/uploads/attachment_data/file/355588/home-school_agreement_guidance.pdf

Haraway, J.D. (2016). *Staying with the Trouble. Making Kin in the Chthulucene.* Durham, NC: Duke University Press.

Sari, D.M., Widyantoro, A., and Octavia, S. (2021). Primary school in the time of Covid-19: Parents' engagement in students' online learning. *Jurnal Pendidikan dan Pengajaran*, 54(2), pp. 207-219.

Yulianti, K., Denessen, E., Droop, M., and Veerman, G.J. (2022). School efforts to promote parental involvement: The contributions of school leaders and teachers. *Educational Studies*, 48(1), pp. 98-113. doi:10.1080/03055698.2020.1740978

9 Teaching assistants

KEY WORDS
Deploy, hierarchy, relationship, pedagogy, audit

Contributors within this chapter:
1. Rebecca Massheder-Stuart
2. Olly Cakebread
3. Sara Alston

Critical question

In the relationship with your TA, who deploys whom?

Introduction

This chapter aims to explore how to manage, or deploy, a teaching assistant (TA) effectively in a busy classroom. It will look at the issues that are involved with the deployment of another adult and how these can be dealt with and managed. Telling another adult, who is usually older than you, how you want them to assist you will take a short time to get used to but will have benefits in developing your pedagogy and the children's learning. Some of this chapter is taken from my 2018 doctoral research into the relationship between trainee teachers and TAs during a school experience. This chapter looks at why a TA will be in your class, how you can articulate your pedagogical and philosophical identity that can be recognised by your TA and how you can use some basic workplace skills to create a relationship. The chapter firmly suggests that it will be your role to take the initiative; it may not always be easy, but it is an ongoing situation in which classroom practice, reflection and open discussion will be to your advantage.

Why do I have a teaching assistant?

Two significant reasons for the further increase of classroom assistants during the 1990s were the introduction of the National Literacy Strategy (Department for Education and

DOI: 10.4324/9781003218098-9

Employment [DfEE, 1998]) and the National Numeracy Strategy (DfEE, 1999) and the bi-lingual language assistant. The prescribed strategies aimed specifically to raise standards in English and mathematics, respectively, by being taught daily. The Literacy Strategy mentioned the use of extra support staff quite categorically:

> Where extra support is available, it should be deployed in the Literacy hour. Additional adults should work in close partnership with teachers as they plan and teach the Literacy hour
> (DfEE, 1998, p. 94).

It was because of these strategies that the role of the TA changed from that of a helper, or ancillary, from the time of the 1967 Plowden Report, to that of someone who became involved with teaching and children's learning. Therefore, the role became pedagogical. Government required these additional adults to be involved, at some degree, with the planning and teaching that before was the sole preserve of the qualified teacher. Pedagogically, the rationale for the Literacy Strategy was that it required whole class teaching at the start of the literacy hour, and then small group work, to be staffed by an assistant. Guided reading and writing programmes were also introduced to provide intensive input, again to be staffed by additional adults. To provide equal access, children with English as an additional language (EAL), or no English at all, were being integrated in mainstream teaching from 1986. This also had an impact on staffing levels and how inclusive teaching was to consider all needs within a primary classroom. HMI (2002) described how this pedagogy therefore influenced the need for increased numbers of TAs.

> Teaching assistants play an important part in implementing these strategies. They support teachers and pupils in the classroom and also have a key role in the related intervention and catch-up programmes...
> (HMI, 2002, p.3).

The report from HMI (2002) reinforced the notion that the TA was now a pedagogical member of staff rather than a practical assistant. Within almost 35 years, from the Plowden Report to this HMI report, the transformation has been significant.

The rise in numbers of TAs was a direct result of centralised government policy within education. The emphasis on financial efficiency and accountability with, for example, more children in mainstream schools led to a significant increase in this element of the workforce. The subsequent National Workload Agreement of 2003 (Department for Education and Skills [DfES, 2003]) saw more TAs being employed in schools but with the emergence of a new role – higher level teaching assistant (HLTA). Their role was to reduce teachers' workload by taking classes in the absence of a qualified teacher

This is important for trainee teachers, as well as qualified teachers and leadership teams, to realise that their management of other adults influences children's learning

How do I deploy a teaching assistant?

Recognising that you can deploy a TA is only the first step in creating a relationship with your colleague. The other steps, which are detailed below, may help you in creating an effective, practical and professional-based relationship that has a clear and definitive purpose.

Consider the existing routine and attitudes of the school

This is what Bourdieu (1984) calls the habitus; in other words, how individuals create a philosophy of how things operate in a particular place and how that organically develops. In a school we may call this how policies are written, how attitudes and pedagogies are developed and sustained, and how teachers, TAs, children and even parents are expected to conform to these. It can also be described as a culture and naturally an expectation to 'fit in'. (This is why it is useful to consider how a school feels to you when applying for a position.) To consider the creation of a relationship with a TA, consider the habitus of the school; how are things done? What is the school's attitude to collaboration, CPD and status (are TAs seen as vital to children's learning and fully involved in decision-making, policymaking)? An inclusive school will be a school where new or inexperienced teachers can contribute, not only to the habitus but also change it for mutually agreed benefits. The habitus of the school environment, in which a trainee teacher finds herself for a placement which cannot be challenged and only in a few instances can any trainee be given some degree of leeway in decision-making, may not be conducive to healthy teaching and learning. In such cases, some trainees quickly realise they have to adapt, accept their place as they conform to policy and practice. For some trainees, this is an easier process according to their work-based history and experience.

Begin the construction of a professional relationship

As a trainee teacher, you may find that you see yourself in a hierarchical position when you first meet your new TA (see Figure 9.1).

What you may find is that your TA is only too willing to be deployed by you providing you appear confident and competent, usually in the form of class control or behaviour management. This is important to remember; the TA accepts that you will deploy him or her. The issue that you may experience is that it is like 'telling your mum what to do' because the TA is likely to be twice your age. The next step is for you to consider how to cross the divide; how exactly do you tell a more experienced member of the school community what to do? This will enable you to perceive the hierarchy of deployment differently (see Figure 9.2).

As a professional you may perceive your role is to establish a relationship with the TA, but for it to be seen as working successfully, you require the cooperation of the TA for the development of your own development; the health of the relationship to grow because of the

Your Teacher

↓

Your Teaching Assistant

↓

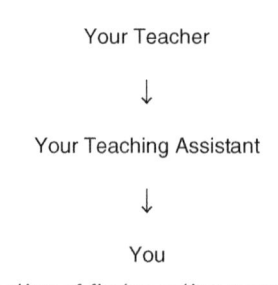

You

Figure 9.1 The hierarchical perspective of first meeting your TA

Your Teacher

↓

You

↓

Your Teaching Assistant

Figure 9.2 Revised hierarchy of TA deployment

necessity of cooperation; and for the needs of the children. The support of the TA is important to you, although it cannot be disguised by notions of teamwork or collegiality in favour of professional relationships. The first point to remember is that you can legitimately deploy a TA, as evidenced by the Core content Framework (for trainee teachers) and the Early Career Framework (for qualified teachers):

> Teaching assistants (TAs) can support pupils more effectively when they are prepared for lessons by teachers, and when TAs supplement rather than replace support from teachers.
>
> (CCF & ECF Standard 8, p. 5)

The trainee teacher, during a school experience, should be able to deploy an assistant, but they choose not always to be willing in accepting their position. Research exploring how trainee teachers deploy their TAs on a school experience placement (Morgan, 2018) discovered that trainee teachers recognise the right to deploy their TAs but appear not to wish to engage in an overt struggle for power – but rather do it subtly, by preferring to adopt a process of 'localized familiarization'. This, in their perception, enables them to work towards 'equality' in the classroom through negotiation and discussion. What was revealed, however, is a surprising amount of power wielded by the TA who may be viewed as a monitor of the habitus of the school. You may know you have the legitimacy to deploy a TA; you may even know how to do it in theory, but in the real-life classroom, physically doing so is more difficult. It is not always a natural skill to design and monitor the duties of another person, especially if you have no experience in doing so (for example from experience in another workplace). The technique of the 'localized familiarization' is defined as the act of a trainee teacher engaging in the process of an informal relationship parallel to that of engaging in the professional relationship of deploying a TA during a school experience. It is a process of appealing to the TA in a social or familiar fashion, and when there is a sense of warm reciprocity, a confidence develops which then enables the trainee to deploy a TA. In other words, 'I think she likes me so I can now ask her to do things'.

This is not surprising, but you do not have time to engage in such a technique because it obscures the purpose of the professional relationship, and to be blunt, it wastes time. Of course, developing a friendly and familiar relationship with another colleague in parallel with a professional relationship is only a benefit to a harmonious school environment. What you can rely on is that the TA is willing to be deployed by you and accepts this, providing you are developing competence in displaying effective behaviour management and a sense that there is order connected to your teaching.

Your identity

As you begin to construct the relationship, with the confidence to take those first steps, it needs to be accompanied by a confidence in your teaching identity. Who are you as a teacher? This is what the TA will be (silently) asking of you. Trainee teachers formed their identity during their training through their engagement with pedagogy (Britzman, 1991; Danielewicz, 2001). Atkinson (2004) regarded becoming a teacher as a process of self-identification and identification of that self by others. This continuous process is necessary because the profession of teaching calls for more than a 'role' of a teacher to be adopted but that an identity must be constructed instead. An identity is the result of interactions between those who are training and the trained within a school context. You would do this by engaging with others (within the habitus) but importantly deciding what your philosophy of teaching is. What type of teacher are you in terms of favoured pedagogy, classroom design, pupil autonomy and organisation. The type of teacher you are determines the deployment of your TA. For example, if you are predominantly a social constructivist in your planning and teaching, then your TA will be deployed in a social constructivist scenario. For example, this could be using talk to gather more informative assessment records or prioritising pedagogical deployment over administrative deployment. Do you need the TA to create the displays, organise reading records and tidy coats and bags areas or can the children do this?

Goffman (1959) argued that a given individual requested to his/her observers to take seriously the impression that was fostered before them. This impression was based on the belief that the individual, as perceived, did possess 'certain attributes' that he/she ought to use to perform the task that was claimed. In other words, if others saw you, for example, as a teacher, they had to believe that your actions, language and appearance were those that would qualify you as a teacher in their presence. The construction and subsequent development of the relationship between you and a TA is characterised by negotiation and the need for a sense of partnership.

So, in your developing teacher identity, it should be clear that your TA is acutely aware of not only what it is you believe in pedagogically, but that it must be carried out in everyday deployment. Some trainee teachers make the mistake of not articulating any deployment whatsoever. They see the TA engaging in a particular task which fosters the impression that she is working on something and that cannot be altered. What the TA is likely to be thinking is that 'if I am not receiving any particular guidance/instruction, then I will do something that I think that should be happening/or what I usually do'. Such a situation may seem to be producing an outcome, but is it one of your pedagogical choosing? For example, is this the most efficient or effective way for the children to be learning? This is where your identity needs to not only be asserted but also communicated; it is no surprise that communication is crucial to the developing professional relationship.

Once this is secure, a dialogue can begin as to how your identity as a teacher and your relationship with a TA can progress to the next stage.

Communication

It is not a surprise that effective communication with your TA leads to effective deployment. Communication in a busy primary school is not just being heard in a noisy classroom, but the ability to find a quiet time to discuss what you perceive to be the important matters. The twin important matters for discussion are, arguably, planning and assessment, which can be followed, if confident, by an appraisal of your teaching. Your TA is likely to have set working and contractual hours, for example 9.00 am to noon. If that is the case, you will have three hours' window in which to work. Consider having ten minutes at the beginning of the period for the assistant to read through and annotate the lesson plan, maybe an opportunity to ask questions. Then consider maybe fifteen minutes at the end of the lesson for the assistant to provide you feedback on the teaching activity they have engaged with (even better if you have already provided a template for the planned teaching activity).

This will mean that a slight reorganisation of the teaching time is required but consider the TA as a direct capital expenditure of which you take responsibility. A TA will, on average, cost the school, anywhere up to £18,000 per year (pro rata). So, any deployment of the TA could be treated as though you are directly spending the school's precious budget. It could make you more confident in applying the effective and efficient rule; that is, is what my assistant is doing at any given point an effective and efficient use of the school's money? Or in another way, if the headteacher were to look through the classroom door and enquire as to how the TA is being used, would your answer be convincing?

The example I quote above can allow you as an early career teacher (ECT) to do two things. The deployment will remind you of your favoured pedagogy at any moment (as described above), and it will allow you to be innovative in your deployment. For example, a TA could receive the plans and assessment via the latest communication platform that is compliant with the school's GDPR regulations, and could upload the assessment records into the school's preferred electronic storage system. From a teaching perspective, perhaps the TA could plan a sequence of lessons, with support from you or another member of staff, for a small group of children, or the child with whom they usually work.

An audit of skills

As a new member of staff, you may not be aware of what your TA is experienced in across the wider curriculum. It is possible that your TA has a wide range of curriculum skills and confidence, or not, particularly if they are usually deployed for mathematics and English. Therefore, an audit of what the TA can do will be beneficial; this is because in the relationship that you have created, you are the lead and you are implementing your style of pedagogy and indeed teaching philosophy, in the classroom, and you would want your TA to fully participate and be supportive.

You may have heard staffroom stories that some teachers, let alone TAs, are 'afraid of year 6 maths' or 'do not want to work with the top group'. There may even be some truth in that, but obviously as the lead practitioner with an obligation to the most effective and efficient use of all school resources this will be something you have to tackle. An audit of what the TA can or cannot do with confidence may lead you to re-evaluate the implementation of the wider curriculum. Your TA may have been employed in other work places, not necessarily education, or may have a hobby or a skill that could be used in the classroom. This could be mathematical skills, linguistic skills, physical education (sports) skills, artistic and music skills or a flair for design, spatial awareness (for re-designing the classroom) or languages. Or it could be that they know someone within their professional or social network who could assist, visit the class or host the class on a trip. You will never know unless you ask and record this information. Naturally it will call for sensitivity and trust, because few people would readily admit to deficiencies, especially in the wider curriculum. This is where you would liaise with the senior leadership team and suggest that career professional development would be one way of promoting or learning new skills, as well as refresher courses in particular subjects, for example newer computational mathematical methods.

The audit may also reveal areas where, with confidence, skills could be shared in subjects. For example, music could be taught or be led by the TA with your support. This could also inform and reinvigorate your lesson planning (albeit with the timings agreed). This is not a one-way process; it would be advantageous for you to participate in this; record where you are confident in terms of subject knowledge and experience of teaching certain subjects (there may be times during the pandemic where some subjects were not taught at all or not covered during your initial teacher training). Your school should support you in your early career development in your deficiencies and the need to be more confident, but taking your TA along with you in this procedure will arguably cement you more as a team.

Issues

Guidance is clear in that you are there either to 'deploy support staff effectively' (Teachers' Standard 8) or to improve at preparing TAs for lessons under supervision of expert colleagues (Core Content Framework professional behaviour 8). This is what gives you the legitimacy to dictate the role of the TA and serves as a reminder of you being ultimately accountable for the children's learning and progress. It is hoped, of course, that your TA will be readily agreeable to working with you. It should be stressed that you are there to construct a productive working relationship that is underpinned by trust, mutual respect and a shared (or understanding of your) pedagogy for the children's best interests. You will be guided by the ethos of the school and its working practices as encapsulated and promoted in its policies. But, what if the TA is somewhat unresponsive to your classroom practice? What if you feel the TA knows a lot more of the school procedures and has a handle on all the seeming working knowledge of a school? What if the TA is like 'telling your mum what to do'?

It is not easy when there is disagreement of any shade. We all want to be liked and respected for what we do and believe in. Sometimes, though it is hard and that is an acceptable way to feel. It is not your fault as long as you are being reasonable (in terms of workload and allocation of task), have the children's interests at heart and are not contravening any school policy or practice. Remember though, that if a TA does not understand what is required of them or has late plans (or even no plans), then they will, by default, resort to doing *what they think they ought to be doing*. This may be an historical class-based decision; in other words, what the previous class teacher would agree for them to be doing. But if this is not what you want, or you feel unable or unconfident to change their practice, then it becomes a case of the *teaching assistant deploying the teacher*.

The solution is to speak to the TA and explain how you would like things to be done. If you feel this can achieve a solution, that is acceptable, providing there will be evidence of a change on deployment. It could be that the TA can offer a perfectly acceptable explanation of what is occurring, and you can accept that. If not, you should approach your line manager who will act on your behalf. If you try the former, then at least you will have spoken to your TA first and tried to see what they have to put forward in the discussion, rather than appearing to bypass them and appealing to more senior colleagues in the school.

Likeability and common sense

Although we want to be liked and feel that we can deploy a TA effectively and efficiently, it arguably all boils down to non-pedagogical matters. Being professional is one thing, but being courteous and considerate are also important. You should opt for a blend. A TA is not only a valuable resource from the school's budget but also probably the only adult you will have much contact within the daytime. If deployment tasks are considered by you as 'reasonable', then what matters next is the human factor; recognising when gratitude is to be expressed, when a cup of coffee can be made or when a tired TA can be given five minutes to sit and do something less exhausting (these are busy classrooms!). You may not wish to engage in extraneous discussion about each other's social lives, but you will have to share a classroom with each other and there is a need for a conversation with another adult. Perhaps some of you reading this chapter were former TAs and will know exactly how good and poor deployment by a teacher felt; those experiences will inform your current practice. Were you deployed effectively and efficiently? Did you have some measure of autonomy and trust, and were you deployed for menial tasks? Did the school have your development as a priority in your appraisal? Then you will know how to proceed with your TA and have some experience to begin your teaching career.

Reflection

Your early teaching career may not be easy, but it can be helped by taking time to reflect on your classroom practice and relationships with other colleagues. The use of reflective practice, as the process of identifying effective teaching strategies and understanding why a strategy is effective, is important to a teacher's use of pedagogy. (Pollard et al., 2014). The need to be a consistent reflective practitioner can be seen in the work of Schˆn (1991) and his examining of 'reflection in action' and 'reflection on action'. The former allows teachers to use experiences, feelings and existing theories to create a repertoire of pedagogy and test them out in a given situation, for example in a classroom. The latter allows for a discussion with a professional staff member in the school to enable teachers to explore and explain why they acted as they did in a given situation. This would allow both parties (the identity of the teacher and the public image of the teacher, viewed by the school) to show progression.

Take time to reflect and build it into your PPA time or your ECT development time. Focus on the relationship with your TA and seek advice where you can.

Deploying the Teaching Assistant

By Rebecca Massheder-Stuart, Teacher, London, UK

I have been there, both sides of it, as a teacher wondering, 'what can I ask my TA to do, so they feel useful?' And, as a TA, wondering, 'how can I make this lesson go smoother?' Here is the thing; a relationship with your TA is going to be one of the most important ones you make every year. They have to feel included, and you need to value everything they do because, I mean, let's face it, without them, how hectic would that class be? After teaching in a private school for a year, I took the decision to go into a state school as a TA; seeing it from the other side has made me realise things I should have done as a teacher.

My first bit of advice would always be, communicate! In the morning before the eager faces come into class ready to learn, tell the TA your plan. Identify with them how strong they are on that subject; what group could really benefit from their attention; and how they could help differentiate the work for the higher or lower ability groups. When TAs know where they are going to be useful the most, they will make sure that group of children do their best work, because that is how they are going to make a difference that day.

Second, treat TAs as your equal, and the children will follow. I cannot stress how important it is to support their decisions in front of the class. Make sure they feel your support, and they will give their all back to you. A lot of TAs I have had the pleasure of meeting throughout my career will always comment on how their teacher supports them; the ones who have great teacher support end up being some of the most amazing TAs I have met because they do their hardest to make life easier for their teacher. Everybody needs reassurance and confirmation that they are doing the right thing, so give TAs that, let them know how you would have handled it, let them be on the same page and show the children there is a team with the same expectations.

Last, give TAs things to do; no matter how small a task might feel, it is so important to feel they are needed and not just sitting there whilst someone is teaching the class. Yes, they can help with behaviour management or children who need extra support, but it is very tedious and frustrating to feel they are not contributing. TAs will not always know what your plan is, how far along in the planning you are and what materials you have or need sourced, so discuss that and ask for help. Let TAs know what you need, and they might come up with ideas that you did not have time to think of; use the strengths of whom you have around you and you may be pleasantly surprised. They are here for the children of course but make a team; two heads are always better than one.

Deploying the Teaching Assistant

By Olly Cakebread, Primary Teacher, Bexleyheath, England

The greatest travesty within the education system is that our TAs are not seen as important as they truly are to the classroom. Many people have them away doing administrative and low-key jobs such as cutting and trimming, and whilst, yes, they

(Continued)

are there to assist a teacher in these ways, they are most importantly there to enhance the learning of the children in the class, and this is exactly what they should be deployed to do.

Before being hired as a cover teacher whilst doing my degree, I was a TA, so I feel as though I have picked up many tips and tricks that I now use to deploy my own TAs in the classroom. If your TA is willing, one of the greatest things I have ever done is use them as a 'mini teacher' to support, not just lower ability children, but any children who need help in covering the learning objectives in a slightly different way. Whilst it would be lovely to personalise every child's learning experience, we just do not have the facilities for that in schools. By deploying a TA to assist in the teaching of a lesson, albeit in a slightly more abstract way using the outdoors or different concrete objects, we can try our hardest to ensure every child gets the ability to learn in a way suited to them. Giving your TA autonomy over their work and saying something along the lines of *'I would like to teach place value but children x, y and z are not accessing it because they need something more creative. Would you mind spending twenty minutes or so planning a little activity for them to do outside and using their bodies that can help teach them this?'* can really help TAs to take ownership over what they are doing and help create creative strategies to things that can be particularly tricky for some children.

Many times, I have been struggling with ways in which to tackle activities with children, and the class TA has been able to think of something so creative that I wonder why they are not the ones leading the class! A collaboration between teacher and TA is just a wonderful thing and creates such an inclusive, varied and rich learning environment for the children to be educated in and really will ensure that their attainment increases beyond anything you could imagine! The only advice I would give though is remember as a teacher you still have ultimate responsibility over the class's learning so I would ensure you are still closely monitoring the progress of the children and intervening if necessary. Oh! Also, as a TA it was very much appreciated when my class teacher brought in a box of chocolates and left them in the cupboard in case of 'emergencies'. Just saying!

Sharing Planning with TAs through Three Key Questions

By Sara Alston, Consultant and Trainer: SEA Inclusion & Safeguarding, Surrey, UK

None of us do our best work when we are not sure what we are doing. Yet, despite years of work by the MITA project and EEF highlighting the key issues of TAs deployment, practice and preparedness, this is the position we put TAs in on a daily basis. TAs will rarely have the same understanding of the planning as the teachers who actually put it together. Their involvement with the planning, when it is shared at all, tends to be reactive rather than proactive: commenting on and asking questions about planning,

(Continued)

rather than creating it. Their lack of understanding of the lesson planning reduces the impact of the support TAs can offer children for their learning.

Many schools say that planning is available for all staff. But there is a difference between planning being available and staff having the time and opportunity to read and understand it. Sharing planning effectively takes time. When time is scarce, we need to reduce the communication about planning down to a useful minimum by focusing on three key questions.

What is the learning intention? Identifying the key focus of the learning is vital. This needs to include enough information to be useful, not just 'addition', but 'addition with exchange using formal methods with two and three digit numbers'.

What is the key vocabulary? The new, technical or unusual vocabulary children will need to access the learning. This can be highlighted on the planning and/or slides or simply listed with an explanation of the language where necessary.

What is the outcome? This is what the children are expected to produce by the end of the lesson. There should be sufficient flexibility in this that tasks can be adapted and differentiated to meet children's needs and allow them different ways of demonstrating their learning. This should support a focus on learning, not just task completion.

These three questions cover only the tip of the iceberg of the information included in teachers' planning. Our communication with TAs needs to move beyond the delivery of instructions. We need to ensure the communication about learning is effective and relevant to the children in the class. A fundamental starting point for this is the effective sharing of planning.

Summary

You will have had experience of deploying a TA to some degree, from your time as a student on school-based teaching placements and recalling the theoretical input from your initial teacher training institutions. Therefore, be confident that you can legitimately deploy a TA; this is an already accepted expectation. The chapter began by asking, 'In your relationship with a teaching assistant who deploys whom?' I have argued then that the relationship is not an equal one; there needs to be a hierarchy of responsibility – how you address that is up to you; you may prefer a subtle hierarchy or a more overt one. If you use the concept of the 'localized familiarization', then it takes time away from your efficient work in the classroom and the deployment of the assistant. I am not saying you cannot be sociable and indeed socialise outside of school hours, but you need to grasp the initiative.

This will be in the articulation of your pedagogical identity. Show and discuss with your TA what it is you believe in philosophically and pedagogically. If you are a social constructivist, you will deploy the TA in a social constructivist way and that will be noticeable within the classroom; if you are a behaviourist, then the same will apply. Note I am not favouring any type of pedagogy; that will be your decision and one in which you feel comfortable to get results (or even what the school favours).

Although pedagogy will be more the frequent characteristic in any deployment, this chapter has shown how remembering the simple but important soft skills of communication, audits and courteousness will also matter. Ask yourself this question – would you be willing to be deployed by 'yourself'? Perhaps this self-reflection is one way where you can make the relationship work for everyone concerned in the classroom.

References

Atkinson, D. (2004). Theorising how student teachers form their identities in initial teacher education. *British Educational Research Journal*, 30(3), pp. 379-394. [Online]. Available at: http://onlinelibrary.wiley.com/doi/10.1080/01411920410001689698/pdf

Bourdieu, P. (1984). *Distinction*. London: Routledge & Kegan Paul.

Britzman, D. (1991). *Practice Makes Practice: A Critical Study of Learning to Teach*. Albany: State University of New York Press.

Danielewicz, J. (2001). *Teaching Selves*. New York: State University of New York.

Department for Education and Employment (DfEE). (1998). *The National Literacy Strategy*. Sudbury: DfEE.

Department for Education and Employment (DfEE). (1999). *The National Numeracy Strategy*. Sudbury: DfEE.

Department for Education and Skills (DfES). (2003). *The School Teachers' Pay and Conditions Document 2003*. London: The Stationery Office.

Department for Education (DfE). (2019). *ITT Core Content Framework*. [Online]. Available at: https://assets.publishing.service.gov.uk/government/uploads/system/uploads/attachment_data/file/974307/ITT_core_content_framework_.pdf

Goffman, E. (1959). *The Presentation of Self in Everyday Life*. London: Penguin.

HMI. (2002). *Teaching assistants in primary schools: An evaluation of the quality and impact of their work*. [Online]. Available at: http://dera.ioe.ac.uk/4532/1/Teaching%20assistants%20in%20primary%20schools%20an%20evaluation%20of%20the%20quality%20and%20impact%20of%20their%20work%20(PDF%20format).pdf

Morgan, R. (2018). *What are the perceptions of the practice of the deployment of teaching assistants by trainee teachers during classroom teaching experiences on a university-based Initial Teacher Training programme in southeast London?* Unpublished EdD Thesis. University of Greenwich.

Pollard, A., Black-Hawkins, K., Hodges, G., Dudley, P., James, M., Linklater, H., Swaffield, S., Swann, M., Turner, F., Warwick, P., Winterbottom, M., and Wolpert, M. (2014). *Reflective Teaching in Schools*. 4th edn. London: Bloomsbury.

Schˆn, D. (1991). *The Reflective Practitioner*. Aldershot: Avebury.

10 Fundamental British values
What is British about them?

KEY WORDS

Democracy, law, liberty, respect of faith and belief, citizenship

Contributors within this chapter:
1. Sally Burns
2. Maritza Masiello
3. Vikki Hurst
4. Natalie Starkey and Lee Hill

Introduction

Fundamental British Values were conceived as a part of the 'Prevent agenda to stop people becoming terrorists', which in turn with 'Pursue to stop terrorist attacks', 'Protect against a terrorist attack' and 'Prepare: to mitigate the impact of a terrorist attack' comprised the government's CONTEST strategy, which has as its aim, to 'reduce the risk to the UK and its interests overseas from terrorism, so that people can go about their lives freely and with confidence' (HM Government, 2011a, pp. 3-6). In summary, 'Prevent' is designed to reduce the threat of terrorism by promoting the spiritual, moral and cultural development of pupils and preparing them for the opportunities, responsibilities and experiences of life (HM Government, 2011b. p. 65).

It was the Department for Education (DFE 2014) that formalised the guidance for the promotion of Fundamental British Values of democracy, the rule of English law, individual liberty and mutual respect and tolerance of those with different faiths and beliefs (DfE, 2014, p. 5) so that promoting such values means 'challenging opinions or behaviours that are contrary' to them. This is to be taught (promoted) under the remit of Spiritual, Moral, Social and Cultural development (SMSC), and with a link to the Core Content Framework Standard 8 - 'Fulfil wider professional responsibilities'. As a reflective teacher, you may be wondering why, in the liberal society the government wishes us to live in, would there be a need for the government to instruct its citizens about what values should be promoted in its schools? Can you be taught a value? And why are British Values only taught in England;

DOI: 10.4324/9781003218098-10

what does that say about the identity that is England, or Britain, or indeed the United Kingdom in the age of devolution?

This chapter does not dwell too much on the questions raised above; you can read critiques of this elsewhere, but it explores values that are important and gives some ideas as how they can be shown/promoted/taught in schools. I shall focus on England primarily in this chapter rather than the United Kingdom, but as I shall argue throughout more a feature on 'values' than their 'Britishness'.

It looks at how values of democracy, law, liberty and respect for faith and belief can be embedded into everyday practice and the environment of the classroom and wider school, as well as some discrete examples through the curriculum.

A liberal heritage

Critical question

What are the Fundamental British Values, and what is their purpose?

England has a proud and noble liberal tradition, and it is worth setting a definition of what liberalism is because I shall argue that British Values, whatever interpretation springs to mind, should be rooted in it. Liberty, according to the dictionary, is the act of being free from captivity, or having rights, or being allowed privileges by an authority. Liberalism is defined by Rousseau as developing a society that is not subject to absolutism but 'lies in the conviction that each person's pursuit of his personal interest leads to the promotion of the public interest' (Manent, 1995, p. 69).

Therefore, it is the promotion of the rights of the individual and the acceptance of rule; that is rule by government and the imposition of law and societal structures. Liberalism is not unbounded; it has rights and responsibilities to other humans, originally property, but now in the modern age to other ethical concerns, for example animals and the environment. Liberalism in England began in earnest with the Glorious Revolution of 1682 which gave the nation a bill of rights, greater freedom of the press, parliamentary sovereignty and habeas corpus (a proper trial and imprisonment). Further freedoms came in the form of economic liberalism (free markets and reduced government interference, classic liberalism (spreading of happiness for the greater good and social reform through government) and social liberalism (increased government reform such as welfare and organising and spending on education and health). Without embarking on too much history, (though it is worth mentioning trade unionism, the creation of the welfare state and the NHS, the role of the country in fighting totalitarian regimes in the twentieth century, freedom of speech, freedom of worship and freedom to vote amongst other British creations), liberty and liberalism can be grossly simplified as the right of a person to express oneself either individually, in relation to others or in institutions: the tension between the self and government.

The United Kingdom is a member of the United Nations (UN) and subscribes to its Universal Declaration of Human Rights and a signatory to the European Convention on Human Rights. This demonstrates the tradition that you as a trainee teacher or early

What is fundamentally British about these values, and does it matter?

Amanda Spielman, the current head of Ofsted, defended British Values in 2018 as serving beyond the remit of preventing terrorism and mentioned the need for a strong government, although there is no evidence of a consensual one, but noted how values would promote trust and the willingness to contribute to the 'common good'. British Values are to be viewed as not being originally British in origin but part of the ethos that makes Britain; in other words, 'values which stand in opposition cannot and should not be described as British'.

Spielman is clear that '…teachers are expected to give children a proper understanding of British Values, and of what these values have contributed – and continue to contribute to – the strength and success of British society… that there is much more that can be done within the existing school curriculum and, in particular, across all the humanities'.

It does not matter those values are British (or even English), although what 'makes Britain' is a harder concept to identify and this chapter does not do this. It is not merely a display of the Union flag with stereotypically British characteristics, attractions, histories, people and so forth on it. Neither should British Values be added to a lesson or within a subject to demonstrate it has been 'covered'. Then again, the British value of democracy, although not original to Britain, is it accepted for children to criticise it, for example calling for its reform or to critique how it was exported to other countries?

This chapter argues that although British Values are flawed, confusing and imposed, it should be seen as pro-liberty and as an opportunity to be central to everyday teaching. For this chapter, this means both the individual child and the class, as a collection of individuals, looking to assert their rights with the acceptance of those who teach them, the interest of the child and how the school protects that.

Democracy

This is the government of the people chosen by the people, usually by the representatives of the people, but according to John Dewey (2008) it is more than that. For him democracy is a way of living with a focus on the recognition of mutual interests and a continuous readjustment from the interaction of social groups. It is a form of associated living which individuals have an interest that relates not only to themselves but also to the interests of others. The individual becomes a citizen as she is aware of the aims of institutions and therefore can share a space with others. Democracy is fuelled by the practice of social equality, and for a modern society or classroom, that is the eradication of practices that favour discrimination and exclusion.

This is your starting point when considering your approach to Fundamental British Values. How far do you believe in the rights of children in everyday classroom situations? This is where inclusive practice should be the defining example of pedagogy, procedure and organisation of the classroom. Inclusion must go beyond adaptive teaching (differentiation) and look at that word 'rights'. What other rights do children possess in the classroom, and how would you encourage it? If you are inclusive, then you are certainly promoting the value that is democracy.

In the classroom, what do you allow? How about a child being able to interrupt you and question you? What about children being given autonomy to choose what to have for their learning and wandering around the classroom to obtain it? How much can children decide about the organisation of the furniture, the quantity of homework or a review of your planning? These decisions will reflect your objective commitment to democracy. It may be that you have never considered sharing your planning with the children (or for younger pupils informing them of what will be happening), but if you welcome their feedback, you are at least showing that it is valued.

The classroom reflects your philosophy of education even when the children are not in it; when they are in the classroom, your philosophy becomes active pedagogy. Consider what you will display on the walls that show how you wish the value of democracy to be appreciated – who are the role models that would appeal to the demography that represents your class? Who, in your opinion, is inspirational from a social justice perspective, history, anti-racism, anti-Islamophobia, anti-homophobia (as I write Alan Turing has been portrayed on the Bank of England's £50 for a year) or from a feminist perspective? What books will you accumulate in the reading corner or in a prominent place in the classroom? What you believe in and what your heritage is will be the best way to determine how you wish to populate your classroom with resources.

For a subjective perspective, the curriculum plan would be your next step. It is an obvious starting place to begin with Personal, Social, Health and Economic Education (PSHE) and relationships education so that *'in primary schools, subjects put in place the key building blocks of healthy, respectful relationships, focusing on family and friendships, in all contexts…'* you extract the values inherent in the guidance and plan for them. A wider curriculum approach will enable you not to follow a stereotypical path by staying with history or English. Look at what you can do in music, art and design or physical education. Democracy is about inclusion and celebrating those who have done exactly that. In physical education, inclusion would be you modifying games, gymnastics, athletics and dance, for example having all children sitting to play volleyball and using a large balloon, displaying a poster of a Paralympian such as Ellie Symonds and describing her opinions on 'dwarfism' (Varley, 2022) Take the subjects to be taught in a half-term and plan to include examples of inclusion (adaptive teaching, consideration of children's feedback, children's access to learning, key resources, key figures and what the children can bring to the subject, for example their own life stories).

Once that is done, the next step is arguably a familiar one. Teach democracy discretely by teaching in an age-appropriate manner, the history of Parliament, the role of MPs, how elections work (ever wonder why elections in the UK are always held on a Thursday? – have a bit of psephology taught!) and how democracy has allowed people today to make protest and secure reform. The teaching of anti-slavery, suffragettes, trade union reform and working practices of children in the Victorian age are obvious examples. That said, however; do go beyond the obvious and look for examples that you think are relevant and stimulating so that you will not be teaching to stereotype or conformity. Promote the engagement of the school council, and do not be afraid to encourage a healthy and respectable discussion that seeks reform. What would the children want to change that will make teachers really notice?

138 *Fundamental British values*

Law

In England and Wales, which shares the same laws owing to the Act of Union of 1536, the main purpose of civil law is to uphold the rights of individuals, whereas criminal law involves offences and the rules and procedures that apply when the police investigate (Elliott and Quinn, 2017). DfE (2014) is clear that the teaching of law is that pupils should understand that whilst different people may hold different views about what is 'right' and 'wrong', all people living in England are subject to it; schools should support the rule of English civil and criminal law and not teach anything that undermines it. Both civil and criminal law in England and Wales are about codifying what cannot be done in order to protect a population, its property, and to uphold its rights. The law in this country is part of the philosophical idea of the social contract, first proposed by Thomas Hobbes who argued that humans would willingly give up their individual claims within a society to the concept of a state and its laws; otherwise humans would be anarchic and revert to unpleasant and selfish actions (Kaye, 2013).

This is your starting point, when considering your approach to the value that is the law. How far do you consider that children should accept the law; that is, do as they are told unquestionably (I am not suggesting this applies to evacuation drills or such safeguarding procedures) or have the freedom to change the law, make new laws or reject it? This will be the same thought process that defines your teaching philosophy, and as above, your thoughts on what you allow in terms of teaching the value of democracy.

Objectively the laws of the land need to be taught because children, especially those in Year 5 and up, need to know that the differences between right and wrong can lead to serious consequences. Children in England and Wales between 10 and 17 can be arrested and taken to court if they commit a crime. They are treated differently from adults and are dealt with by youth courts, given different sentences and can be sent to special secure centres for young people (HM Government, 2022). If a fire alarm sounds, the children will be drilled into following it and, for their own sake, must accept it that is acceptable. If a child discloses to a teacher an incident that requires safeguarding procedures to be implemented, the law must be followed and the teacher, for example, cannot promise to keep the matter away from colleagues in authority who need to pursue it further. Apart from these examples, daily situations that involve the implementation of school policy also need following; they may not be changed, but they can be explained as to why they are written, and the benefits are to the children for agreeing not to challenge them. This will be about personal and collective safety, trusting the judgement and experience of teachers, protection and accountability.

Outside of this common sensical approach, and becoming more subjective, it can be argued that other forms of law within the school environment may be more contestable. An obvious contender is the formation of the classroom rules. Advice may be to frame these as positive statements prefaced by 'do' rather than 'do not' in behaviour management textbooks, but it is important to consider the rights that are being upheld for the children's benefit. All children have the right to learn and have equal access to it (as written in Education Acts) and to be free from discrimination and bullying. They have the right, amongst other things, to have their voices heard, their property protected and their safety being guaranteed; so how would you construct a short classroom set of rules that the children also have a say in? What would be the rights that you as a teacher would want to uphold that the children recognise as important and assent to? What about a reward and sanction system to follow, and how would you facilitate that (bearing in mind that children can be quite severe in deciding sanctions!)?

In terms of the curriculum, you would be teaching about the law from a historical perspective; knowing how laws originate in England and the function of Parliament, the judicial system, the ceremonial role of the monarch, the work of the police and the curious fact that the United Kingdom does not have a written constitution (but at the time of writing it will be interesting to read what the current government's intended 'Bill of Rights' will set out to achieve). From a PHSE perspective, this can be widened to develop children's skills of debate, reasoning, world affairs and empathy. An opening gambit is the notion of whether some laws should be kept or even broken – how did universal suffrage in the United Kingdom occur without the law-breaking activities of the suffragettes; the United States and its history of race reform; or South Africa's ending of apartheid; should a young mother be arrested who, facing hardship under a 'cost of living crisis' be arrested for stealing baby food? This latter scenario could be enacted with a judge and jury in the classroom and developed as a series of planned lessons, planning for the defence, the prosecution and a team of judges. Such examples are only posited by world events; how should children's interpretation of the law be extended to asylum seekers, environmental campaigners who disrupt civil life and whether British museum artefacts should be returned to former colonial countries?

Yet if laws are about upholding rights and a consensual agreement (with some elasticity), how would this manifest itself in other subjects? Religious education provides discussion for upholding (or otherwise) the teachings of religious figures; English provides an obvious medium for recording learning in the written word; geography can look at international law (Antarctica, the Amazon Rainforest and disputes over water supply); art and design would be exploring propaganda as a way of how humanity was coerced into obeying law, or the works of artists who encouraged liberation. Mathematics is a bit different; however, there are laws in mathematics, such as formulae that are required to be learned – slightly tenuous but still something that can be useful for children to know; a formula will enhance your mathematical knowledge and application.

Liberty

In 1953, former HM inspector and teacher educator, Christian Schiller wrote, 'freedom is not a gift which is given or taken, but a power which grows or fails to grow and it is a power of special value to children at school' (Schiller, 1984 p. 48). He added that children learn best when they 'exercise their growing power to choose' (Schiller, 1984, p. 49. Schiller was clear that the issue rests with teachers in deciding how to help children develop their ability to choose and that the way to accomplish this was to create a 'climate of feeling and a range of material' to aid growth.

Schiller's point reinforces a key theme of this chapter so far; in that in order to teach children British Values (or rather develop them mutually), the teacher and her values need to be examined first. This reflective practice determines classroom practice. The British Value that is 'individual liberty' is not individualism; it is about the rights of the individual, the promotion of freedom and, crucially, the relationship of the individual with others and institutions.

This is our starting point for considering individual liberty; objectively it is about two issues, the power of choice and that power resting with consideration of others. Let us start with the amount of choice afforded to children. Consider a typical day where you have taught the children; how much choice did you plan for them? This may be an obvious question for Early Years' practitioners as it is the basis of their pedagogy, but in Key Stage 2, for example, do you allow the children to decide on the organisation of the learning, in terms of seating or resources? Do you tend to want to 'tell them the answers' rather than risk a protracted period where they must work it out? Do you allow for long and meaningful discussions instead of 'talk to your partner for 30 seconds'; do you set homework rather than negotiate it? You may reply that the school does not really operate in that way, but it is an opportunity to consider how much can be negotiated with management as to what change can be effected; something small is probably better than no change at all. Such reflection is about the balance of power in the classroom, rather as has been written about in chapter x, behaviour management. This chapter, however, is asking you to think about how much autonomy you are willing to give to your children without there being a total loss of your authority.

The second issue is the right of children having choice and the effect that has on other children. Child development theory has taught that children are naturally selfish before developing empathy. This is something that arguably informs most of your behaviour management, social skills teaching and modelling; for example, sharing. Children are taught about consequences and the emotional and physical outcomes their actions have on others. This is teaching the children about liberty, and you already do it. It is related to children's acceptance or disregard of the law (as discussed above). If children cannot see the need to comply with classroom values, it not only means they are sanctioned but it can mean that others are affected. For example, name calling spreads hurt to others, destruction of property means others cannot use it, or that if someone does not confess to a misdemeanour, the whole class could be sanctioned!

In terms of the curriculum and the more subjective application of liberty, you can begin with planning: deciding what the children can do and what they should be encouraged to do (so that they acquire independence and less reliance on you, which is probably good for your own workload). The whole curriculum lends itself to developing children's autonomy when you consider ability grouping and assessment (how much can the children contribute to their own or peer assessment and record keeping); what if an activity has captured their enthusiasm, would you allow them to continue with it or end it because there is a need to move on? Conduct an audit of the children's dependency (regardless of age) and consider how to reduce that.

For discrete subjects, the teaching of the value of individual liberty and the need to consider others, rather much like law, is probably easier in the humanities-based areas. History (and again PSHE) is where liberty is usually taught with examples of ending slavery (one cannot want to enslave another human being without having to realise the dreadful impact that has on the enslaved), and the focus on decolonisation is rich in terms of opportunity, as any watching of current affairs will suggest. Other ideas would be freedom from totalitarianism; reducing hate crime; welcoming those in need; the right to access work, leisure and housing free from discriminatory institutions; and the right of an individual not to be attacked physically, sexually or verbally. There is a wealth of case studies, contemporary role models and stories from which to choose across the world, but one tip may not to go to stereotypical (well-known) countries, but to look at where your children originate and find examples from there. For instance, the rights of all citizens to live without prejudice or restrictions on religious freedom in India (see below), the rights to stop mineral exploration in the Democratic Republic of Congo, the right of

Brazilians to be educated through mass literacy programmes so they can end their poverty or the rights of displaced and interned peoples globally. Liberty can be taught in art and design; rather than you waste time modelling what should be painted, eschew that part of the lesson and literally provide a blank canvas; let the children decide what to paint; in music give the freedom of choice to arrange a composition; in reading provide more of a range of literature that reflects the demography of the class and reflects liberty stories, so the children can choose. Children can only choose if there is a concerted effort by the school to widen choice or if the children are confident enough to make demands for extra books!

Mutual respect and tolerance of those with different faiths and beliefs

The foreword to the Royal Borough of Greenwich's agreed syllabus for religious education, under the heading 'families of faith and belief', has a focus on inclusion, diversity and respect,

> The syllabus is to be transformed into a freedom of pedagogy that meets the needs of critical thinking learners, whatever their faith and belief, as it exists during their learning. Good religious education throughout all seventeen wards in the borough will be contemporary, innovative, inclusive, searching, and challenging. It will deepen understanding, develop skills and show how all learners can live and learn in a cohesive community… [and] be used to explore and celebrate the Royal Borough of Greenwich's diversity, energy and growth. It will prepare confident and mature learners to explore faith and belief at a local level to prepare and equip them for the future's national and global challenges.
>
> (Morgan, 2018)

That, in a nutshell, is good religious education; it does not focus on the phrase 'tolerance' per se but looks to aim for respect and understanding, a leaning toward curiosity, shared values and openness. The caveat for the DfE's (2014) guidance is that children are taught the difference between the law of the country and religious law; with religious law being, for example, Christian Canon law, Jewish Halakha law and Islamic Sharia law. In England and Wales, the law of the state overrides religious law, although people of faith's conscience and attitudes are shaped by religious law; such a circumstance can be taught in school, for example the upholding of a day for worship or treating the elderly with care.

Every child will have a belief, but not every child will have a faith. It will be simple, for the purposes of this chapter, to define a religion and faith as the same thing, that is a belief in explaining humanity's understanding of the self, each other and the environment with a reliance on a superhuman entity to which is ascribed worthy attributes and names, whereas a belief is more generic and can have foundations in ideology, lifestyle or qualities broadly considered to be universal, for example charitable giving and accepting strangers. The Core Report (Commission on Religious Education 2018) explores both religious and non-religious worldviews which are 'a person's way of understanding, experiencing and responding to the world… a philosophy of life or an approach to life', and Smart (1992) provides excellent in-depth definition of what a religion is through the seven dimensions, including understanding secular world views.

This is your starting point: every child will believe in something. The skill of fostering respect for children of any belief is to find the common ground, to explore and accept the differences and to wonder at different practices and interpretations. If a Jewish child keeps Shabbat (Sabbath) special, then the idea of keeping it special is also applied to the Christian and church attendance on Sunday, and the Muslim and Friday. For those with a non-faith background, the concept of 'a special day' is not lost on these children; they can experience their special day as a birthday or an important family occasion. The skill for you as a teacher is to extract and showcase the themes that are applicable to all children, notably excitement, reverence and memories.

You are going to be heavily guided and supported by the subject of religious education for this British value, whether that is from an agreed syllabus from the appropriate SACRE, external provision or from belonging to a faith school. Most curricular, by law, will have a focus on Christianity, up to 50 percent of the coverage, but you should conduct an audit of faith and belief of your class. Outside of the six widely observed faiths (Buddhism, Christianity, Hinduism, Islam, Judaism and Sikhism), what else is there? How many adherents are there of Humanism, Ethical Veganism (which is the latest belief to have protected characteristic in law), Paganism, Atheism, Bah·'í, Zoroastrianism, Shintoism, Unitarianism or Taoism? Once you know who believes in what, this can help you to celebrate and inform the class of such beliefs.

The academic year is organised based on the Christian festivals of Christmas, Easter and Whitsun. Recent focus has allowed schools to celebrate or allow awareness for Ramadan and Eid, Chinese New Year or Vaisakhi. The focus should not always be on these festivals because that will draw you into stereotype and will not allow for inclusion and a sense of developing an inclusive community. If children are not exposed to wider faith and belief, then they will be in ignorance. It is appropriate to celebrate St George's Day from a faith perspective (Christianity) and from a cultural perspective to inform children about the Christian teaching of upholding one's beliefs and to celebrate the importance within English culture which is about inclusion and acceptance.

You will have realised at this stage that there is no mention of extremism. Having a respect for a faith requires you to learn about what a religion truly stands for and the way its followers practise it. A faith is about human values, environmental values and a way of appreciating the divine entity that is to be interpreted for the modern society for togetherness. That is the acceptance. Dismissing extremism is recognising a false interpretation of a particular faith and belief.

Practical Activities for Exploring British Values

By Sally Burns, The Values and Visons Foundation, (online), UK

Whether consciously or unconsciously, nearly everything we do, think and feel is coloured by what we believe matters; what we give value to.

Since 2014, the DfE has decreed that four values should be embedded in classroom teaching:

- Democracy
- Rule of law
- Respect and tolerance
- Individual liberty

(Continued)

How can we teach these four values? It may seem daunting but need not be if we follow some simple guidelines.

One of the first steps to take is to establish ground rules in your classroom. Over the last thirty years, we at the Values and Visions Foundation have found that six simple ground rules create a safe place in which to share and an effective way of working together to get results. Try them out! They are the following:

- Confidentiality
- Mindful: listening, with two ears, two eyes and an open heart
- Pacing: sharing the responsibility for using the time fully and well
- Pass: there is no pressure to share
- No observer status: although anyone may choose to pass, everyone stays involved
- No criticism, complaining and blaming

These will help you to establish a calm, listening-engaged classroom where you can all work more effectively. They enable democracy. They allow for the discussion of sensitive issues. They engender respect. They create an atmosphere for sharing what is dearest to us: our values.

How do you begin to talk about values? Let us take one of our activities: *When You're 85*. Ask your pupils to sit in a circle, relax and close their eyes and to project themselves into the future when they are 85 years old, sitting comfortably in an armchair and thinking back over their life. From this perspective, ask them to become aware of what they have achieved and what has been important to them. Finally focus on the three qualities which have most influenced their life. The pupils write these down and then read them out to others. What is striking is to find that many share the same values even though they will have arrived at them individually. One of my pupils reflecting on this activity wrote, *'I chose integrity, perseverance and being humble because those are characteristics my grandfather had, and I aspire to be like him'*. He found he was not the only one who held those values dear.

I like to get pupils to take each of the values they have jointly come up with and brainstorm what it looks like in practice. If there is respect, what will you see, hear and feel? What will be happening? This way the values become concrete principles by which to live. The process is strengthened by displaying the values as a poster which everyone signs. When a new decision or course of action comes up, the class passes it through the prism of these values and ensures it works for them all. The process leads to a sense of ownership of the values and will engender a commitment to living by them.

Young people need inner strength which comes from living by what they believe in. Being confident about their values enables them to find meaning and purpose in the volatile world in which they live.

Now check back to the British Values: you are doing them!

The Importance of Representation in the History Curriculum

By Maritza Masiello, Podcaster, Writer and Business Owner, London, UK

Imagine sitting in a classroom, learning alongside your friends. The topic is the invasion of the Vikings – you find it gory but fascinating. Last year your class learnt about Henry the 8th and all his wives. Although it was interesting, you wish you could also learn about people who had brown skin and looked like you, but you forget about that thought just as quickly as it came into your mind.

It cannot be underestimated how important identity is; similarly, it is paramount for any child to feel a sense of belonging through representation, including in the teaching of the history of Britain. The concepts surrounding 'nation' and 'nation identity' arrive through the teaching of mass migration and settlements of the British Isles. However, a dominant part of the history curriculum dictates that students are taught about Vikings and Anglo-Saxons as part of compulsory teaching, ignoring Black and Asian migration. Aside from migration, there are suggestions of Black historical figures to study within the History Programmes of Study, such as Martin Luther King and Rosa Parks, but these are not compulsory; therefore, a disjointed understanding of a diverse history is evident throughout English primary schools (Charles, 2019).

The number of pupils from diverse heritage in England is increasing, yet this is not reflected in the number of Black and ethnic minority teachers or the compulsory history subjects studied in primary schools. The curriculum was designed through the lens of the White and Eurocentric perspective, and children with brown skin do not see themselves in the history taught in classrooms. Additionally, the non-compulsory suggestion to learn about two American Black figures discounts the importance of acknowledging a diverse British history. Many have argued that schools are societal institutions that replicate the reproduction of the dominant culture, attitudes and beliefs of society (Asante, 1991). If children are not taught an inclusive curriculum that reflects a multicultural England and Britain, in all schools, even those that are in predominately White areas, then what does that say about what is seen as 'important' history? This is particularly significant as one of the reasons children attend school is to prepare for life as part of wider society, yet representation of wider society in England and Britain is not reflected in compulsory history lessons. There are of course tokenistic attempts at diversifying what is taught, such as during Black History Month and International Food Day, but surely non-White history should not be confined to just one month or one day. Furthermore, it has been argued that diversity and ethnicity focus almost exclusively on emphasising the discourse of culture and religion, excluding other aspects of diversity, such as society and history (Maylor et al., 2007).

The Macpherson Report and The Black Lives Matter protests represent significant moments in time that highlighted the racial inequalities that exist both in Britain and internationally. Both events focused our minds and were seen as a catalyst for change in the education system and society as a whole. Considering education is the main driver for change, the English primary curriculum has remained stagnant, leaving the principles of inequalities untouched, despite the knowledge that those inequalities continue to

(Continued)

exist in society (Gillborn, 2008). The consequences of this is that classroom pedagogy has struggled to keep pace with public understanding of anti-racism, and nowhere has this been more keenly felt than in the history curriculum (Doharty, 2017).

The reading material used in classrooms and the unconscious bias of some White teachers could have adverse effects on children. Unconscious bias can be learned and absorbed over time and, although subtle in action, can negatively impact pupils and have detrimental long-term effects (Benson, 2019). Teachers are key figures and a major component of the 'change making' that is required to teach a more representative curriculum, yet the subtleties in unconscious bias can result in the omission of studying important non-White figures (Johnson and Mouthaan, 2021). Although this is partly addressed in the Teacher's Standards, we need to go further. Until diversifying the primary curriculum becomes a top-down governmental priority, teachers need to develop an understanding of their own values, prejudices and attitudes and view diversity as a curriculum opportunity rather than as a threat. (Maylor et al., 2007; Charles, 2019; Moncrieffe et al., 2019).

Now imagine sitting in a classroom, learning alongside your friends. The topic is the invasion of the Vikings – you find it gory but fascinating. Last year you learnt about Black and Asian migration, and you see yourself and your friends in history lessons. You see people who look like you, and you understand the invaluable contribution that different races have had on the country you call home.

The Importance of School Councils

By Vikki Hurst, Primary School Teacher, Greater Manchester, UK

In preparation for writing this, I asked my Year 5 class why they thought school councils were important. Hasib* (who, interestingly, has never seemed interested in our council) chimed up, 'It's how we get things we care about to change'. In saying this, he's superseded any need for me to write more – that's the crux of it. The things that our pupils care about are often different to the things their teachers and school leaders care about – not lesser and not trivial, but different. They have a different outlook on school life and notice different things: the blind corner just outside the gates where older kids lurk with seeming menace; that Year 2's later break time means there are never any oranges left in the snack bowl when they get out; that they really enjoy the history topic your KS2 lead is considering swapping out and want to be part of the conversation; that the library only has two books about skateboarding even though it's the latest craze; that it might be really cool to plant the sunflowers Reception are growing in that weedy patch along Year 4's classroom wall. Of course their perspective needs to have a voice, an authentic one – it's their right, says the UN, to have a say in the things affecting their lives and to have that say considered seriously (UNICEF, 2017).

There are other reasons too. Research shows that where school councils are effective, pupils have a better view of the school's social and academic offer, feel listened to by

(Continued)

teachers and tend to behave better (Alderson, 2000). This makes sense – if students have a say in creating rules, culture and opportunities, they are more likely to be pleased with what's offered. And if they are not happy, we can use the school-council system as a pathway to help them appropriately and positively communicate that dissatisfaction. At their best, school councils operate as democracies, and we all feel happier in our democracy when our opinions are listened to and we are represented. The commonly used structure (student representatives for each class or year group, chosen by pupil vote) mirrors in many ways the UK system of MPs and so can offer a direct learning opportunity about how parts of our parliamentary organisation operate. Participation in student council – as a representative, guest speaker on a particular issue or simply as a 'constituent' discussing considerations on the playground – provides opportunities to engage proactively in democracy, and the hope is that this encourages continued engagement as active, voting citizens or even as politicians. Explicit teaching about voting systems links to increased civic engagement (CIRCLE, 2020), so it would seem that actual participation in such a system should further reinforce this outcome. School council participation is also an important opportunity to recognise and develop leadership skills in our young people – practising speaking and listening to a range of people (including in often formal settings), using those English-lesson persuasive devices in a real-world setting and carefully considering the future implications of change with logical skills and sociological understanding.

But, buyer beware – a school council must go above and beyond being a tickbox to demonstrate commitment to those good-old British Values when Ofsted come to call. All too often, school councils are an exercise in lip-service only; the children can tell this and know that it's not worth their time to engage with such tokenism. Thus, the council is ineffective, and its irrelevance becomes a self-fulfilling prophecy. Your school council needs to be thoughtfully and realistically implemented so that it reflects the real opinions of a majority of pupils, and so that it actually can create real change. That's not always easy to achieve, and doing so will vary from context to context – but it's worth it.

Tips for an effective school council

- Get school leadership on board – not necessarily coming to meetings, but open to what gets fed back.
- Be honest and open with the children – if they suggest something unrealistic, tell them the truth and why; talk about alternatives. Take what they say seriously, even if it seems unimportant to you.
    o Ensure student representatives are actually representative of your community – not all high achievers or with parents on the PTA. Class teachers can help with this.
    o Meet regularly – once a half-term is usually a good balance between being effective and achievable.
    o Celebrate successes – make sure everyone knows the impact that their voice has had.

*name changed

Pupil Voice at Howden Junior School

By Natalie Starkey (Pupil Voice Champion) and Lee Hill (Headteacher) at Howden Junior School, Howden, East Yorkshire, UK

At Howden Junior School, in an effort to increase pupil engagement and motivation (Rudduck and Flutter, 2000; Biddulph, 2011), we have reviewed and overhauled how we approach pupil voice. Pupil voice, whereby pupils have a 'voice' in decision-making that results in the students having meaningful learning experiences (Mitra, 2003), involves students discussing matters with teachers, and their peers, related to the operational running of the school. We recognised, however, that the school needed to make more effort to ensure that the student participation was genuine and not tokenistic (Lundy, 2007). As busy teachers and leaders, we wanted to make sure that this was not solely a 'box ticking exercise' so we spent time in the implementation phase to ensure the conditions were right so that all students speak up or had their say through other methods – subsequently contributing to decision-making, which is tangible and impacts positively on the whole school.

This is achieved in many ways:

- A Communications Team who works to set up class meetings, deliver messages, plan assemblies and participate in Action Team meetings.
- Actions Teams (small groups set up by children with a certain topic or action in mind). For example, Jubilee Action Team, Eco Action Team and Girls in Sports Action Team. These teams are generated and run by the pupils under the supervision and guidance of a staff member, where needed.
- We link it all to our House Leaders who work with the Communication Team on whole school events, such as Red Nose Day, Children in Need and MFL Celebration Days. To further enhance pupil voice in school, our House Leaders apply and are chosen by existing leaders rather than staff.
- Each class completes a Class Meeting weekly. These can be debate topics which support speaking and listening, or action points to be decided by pupils linked to an ongoing Action Team or questions from teachers linked to their subjects. Curriculum Champions (Subject Leaders) can send our Pupil Voice Champion (Miss Starkey) survey questions or action points to out to all the children in these class meetings.
- A whole school display board shows progress made by Action Teams on their projects and achievements in school.
- Pupils' research, presented on and voted for our new House names, linked values and how we weave these into our curriculum.

Through these opportunities for pupils to have meaningful engagement, they help to establish the school direction, vision and values by sharing their knowledge and perspectives on a range of topics (Levin, 2000; Rudduck and McIntyre, 2007). The increased level of pupil engagement is amplified by recognising and valuing students'

(Continued)

'interests', where they are able to bring their culture and experiences into the discussions, whole school initiatives and, where possible, their learning (Bishop and Berryman, 2006). Therefore, through increasing opportunities for pupils to have a 'voice' in the school, we are encouraging them to see their education as a joint effort – whereby everybody is on the 'same page' working in the same direction aligned by the clear whole school vision and values (Flutter and Rudduck, 2004; Biddulph, 2011). This can be highly empowering and motivating for students and increases self-efficacy as they see their teachers in a new light; as a supporter, not an enforcer of prescriptive learning (Bevan-Brown et al., 2011).

Not only does student voice have the capacity to shape decisions that are made in schools, but it is also directly linked to self- efficacy and students' sense of place in the local community. Self-efficacy is a student's belief in their own ability to succeed in a particular situation (Bishop and Berryman, 2006; Beaudoin, 2013), as well as recognised as key to student empowerment, motivation and engagement to learn (Bishop and Berryman, 2006). Therefore, by ensuring the conditions were right for student voice and by giving our pupils increased opportunities to be part of and lead Action Teams, we are engineering opportunities for them to identify their place in the school community, model this and articulate their perspective to other students and influence whole school practice (Hart, 2002; Absolum et al., 2009; Biddulph, 2011). Self-efficacy is the foundation of student empowerment, motivation and engagement to learn.

Our next step is to develop a Pupil Mentor Scheme, whereby successful applicants and pupils who show an outstanding attitude/passion for a certain subject work with Subject Champions (Subject Leaders) to shape the direction of teaching and learning and curriculum development. As research shows that to take student voice a step further, it is a process where students take more control of the curriculum and share their ideas and thoughts around curriculum delivery (Absolum et al., 2009; Robinson et al., 2009; Biddulph, 2011).

Summary

Fundamental British Values are requiring you as the trainee teacher or ECT to reflect on your philosophy of what you believe in, in terms of pedagogy and practice. It asks you to think of how you can operate your school, with its ethos, procedures and policies. It asks of how much freedom and respect for others children are able to have so they can enjoy this liberty. British Values are designed for children to prepare for life in modern Britain. Being able to express individual liberty whilst not encroaching on the rights of others, in terms of unfairness or oppression or violation of the law or freedom to express beliefs, is what it is designed for. Therefore, this ultimately is about safeguarding; children are being taught to recognise that any infringement of their rights or the rights of others is not acceptable. British Values are a constant in your classroom; it is not restricted to one-off events or displays, neither is it confined to certain subjects. It is wider than that, and the children deserve it to be.

References

Absolum, M., Flockton, L., Hattie, J., Hipkins, R., and Reid, I. (2009). *Directions for Assessment in New Zealand: Developing students' Assessment Capabilities*. Wellington: Ministry of Education.

Alderson, P. (2000). *School students views on life at school and school councils*. [Online]. Available at: https://www.researchgate.net/publication/227645003_School_students'_views_on_life_at_school_and_school_councils [Accessed May 2022].

Asante, M.K. (1991). The Afrocentric idea of education. *The Journal of Negro Education*, 60(2), pp. 170–180. doi:10.2307/2295608

Beaudoin, N. (2013). *Elevating Student Voice: How to Enhance Student Participation, Citizenship and Leadership*. Abingdon: Routledge.

Benson, T. (2019). *Harvard EdCast: Unconscious Bias in School*. Available at: https://www.gse.harvard.edu/news/19/11/harvard-edcast-unconscious-bias-schools [Accessed 10 April 2022].

Bevan-Brown, J., Mc Gee, A., Ward, A., and MacIntyre, L. (2011). Personalising learning: A passing fad or a cornerstone of education. *New Zealand Journal of Educational Studies*, 46(2), pp. 75–88.

Biddulph, M. (2011). Articulating student voice and facilitating curriculum agency. *The Curriculum Journal*, 22(3), pp. 381–399.

Bishop, R., and Berryman, M. (2006). *Culture Speaks: Cultural Relationships and Classroom Learning*. Wellington: Huia Publishing.

Charles, M. (2019). Effective teaching and learning: Decolonising the curriculum. *Journal of Black Studies*, 50(8), pp. 731–766.

CIRCLE (Centre for Information and Research on Civic Learning and Engagement). (2020). *Youth who learned about voting in high school more likely to become informed and engaged voters*. [Online]. Available at: https://circle.tufts.edu/latest-research/youth-who-learned-about-voting-high-school-more-likely-become-informed-and-engaged [Accessed May 2022].

Commission on Religious Education. (2018). *Religion and worldviews: The way forward* (Executive Summary). [Online]. Available at: https://www.commissiononre.org.uk/wp-content/uploads/2018/09/Final-Report-Exec-Summary-of-the-Commission-on-RE.pdf

Department for Education (DfE). (2014). *Promoting fundamental British values as part of SMSC in schools*. [Online]. Available at: https://www.gov.uk/government/publications/promoting-fundamental-british-values-through-smsc

Dewey, J. (2008). *Democracy and Education*. Radford VA: Wilder Publications Ltd.

Doharty, N. (2017). I FELT DEAD: Applying a racial microaggressions framework to Black students' experiences of Black history month and Black history. *Race Ethnicity and Education*, 22(1), pp. 110–129. doi:10.1080/13613324.2017.1417253

Elliott, C., and Quinn, F. (2017). *English Legal System*. 18th edn. Harlow: Pearson.

Flutter, J., and Rudduck, J. (2004). *Consulting Pupils: What's in It for Schools*? London: Routledge.

Gillborn, D. (2008). *Racism and Education: Coincidence or Conspiracy*? London: Routledge.

Hart, R. (2002). *Children's Participation. The Theory and Practice of Involving Young Citizens in Community Development and Environmental Care*. London: Earthscan Publication.

HM Government. (2011a). *CONTEST: The United Kingdom's strategy for countering terrorism*. [Online]. Available at: https://www.gov.uk/government/publications/counter-terrorism-strategy-contest

HM Government. (2011b). *Prevent strategy*. [Online]. Available at: https://www.gov.uk/government/publications/prevent-strategy-2011

HM Government. (2022). *Age of criminal responsibility*. [Online]. Available at: https://www.gov.uk/age-of-criminal-responsibility

Johnson, M., and Mouthaan, M. (2021). Decolonising the curriculum: The importance of teacher training and development. *Runnymede Trust*. Available at: https://www.runnymedetrust.org/blog/decolonising-the-curriculum-the-importance-of-teacher-training-and-development [Accessed 28 March 2022].

Kaye, S. (2013). *Philosophy*. London: Hodder & Stoughton Ltd.

Levin, B. (2000). Putting students at the centre in education reform. *International Journal of Educational Change*, 1(2), pp. 155–172.

Lundy, L. (2007). 'Voice' is not enough: Conceptualising Article 12 of the United Nations Convention on the Rights of the Child. *British Educational Research Journal*, 33(6), pp. 927–942.

Manent, P. (1995). *An Intellectual History of Liberalism*. Princeton, NJ: Princeton University Press.

Maylor, U., Read, B., Mendick, H., Ross, A., and Rollock, N. (2007). *Diversity and Citizenship in the Curriculum: Research Review*. The Institute for Policy Studies in Education, London Metropolitan University. Available at: https://dera.ioe.ac.uk/7782/1/RR819.pdf [Accessed 28 March 2022].

Mitra, D. (2003). Student voice in school reform: Reframing student-teacher relationships. *McGill Journal of Education*, 38(2), pp. 289-304.

Moncrieffe, M.L., Asare, Y., and Dunford, R. (2019). *Decolonising the Curriculum: What are the Challenges and the Opportunities for Teaching and Learning?*. Researchgate. Available at: doi:10.13140/RG.2.2.26574.72003 [Accessed 16 March 2022].

Morgan, R. (2018). *Foreword to the Royal Borough of Greenwich faith and belief 2019-2024 agreed syllabus for religious education*. Unpublished. Link to the Agreed Syllabus. [Online]. Available at: https://www.royalgreenwich.gov.uk/info/200285/about_our_schools/1152/teaching_religious_education_re_in_our_schools

Robinson, V., Hohepa, M., and Lloyd, C. (2009). *School Leadership and Student Outcomes: Identifying What Works and Why: Best Evidence Synthesis Iteration (BES)*. Wellington: Ministry of Education.

Rudduck, J., and Flutter, J. (2000). Pupil participation and pupil perspective: 'Carving a new order of experience'. *Cambridge Journal of Education*, 30(1), pp. 75-78.

Rudduck, J., and McIntyre, D. (2007). *Improving Learning Through Consulting Pupils*. New York, NY: Routledge.

Schiller, C. (1984). *Christian Schiller in His Own Words*. London: A & C Black Ltd. and National Association for Primary Education.

Smart, N. (1992). *The World's Religions*. Cambridge: Cambridge University Press.

Spielman, A. (2018). *The ties that bind: Amanda Spielman's speech to the Policy Exchange think tank*. [Online]. Available at: https://www.gov.uk/government/speeches/amanda-spielmans-speech-to-the-policy-exchange-think-tank

UNICEF. (2017). A *summary of the UN convention on the rights of the child*. [Online]. Available at: https://www.unicef.org.uk/rights-respecting-schools/wp-content/uploads/sites/4/2017/01/Summary-of-the-UNCRC.pdf [Accessed May 2022].

Varley, C. (2022). *Ellie Simmonds: A world without dwarfism? – Documentary explores views on new drug*. [Online]. Available at: https://www.bbc.co.uk/sport/swimming/60934176

11 The wider curriculum

KEY WORDS

Wider curriculum, cross-curricular, humanities, foundation subjects, PSHE, D&T, Music, R.E., PE, Art, Modern Foreign Languages, Bruner, Bloom's taxonomy, Gardner

> **Contributors within this chapter:**
> 1. Leah Downie
> 2. Natasha Nechat-Murphy
> 3. Matthew Flynn
> 4. Rachel Kerridge
> 5. Allen Tsui
> 6. Ami Crowther and Polly Ward
> 7. Dan Young
> 8. Ted Samaras
> 9. Agnes Kosek
> 10. Jordan Wintle
> 11. Annelies Paris

Introduction

In this chapter, we explore the role that the wider curriculum plays in a child's primary education. Despite the dominant focus on English and mathematics in England's National Curriculum (DfE, 2014), it cannot be denied that these wider curriculum subjects all have parts to play in a child's holistic development. The wider curriculum subjects are as valid as the core ones (McDonald and Gibson, 2021), and part of the defence for making timetable time for these is the ways in which these subjects can embrace creative teaching and learning (Piasecka, 2021).

We begin by asking what the wider curriculum involves and how these subjects can offer creative opportunities for teachers and learners. We go on to find more about Gardner's Multiple Intelligences theory, Bloom's taxonomy of thinking skills and Bruner's spiral curriculum and consider the planning and teaching of wider curriculum subjects in the light of these

DOI: 10.4324/9781003218098-11

three key theories. This chapter contains a brief evaluation of each of the wider curriculum subjects, before offering a consideration of the role that teacher training programmes must play in preparing students for planning and delivering the wider curriculum, and the commitment that schools must show to teachers' continuing professional development (CPD). This chapter ends with a reminder of the key points for the reader to take away about the importance of the wider curriculum in a child's development.

Marginalisation of subjects in the curriculum

> **Critical question**
>
> What are the wider curriculum subjects, and what value can they offer?

The marginalisation of some subjects in the primary curriculum is a concern for many teachers, especially with regard to arts and humanities (Caldwell et al., 2021). With lack of focus also may come lack of funding and teacher CPD opportunities.

The very first National Curriculum (NC) in England was born in 1988 under the Education Reform Act under Conservative rule. Interesting, the curriculum had three core subjects (English, mathematics and science), six foundation subjects and a total of 14 subjects in all. We may argue that over 30 years later, as we use the most recent NC (published by the Department for Education in 2013 and rolled out into schools in 2014), that the focus on subjects has hardly changed, with the same structure of three core subjects and six foundation subjects. Of course some things within the NC have changed more readily, such as our current subject of 'Computing' which didn't exist in 1988, and also Modern Foreign Languages (MFL) which became statutory in Key Stage 2 (KS2) from 2014, but overall the core subjects still dominate the primary timetable, and namely mathematics and English which are the two currently assessed subjects in Year 6 SATS, leading to marginalisation of the other subjects.

But what can these other non-core subjects offer that English and maths may not?

Howard Gardner's Multiple Intelligences theory

Individuals can come to understand their **multiple intelligences** (MI) (Gardner, 2000).

The theory of MI was set forth in 1983 by Howard Gardner. The theory holds that all individuals have several, relatively autonomous intelligences that they deploy in varying combinations to solve problems or create products that are valued in one or more cultures. Together, the intelligences underlie the range of adult roles found across cultures. MI thus diverge from theories entailing general intelligence, or g, which hold that a single mental capacity is central to all human problem-solving and that this capacity can be ascertained through psychometric assessment (Kornhaber, 2019). Application of Gardner's theory presents significant changes in the modern-day classroom. However, these changes have been shown to increase effectiveness and understanding of various topics by students (Khamo and Johnson, 2019). The act of synthesising can draw on various **intelligences**, and combinations of **intelligences**, in various ways (Gardner, 2020).

Constructive alignment in learning outcomes

Learning institutions should provide a balance of challenge and support (Larkin and Richardson, 2013). By getting to know learners and their diverse needs, educators can best provide appropriate teaching and learning environments. Whenever we produce a lesson plan, we should see it as part of a sequence of learning, rather than a stand-alone lesson, and taking learners' prior learning into account is important too; this is why we should show the contextual information on the plan.

Biggs (1996) highlighted the use of constructivist learning theory to create 'constructive alignment'. Constructive alignment encapsulates the idea that the learner constructs their own learning through the activities they engage with (Biggs, 2003); therefore, the lecturer's role is to facilitate this learning through an appropriate environment and using strategies to encourage interactivity. Setting clear lesson outcome (LO) statements is a key part of constructive alignment (Biggs and Tang, 2015), and I have thought carefully about the verbs used in my LOs. **Bloom's Taxonomy Verbs for Critical Thinking** may be a useful resource for you to look up.

Trigwell and Prosser (2014) agree that constructive alignment can be a powerful tool but highlight that a teacher's awareness of their own pedagogical style and approach can affect the way that learning occurs. As teachers, we should continue checking that lessons work as a sequence and that these have measurable outcomes. One of our key priorities should be making learning visible for the learners and ensuring that the outcomes are measurable using verbs from Bloom's taxonomy.

Creativity and possibility thinking in the wider curriculum

At its most fundamental, it involves posing, in many different ways, the question, 'What if?', and therefore involves the shift from 'What is this and what does it do?' to 'What can I do with this?' (Craft, 2010).

Without SATS or formal assessment administered in many of the wider curriculum subjects, there is scope for teachers to use creativity in these subjects that may not always be possibly in the daily rigidity of England and maths teaching, for example.

The following ten contributions will encourage us to consider how we can deliver these wider subjects in a way that is meaningful and relevant to learners, developing skills that may be useful in their futures, as well as offering a more holistic approach to education.

A Basic Toolkit for Teaching Foundation Subjects and the Wider Curriculum

By Leah Downie, Primary School Teacher, Cardiff, Wales

I taught English in primary schools in France in 2000. The emphasis back then was teaching orally through games, songs, etc., and making it fun for the children. I'm not sure what they recommend now, but I use the same idea of focusing on oracy but teach the children Italian/French/Welsh. For me the emphasis should be on oracy and

(Continued)

repetition so that the children have plenty of practice of new language sentences, etc., and are developing their confidence.

Here are some games I use which are successful and you can use for any language:

'Walk and talk': I have an assortment of hats and wigs which I put on the table. I shake a tambourine, and the children choose a hat or wig. They walk around, and when I tell them to stop, they converse with the person nearest to them in the foreign language. They then choose a new hat/wig and walk/jump/dance again around the classroom, and when I ask them to stop, they converse with another person and so on. This is repeated many times so that they have ample opportunity to practise the language they are learning.

'Budge': This is a game whereby they stand in two rows so that they are opposite a partner. They converse with the person opposite until the two at the top end have finished. In which case they shout 'budge' and the person at the top (on one side only) goes down the middle, whilst the others make an arch with their arms for the child to go under. Whilst they are going through, we shout 'allez Bobby' in a chant. When they are through the arch and at the bottom, that child shouts 'budge!' (or an equivalent word in the chosen language) and the children on just one side budge up so that each has a new partner. This exercise repeats until all the children on the one side have had their turn going through the arch and are back with their original partner.

Zap: All children stand up in this game. They practise something they have learned, e.g. Comment ca va, which we chant together as a class. The teacher then chooses someone to answer. I might give them one or two zaps, and they 'zap' someone out of the game. This continues until there are only a few left.

Balloon game: This is fun for learning colours. You have lots of balloons in the air, and the children have to keep tapping them to keep them in the air, but they tap it whilst remembering the colour in that language, e.g. they will only tap a red balloon by shouting 'rouge' at the same time.

Around the world: The children are seated, and one person stands behind another person's chair. They answer a question in the language they are learning, and whoever gets it right moves on to the next person. If the person standing gets the answer wrong, they swap places with the person sitting down who they are against. The winner is the last person standing at the end.

Mallet's Mallet: There used to be a programme on TV hosted by Timmy Mallet when I was a child! I used this idea as a game which works well with colours or numbers. I have a giant inflatable mallet which I use. Here is a video clip which is how I present the game (like the game show): Mallett's Mallet - YouTube

Art

By Natasha Nechat-Murphy, Teaching Assistant and Primary Education student at Anglia Ruskin University, London, England

Art is an enriching experience that allows ideas from your imagination to flow and come to life! From a very young age, I have always had a huge passion for art. Producing your own art can help you create a visual representation of what is in your inner mind whilst giving you an escape from reality. Art is a form of self-expression and communication. In practice, art significantly improves concentration skills and develops critical thinking.

Art does not discriminate. It is accessible to all adults and children, regardless of their needs and ages. In the Early Years, explore different textures and use bright colours. Teach them the works of Vincent Van Gogh, by recreating 'Starry Night' as a sensory experience. Use coloured rice and pasta, and even sand to create the swirls.

For Early Years and Key Stage 1 (KS1), engage children in the vibrant world of Claude Monet and his water lily pond. You can recreate this by using watercolour paint, salt and oil pastels. Paint the background using watercolour paint first; then whilst the paint is wet, sprinkle salt onto the paper. Witness the salt submerge into the paint and leave to dry. Finally, draw on the water lilies using oil pastels. You have produced a mixed media piece!

In KS2, focus on refining technique and adopting a personal style. A particular activity I really enjoyed for this group was looking at the work of Georgia O'Keefe. Involve children in the experience by taking them on an outing to the local park and encouraging them to take their own photographs of flowers. Then use the photographs to observe and draw different shots of the flower.

To help introduce a particular artist into your art lesson, especially for Early Years and KS1, look at sources of literature. I highly recommend the collection of artist storybooks by Laurence Anholt. He has written captivating stories about Claude Monet, Vincent van Gogh, Pablo Picasso and many more. Each book is wonderful at storytelling, whilst including reproductions of the artist's work.

To teach art effectively, model art in practice. Show each detail step by step, whilst displaying care and appreciation. Show patience and a willingness to try again, even if you make a mistake. Remember in art, you can turn your mistake into a new idea that you may not have thought of before. Be willing to do your own research about the topic or artist you will be teaching. Adopt a passion for art, by visiting art galleries to gain further interest and even practise your art lesson at home to develop your artistic skills. Lastly, never be afraid to experiment! Art is in the eye of the beholder; all art is beautiful!

History

By Matthew Flynn, Matt Flynn, History Leader, Chartered Teacher of History at Ryders Hayes School, Walsall, England

I wanted to create a primary history curriculum that inspired our children, offered challenge and helped them to grow into young historians. I am passionate about getting this right as for many children, the majority of their history education is at primary school.

Relevance was key – drawing on local sources, such as museums and visitors, meant that children could make links between local, national and global history more easily and see how their own locality has made an impact or been impacted upon throughout history. In addition, I wanted to be confident that all our children could see themselves in the curriculum, but also be introduced to other ways of life. As a result, I looked to diversify what we were teaching. I wanted to see the learning journey from a child's perspective, so I asked myself 'What do children see as they move through our history curriculum?' For example, our Gypsy, Roma and Traveller children needed to see their heritage reflected in what they were learning and so, by planning opportunities for this through stories and the study of significant people, a shift in their interest in the subject became evident. Consequently, other children were also able to learn about and celebrate the rich heritage of their peers – something that they may not get an opportunity to do again.

Our curriculum is sequenced in a way to support children to build knowledge cumulatively and episodically. After training on retrieval practice, teachers regularly revisit previous content and tap into prior knowledge, which is supported using the bespoke in-house designed Knowledge Mats for each unit and subject. The introduction of 'Curriculum Working Walls' has supported our children not only to make links within and across different periods but also to make links with other subjects; for example, when studying an artist in art, teachers and children can add this to the working timeline on the working wall to see how this relates to other subjects, topics and events studied. We also created key strands to build general knowledge known as 'knowledge categories' (each with an image) as golden threads throughout the whole curriculum. These include 'location', 'food and farming', 'careers', 'settlement' and many more. They support children to make meaningful links across subjects, whilst maintaining subject integrity. For example, children might learn about 'food and farming' in different periods of history, and this will support their understanding of 'continuities and changes' over time but also make links in geography as they learn about where their food comes from, and science when learning about nutrition.

A passion for history can be felt throughout our school amongst children and teachers. It is clearly evident from the extra home learning completed that our children love history and have a growing understanding of what is meant by a historian!

A Toolkit for Teaching Primary Dance

By Rachel Kerridge at Wentworth Primary School (Academy), Kent, England

Dance is a statutory element of the physical education (PE) curriculum for KS1 and KS2 and also features in the Early Years' curriculum. However, it is not always regarded as a high priority subject and teachers can lack the knowledge, skills, experience and training to plan and deliver effective dance lessons. Since the introduction of the Sports Premium Funding, some schools have increased the dance provision in their schools by outsourcing teaching to specialists. This could have led to more primary school teachers lacking in confidence and experience. This toolkit aims to provide some handy tips to help less experienced teachers get the most out of their dance lessons.

Cross-curricular links: Dance in primary school can often be linked to other subjects within the curriculum, most notably history. The retelling of stories and events using movement can be an effective way for children to consolidate learning and also offer opportunities for deeper understanding. There are many sources of inspiration available on the internet to provide ideas for linking dance to an array of cross curricular topics (see essential websites below).

Music: Availability of music can pose a challenge for some teachers. Firstly, remember that music is not essential for every dance lesson. Music can even provide an unwelcome distraction when children are responding to a different, more specific stimulus such as a story or an illustration. When you are ready to perform to music, YouTube can be an accessible resource for music and playlists can be created in advance and saved prior to the lesson. Your school may be willing to open a Spotify or iTunes account to support dance; often the music coordinator can help with this.

Be Positive! The children in your class will not be expecting you to perform like a west end professional! Just like in other areas of the curriculum, your most important role is to create a safe, happy, learning environment where children feel able to explore, discover and express themselves. A teacher with a positive, can-do attitude will be beneficial to all of the children whether reluctant dancers or highly skilled performers. Lead by example, but know that it is perfectly acceptable to use high-quality video clips or confident and more able children to model and demonstrate specific movements or patterns of movement.

Essential websites

www.afpe.org.uk
www.onedanceuk.org
www.ukcoaching.org
www.Artscouncil.org.uk
www.TES.com
www.imoves.com

Introduction to Primary Computing

By Allen Tsui, Subject Lead for Computing at Willow Brook Primary School Academy, London, England

Amidst the perennial controversies over public examination results for schools in England, one of the headlines that the mainstream media appeared to miss in 2022 was the rise not only in the number of students recruited to computer science-based degree programmes but also apparently computer science emerging as one of the fastest growing school subjects (source: BCS, Chartered Institute for IT https://www.bcs.org/articles-opinion-and-research/record-numbers-of-students-choose-computer-science-a-level-in-2022/ last accessed 23 August 2022). For a subject that was as the Royal Society described given a 'reboot' in 2014 and was only introduced to schools in the 1980s, its rise amongst more traditional subjects might be considered extraordinary.

But what of its pedagogical origins and how can primary school teachers secure its success in their settings? The Department of Education for schools in England placed an £84 million over three-year value on the subject in 2018, funding the formation of the National Centre for Computing Education (NCCE) from a consortium of the National STEM Learning Centre, Raspberry Pi Foundation and BCS, the Chartered Institute for IT. The global public health crisis that emerged in 2020 meant that the funding to support the development of subject knowledge for any teacher interested in teaching Computing or computer science was extended to Summer 2022. Participants could at their own pace work towards a Certificate in Teaching Primary Computing, Secondary Computing or the GCSE-focused Computer Science Accelerator Award. According to the NCCE by July 2022, approximately 11,000 had either registered for, begun or completed the Teaching Primary Computing Certificate.

Supported by the BCS, the Computing at School 'Community of Practice' exists, according to one of its founding members, Simon Humphreys, 'to establish computer science as a foundational subject that every child should have the opportunity to learn, from primary school onwards, just like mathematics or natural science' (source: https://royalsociety.org/blog/2021/01/computing-at-school/ last accessed, 23 August 2022).

By being part of the Computing at School Community of Practice has enabled me personally to formulate and fine-tune my ideas on what I should be teaching and how I teach it. Computing can essentially be organised into these five strands, or blocks as illustrated in this pastiche of the block style computer programming that the Massachusetts Institute of Technology has made globally ubiquitous since 2007:

Despite the policymakers' rhetoric about the NC for schools in England not being prescriptive and 'free' schools or schools with Academy (independent of local authority control) status being able to 'design' their own curriculum, based on my decade plus of experience working in a range of schools across the primary setting spectrum,

(Continued)

the centrally produced guidance continues to be broadly followed. Using the NC as the starting point, the NCCE and Computing at school have previously published a competency-based framework to break down the NC statements into learner end points. This is where Computing slightly deviates from other subjects. Learner end points replace 'age related expectations' because technology has enabled children as young as Reception to be able to learn about Computational Thinking and become digitally literate to a standard that was or is according to the NC expected by the end of KS1. This is made more possible especially if rather than dwelling on the technical aspects of Computing, teaching the subject focuses on the qualities of computer scientists adapted from the 'Engineering Habits of Mind' developed by the Centre for Real World Learning at University of Winchester and the Royal Academy of Engineering (2014).

Children as the Drivers of Change: Supporting them through Sustainable Education

By Ami Crowther, Researcher at Anglia Ruskin University, and Polly Ward, Teacher, Manchester, England

The importance of adopting sustainable practices is being increasingly emphasised in both policy and everyday discourse. The United Nations has recognised children as 'drivers of change for a sustainable future' (UNESCO, 2018). The role of children in supporting the adoption of sustainable practices has been highlighted through research conducted by Hosany et al. (2022), where they found that children influence household sustainability practices by 'transmitting acquired values, beliefs, norms, knowledge and skills back to their families'. The translation of sustainability messages by children to their families highlights the value in providing sustainability education and supporting sustainable practices within schools.

The UK Government recognises the importance of sustainability education in their 'Sustainability and Climate Change' education strategy (UK Government, 2022), which aims to prepare all young people for a world impacted by climate change through learning and practical experience. Schools and teachers play an important role in educating students and providing them with the practical skills required to communicate sustainable ideas and undertake sustainable practices, both in the classroom and perhaps more importantly at home.

Educating students about *why* sustainable practices are important and the potential impact of not adopting sustainable practices can support behaviour shifts. It also provides arguments which can be used to encourage the adoption of more sustainable behaviours at home. Using recycling as an example, educating children about the process of waste collection and the realities of landfill demonstrates why it is important to recycle. For older children, waste practices can be

(Continued)

linked to the larger scale issue of climate change, whilst for younger children the focus can remain on their household practices.

To enable children to become the 'drivers of sustainable futures', sustainability education needs to extend beyond *why* certain behaviour changes are important to present *how* behaviours can be changed and what can be done. Demonstrating the *how* of sustainable behaviour helps makes sustainability more relatable to the lives of children. Schools provide a space to learn and practise sustainable behaviours, and there is the need to ensure opportunities and resources are available for these behaviours to be practised. Continuing with the example of recycling, providing recycling bins in the classroom and actively encouraging their use helps ingrain this sustainable behaviour in children.

As well as educating children about *why* sustainable behaviours are important and allowing them to *practise* different sustainable behaviours at school, further actions can be undertaken to support the translation of sustainable behaviours from the classroom into the home. In the case of recycling, having the recycling bins in the classroom match the colours of the recycling wheelie bins at home will help translate the behaviour. For example, in Greater Manchester the blue wheelie bins are for paper and brown wheelie bins are for plastic/glass/tin, so classrooms could have blue bins for paper and brown for plastic.

For children to become the drivers of change for a sustainable future, they need to be provided with information and resources related to sustainable behaviours, with schools and teachers playing a critical role in this.

Physical Education: Supporting Non-Specialist Teachers in PE

By Dan Young, i-PEP Curriculum and coaching manager at Complete Education Solutions, Cheshire, England

I always like to view PE as two separate entities. The 'Physical' introduces pupils to a range of movements and skills which are transferrable across life – not just sports. The 'Education' aspect of the subject provides pupils with the knowledge and understanding of their bodies, fitness and the benefits of physical activity. For me, personally, it is the education side that is crucial for pupils. Ultimately, we want our pupils to be fit and healthy – alongside living fulfilling lifestyles. You need to remember that we are not producing super athletes!

It is the enthusiasm and passion for the subject that makes you an excellent PE practitioner. You can spend hours and hours researching perfect technique and planning detailed lessons to find out that your sports hall has been commandeered for exams or the weather has dictated an indoors lesson.

Firstly, TAKE RISKS! Don't be afraid of something not working. Everyone at some stage – sports professionals, tech leaders and politicians – they've all had an idea and

(Continued)

just ran with it. If it works, fantastic, you've a foundation to build on, confidence will be boosted and you've got your pupils eating out the palm of your hand. If it doesn't work, 'it is what it is' – you've tried something different and know that it doesn't work for next time; it hasn't had catastrophic effects!

Secondly, LESS CAN BE MORE! Don't feel like you have to reinvent the wheel – granted do some research (TES, NGB's and YouTube as a solid starting point) and find new and exciting ways of delivering PE (Twitter can be amazing for this!). Decide on your skill(s) that you're delivering that lesson, and think of as many fun and engaging games/activities to develop this. Linking to this, I always used to laugh and joke that my teaching file would just be a collage of post-it notes – there is nothing wrong with having notes to support your lesson. My background is football; put a football in front of me and I'm in my element; when it came to athletics (especially throwing techniques) or dance (again two left feet), I'd always come home from teaching with a wad of post-it notes overflowing out of every pocket. It was like a crutch when I was teaching something unfamiliar, and then overtime, the post-it notes reduced and my confidence grew.

Next, STAFF SUPPORT! I've genuinely lost count of how many times I've asked for reassurance or shared ideas; we're all in this together! Again, going back to my PGCE studies, it was a very quiet day if someone's USB stick wasn't being shared for a range of ideas or sample lesson plans. Use your colleagues; they're called colleagues for a reason! Whether you want an informal observation (I used to love these – just popping your head into a lesson to see how a particular skill was delivered) or just to discuss and collaborate different ways of teaching a specific skill.

Personal Growth through Technology Education

By Ted Samaras, Instructional Technology Coach at Franklin Township Public Schools, Somerset, New Jersey, America

Students and staff members need to feel valued and heard. Listening and internalising what people are saying and what they need is truly at the heart of learning and teaching and allows for relationships to develop and trust to grow. In my experience as an instructional technology coach, this could not be truer.

It is the coach part of my job that is the most crucial; the technology is just the gateway to connect. Sometimes, when teachers hear the word 'technology', they become intimidated or not sure how to incorporate it in a valuable way. They are afraid of it becoming one more thing in their already hectic day.

When using technology in the classroom, teachers are really problem-solving with their students. They are trying to enhance their experience and make it more efficient and effective. In the short term, this is true and to save time and learn a quick skill is wonderful. However, the longer view of technology education is more about sparking

(Continued)

curiosity for students and igniting their willingness to problem solve through productive struggle. (I have found that this same spark and excitement happens for teachers that I work with as well!) Students will be working in jobs and creating technologies that do not yet exist. In fact, many of us already work in positions in education that did not exist a generation ago. Learning about technology in schools at any age is about learning to set goals, creating different pathways to reach or exceed these goals and building an environment of confidence to take educational risk.

Once teachers believe that learning about technology is not the sterile and neat environment of pressing buttons and using machines but rather the creative and messy world of problem-solving and risk-taking, learning and engagement for students and teachers can truly begin collaboratively and effectively!

What are the Benefits of Philosophical Talk in Primary Classrooms?

By Agnes Kosek, Lecturer for BA Hons Child and Educational Psychology, Maidstone, England

There are various benefits of fostering philosophical enquiry in primary classrooms. According to Matthews and Sheffer (2021) and Burgh (2018), philosophical talk is often deeply engaging, open ended and child led and offers various possibilities to stimulate children's enquiring minds. The use of a given stimulus such as a video, newspaper or picture story as a part of philosophical inquiry might trigger various questions and extend children's knowledge of curricular concepts, not only developing their higher order thinking skills but also promoting individual meaning-making and independence of thought. Sprod (2020) and Lipman (2010), for example, state that such appropriately facilitated philosophical discussions provide children with opportunities to ponder life's big questions regarding morality, fairness and social justice, enabling them to reason, exchange viewpoints, express themselves and think creatively beyond the given. Philosophical discussions, therefore, not only are vital for children to grow into curious and independent lifelong learners, but are also important components to a child-centred, democratic education.

However, due to the test-focused, overloaded primary curriculum there is limited time for children to engage in philosophical thinking. Mercer (2021) and Alexander (2020) point out that the majority of lessons in primary classrooms focus on closed-ended questions and 'right-or-wrong' answers. This is not only thought to prevent many children from engaging with the curricular content and thinking for themselves, but also encourages dependence on the information provided by 'the more knowledgeable other' (Vygotsky, 1962) that cannot be justified by their own reason. It is crucial, therefore, that in the age of fake news and misinformation, policymakers and primary school educators bring philosophy back into the classroom and make it a central aspect underpinning all curricular subjects.

Physical Activity Promotion in the Primary School

By Jordan Wintle, Senior Lecturer in Sport and Exercise at University of Gloucestershire, Gloucester, England

Our health is often referred to as our greatest gift, with physical activity (PA) being lauded as a 'magic pill' for the prevention and cure of many ailments including cancer, diabetes and a host of cardiovascular diseases (Arem et al., 2015; Ekelund et al., 2020). The latest figures from Sport England (2021) and the National Health Service (2020) demonstrate a worrying decline in PA in youth populations and an increase in those classified as overweight or obese. On a more positive note, those who do engage in PA not only benefit from improved physical health but make notable improvements in mental and social well-being as well as academic attainment (Bailey et al., 2013; Biddle and Vergeer, 2020).

Recent work has advocated a whole-school approach to the promotion of PA through the Active School Framework (ASF) (Daly-Smith et al., 2020). The ASF has been developed by researchers and practitioners to sustainably embed PA throughout the school so that everyone understands its benefits and can easily implement it in their practice.

In this section, we pay particular attention to highlighting the opportunities within the primary school setting to integrate PA in many areas of school life. The opportunities are determined by what the school can closely control (from the centre to the left) and opportunities that the school can only influence (to the right of the centre). What is clear is that the culture and ethos created around PA are pivotal in maximising the opportunities presented; this includes school policy, teacher attitudes and the physical environment.

Curricular lessons (non-PE)

Integrating PA into curricular lessons other than PE is a great opportunity to increase the amount of movement integrated into the school today. Examples could include active maths and English programmes (Youth Sport Trust, 2022) that help to teach concepts from these subjects in active ways through a range of problem-solving tasks. You could also consider aspects of science and geography that could make use of the school site to teach concepts linked to nature or map reading.

Physical education

Ensure your school is meeting the recommendation for PE lessons to be delivered at least twice weekly and perhaps, most importantly, the lessons should rarely be cancelled (this sends a message to pupils that it is of lower importance). PE lessons should be age appropriate and adapted to meet the needs of all pupils with a focus on mastery and enjoyment. PE in the primary school should set the foundation to access a broad range of activities by enhancing pupils' competence, confidence, motivation, knowledge and understanding of PA.

(Continued)

Active travel

Making walking, cycling or scooting to school more accessible is a really helpful way to increase PA for many pupils. Schools should ensure they provide suitable storage for bikes/scooters and should engage in programmes such as Bikeability to develop pupils' confidence and competence to cycle safely. Increasing walking to school could be supported by creating a 'walking bus' for pupils and carers.

Family and community

Schools should provide opportunities and guidance for families and communities to continue PA participation at home and in the local area. This could be increased knowledge of where and how to be physically active (e.g. venues and clubs), setting active homework and/or creating displays of pupils and staff engaging in PA outside the school to create that culture of PA we want to see.

PA has the potential to have a significant positive impact on the entire school community (and not just the pupils). If you haven't done so already, I would recommend adding this to the agenda of your next staff meeting.

Modern Foreign Languages

By Annelies Paris, Primary Teacher and YouTube Content Creator as 'Petite Primary', Dorset, England

Imagine being put into a work environment that you have no experience in. Maybe you do a degree in English and get placed into a hospital? Or maybe your degree is in philosophy and you get put in the police force? Now, consider being faced with the sole responsibility of teaching a foreign language to 30 pupils.

For some of you, you may only speak English; for some you may have hated this subject in school; and for others, not had exposure to any of the ones taught in England (commonly French or Spanish) but already speak different languages. Indeed, it's a subject that people either love or hate. Teachers either approach it enthusiastically or try to put it in their PPA slot so somebody else teaches it. Attitudes in schools to Modern Foreign Languages vary too: from employing external agencies to cover these lessons, or being very proud about their provision from native speakers. Nevertheless, as trainees (particularly in primary) or early career teachers, you should be prepared to enter either of these schools and be prepared to deliver the best lessons possible, with the same expectations as any other foundation subject.

Make lessons fun! Don't be scared to get a Year 6 up and dancing or singing 'Heads, Shoulders, Knees and Toes' to a silly video. If they like Disney, watch a clip in French and see what words they can identify as similar or allow them to guess the context based on a few words you have pre-taught them. For little ones, movement and repetition is

(Continued)

key. Big facial expressions and use of body language, for example, when learning emotions and dual coding for any vocabulary or phrases, are crucial to them recalling it later on.

The next tip I would give is about ensuring they know the importance of this information in order to promote enthusiasm and an intrinsic motivation to learn. With English being so well known worldwide, it can be easy for students to feel demotivated to pursue a language. However, with events such as Brexit, learning languages is becoming ever more useful. I pitch languages as a way to open up new doors and to learn what life is like for other people. As a result, I introduce to them traditions and get them hooked on making comparisons, and the amount of 'woah' or 'no way' that you hear is surprisingly very rewarding. It's easy to feel like we're in a bubble and that everyone lives the same way, but as we know this isn't true, it also opens up a whole new world of literature and understanding of historical events and media.

I will leave you with the quote from Haruki Murakami who said that 'Learning another language is like becoming another person'. Set your fears aside, immerse yourself into a new culture and world and cast those worries away so that you can enjoy learning and teaching alongside your pupils.

Summary

- Children learn in different ways and in different environments.
- Offering a creative wider curriculum can help to nurture a range of strengths and skills.
- Making learning outcomes measurable helps learners to engage with tasks and be able to measure their progress independently.

References

Alexander, R. (2020). *A Dialogic Teaching Companion*. London: Routledge.

Arem, H., Moore, S.C., Patel, A., Hartge, P., De Gonzalez, A.B., Visvanathan, K., Campbell, P.T., Freedman, M., Weiderpass, E., Adami, H.O. and Linet, M.S. (2015). Leisure time physical activity and mortality: A detailed pooled analysis of the dose-response relationship. *JAMA Internal Medicine*, 175(6), pp. 959–967. doi:10.1001/jamainternmed.2015.0533

Bailey, R., Hillman, C., Arent, S. and Petitpas, A. (2013) Physical activity: An underestimated investment in human capital?. *Journal of Physical Activity & Health*, 10(3), pp. 289–308.

Biddle, S., and Vergeer, I. (2020). 'Mental health benefits of physical activity for young people'. In T.A. Brusseau, S.J. Fairclough, and D.R. Lubans (Eds.), *The Routledge Handbook of Youth Physical Activity* (pp. 121–147). New York, NY: Routledge.

Biggs, J. (1996). Enhancing teaching through constructive alignment. *Higher Education*, 32(3), pp. 347–364. Available at: https://link.springer.com/article/10.1007/bf00138871 [Accessed 30 October 2021].

Biggs, J. (2003). Aligning teaching for constructing learning. *Higher Education Academy*, 1(4). Available at https://www.cardiff.ac.uk/__data/assets/pdf_file/0020/584030/Aligning-teaching-for-constructing-learning-John-Biggs-HEA.pdf [Accessed 20 October 2021].

Biggs, J., and Tang, C. (2015). 'Constructive alignment: An outcomes-based approach to teaching anatomy'. In *Teaching Anatomy* (pp. 31–38). Cham: Springer. Available at: https://link.springer.com/chapter/10.1007/978-3-319-08930-0_4 [Accessed 1 November 2021].

Burgh, G. (2018). The need for philosophy in promoting democracy: A case for philosophy in the curriculum. *Journal of Philosophy in Schools*, 5(1), pp. 38-58.

Caldwell, H., Whewell, E., Bracey, P., Heaton, R., Crawford, H., and Shelley, C. (2021). Teaching on insecure foundations? Pre-service teachers in England's perceptions of the wider curriculum subjects in primary schools. *Cambridge Journal of Education*, 51(2), pp. 231-246. Available at: https://www.tandfonline.com/doi/full/10.1080/0305764X.2020.1819202

Craft, A. (2010). 'Possibility thinking and wise creativity: Educational futures in England?'. In R.A. Beghetto and J.C. Kaufman (Eds.), *Nurturing Creativity in the Classroom* (pp. 289-312). Cambridge, MA: Cambridge University Press.

Daly-Smith, A., Quarmby, T., Archbold, V.S., Corrigan, N., Wilson, D., Resaland, G.K., Bartholomew, J.B., Singh, A., Tjomsland, H.E., Sherar, L.B. and Chalkley, A., (2020). Using a multi-stakeholder experience-based design process to co-develop the creating active schools framework." *International Journal of Behavioral Nutrition and Physical Activity*, 17(1), p. 13. doi:10.1186/s12966-020-0917-z

DfE, (2014). National curriculum in England: framework for key stages 1 to 4 - GOV.UK. [online] Gov.uk. Available at https://www.gov.uk/government/collections/national-curriculum

Ekelund, U., Ekelund, U., Dalene, K.E., Tarp, J. and Lee, I. (2020) Physical activity and mortality: What is the dose response and how big is the effect?. *British Journal of Sports Medicine*, 54(19), pp. 1125-1126. doi:10.1136/bjsports-2019-101765

Gardner, H. (2020). *A Synthesizing Mind: A Memoir from the Creator of Multiple Intelligences Theory*. Cambridge, MA: MIT Press.

Gardner, H.E. (2000). *Intelligence Reframed: Multiple Intelligences for the 21st Century*. London: Hachette.

Hosany, A.R.S., Hosany, S., and He, H. (2022). Children sustainable behaviour: A review and research agenda. *Journal of Business Research*, 147, pp. 236-257. doi:10.1016/j.jbusres.2022.04.008

Khamo, A., and Johnson, A. (2019). 'Literature review of multiple intelligences'. In *Global Learn* (pp. 195-200). Association for the Advancement of Computing in Education (AACE). Available at: https://www.learntechlib.org/p/210413/

Kornhaber, M.L. (2019). 'The theory of multiple intelligences'. In *The Cambridge Handbook of Intelligence* (pp. 659-678). Cambridge University Press. Available at: https://pennstate.pure.elsevier.com/en/publications/the-theory-of-multiple-intelligences

Larkin, H., and Richardson, B. (2013). Creating high challenge/high support academic environments through constructive alignment: Student outcomes. *Teaching in Higher Education*, 18(2), pp. 192-204. Available at: https://www.tandfonline.com/doi/abs/10.1080/13562517.2012.696541 [Accessed 20 October 2021].

Lipman, M. (2010). *Philosophy goes to School*. Philadelphia: Temple University Press.

Matthews, G.B., and Sheffer, S. (2021). *Children as Philosophers*. London: Routledge.

McDonald, R., and Gibson, P. eds. (2021). *Inspiring Primary Learners: Insights and Inspiration Across the Curriculum*. London: Routledge.

Mercer, N. (2021). *It's only words: Why classroom talk is important*. Available at: https://www.tc.columbia.edu/media/centers/lansi/LANSI-talk-NMercer.pdf [Accessed 28 May 2022].

National Health Service. (2020). *National Child Measurement Programme, England 2019/20 School Year*. Available at: https://digital.nhs.uk/data-and-information/publications/statistical/national-child-measurement-programme/2019-20-school-year

Piasecka, M. (2021). 'Creativity, live art and the primary school curriculum'. In D. Watt and D. Meyer-Dinkgrafe (Eds.), *Theatres of Thought: Theatre, Performance and Philosophy* (p. 140) Newcastle: Cambridge Scholars Publishing.

Sport England. (2021). *Active lives children and young people survey academic year 2019/20*. Available at: https://sportengland-production-files.s3.eu-west-2.amazonaws.com/s3fs-public/2021-01/Active%20Lives%20Children%20Survey%20Academic%20Year%2019-20%20report.pdf?4Ti_OVOm9sYy5HwQjSiJN7Xj.VInpjV6

Sprod, T. (2020). Philosophy in classrooms and beyond: New approaches to picture-book philosophy, by Thomas E Wartenberg. *Journal of Philosophy in Schools*, 7(2), pp. 106-110.

Trigwell, K., and Prosser, M. (2014). Qualitative variation in constructive alignment in curriculum design. *Higher Education*, 67(2), pp. 141-154. Available at: https://link.springer.com/article/10.1007/s10734-013-9701-1%23page-1 [Accessed 10 October 2021].

UK Government. (2022). *Sustainability and Climate Change: A Strategy for the Education and Children's Services Systems*. London: Department for Education.
UNESCO. (2018). *Global action programme on education for sustainable development* (2015-2019). Available at: https://en.unesco.org/gap/priority-action-areas
Vygotsky, L. (1962). *Thought and Language*. Cambridge, MA: MIT Press.
Youth Sport Trust. (2022) *Teach active*. Available at: https://www.youthsporttrust.org/resources/physical-and-mental-health/teach-active [Accessed 17 June 2022].

12 Career progression and further study

KEY WORDS

Passion, career, progression, study, further study, development, motivation, train, professional

---

Contributors in this chapter:

1. Matthew Tragheim
2. Becky Ellery
3. Lynsey Hunter
4. Andrew Jack
5. Harry Garland
6. Sam Crome
7. Daniel Davies
8. Chris Ball
9. Emma Longley
10. Mary Leighton
11. Ashley Brett
12. Seraphina Simmons-Bah
13. Stella De Larrabeiti
14. Belinda Benatar-Kotler

Introduction

Critical question

Where do I want to be, what do I want to do and how might I get there?

This chapter discusses different career pathways within primary education, including lecturing, to help guide the necessary professional development that can help reach those goals. This chapter also explores further study, such as Masters' level study, or doctoral work, and explains what these look like in the world of education. Considerations of further study and

DOI: 10.4324/9781003218098-12

professional development/training are interspersed with those for career progression. A common theme underlying the contributions from professional colleagues is the passion, dedication and motivation that they bring to education.

This chapter begins with the theme of motivation and passion, which is encapsulated within Matthew Tragheim's thought piece and Becky Ellery's reflection of her development as a maths lead and a student mentor for her school. Lynsey Hunter then reminds us about the importance of investing within yourself as an early career teacher (ECT), whilst Andrew Jack provides a thought piece around considerations of continuing professional development. The theme of lifelong learning as professional development through education and qualities of leadership are then explored. This starts with Harry Garland's contribution of being a leader as an ECT and consideration of leadership qualities which may be galvanised from the start of entering the teaching profession. It is then considered that a key feature of developing leadership qualities is to harness a smooth transition from initial teacher training to entering the professional world, underpinned by career aspirations and opportunities for professional development. This educational transition is considered through reflection on current, government policy and how initial teacher training, ECT training and later professional development are connected through the idea of learning communities.

Before consideration of making formal career decisions or undertaking further study, we are encouraged to explore the value of coaching by Sam Crome. The chapter then presents some ideas around further study options which are (a) the National Professional Qualifications (NPQs) (DfE, 2022c) and a reflection of becoming senior leaders provided by Daniel Davies and Chris Ball, assistant headteacher and headteacher, respectively and (b) Postgraduate Diplomas and Certificates (which includes a description of the PGCert for Special Educational Needs Coordinators (SENCos) by Emma Longley) and Masters (which includes a thoughtful reflection by Harry Garland about why he is venturing off and starting his Masters). These further study options are followed by a reflection of becoming an educational psychologist by Mary Leighton who took up this position following Masters' level study. Opportunities for doctoral studies are then explored with a contribution from Ashley Brett, tracking his journey from being an education consultant to deputy head to senior lecturer. This is followed by discussion of becoming a university lecturer, which has a think piece by Seraphina Simmons-Bah about what inspired her to enter this profession, and two reflective pieces about being mentors, supporting those training to become teachers, by Stella De Larrabeiti and Belinda Benatar-Kotler.

Motivation and passion to do something about career progression and further study

Critical question

How may I get motivated for career progression or further study? Does it matter if things seem unclear and I do not know where I am headed in my career pathway?

170 *Career progression and further study*

This chapter's themes of career progression and further study may be considered as being intrinsically healthy if we were to link it with elements of intrinsic motivation and Maslow's hierarchy of needs (1943, 1954), honing in on self-actualisation and 'to become everything that one is capable of becoming' (Maslow, 1943, p. 383). Whilst, Maslow's theory has been critiqued for its methodology, Tay and Diener's (2011) research supports the notion of a worldwide universal concept of needs. It is important to recognise that even Maslow (1987) came to conclude that levels of the hierarchy of need were not dependent upon satisfying other levels of need. Indeed, there is recognition that needs are dependent upon individuality and circumstances. It is also important to acknowledge that self-actualisation is not an end point, but a continual process in which an individual aspires to achieve higher levels encompassing dimensions of well-being, creativity and fulfilment – a feeling of wanting to develop as an individual (Maslow, 1943). These dimensions could echo some of the characteristics that might underpin an individual's pursuit for further study, professional development or career development.

The theme of motivation is also taken up by Kowalczuk-Walędziak et al. (2017), whose research focuses on doctoral studies. The researchers suggest that motivating factors to pursue study are accounted by a requirement for professional development, a desire to improve their students' learning and personal fulfilment. This latter aspect complements that of Maslow's self-actualisation.

Matthew Tragheim's reflection starts us off with some pertinent and sage advice about future pathways and what they may hold; his ideas are underpinned by motivation and a passion for learning.

A Passion for Learning

By Matthew Tragheim, Lecturer in Primary Education, London, England

The famous author, Arthur C. Clarke, once wrote 'Any sufficiently advanced technology is indistinguishable from magic' (Clarke, 1968). As a fan of science fiction, and someone who has witnessed the magic first hand, I think this quote can be equally applied to outstanding pedagogies. Their wealth of knowledge, dexterity of skill and ability to intuitively understand the needs of learners are both mesmerising and magical. Whether at some level of school management, a subject leader, the school SENCo, a lecturer, a researcher or education influencer, exceptional educationalists are united by a single driving force, which is a passion for learning.

When considering your pathway through career progression, my advice would be to reflect on the aspects of education that light your passion and connect this with how you can positively impact the learning of others. Aligning your priorities with the needs of your community (children in your class, fellow practitioners, senior leaders, online social network, etc.) will ensure that you're purposefully preparing for future opportunities, however and whenever they may arrive. For some, career progression means

(Continued)

honing skills within the classroom. For example, this may be through wanting to becoming the best classroom teacher that you can be, by developing pedagogical knowledge, innovating approaches or practice, engaging every child or devising curriculum content. For others, they envisage one day lecturing future teachers and so set about building their knowledge and experience, and gradually growing their influence and extending their network. Whatever your pathway through career progression, outstanding educationalists are often specialists who have reached their current destination by using their passion to supercharge and sustain their dedication. They stand out because they have been well prepared for opportunities such as the entirely unexpected, the carefully orchestrated and the hard-won.

From my own experience, I remember having an absolute aversion towards technology and its creeping influence in education during teacher training. However, the opportunity arose to work in a very technology literature school, and, due to its unusual approach at the time, I thought it would allow me to clarify and galvanise my own criticism. Instead, my time there completely challenged my preconceptions. I have since taken opportunities to advance my learning, focusing on the impact of technology on education through an MA in education leadership. I have also published research and case studies about how technology has the potential to enhance collaboration in the classroom and school community. Although I am not always certain of where my career pathway will take me, I believe that having a passion for learning will give me the resilience to learn from my failings, explore new experiences that enrich my own education and prepare for every opportunity.

Becky Ellery considers her pathway from reticent mathematics student to passionate mathematics lead at her school and not putting a ceiling on your abilities. It is an example of professional development and being open to what life's opportunities may bring.

Maths Specialist to Maths Lead and Part-Time University Lecturer

By Becky Ellery, Mathematics Lead at Hook Lane Primary School, London, England

'Maths is one of the main reasons I hate school' – a Facebook status I made in 2011, the year of my GCSEs. Maths was never my strongest subject. It has always been something that I have had to work hard at, and it does not come naturally to me. With all that being said, I can say it is something I enjoyed during my time in school. The issues started, however, with being grouped according to ability and there being a stigma around being in the 'bottom set'. Bottom set maths, at times, could feel like you were forgotten about. We were given pages and pages of questions to answer, and everything was rote learning. If you did not understand, you were shown an example and then simply given more questions to answer – then given even more as homework.

(Continued)

When I had the opportunity to do my PGCE with Maths Specialism, I took this as my chance to ensure that those children who find maths more challenging would have a teacher who will spend time working through problems with them, have the confidence they needed to identify which elements of the learning they are struggling with and, ultimately, gain a deeper understanding of the 'why'. That PGCE year completely shaped my attitude towards the teaching and learning of maths.

After finishing my NQT year, I was fortunate enough to be given the role as maths lead across my school. I was terrified! However, the support and encouragement I received from my colleagues meant that I could put my learning into practice outside of my classroom. Since then, I have had the opportunity to work with so many experienced and knowledgeable colleagues who have helped shape the children in our school into those who look forward to learning. We have been working hard on ensuring that all of our children can confidently and independently use concrete resources to form the basis of their abstract understanding, they are able to use number facts fluently to reduce cognitive overload and they are all working towards reaching a deeper understanding of their learning.

Over the past 4 years, we have worked closely with the London South East Maths Hub on the Teaching for Mastery programme across the school, we are developing our whole-school approach to learning times tables and we have introduced the Mastering Number programme in Early Years and Key Stage 1. I have been working alongside the University of Greenwich as a mentor for Maths Specialist students, I am on the publications committee for the Mathematical Association and I am an advocate for not putting that glass ceiling on abilities. In the last academic year, I have become a mathematics lecturer for primary teacher trainees two days a week and work in my school as class teacher and maths lead the rest of the week. If I could tell a 16 year old me that this was now my career, she would laugh out loud!

Investing in yourself

The importance of continuing professional development (CPD) and lifelong learning is worthy of consideration as these can contribute to your career trajectory. Lynsey Hunter details the importance of investing in yourself as you start the pathway of being an ECT.

Being an Early Career Teacher

By Lynsey Hunter, Senior Lecturer at Sheffield Hallam University, Sheffield, England

As an ECT, you are not the completed teacher product and no one expects you to know everything. The Early Career Framework (DfE, 2019b) in England supports this view and is underpinned by an entitlement to two years of continued professional development as an ECT. This will enable you to apply what you are familiar with from your Initial Teacher Education and begin to adapt and apply it in your new context.

(Continued)

Do not see professional development as something you 'have' to do for the sake of it or as another 'tick box' exercise. Look at it as an investment in you; something which is for your benefit and that of your class. The more you look at your early career as a chance to be in control, to be empowered and to lead conversations with your mentor, the more you will continue to become the confident teacher that you want to be. Use an iPad and record examples of your practice ready for discussion. Refer back to your ITT course materials and find strategies from reading or discussions with others that you want to try and test for impact. Think about what you want to do next in relation to all those key domains of professional behaviours, pedagogy, curriculum, assessment and behaviour for your own practice and to benefit your pupils.

Being an ECT is not all about developing classroom practice. It is also about developing good habits which support your longevity in the profession. Look after yourself above all else. YOU are your best resource and need looking after. Nurturing and teaching the future generation the skills and values they will need to make the world a better place is a big job, so get into good habits now. Have at least one night a week and one complete day at the weekend of *you* time as a bare minimum and do not compromise on that. Invest not only in your practice, but in yourself.

Andrew Jack provides important food for thought around professional development and learning and how we need to stand up for elements of relevance to our own career trajectory

Reflections on Continuing Professional Development and Career-Long Professional Learning

By Andrew Jack, Probationer/Student Regent, PTC Science at St. Kentigern's Academy, Blackburn, Scotland

I feel that there are important nuances between CPD and career-long professional learning (CLPL). I like to consider the CLPL as being my aspirational pathway that evolves over time based on external influences and establishments I work within, and reflects the needs of my career progression. In essence it is my path, my journey and my road. When I then think about CPD, it does not necessarily fit that description; however, CPD could be considered my stepping stones, my tools and the development I need to progress on that journey. The issue with CPD is that as part of our ongoing development as a profession, there is an onus to continually enhance our skills, knowledge and approaches to education. This is due to many pressures from government, policy, internal school pressures and also a personal drive to deliver the best outcomes for our pupils.

I firmly believe the learner should be at the core of everything we do in education and learning, and teaching is the bread-and-butter of what we do as educators.

(Continued)

> As such, I fully recognise the importance of upskilling and making myself aware of new pedagogies and theories in order to provide the best experiences for my pupils. However, the reality of our profession is that there are always external pressures put upon us, which can lead us to struggle with time management and prioritisation of learning and can lead to an apathy towards professional learning.
>
> How often do we encounter a CPD training session that is not felt to be relevant to our development but delivery has been demanded from the powers that be, so we attend and go through the motions? Then, in contrast, how much better does it feel to go to a training that is for us as individuals, one that we have signed up for as it is something we are, dare I say, excited to learn more about? Which is going to be more sustainable in our practice and suitable for us as professionals? Speak up, ask why we are doing what we do; be an activist in this sense and retain that professionalism we are all striving to show the world.

Career progression and further study

> **Critical question**
>
> How might I begin to show leadership qualities, which can then translate into something bigger?

The concept of being a lifelong learner as an educational practitioner underpins further professional study, professional development and career progression. Ideas developed through learning might be conceived from reading professional articles or scholarly research, through continued professional development training, early career teacher networks, formal education or other professional reflection. We can also all be open to ideas provided by new entrants to the profession, who have completed training and are quite knowledgeable about the latest theories, research and practice. We can see new entrants to the profession as informed leaders within their class and year group, which Harry Garland encourages us to reflect upon.

> ### Leadership Whilst not Being a Leader
>
> *By Harry Garland, Early Career Teacher, Maidstone, England*
>
> There are many different types of people who choose to teach. Some are, or have aspirations to be, a senior leader. Some have taken that role and chosen to return to classroom practice; many have no desire to be anything other than the best classroom practitioner they can be, whilst others do not want to be there at all and are only encouraged by the fact their bills need paying. All are leaders.
>
> *(Continued)*

This sentiment was news to me as an ECT. I have no title to say that I am a curriculum lead, but working within a team I have no choice but to lead. That is not to say I am not led. One has to accept that as an ECT, one cannot have control over every element of one's practice. For instance, I wrote an essay at university bashing the notion that marking every piece of work was essential practice, with support from all sorts of recognised literature. My school's marking policy disagrees with my firmly held notion. It is important, therefore, to acknowledge that leadership does not mean control. I cannot simply turn to my headteacher and say 'Thanks for taking the time to write this policy, I however know far better and will choose to ignore it'. Leadership does not mean deliberately sabotaging one's own career! A better response is to accept the policy for what it is, follow the direction, realise that it could be a lot worse than it is and get on with it. If I were to disagree wholeheartedly with the direction of policy, I would have the option to find another school.

In my current team of three teachers, a higher level teaching assistant (HLTA) and four teaching assistants, I am one of three main leaders. Amongst the team, including support staff, we all take on varying degrees of leadership, even if it is not clearly defined. For instance, I have a love and passion for the teaching of RE and maths, backed up by my knowledge of the latest research my shiny new teaching certificate proves I have. This enables me to lead the direction we take in those subjects for Year 4. Two of the teaching assistants (TAs) have a real flair and passion for art and become valuable leaders when it is time to change the displays. Another teacher in the year group is the science lead for the multi-academy trust, so his leadership role is clearly defined. My point here is that everyone who works in a school, at any level, has the potential to lead and make positive change. They can do this by being a role model and demonstrating the change that they would like to see.

Harry's thought piece captures that we can be seen to be leaders even if we are not yet formally recognised leaders through our job title. The transition between training to be a teacher and being an early career teacher whilst recognising and developing leadership qualities in our workforce is important. A need to create a smooth transition from training into the teaching profession is at the heart of government policy so that the profession maintains committed, quality workforce who are inspired and see teaching as a career with longevity and in which they can develop and progress. Within the 'Initial teacher education (ITE) inspection framework and handbook' (DfE, 2022b), guidance on career progression and further study are detailed under the heading 'professional behaviours':

> Trainees are taught how to... engage with relevant subject and/or scholarly communities, including communities of practice relating to technical and vocational training, where relevant.
>
> (DfE, 2022b, no page)

A leadership component may be engrained within the transition document, which a graduate takes with them to their new employing school to help begin their transition from trainee to ECT. The document may prompt trainees to set targets based on their final school experience assessment report and to consider what career ambitions they have, honing in on what professional development opportunities, actions and strategies might support them.

The process of training to be a teacher in England is now supported by the Core Content Framework (DfE, 2019a), as part of Initial Teacher Training, and the Early Career Framework (DfE, 2019b) during teachers' first two years of practice within the profession to support their induction (DfE, 2021) and leading to a final decision as to whether their performance meets the Teachers' Standards (DfE, 2022a).

The baselines of the frameworks' contents have been designed to help trainers and trainees consider the components of 'learn that' (e.g. around key pedagogical thinking) and 'learn how to' (what does this look like in practice). A baseline of relevant material is provided, incorporating research articles and other educational literature, to support trainers and, importantly here, trainees/teachers at the beginning of their career for their professional development. A similar format is employed for the NPQs (DfE, 2022c) for consistency. The process of professional development utilises a three-pronged approach: material approved by the DfE for consistent practice across the country, an expectation of base coverage by those institutions providing the theoretical training ('learn that') and the practical training ('learn how to'), and a resource tool for the trainees. Learning, therefore, is seen as a partnership between key people, and this meshes very well with the idea of socially situated learning and communities of practice, which we now briefly explore.

A community of learners

> **Critical question**
>
> What learning do you engage with, within your setting? Where might it take you with your aspirations?

From training to be a teacher through to following career aspirations and undertaking further training or formal qualifications, as educational professionals we are invited to engage within a community of learners to advance and refine our teaching craft. Lave and Wenger's (1991) concept of socially situated learning and Wenger's (1998) highlighting of communities of practice centralise the relevance of learning in a process involving multifaceted components including relationships and culture. As novice learners become involved in their communities supported by other experienced practitioners to enhance and refine practice, they eventually become esteemed members themselves of that community of practice. The relevance of Lave and Wenger's ideas for this chapter is that the learning of practice within a community focuses in on belonging to the community, contributing to the community and how to change the community. These elements are fundamental to career progression and further study and how we may develop our identity within our educational community. Indeed, community and identity are two components proposed by Wenger (1998) as part of socially situated learning.

(NB You may also wish to refer to Chapter 13 for the role of professional learning communities as part of action research.)

Career progression and further study – where might I head?

> **Critical question**
>
> How may I gather my thoughts together before making a decision about my career progression or further study?

Before we start out with undertaking further study or training to further develop our teaching or our careers, we may consider taking a step back to reflect. A contribution from Sam Crome advises us about the power of coaching to help crystallise our thoughts as to where we might progress to in our professional roles.

Coaching

By Sam Crome, Deputy Headteacher and Executive Coach, London, England

After your early career teaching years and mentor support, you will feel more confident with your practice and yet will continue to identify areas to improve. This is the perfect time to find a coach to help you unlock your potential. Coaching sessions prompt the coachee to think through their ideas, challenges or views, with the questions from their coach helping them to find a new perspective, but which is always focused on solutions. Sometimes, our best thinking happens out loud, when we articulate beyond our internal conversations and which seems to make them become more actionable. The coaching conversation will help you discuss and reflect upon a range of ideas, with a skilled, supportive professional to guide you with targeted questioning, summary and paraphrasing.

Christian van Nieuwerburgh (2015) identifies benefits of coaching as follows: increased self-awareness and emotional intelligence, enhanced interpersonal skills supporting stronger relationships, stronger self-confidence and leadership skills, increased loyalty to the organisation, renewed passion to support the development of others, and better work-life balance. There is a large body of research that advocates coaching as a process to develop and empower coach and coachee. Here is a quick summary of other benefits to having a coach:

Establishing the 'real' thing: In his book, 'The BASIC Coaching Method', Andy Buck (2020) warns of the danger of getting hung up on something, wrongly attributing an idea or issue to being 'the main thing'. But what if it isn't? Coaching conversations often establish how we really feel about an issue; after some deliberation and discussion, it can become apparent that the background to a challenge might not have

(Continued)

> been the root cause, and the intended course of the conversation needs to change. Goal setting is more effective once the background is clarified.
>
> **And what else:** This key question, suggested by Michael Bungay Stanier (2016) in 'The Coaching Habit: Say less, ask more and change the way you lead forever', represents what your coach will help you do. Through their questioning, and in particular their reluctance to let you settle with your initial thoughts or ideas, your coach will encourage you to find a way ahead.
>
> **Control and autonomy:** Feeling a sense of autonomy over our work can have a huge impact on how we feel about it. Coaching allows a coachee to come up with their own solutions and to take control of a situation, leaving the coachee to feel empowered and rejuvenated about their next steps.
>
> **Perspective and impetus:** In the first part of the conversation, the coachee will gain perspective over their context and goals. In the latter stage, they will plot a course of action in tangible, chunked-up steps. Leaving a coaching conversation with an immediate set of tasks creates confidence and impetus to put words into action with a sense of accountability and a desire to improve.
>
> Coaching is an exciting process that will be the best investment of your time you can make!

Further study

This section considers further study and the opportunities that it might bring.

Further study – thinking about 'National professional qualifications'?

> **Critical question**
>
> What might further study look like, and what should I be considering if I were to undertake such study? How do I know if I am ready to study?

The DfE and Gibb (2021) announced plans to establish in September 2022 a new Institute of Teaching in England to support teachers and school leaders with CPD. Alongside teacher training, it will also provide mentoring and early career support as part of the Early Career Framework reforms and NPQs (DfE, 2022c). At the time of writing, it is proposed that the training at the institute will combine online, face-to-face and school-based (self-directed) elements linked to evidence-based practice. The summative assessment for NPQs is a short case study (DfE, 2022c) (see also National Institute of Training https://niot.org.uk/).

A revised NPQ collection has been launched, to support recruitment and retention (DfE, 2019c), in senior leadership, headship, executive leadership (supporting those interested in leading trusts) and Early Years leadership, and there has been replacement of the middle leadership qualification NPQ with a focus for teachers and leaders wanting to enhance their practice in leading teacher development, leading teaching, leading behaviour and culture, and leading literacy. Funding, at no cost to the participant, is available. The DfE explains that the duration of the studies last from 12 to 27 months according to the NPQ, with the trainee's provider determining the content, delivery mode and course structure. The DfE further explains that the studies will enable those training to make improvements in their current role or to progress in their career. Further details are available from the DfE website (see DfE, 2022c). The professional training and development routes are intended to provide rigour based on a baseline of research, though that is not to say that other research or other sources of professional development should be discounted.

The NPQs include courses for those wanting to progress in senior leadership. The professional development of Daniel Davies and Chris Ball, in relation to these senior positions, is now presented.

Developing my Leadership and Ideas to Help you Develop yours

Daniel Davies, Assistant Headteacher, Woodland Academy Trust, London, England

After working as a performer, I reached the stage in my life where a career change was needed. Wanting a regular 9–5 office job, I became a personal assistant to the CEO of a primary multi-academy trust and was encouraged to explore teacher training options; goodbye 9–5. I was lucky enough to be offered a salaried school-based route to gain my QTS with the same trust and began my NQT year. My previous experience working with the CEO had provided me with an insight into the world of senior leadership, and I knew that this was the direction I wanted my career to go in.

My first piece of advice with leadership is to get classroom practice right first. In almost all leadership positions, you need to reflect back on your time in the classroom and be able to offer support and advice based on this. Moreover, utilise your colleagues, seek advice and be accepting of feedback.

Before applying for leadership positions, there are a few easy ways to gain some initial experience. These could include shadowing a subject or phase lead, standing as a staff governor, volunteering for any staff working parties or taking a proactive role in the organisation and planning of whole school events such as sports days or charity days. This provides examples of your impact as a leader to discuss during the application and interview process.

Some top tips to support development in an early/middle leadership position include the following:

- Joining local and national networking groups
- Gaining early leadership qualifications/participating in research projects
- Working with school finance staff to understand departmental budgets
- Working with senior leaders to understand how to lead courageous conversations
- Developing knowledge of whole school documents and assessments

(Continued)

The next stage in my career allowed me to gain more experience of leadership across a whole school as a subject lead. This has many benefits, e.g. developing knowledge of what this subject looks like beyond the key stage you are working in and building relationships with members of staff across the school. The completion of my NPQ for school leaders supported me in securing my first assistant headship, responsible for personal development and digital strategy across four primary schools. To support my leadership in these areas, I enrolled on a Masters' degree in Educational Leadership and Management, to enhance my skills, knowledge and behaviours as a leader. It may be of relevance to readers to note that many of these Masters' courses are built to incorporate a Level 7 apprenticeship qualification allowing them to be funded as part of the apprenticeship levy, without any cost to yourself. Incidentally, the trust for which I work has recently been recognised as an Apple Regional Training Centre, where I have taken up the role of centre manager and lead trainer, allowing me to facilitate opportunities for teachers to develop skills and build on their confidence to use Apple technology in the classroom.

An Accidental Entry into the Wonderful Profession of Education

By Chris Ball, Headteacher at Rangefield Primary School, London, England

I fell into teaching by accident…. Having been a commercial manager for Marks & Spencer at 18, skipping university much to the anguish of my grammar school, I found myself redundant at 19. It was one of those times where jobs were not easy to come by, so I headed north to Liverpool for university. Halfway through I was standing for election to a London borough council, and home I came. The University of Greenwich took me on, and moving into their education department to train as a teacher seemed to be a workable plan. Little did I know that nearly 20 years later I would be back helping train the next generation of teachers as an academic.

My career path has been unconventional as my route in. I knew from an early age that I wanted to lead and teaching was where I found myself. I looked, initially with intrigue, at how senior staff operated and both consciously and subconsciously watched to see what was effective. The fact I also found myself involved in local government exposed me to a range of other leaders, both political and officers.

Back at school I found myself enjoying the single most magical, memorable and rewarding year of my career. I loved being an NQT and built such a strong bond with my class that I still know what many of them are doing now. As was common then, subject leadership followed in my second year and year group leadership immediately after that. By this point I was much more focused on career progression and moved onto a different school as a phase lead and assessment lead.

I had become increasingly keen to climb ladders and found myself leader of my political group on the local council, undertaking a successful year as mayor, and then

(Continued)

Career progression and further study 181

> following elections the leader of the council. Without doubt, this experience gave me a real insight into strategic leadership and motivation of colleagues and sharpened me to be able to say 'no' with conviction. It did, however, make a real difference with my teaching career, going part time for a while. I fell into a job doing some supply work in a school that was at the very start of its journey of improvement. The journey included the departure of the deputy head, me filling that gap, and, when the head found promotion, I became the headteacher. Adrenalin and an amazingly good group of colleagues carried me through that first year.
>
> I have delivered school improvement in a number of challenging schools, and this has been interspersed with teaching the next generation of teachers as a lecturer. Opportunities have presented themselves in a timely way. My experience of most leaders is a deep sense of imposter syndrome; some disguise this better than others. I have felt that pain and still do at times. Living on the edge can be fun. Go for it!

Further study - in a postgraduate

> **Critical question**
>
> How might a Postgraduate Diploma or Postgraduate Certificate be right for me in my career progression?

There are a host of postgraduate qualifications for educational professionals to pursue which may support career progression. This section considers Postgraduate Diplomas (PG Dips) and Postgraduate Certificates (PG Certs), Masters and Doctorates. Credits from PG Dips and PG Certs may often be used towards a full Masters, but check with the institution at which you will be studying.

PG Diplomas and PG Certificates

PG Dips and PG Certs can support your career development. They are the same advanced level of study as a Masters' degree, with the difference being that they are of a shorter duration and worth less credits (PG Dips and PG Certs are worth 120 and 60 credits, respectively, as opposed to 180 credits from a Masters) and do not require a dissertation to be completed (Smith, 2022a). Study may be full time or part time – e.g. two terms for a full-time PG Dip and one term for a PG Cert (Smith, 2022a). Distance or online learning may be available, delivery is provided through lectures and seminars, and assessment is undertaken through practical assignments and short written essays (Smith, 2022a). Universities normally provide details of the PG Dip and PG Cert alongside their Masters programmes.

Emma Longley, who had experience as a lead for the PG Cert for SENCos, explains the framework for training to be a SENCo.

> **Interested in Leading Provision for Children with SEND?**
>
> By Emma Longley, Experience of Programme Lead PGCert SENCo at The University of Greenwich, London, England
>
> Since 2008 it has also been a requirement that all SENCos complete a postgraduate qualification, the National Award for Special Educational Needs Co-ordination (NASENCO), within three years of being appointed to a position (see NCTL, no date) for the NASENCO).
>
> This programme provides a detailed understanding of the knowledge and attributes of a SENCo, underpinned by research, rigorous theoretical grounding and engagement with the practical expertise shared by a variety of experts in the field. Taught sessions, visits to schools and independent research support development of a critical awareness and understanding about key issues in equality, diversity and inclusion, and how to respond effectively and adapt provision to meet SEND children's individual needs. It will help leaders to define aspirations, develop confidence and explore the skills, knowledge and understanding to be able to respond to diverse opportunities and challenges and the ability to solve problems in creative and innovative ways.
>
> Programmes will vary in terms of organisation and delivery; however, they share the same overall intention which is to equip leaders of SEN with the professional knowledge and understanding to lead and coordinate provision and understand the personal and professional qualities to fulfil the role. The learning outcomes involve learning about the statutory, legislative context and how this impacts upon the setting, leadership, how SEND affects pupils' engagement with learning and how to improve their outcomes (NCTL, 2014). It also includes consideration of how to strategically work with and challenge colleagues, senior leaders and governors (NCTL, 2014). Furthermore, the programme enables critical evaluation of evidence about learning, teaching and assessment to enable practitioners to monitor those used within SEND provision (NCTL, 2014).
>
> If you are interested in pursuing this avenue of career progression, details of providers can be found at https://nasen.org.uk/page/nasenco

Further study - Masters

> **Critical question**
>
> Where might a Masters lead, and am I ready for it?

Masters level study is characterised by an increased intensity and complexity, compared to an undergraduate degree and PG Dips and PG Certs, often encompassing a piece of research or scholarly exercise (FHEQ, 2014). Smith (2022b) details key points of a Masters degree, but for this chapter, elements have been tweaked, tailored and refined towards those working in schools, who indeed might choose to study a Masters degree in Education. Full time study of the 180 credit programme may last a year, though school practitioners are likely to study part time. Being a school practitioner will facilitate reflection and linking theory with practice. The programme is delivered through lectures, seminars and practical tasks, and assessment is through essays, group tasks, presentations and a dissertation around a research project. Independent study is critical, but tutor support enables work to be managed and reflection to be developed. Weekly contact time (through lectures, seminars, group activities and tutorials) might be about ten hours weekly (for full-time study and significantly less for part time), with expectations for independent study to be about 3–3.5 times the contact time. Costing will need to be considered, though your school might fund you. Forethought of ways to manage a work-study-home life balance, especially when considered against the background of intense workload within the classroom, will also need to be contemplated to enable positive engagement. Alternatively, some people might choose to work part time and study part time. It is also worth asking your school if you can be granted study leave as part of your professional development if you are working full time.

Harry Garland (early career teacher) and Mary Leighton (educational psychologist) reflect on their motivations of undertaking their Masters.

Why Would an ECT do a Masters?

By Harry Garland, Early Career Teacher, Maidstone, England

When I told some of my university friends that I had successfully applied for a Masters in Education, I received a mixed reaction. One common theme was 'rather you than me'. At the time of writing, I am yet to start, so I cannot suggest that this will be as successful a decision as I hope it will be. The risks are obvious. The prospect of juggling an additional twenty hours a week of study on top of what is a hectic jumble of ECT work and the unrelenting hours being a classroom teacher is far from appealing. I am sure my health will cope with the prospect of less television and more ready meals.

The potential gains of surviving the process of study are, in my opinion, worth it. I trained as a teacher, after several years of working as a TA, with a view to make proactive changes to what I believe is a fundamentally flawed system. I have come to realise, both through study of a bachelor's degree in education and my first year working as a teacher, that I am not yet in a position to make those changes. I want to progress into a leadership role quickly, and I believe that having the weight of further study behind me will support me with that.

There are, I believe, other benefits to taking on further study early in my career, in addition to the prospect of fast-tracking my career. In the short term, I believe that the knowledge I will gain from further study can only but help me as a classroom practitioner. We also know as teachers that new knowledge is built around prior knowledge. By undertaking further study soon after finishing and in the same field as my

(Continued)

bachelor's degree, I am ensuring that the knowledge I have is as fresh, up-to-date and relevant as it can be.

Furthermore, having finished my degree in the auspices of a national lockdown, the idea of online study does not phase me as much as it would have had before the pandemic. I have a great understanding of how I work at home (thanks pandemic) and how I work at school, and this enables me to maximise the hours I have to study whilst still making time for self-care.

I think the time is right to go that little bit deeper into the field and learn as much as I can. For others, it might be different. If you agree with the sentiment of my friends; 'rather you than me', then it is not the right time. If there is an inkling inside you that says it might be the time, it is certainly an avenue worth exploring.

Career progression – what might you do with a Masters?

> **Critical question**
>
> Where might a Masters lead to? Does it matter if you don't end up doing what you thought you might do?

People undertaking a Masters may have a specific goal in sight – perhaps for a new role or a career change, or they are aware of the need for a new challenge. Mary Leighton reflects upon where the journey took her.

Becoming an Educational Psychologist

By Mary Leighton, Educational Psychologist, Doncaster, England

Initially, I had no particular intention to work with children and young people (CYP) with SEND; in fact, I did not label CYP; rather, I did my best to cater for whatever they needed. In a twist of fate, I became a SENDCo at a school. Even though I had no experience of being SENDCo, the school saw something in me, and despite its demands I found it exhilarating.

Unbeknown to me, my pathway was slowly being paved towards becoming an educational psychologist (EP): whilst unable to work for several months, due to ill health, a light bulb moment came about as I contemplated my future as I felt that I was going to burn out if I continued as a teacher. I phoned the EP of my school to discuss her role. Her job sounded appealing, even though it meant me attending two university courses and making financial sacrifices to pay for them. However, whilst studying for the first

(Continued)

degree (MEd Educational Psychology) (two afternoons into the evenings per week) I found plentiful work as a supply teacher. As luck would have it, I was able to volunteer as an assistant EP one day per week at a neighbouring local authority (LA) at the same time as I was studying. The degree was completed in a year.

Again, fate was on my side as the LA I was working for had a vacancy for an assistant EP. I was interviewed and gained the role. I applied for the EP training course (MSc Educational Psychology) and was offered a provisional place, but it did not work out. However, bumps along the way are to be expected and I still had my job as an assistant EP. Besides, gaining a place on the course is extremely competitive with individuals applying for several years, so gaining a provisional place in my first year of applying was an achievement. The following year I *was* successful. (NB Subsequent to my studies, the Masters became a three-year course, opening up to a wider range of individuals which meant it was no longer a requirement to have a teaching degree. Another change was that the course became a doctorate.)

I qualified as an EP and went to work with a LA who, subsequently, funded me for my doctoral studies, though this was not a necessity at the time. I thoroughly enjoy my job – it does not feel like a job to me – it is definitely a vocation. I have never looked back. The work is fascinating since no two days are the same and I feel I am learning which keeps me stimulated. I consider it a privilege to be able to work with CYP, their families and settings along with a wide variety of support agencies and trust that I am making a positive difference to the lives of CYP.

Further study – Doctorates

Critical question

What is the point of doing a doctorate? What might be the impact of undertaking a doctorate upon your professionalism?

Studying to become a Doctor in Education (Ed.D.) or a Doctor in Philosophy (PhD) where the PhD may be linked to education can be the beginning of an interesting learning and career journey. Completion of study at a doctoral level 8 requires the formation and analysis of new knowledge undertaken through original research, developing the discipline, work being worthy of publication and being subject to peer review (FHEQ, 2014). Professional doctorates (e.g. Ed.D. for Doctor of Education) 'aim to develop an individual's professional practice and to support them in producing a contribution to (professional) knowledge' (p. 30). Duration of study can last from the equivalent of three full-time calendar years to substantially longer for part-time study.

An extract from Ashley Brett, senior lecturer, reflects his motivation behind his doctoral studies.

From Consultant to Deputy Head to Senior Lecturer

By Ashley Brett, Senior Lecturer in Primary Education at The University of Greenwich, London, England

My interest in pursuing doctoral studies began whilst I was a numeracy consultant for a local authority (LA). One of my professional duties as a maths consultant was to facilitate primary school improvement. The catalyst for my research stemmed from my professional encounters whilst supporting underachieving schools that found change challenging, and where I was aware of negative perceptions, including despondency, from some school-based leaders and their teachers about the nature of my support. On one occasion, I visited a school and, during a routine meeting with the head and her deputy, I was met with a barrage of angry comments. They felt little sense of professional autonomy in their dealings with the LA - specifically, they felt they had to comply with LA recommendations, even if they did not agree. This emotional reaction caused me to become inquisitive about how my peers supported teaching staff in schools to recognise and modify their educational practice in order to improve their pupils' academic achievement. This subsequently became refined to researching how senior leaders might support their teachers to become engaged as learners within the context of change, as I transitioned between careers within education. This refinement mirrors the expectation of a professional and personal journey and the maturation of research ideas during the Ed.D, as described by the programme lead at the commencement of my studies.

Following the demise of the National Strategies, I became a deputy head for my professional development and to utilise what I had learnt during my consultancy. Although I had engaged in successful consultancy experiences alongside my extensive studies at doctoral level, garnering a knowledge about school improvement strategies, I deemed that the pressures and activities of potential future headship at any school requiring change (which seemed to be reflected in LA leadership meetings as being most schools responding to the continual tide of educational changes) would be unsustainable for me to manage as part of a sensible work-life balance. Simultaneously, I realised through my Ed.D professional studies that I wanted to develop my career within an academic environment. Within a fortuitous sequence of events, I applied for my current role as a university senior lecturer for initial teacher training (ITT).

(Extracted and adapted from Brett, 2018, by Ashley Brett)

Lecturers/training teachers/mentoring

> **Critical question**
>
> What other career choices or positions might be out there?

Lecturing is an extremely privileged position and is a rewarding and fulfilling career. To be of benefit to trainees who themselves are each going to have a positive impact upon the lives of hundreds, possibly thousands of children – the future of our society – is a humbling and incredibly worthwhile and positive experience. Some practitioners may experience 'imposter syndrome' as they grapple with a transition from school classroom to university classroom, but one strategy to overcome this is to present at conferences and make use of 'reflection, feed-forward, perspective, support network[s] and talk' (Gibson and Coombes, 2020).

Seraphina Simmons-Bah recounts her journey and motivation for entering the world of academia as a professional.

Becoming a Senior Teaching Fellow

By Seraphina Simmons-Bah, Senior Teaching Fellow in Primary Education at University of Greenwich, London, England

I started my career in education working as a TA in Early Years settings, gaining experience in both day nurseries and schools. In this time, I became fascinated by the processes children go through as they learn and developed a desire to become a teacher. Thus, I decided to apply for a place on a BA Primary Education with QTS programme. When I first started my degree, my focus was on getting my qualification and returning to the classroom above all else. However, I quickly realised that I would want to have a career in higher education in the future. I enjoyed the space there was within higher education to question and challenge the education system and to explore a range of approaches to teaching and learning. I became fully immersed in both study and wider university life, taking on various student representative positions which gave me opportunities to learn more about the machinations of universities.

During my time studying for my BA, I developed a keen interest in children's literature, which I chose to pursue further through studying for a Masters. I completed my Masters in children's literature whilst working as a class teacher in both the Early Years and upper Key Stage 2 in a number of schools across South East and East London. I was able to develop my skills as a researcher and teacher in tandem, and my diversity of experience gave me an insight into how different contexts and individual and collective ideologies influence the practice found in a school. Throughout this time, I kept in contact with my university tutors. When the opportunity to work as an hourly paid part-time lecturer arose, I was able to draw on the range of skills I had developed in schools and through further study, to teach several subjects at the level required for both undergraduate and postgraduate programmes. In turn, the experience I gained as an hourly paid part-time lecturer and my commitment to academic development set me in good stead to secure a full-time university teaching position.

Working as an academic gives me the opportunity to continue teaching, which I consider to be my vocation, whilst also continuing to develop as a researcher through PhD study. Importantly, I am able to work with a wide range of schools and collaborate with both university- and school-based colleagues to explore ways of enhancing student teachers' practice. I have just been appointed as the programme leader for the BA primary education with QTS – what an amazing few years I have had and what a great future to look forward to.

Mentoring

It should be noted that the world of teacher training in England is currently altering and, from September 2024, any institution leading training has to have been (re)accredited by the DfE. Changes will also occur with processes of mentoring trainees. Nevertheless, key skills will remain fundamental, and two contributions follow from educational colleagues, which highlight the benefits of mentoring those training to become teachers when they are on school placement.

Mentoring

Stella de Larrabeiti, Redbridge Primary School, Mentor Lead, London, England

Mentoring is more than just meeting P10 of the post-threshold teaching standards and a means of attaining and being kept on the upper pay scale. As teachers and leaders, we are driven to achieve the best possible outcomes for the children that we teach. By mentoring, we are ensuring and securing this for not only the children within our immediate environment but for those further and wider afield, for many years to come.

There is no denying that being a mentor is a responsible, powerful and extremely privileged role to be in, but it is not one to be feared. We often think of a mentor as a wise and experienced teacher who knows everything about the profession, and this can sometimes be overwhelming. But the most important role of an impactful mentor is to inspire, to be supportive, to share what they know and to facilitate a nurturing environment so that their mentee can grow, thrive and in turn develop their own professional identity as a teacher. Benjamin Disraeli once said, 'The greatest good you can do for another is not just to share your riches but to reveal to him his own' (no citation), and this is what mentoring is.

Just as we professionally develop the children within our classroom, the same can be said for mentoring and coaching colleagues and trainee teachers. The exact same processes apply, and it is a matter of showcasing and sharing effective practice, and providing practical and useful advice and feedback. Something that we do on a daily basis!

In my time as a teacher, a leader and a mentor, I have experienced positives and negatives but, for me, mentoring colleagues and trainee teachers provides job satisfaction like no other role. It is an opportunity that allows you to make a difference to the lives of many, to create a legacy in some respect, and is essential and key to future teacher retention if done well. It also keeps you at the top of your game and ensures that you remain up-to-date with your practice. Quite truly, mentoring is a blessing for all stakeholders involved, the mentor, the trainee teacher and the children, and is an opportunity not to be passed up if you are offered this position.

The Power of Being a Role Model

By Belinda Benatar-Kotler, SEN Teacher, Zevulun, Israel

I believe that there is a lot of reciprocal learning which can go on between those learning their craft and those supporting them to become teachers. Looking back on my personal experience as a student teacher, I believe the only way to gain needed skills in order to be a successful teacher comes from standing in front of a classroom of children, dealing with their needs and catering for them academically and emotionally, with the guidance and support of the class teacher/mentor. When I was in training to be a SEN teacher, we visited a special needs class once a week. I was placed in a primary class of children with learning disabilities, and most of the pupils had behavioural problems. I remember my personal excitement from the beginning as I wanted to help the children to flourish. In the first term, we were required to base our learning upon what we observed from the teacher and the methods they used, and in the second term we taught a unit that we developed ourselves from the teacher's guidelines from taking into account the pupils' needs.

When I agree to tutor student teachers in my classroom, my mission is to allow them as much practical work as possible, to support their confidence and self-esteem, whilst guiding them through the process of putting theory into practice. I base my approach and belief on the fact that we have a mutual goal to accomplish – it is ultimately to do with what is in it for the children and how they may ultimately benefit, both for those children in my current class and the children of the trainee in the future. I have found that whilst achieving this goal requires my commitment of time to mentor and help train the teacher, the process yields dividends. Both mentor and mentee come together in a tour de force nurtured, in my belief, by motivation and belief in the possibility to make a change in the life of children with whom we work. Over the years, I have found that the more time I dedicate to my student, the more fruitful it becomes, as long as there is that mutual motivation and commitment.

In hindsight, I (as a student teacher) never felt important or meaningful in the class I visited each week. Despite my excitement and passion to practice, I found myself feeling a burden on the teacher rather than an asset. From this experience, I have pledged never to agree to have a student teacher if I am not ready to commit and apply myself to the mission as a mentor. The bonus of tutoring comes from the opportunity to think out loud and share mutual thoughts and experiences – knowledge, opinions and attitudes – and create time for student and self-reflection. It is a win-win situation in a demanding profession.

Conclusion

This chapter has considered different career progressions and study options post-undergraduate degree. The contributions from educational colleagues have provided some inspirational and honest reflections. What binds them together are underpinnings of passion, motivation and a love of learning. The sky is the limit for anything you want to achieve; it may involve some extra time and commitment on your part, and only you know what you are ready for. Just finding out what might be out there and what you have to do to achieve it can be a useful first step. Happy new beginnings everybody!

References

Brett, A. (2018). *Primary school leaders creating conditions for teacher learning associated with change: developing an understanding with reference to transformative learning theory*. Doctoral thesis (Ed.D). UCL (University College London). [Online]. Available at: https://discovery.ucl.ac.uk/id/eprint/10058697/ [Accessed 1 October 2022]. Unpublished.

Buck, A. (2020). *The Basic Coaching Method*. London: Cadogan Press.

Clarke, A.C. (1968). Clarke's third law on UFOs. *Science*, 159(3812), p. 255.

Department for Education (DfE). (2019a). *ITT core content framework*. [Online]. Available at: https://assets.publishing.service.gov.uk/government/uploads/system/uploads/attachment_data/file/974307/ITT_core_content_framework_.pdf [Accessed 1 October 2022].

DfE. (2019b). *Early career framework*. [Online]. Available at: https://assets.publishing.service.gov.uk/government/uploads/system/uploads/attachment_data/file/978358/Early-Career_Framework_April_2021.pdf [Accessed 1 October 2022].

DfE. (2019c). *Teacher recruitment and retention strategy*. [Online]. Available at: https://www.gov.uk/government/publications/teacher-recruitment-and-retention-strategy [Accessed 1 October 2022].

DfE. (2021). *Induction for early career teachers (England)*. [Online]. Available at: https://assets.publishing.service.gov.uk/government/uploads/system/uploads/attachment_data/file/972316/Statutory_Induction_Guidance_2021_final__002_____1___1_.pdf [Accessed 1 October 2022].

DfE. (2022a). *Changes to statutory induction for early career teachers (ECTs)*. [Online]. Available at: https://www.gov.uk/guidance/changes-to-statutory-induction-for-early-career-teachers-ects [Accessed 1 October 2022].

DfE. (2022b). *Initial teacher education (ITE) inspection framework and handbook*. [Online]. Available at: https://www.gov.uk/government/publications/initial-teacher-education-ite-inspection-framework-and-handbook/initial-teacher-education-ite-inspection-framework-and-handbook [Accessed 1 October 2022].

DfE. (2022c). *National Professional Qualifications (NPQs)*. [Online]. Available at: https://www.gov.uk/government/publications/national-professional-qualifications-npqs-reforms/national-professional-qualifications-npqs-reforms [Accessed 1 October 2022].

DfE and Gibb, N. (2021). *New institute of teaching set to be established*. [Online]. Available at: https://www.gov.uk/government/news/new-institute-of-teaching-set-to-be-established [Accessed 1 October 2022].

FHEQ. (2014). *UK quality code for higher education part A: Setting and maintaining academic standards. Part A the Frameworks for Higher Education Qualifications of UK degree-awarding bodies*. [Online]. Available at: https://www.qaa.ac.uk/docs/qaa/quality-code/qualifications-frameworks.pdf [Accessed 1 October 2022].

Gibson, P., and Coombes, S. (2020). Confronting the impostor: The role of conference presentation for confidence-building in academics: Conference reflections. *Compass: Journal of Learning and Teaching*, 13(2). [Online]. Available at: https://journals.gre.ac.uk/index.php/compass/article/view/1033

Kowalczuk-Walędziak, M., Lopes, A., Menezes, I., and Tormenta, N. (2017). Teachers pursuing a doctoral degree: Motivations and perceived impact. *Educational Research*, 59(3), pp. 335-352.

Lave, J., and Wenger, E. (1991). *Situated Learning: Legitimate Peripheral Participation*. New York, NY: Cambridge University Press.

Maslow, A.H. (1943). A theory of human motivation. *Psychological Review*, 50(4), pp. 370-396.

Maslow, A. (1954). *Motivation and Personality*. New York, NY: Harper.

Maslow, A.H. (1987). *Motivation and personality* (3rd ed.). New York: Harper & Row.

NCTL. (2014). *National award for SEN co-ordination learning outcomes*. [Online]. Available at: https://assets.publishing.service.gov.uk/government/uploads/system/uploads/attachment_data/file/354172/nasc-learning-outcomes-final.pdf [Accessed 1 October 2022].

Smith, J. (2022a). *Postgraduate diplomas and certificates*. [Online]. Available at: https://www.prospects.ac.uk/postgraduate-study/postgraduate-diplomas-and-certificates [Accessed 1 October 2022].

Smith, J. (2022b). *What is a masters degree?* [Online]. Available at: https://www.prospects.ac.uk/postgraduate-study/masters-degrees/what-is-a-masters-degree [Accessed 1 October 2022].

Stanier, M.B. (2016). *The Coaching Habit: Say Less, Ask More and Change the Way You Lead Forever*. Toronto, ON: Box of Crayons Press.

Tay, L., and Diener, E. (2011). Needs and subjective well-being around the world. *Journal of Personality and Social Psychology*, 101, pp. 354–365.

Van Nieuwerburgh, C. (2015). *Coaching in Professional Contexts*. London: Sage.

Wenger, E. (1998). *Communities of Practice. Learning, Meaning and Identity.* Cambridge: Cambridge University Press.

13 The power of actioning action research

Becoming an education researcher

KEY WORDS

Action research, reflection, collaboration, ethical, learning, autonomy, value(s)

> **Contributors in this chapter:**
>
> 1. Katherine Richardson
> 2. Leeza Ahmed
> 3. Ashley Brett and Robert Morgan
> 4. Madeeha Kashif
> 5. Matthew Tragheim
>
> (With thanks to Dr Mary Clare Martin for support in developing the ethics forms – see **Tables 13.3-13.5**)

Introduction

> **Critical question**
>
> How might classroom teachers be active in promoting research in their everyday classroom practice to inspire their pupils and help them progress?

This chapter considers how classroom teachers can be active in promoting research in their everyday classroom, using action research at grassroots level to continually inspire their pupils and help them progress. The chapter considers why educational research is important and encourages the reader to contemplate how they may wish to carry out action research in an ethical way in their classroom.

The chapter starts with a brief background to the nature of action research and a contribution by Dr Katherine Richardson, University of Leeds. Next, action research as a transformative experience and as a collective endeavour within a school context are briefly considered before reflecting on three types of action research and the theme of autonomy

DOI: 10.4324/9781003218098-13

which undertaking action research may bring. This is followed by an example of how an early career teacher, Leeza Ahmed, undertook an action research project to motivate her pupils. After this, an example of a cycle of action research is presented followed by consideration of the development of criticality and reflection which can underpin the processes. Following this, an example of how the University of Greenwich facilitates classroom-based research, in which one of the authors of this book has been involved, is explained. This also draws on research by Lambirth et al. (2021) around these supportive processes and zones of proximal and contributory activity which occur before, during and after collaboration. Next, how to deal with some challenges of action research is presented, which is adapted from Lambirth et al.'s research. The chapter then presents how two co-authors of this book, Ashley Brett and Robert Morgan, have led mini-action research projects for PGCE ITE providers; an example of what one trainee, Madeeha Kashif, undertook is also included. Following this is consideration of Roche's (2017) school-college partnership experiences for undergraduate trainees. The chapter moves on to consider ethical processes, which include a pertinent grassroots reminder by the contributor, Matthew Tragheim, about ethical questions to consider, followed by presentation of adaptable ethical templates used by Ashley Brett, a co-author of this book, which the reader may find useful. The chapter concludes with a brief consideration around who 'owns' the research, which also links to ethics.

Action research – a brief background

If it is considered that the educational profession is partly responsible for shaping future society, then questions around the nature and effectiveness of education and learning and teaching are pertinent to ask; these questions go to the very heart of educational research. Even educational accountability mechanisms – e.g. OFSTED or examination results – may partially contribute to a rationale for engaging with educational research, because through learning about our practice and the effects upon our learners we do not just accept a status quo of accountability; we take it further and enquire and gain autonomy within the parameters of accountability.

At the heart of action research is the notion of the researcher being informed by their values, norms and assumptions (Roche, 2016, 2020). It centralises the value of reflective practice (Dewey, 1910) as 'the active, persistent and careful consideration of any belief or supposed form of knowledge in the light of the grounds that support it' (p. 6). This aligns with having an inquisitive stance to teaching and education and, Dewey proposed, having foresight to inform our actions – a critical aspect of teaching practice. Schön (1983) presented two components of reflection – reflection-in-action and reflection-on-action. The former is positioned during action, e.g. during teaching and a teacher's immediate response to a situation such as a lack of understanding by pupils, whilst the latter manifests itself after the action and reflection about the event and the responses made.

Educational self-study action research may be conceived as authentic professional development (Roche, 2020) because it is research about one's own practice and based on themes of collaborative exploration, improvement and values, agency and situational learning (Day and Sachs, 2004) where there is reciprocity between understanding informing action and vice versa. Action research is an embodiment of our lived professional experiences and our critical reflection upon these (Roche, 2020) and can incorporate the past into the present time frame and be a view for the future (Whitehead and McNiff, 2006). 'Developing a better *understanding* (sic) of one's practice is intertwined with the idea of enhancing the practice itself' (Glenn, 2020a, p. 60). Praxis, considered as 'doing action' (Carr and Kemmis, 1986, p. 33) may be considered as being instigated 'following an action that is taken as a result of reflection' (Glenn, 2020a, p. 70); the action is reflected upon which subsequently influences the initial thinking that triggered the action and may alter future actions (Glenn, 2020a).

Whitehead (1989; see also Whitehead, 2019) spotlights an association between the nature of Living Educational Theory and action research enabling practitioners to garner explanations around their theoretical, educational influences through asking, researching and answering questions about how they may improve their practice. For teachers, action research may provide a living experience of continuing professional development which can change them and their practice in profound ways as they self-reflect on their work; it can support different ways of acting as a result of learning and can reshape practice rather than be seen as a process of imposing new materials, methods or theories (Roche, 2020). The uniqueness of your experience is acknowledged in action research, since no other teacher will experience exactly the same teacher-pupil interactions as yourself and have the same reflections and insightful cognitions about practice (Glenn, 2020a). Action research is different to most educational research written by an outsider researcher; it is about your practitioner perspective and your connection with others (Glenn, 2020b).

Dr Katherine Richardson gives some very brief considerations to start the ball rolling about undertaking action research.

Getting Started with Practitioner Research

By Katherine Richardson, University of Leeds, Leeds, England

Enhancing your practice through practitioner research (teachers researching an aspect of their practice) can be fascinating and rewarding. It places you – as the teacher – at the heart of the research, by focussing on your children, classroom or an aspect of your practice. It could be triggered through lesson evaluations, igniting you to explore literature and undertake your own empirical research (gathering your own data) to further your practice – enabling you to deepen your understanding of the teaching and learning situation and identify or explore alternative approaches, solutions or opportunities. Furthermore, it can be used to make a case for change.

You might focus on an aspect of practice which has been niggling you or explore why an approach or resource is effective, perhaps with a view to adapting it to other contexts (e.g. another curriculum area or with a different group of children). Maintaining a tight focus can be challenging, especially when the focus is related directly to your practice and interests. This focus is used to identify the research question(s) which your study seeks to answer. Examples include the following: what are pupils' perceptions of the reading corner? What motivates Year 6 girls to attend football club? What are the key benefits and challenges of using talking frames to support peer assessment?

(Continued)

> Keep reading around your research topic! This helps to contextualise the issue and support your case as to why researching the area is important. Moreover, reading enables you to explore appropriate research methods and how to collect data to answer the research question(s), e.g. will you be collecting quantitative data (numerical data), qualitative data (views, experiences and emotions) or mixed (a combination of both quantitative and qualitative data). Additionally, as part of data collection, you need to consider how to gather data to answer the research questions through the use of data collection tools, e.g. via a questionnaire or interviews. Practical activities, such as sorting activities or using a picture or other stimulus to prompt discussion, can be effective and make the situation less formal than an interview. Or you might choose to do group interviews or hold focus groups rather than individual interviews.

Action research as transformational learning

Action research links with transformative learning theory (Mezirow, 1991; Christie et al., 2015), an adult learning theory about making changes which have been generated by a dilemma. The theory proposes that our self-reflection generates a perspective transformation enabling us to then act differently (Mezirow, 1990a, 1990b, 1991). With reference to teachers' professional learning and action research, this could be deemed as a 'move from non-reflective habitual action to a more conscious practice', which could 'bring teaching issues to the forefront of their mind' and expose teachers 'to a range of ideas that could enhance their teaching practice' (Kligyte, 2011, p. 209). This professional learning engenders a 'change in perspective, [which is] a more sophisticated view of teaching than was previously held' (ibid.). Commonalities between action research and transformative learning theory encompass planning and undertaking action, and making observations and pinpointing outcomes to reflect upon and influence future cycles (Mezirow, 1991; Taylor, 2007; Christie et al., 2015).

Of course, it is important to acknowledge that teachers may alter practice without experiencing transformative learning. Indeed, Mezirow (1991) professes that whilst learning involves change, 'not all learning is transformative' (p. 223). Nevertheless, action research may be considered experiential learning in terms of having a new experience, reflecting on and understanding this experience, leaning from the experience and taking action based on what has been learned (Kolb, 1984).

Critical question

What teaching issues come to the forefront of your mind which might affect your teaching practice and you feel you could enhance?

Action research as a collective endeavour

Whilst action research may be undertaken individually, it could also be part of a collaborative enterprise within a professional learning community (Sullivan, 2017) where staff engage with change to enhance pupil outcomes (Louis, 2006; Fullan, 2016), alongside debate and challenge within a conducive environment of openness and trust (Nias et al., 1992). Southworth (2009) promotes professional dialogue as a foundation for teacher learning, advocating reflection as professional learning opportunities. Dialogue may also occur with the pupils you are engaged with around the action research (Glenn, 2020b). Moreover, the collaboration may be seen to have relevance to Wenger's (1998) notion of communities of practice, which emphasises mutual engagement through members working and supporting one another, joint enterprise (collective understanding of the community's activities and its function) and a shared repertoire (where members have agreed ways of working and communicating).

Three types of action research

Carr and Kemmis (1986) differentiate between three types of action research: technical, practical and emancipatory. Technical action research involves external facilitators asking practitioners to assess the outcomes of external research within their own practices to inform external research literature. Scant focus is made upon developing the practitioner, and instead there is an alignment with externally created questions and teachers co-opted into research. Nevertheless, this could serve to entice teachers to start more intense reflection of their practice.

Practical action research involves a more equal status quo between an external facilitator and a practitioner and is not imposed externally. It is called 'practical' since it 'develops the practical reasoning of practitioners' (Carr and Kemmis, 1986, p. 203). Practices are 'open to development through self-reflection' (ibid.), and facilitators support strategic action plans for change, monitoring problems and noting impacts of change. Practitioners explore ideas and their reasons for action and engage with self-reflection.

Emancipatory action research is where the practitioner group takes responsibility for developing practice and deems whole school determination and decision-making as integral and reciprocal between group and individual (Carr and Kemmis, 1986). It is emancipatory in that it explores issues, including habits, customs, bureaucracy and control, to identify elements which are irrational or contradictory, and empowers participants, engaging them in conflicting debates for increased, just democratic education (ibid). Nevertheless, it acknowledges the limits of power to alter things through its own actions. A facilitatory role can be taken by a member of the action community group. Whilst emancipatory research would lead towards and generate more of a social transformation (e.g. see Glenn et al., 2017), it would require most likely high-risk change and classroom-based practitioners would need authority to act for themselves. Due to conditions related to educational performativity and accountability, this is unlikely to occur. Therefore, it is most likely that as an outcome, a classroom practitioner will veer towards practical action research. Nevertheless, Glenn (2020b) advocates that it is still possible to locate one's research in a broader context where critical pedagogy (see Freire, 1970) exploring political issues of power, oppression and culture may be intertwined with everyday practice in the classroom. For example, Glenn relates a dilemma she had around a pupil she taught whose social skills were more developed but generally deemed, through accountability mechanisms operating within the educational system, not as important as assessed academic ability in maths and language skills.

Autonomy

Action research, undertaken within school practice, is likely to come under the remits of school improvement strategies, with school improvement conceived as enabling the occurrence of change and impact upon children's learning (Thomson, 2010). This aligns more with the framework of practical action research described in the previous section. The parameters of school improvement raise inherent tensions between free choice and limitations of what teachers, engaged in action research projects, are permitted to do within the confines of national directives and school direction (Bubb, 2010; Lambirth and Cabral, 2017; Lambirth et al., 2021). This may also seep into a choice of whether or not an individual has a choice of engaging in action research in the first place. It may be argued that there are degrees of freedom around how a teacher may take ownership for developing their practice and that instead of accepting the educational status quo, they may explore and challenge elements of policy implementation and practice if these are not producing what is desired. Coughlan and Coghlan (2002) articulate the dilemma and seem to provide a resolution, at least for a degree of autonomy. They assert that whilst we may not have control over the forces requiring action,

> there is likely to be a great deal of control over how to respond to those forces. In that case there is likely to be a good deal of scope as to what changes, how, and in what time scale the action can take place
>
> Coughlan and Coghlan (2002, p. 231)

It should also be acknowledged if reflecting on your values is a critical aspect of and trigger for action research, then surely autonomy over your (pedagogical) values plays a major part. A challenge within action research is that of 'experiencing oneself as a living contradiction' (Whitehead, 1989, 2019, p. 5; Glenn, 2020b, p. 84) where values may be at a tangent with what you experience/practice in your daily professional life. Nevertheless, this may act as a catalyst for change, and the term 'contradiction' allows for a resolution.

Before we consider the cycle of action research, Leeza Ahmed considers how action research was used as a tool to motivate pupils in her class. This is relevant because action research should not only motivate and benefit the researcher, but also the children.

Motivating Pupils by Encouraging Pupils to 'Think Hard'

By Leeza Ahmed, Early Career Teacher, Colchester, England

Many educators would agree that motivating pupils can be challenging, yet it is one of the most important predictors of success (Capel et al., 2016). Similarly, cognitive engagement, the 'psychological effort that students put into learning and mastering content' (Fisher et al., 2018 p. 135), is a fundamental contributor to pupil attainment. Cognition and motivation have a reciprocal relationship which can work effectively to fully reap the rewards of enhanced learning.

After teaching an unmotivated and low attaining group of pupils during my teacher training year, I was determined to uncover a strategy to heighten their motivation and,

(Continued)

in turn, their attainment by utilising action research. My action research project aimed to investigate the impact of tasks which had varying demands of cognitive engagement on pupils' motivation. The results suggested a positive correlation - when tasks required increased demands of cognitive engagement, the levels of pupil motivation increased too.

After conducting my action research assignment, I reached two conclusions:
1. **Pupils enjoy autonomy**
   I align myself with the view that children enjoy autonomy because empowering pupils to take ownership over their learning enables them to develop a sense of responsibility and self-motivation (McCombs, 2011). This aligns with Bruner's (1961) argument that discovery learning is beneficial for pupil learning. Instead of providing pupils with information passively and directly, pupils must think hard by exercising their prior and existing knowledge to discover new knowledge independently or collaboratively. Examples of discovery learning include researching information, manipulating objects, carrying out experiments and solving problems.
2. **A creative classroom culture fosters a thinking culture in the classroom**
   I believe that a creative approach to teaching and learning helps to develop children's thinking. I use many simple but effective strategies to incorporate creativity in my classroom such as asking pupils to create a song, mnemonic or rhyme or design a poster, story or book cover. Additionally, I nurture the way in which my pupils can illustrate their learning or make connections, e.g. through asking them to create infographics.

   According to the revised Bloom's taxonomy (see https://bloomstaxonomy.net/), tasks set at and towards a more creative level require higher degrees of cognitive engagement. This is because it compels pupils to draw connections, be critical and inventive. In a report published via OFSTED (2010), creative learning was characterised by being challenging, making connections, seeing relationships and reflecting critically on ideas. In OFSTED's survey with outstanding schools, pupils expressed how creative tasks heightened their motivation, stating, 'We are given the freedom to explore ideas and are encouraged to go as far as possible' and 'we get to THINK about things!' (OFSTED, 2010, p. 13).

   Ensuring that activities I set are challenging, yet achievable, encourage autonomy. Through utilising elements of creativity, and increasing cognitive engagement in my classroom, I encourage my pupils to think hard about their learning. This yields benefits in motivating them.

   (Extracted and adapted from Ahmed, 2021, by Leeza Ahmed)

Round and round it goes - where it stops, nobody knows

The nature of action research is a cyclic process which is detailed in Figure 13.1 and has been influenced by the steps of action research suggested by Creswell (2012) of identifying a problem, locating resources to help address the problem, planning for gathering data, collecting

The power of actioning action research 199

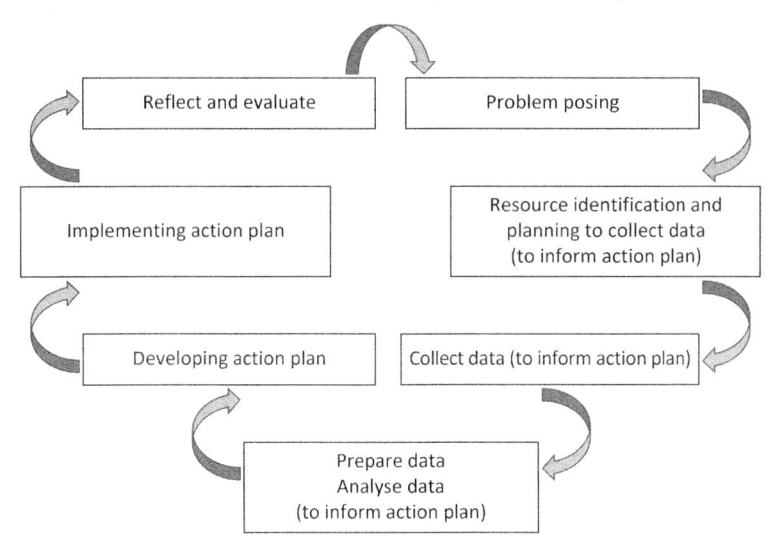

Figure 13.1 The action research cycle

(and preparing) and then analysing data, developing and implementing an action plan, and reflecting on the action taken.

The nature of the cycle may be summarised in the following list:

Step 1: Problem posing – identify the problem to be researched.
Step 2: Resource identification and planning to collect data which will inform an action plan – e.g. consider where the data may come from, who may be involved and how data may be collected. Data may come from a variety of sources such as literature, staff meetings, training courses, visits to other schools or organisations, discussions, interviews, meetings and observations – formal and informal, pupil data or surveys within the school. The data may be 'hard', e.g. of a statistical nature, or 'soft' which may be based on an individual interpretation.
Step 3: Collect data to inform the action plan – the action researcher gathers data around the area they wish to research.
Step 4a: Preparing data – data gathered is collated for analysis for the individual teacher researcher or group.
Step 4b: Analysing data to inform the action plan – the data is analysed by the individual researcher, or group, and discussed, as appropriate, with a facilitator.
Step 5: Developing an action plan – now that this pre-stage of data collection is complete the action being researched may be planned for, and liaison may occur within a group or with a facilitator, as appropriate.
Step 6: Implementing the action plan – the action around the area of research is implemented.
Step 7: Reflect – the impact, both expected and unexpected, of the research is evaluated, to inform further cycles. There is no guarantee that the action undertaken by the research will have the desired effect, but the nature of action research allows tweaks to be made and a new cycle to begin.

> **Critical question**
>
> Why can being critical as a teacher have value?

Becoming critical in more than one sense

McDonagh (2016) promotes that a central tenet in the action research process is to deeply integrate thinking critically by identifying and evaluating your values and noting your thinking at all stages. A key component of undertaking research is that the trigger is likely to stem from a moment of critical reflection. This links back to the concept of possibilities for teachers to experience episodes of reflection and transformative learning, discussed earlier, which meshes with the idea of self-study action research enabling examination and problematisation (looking at a situation from a critical stance and from multiple perspectives) of teaching and evaluating against one's own educational values (Roche, 2016, 2020). Research then becomes a personal endeavour to interrogate your values, practice and the rationale behind these which can potentially uncover uncomfortable realisations (Roche, 2016). Questions may be challenging to pose, but unless this is engaged with, then teachers are limited in their ability to improve pupil learning and their own teaching. Through posing challenging questions, we can be inspired to have freedom of interpretation against multiple perspectives and not accede to the status quo – instead 'reaching for new possibilities and potentials' (Roche, 2016, p. 34). Through questioning, reflection and, most importantly, critical awareness to challenge and alter pedagogy in line with deeply held values, a teacher becomes a learner (Roche, 2016).

Becoming critical also extends to evaluating what information is currently out there. From mapping out the educational landscape through careful critical reading of literature, a researcher may feel more confident with piecing together, formulating and presenting key arguments upon which their research is based. Literature sources may emanate from theory, research, policy or practice literature, and critical reading of these involves evaluating the claims they make (Wilson, 2016). This involves reading between the lines to assess the writer's 'values, beliefs and/or assumptions' (p. 5) which may affect their arguments. That is not to indicate that the writer's perspectives are incorrect; indeed writer objectivity is impossible, and the purpose of their work is to assert their particular view. Nevertheless, the researcher's sceptical approach is warranted.

Supporting reflection

When engaging with critical reflection, it can be most supportive to work alongside other colleagues, in a group or at least with one other person. Constant question posing with others can help to clarify ideas and structure action research. For example, 'What is the important situation in my class and why is it important?', 'How may I understand the situation?', 'What assumptions may underpin interpretations of data collected?', 'Is there another way of interpreting the data set?', 'What questions may be posed from the data analysis?' and 'How may I transform a situation?' (Wilson, 2008).

Historically, there has been limited recognition about the robustness of action research as a 'public knowledge-generating process' (Wilson, 2008, p. 117). Whilst the primary goal of action research is to develop new knowledge for your own classroom practice based on your own critical reflection, this reflection could be prone to bias or procedural irregularities if undertaking self-generated research. Nevertheless, the processes that would be encouraged should demonstrate academic validity as part of rigorous research procedures (see Wilson, 2008, pp. 118-119 for further details). This also includes considering ethical aspects of the research, which is discussed later in this chapter. Perhaps the most powerful element to consider is that action research happens at the chalkface in the classroom, enabling immediate action, and situations are unique. It may be appropriate to undertake further training to support methodology, for example by drawing on the support of academic institutions such as universities to help critical reflection, which is discussed in the next section.

> **Critical question**
>
> How can universities support action research projects in schools?

Classroom research support

A co-author of this book, Ashley Brett, has supported a university programme to encourage teachers to engage with action research within their individual schools. The University of Greenwich's School of Education runs a 'Professionals as Researchers' programme, supporting educational settings with their continuing professional development focused around teaching and learning. One of the projects focuses on action research, where a university colleague supports groups of teachers in their particular setting to identify a focus for a cycle of action research across an academic year. The programme links to and facilitates the elements detailed earlier about the separate components of a research cycle. Meetings to explain the process and to reflect on progress are held half-termly. These meetings are not to replace relevant discussions which occur internal to the setting, but give voice to the progress and a chance for the university facilitator to support colleagues and liaise with them about timely next-step actions in line with the action research cycle, advise them on appropriate literature or answer imminent questions.

The meetings generally would cover the following stages: an introduction to the programme and an overview of the action research cycle to consider a pertinent focus; stages and ideas for data gathering, data feedback and data analysis (autumn term); planning for the action and implementation (around the spring term/early summer term); evaluation and dissemination (summer term). Of course there is flexibility within these parameters, but the key message for teachers is that it is not about undertaking instant research with their pupils in the first term, but to allow for time during the year for their ideas to develop and to engage with that important initial area of data gathering, feedback and analysis before planning any actions. The dissemination is a key aspect of the research process and may align with a teacher/school's action plan. For example, the dissemination may occur through attending conferences, engaging with publications and feedback to the colleagues within the setting. Colleagues who participate are also invited to submit a structured report for Masters credits, should they wish, and for some this can provide additional motivation. (For more details of the process, refer to Lambirth et al., 2021.)

Lambirth et al. (2021) present a model of action research and facilitation, which comprise the three areas of before, during and after collaboration of the Professionals as Researchers programme. The authors acknowledge a 'zone of proximal activity' (McNiff and Whitehead, 2005; Kemmis et al., 2014), which refers to the strengths that both the participants (teachers) and facilitators (university-based colleagues) may bring to the research project. Furthermore, there is recognition of zones of contributory activity (participant-facilitator interaction) and collaborative activities where the skill sets from the participants and facilitators merge to enable reflection, discussion and peer review during the main research process. Lofthouse et al. (2016) distinguish contributory and collaborative activity to denote the likelihood that during collaboration

> the partners [participants and facilitators] do not always work collaboratively on the action research project. Each partner will typically take on activities that make a direct contribution to, or are a direct response to, the collaborative activity but which draw on their individual skills or designated roles.
>
> (Lofthouse et al., 2016, p. 530)

Nevertheless, there is a 'reciprocal and reliant relationship' (p. 531) between the two zones. An 'after collaboration' period returns to a proximal activity zone for dissemination (and further study if relevant for participants). This acknowledges and celebrates the notion that 'the action research study exists in some form or other after the end of the official project is over [and] is part of the long-term sustainability criterion of action research' (Lambirth et al., 2021, p. 822).

Lambirth et al. (2021) consider that this model enables a potential to develop for teacher research 'with teachers finding ways to professionally develop within a specific context' (p. 830).

Dealing with challenges

> **Critical question**
>
> How may you overcome some of the challenges which might arise by undertaking action research?

Undertaking action research does not go without experiencing challenge. Detailed in Table 13.1 are some issues which need to be attended to and possible ways to overcome them. The areas have been adapted from issues highlighted in greater detail by Lambirth et al. (2021) where a team of colleagues from the University of Greenwich supported year-long action research projects in schools.

The power of actioning action research 203

Table 13.1 Challenges and possible ways to overcome them

Challenges	Overcoming challenges
Feeling that you have to participate because senior leaders have told you that it is part of the school development plan	Recognise the potential for your transformation that can stem from engaging with action research. We can also learn from our colleagues' action research experiences to help develop our intrinsic motivation and gain a sense of purpose, independence and autonomy. It also enables us to acknowledge that our work really does matter and has value.
How much independence or autonomy do I really get? Aren't there conflicts of interest?	It is too with negotiation. Facilitated peer discussions with colleagues at school and with senior leaders enable you (and those working with you, perhaps as facilitators from a university) to negotiate your roles and responsibilities, which are set within the context of accountability. The tension, between ownership of your practice and challenging the status quo at odds with your values and beliefs, can lead to a professional identity crisis. Nevertheless, by working through this, the dissonance eventually becomes part of your developing professional identity.
What if I am not aware or do not feel so confident with the practical bits linked to research?	You might get support from outside agencies who are researchers or perhaps you may seek support from an online group. They can help you to design and trial out data collection tools (e.g. surveys, observation grids and interview schedules) and undertake data analysis and appropriate reflection. There may be colleagues within your school who feel more proficient with undertaking research, and they can be sources of support.
Research put out in the educational world can sometime feel a bit up there, beyond my understanding (using a formal academic language for an academic audience) and inaccessible to me if I do not have membership to a particular source. Some research can also be inconclusive. Additionally, I do not have sufficient time to engage with academic reading or to discuss it. I do not feel confident to write, present or share my work, especially if it is for the wider academic audience where particular academic conventions are adhered to. I am anxious that, if shared, my research will not influence other practitioners.	A lot of efforts have been made to align research findings with practice, to make it evidence informed, sharing best practices and 'what works'. Moreover, more accessibility is facilitated nowadays with the use of search engines and open databases. If there is dedicated time, e.g. in staff meetings or on training days, allotted by senior leaders to colleagues engaging in discussion, then this can be used as a vehicle to unpick relevant literature, peer reviewing ideas and analysing themes based on your own knowledge and personal experience, and that of others. Critique of research evidence can support risk-taking, development of new perspectives and changes in practice. Of course, it is important to acknowledge that if facilitated by an outside agency, tensions still might exist between controlling and nurturing (autonomous) approaches to, and discussion of, research. As for discussion – talk is what gives us agency; we use it within our work, within our social contexts. If you work with facilitators from an outside agency, they can support you with that process; within your own school, you are going to be working alongside nurturing colleagues – maybe you can produce a piece of work collectively to celebrate with other schools within your catchment area, or within a trust, or for a non-academic audience or a professional organisation which hosts conferences. It is all about the research having meaning for you, and the process can be a transformative, rather than a transmission, model of professional development. Planning for dissemination of your own learning can be part of what you consider at the beginning of the project. Start small and let the ripple effect take hold for wider communication.

Initial teacher education and partnerships

Ashley Brett and Robert Morgan (co-authors of this book) have led action research projects with postgraduate initial teacher education (ITE) providers, which their university accredits.

PGCE Action Research Projects

By Ashley Brett and Robert Morgan, Present and Past SCITT Leads for PGCE Action Research Projects at The University of Greenwich, London, England

Action research projects have been developed with PGCE SCITT institutions for their trainees, and credits are awarded at level 7, which can be used towards a Masters. There are two components to it: (1) a written assignment around methodology to understand the principles of action research and (2) a small-scale action research project within the school in which they are training. The first unit of study enables students to explore the literature and review methods, ethics and steps of analysis. Within this, students write up a proposed action research project and complete a mock ethics form, but do not actually collect data. Analysis occurs by reflecting on what the student thinks they might have found out with reference back to their literature review. The second unit of study, a small-scale action research project undertaken within the school at which the student is training, is centred around an issue which the student has identified around teaching and learning.

One of the purposes of engaging with the action research within a PGCE programme is that the trainees can go out into the world of teaching with some insight of how to undertake (action) research; this promotes a degree of autonomy for the trainees to not take ideas at face value (not accept the status quo), but to be able to explore areas of importance to them which can then have an impact on their teaching and the children's learning. Moreover, the trainees also develop an ethical understanding of approaches to research and considerations they would need to reflect upon if undertaking research within their own classes at a point in the future. A tribute to its success is that we have some trainees who have contributed their practitioner voice to this book: Leeza Ahmed and Madeeha Kashif within this chapter, and Charlotte Nohavicka and Laura Whiteman in Chapter 7 on 'Formative Assessment'.

The quality of the action research projects is strong, and the school-centred initial teacher trainers (SCITTs) have been creating a database of PGCE action research titles and assignments, providing a legacy of trainees' work and inspiration and support for new trainees. At the end of programme celebration event, trainees are given the opportunity to present and showcase their action research to their peers, tutors and invited guests. This also mirrors professional development within a learning community of a school, where a member of staff may engage with others in discussion

(Continued)

around an area they are researching. They may invite colleagues' feedback about the research findings, and possible implications for the children and the school as next steps' actions.

The action research links to the Early Career Framework (Department for Education [DfE, 2019a]), mirrored in the ITT Core Content Framework's (DfE, 2019b) spotlight on professional responsibilities, because 'learning from educational research, is … likely to support improvement' and 'engaging critically with research and using evidence to critique practice' (DfE, 2019a, p. 29) is something early career teachers will be supported with to develop.

Following is how Madeeha Kashif undertook action research projects within her PGCE SCITT programme. (Madeeha's cohort undertook two action research projects, whereas the current format is as described earlier – an assignment to help trainees understand the principles of action research, followed by undertaking a small-scale action research.)

What my Action Research Project Looked Like in Practice

By Madeeha Kashif, Early Career Teacher, Colchester, England

Refining teaching techniques requires a lot of practice, and undertaking research about teaching helps practitioners to examine pedagogy. The PGCE programme in my training year provided me with an opportunity to do this and complete research in elements of teaching and learning that I would not have explored in such depth otherwise. To be an effective teacher, it is crucial to learn about and understand different ways of teaching and be able to draw upon a variety of techniques to suit learners' needs. The foci in my action research projects enabled me to hone in on particular strategies which I could then adopt into my teaching practice with ease. I also believe that this afforded me more opportunities to help the pupils achieve above their current level and make better achievements.

During the research process, I read from a variety of sources – articles, academic books and published research papers. Once I had selected a research focus, I devised a research plan and began to create resources that would help me to conduct the research. Furthermore, I took advice from my mentor in choosing potential participants to approach and referred to relevant books to support me with understanding research methods.

My first research project was to explore the impact of questioning in the light of Bloom's taxonomy of six levels of questioning (e.g. see https://bloomstaxonomy.net/). I explored how the types of questions worked in practice in different scenarios and began to embed techniques into my practice, which I still use today. By doing this research, I realised the importance of effective questioning and how it improved my pupils' understanding and helped them make better progress within their learning. Moreover, effective questioning helped me to identify any misconceptions my pupils had so that I could

(Continued)

> correct pupils' misunderstandings in their learning. Finally, it also enabled me to develop assessment for learning techniques which informed subsequent planning.
>
> For my second piece of research, I examined the benefits and impact of positive reinforcement (short- and long-term rewards). This helped me to form a menu of techniques to choose from as appropriate to the teaching and learning situation. They proved to be very useful and effective in my teaching training practice, and I have implemented techniques into my current practice. I often use rewards and praise in my lessons to help create a positive learning environment, and it motivates my pupils to learn.

Whilst Madeeha's mini-action research projects revolved around some key elements of whole school priorities in her teacher training school and personal professional practice for her first and second research projects, respectively, there is scope for development of other ideas on other programmes depending upon the school setting in which students train. Roche (2017) explores the ITE and school-college partnership and presents a case study exploring how trainees undertaking self-study action research within their placement, facilitated by ITE tutors and school placement supervisors, can enhance practice and pupil learning.

The hook of a focus of action research through engaging in an inquiry may act as a motivational tool. However, a third space is advocated by Roche which is where both schools (involved in school-university partnerships) and the ITE providers may agree objectives so that all stakeholders can be research informed and research informing (Roche, 2017). Roche details an undergraduate degree provided by her college, and key aspects have relevance to primary trainees. Students reflect on their first two placements, underpinned by key modules to develop criticality around their assumptions of education, to identify and inform their final self-study research project in their third year. This is facilitated by researching literature not as a traditional review, but as 'How do I deepen my understanding of' (Roche, 2017, p. 110). Additional components include opportunities to engage with annual symposiums which reflect the different stages of students' developing research, poster presentations and peer- and self-evaluations. Student reflection of their self-study action research acknowledged that it enabled them to identify their teaching values (personal values translated into student and then professional values) central to their teaching philosophy and to reflect and demonstrate how it translated into practice. This was also enabled by consideration of key questions such as 'what am I doing?', 'why am I doing it?', 'how do I improve what I am doing?' and 'how do I live my values more fully to engage in my practice?' (Roche, 2017, p. 115)

Ethical considerations

> **Critical question**
>
> What ethical considerations do we need to bear in mind when undertaking action research?

This section reflects on the importance of ethical considerations within action research. Given that an action research project is undertaken by teachers in schools about their own practice, the potential for harm might not seem great and the activities similar to those encountered normally by the pupil participants. Nevertheless, because the activities are being monitored for research purposes, ethical procedures need to be considered.

Consent to participate in research needs to be gained. Under the UK General Data Protection Regulation (EU GDPR) (see UK Data Service, no date; ICO, no date) implemented in 2018, 'Consent requires a positive opt-in. Don't use pre-ticked boxes or any other method of default consent'. (ICO, no date). Moreover, it 'also requires distinct ("granular") consent options for distinct processing operations', requiring specific and 'granular' details to enable 'separate consent for separate things. Vague or blanket consent is not enough' (ibid.). Additionally, there needs to be clarity about participants' right to withdraw and offers of an easy way to action this (ibid.). Researchers in Britain often pay due regard to BERA (2018) guidelines for ethical procedures. Nevertheless, it is relevant to acknowledge that ethical details from the British Psychological Society (BPS) (2021) are regulatory and, therefore, merit greater weight than BERA guidance.

Matthew Tragheim reminds us of grassroots, ethical considerations for action research.

Ethical Considerations

By Matthew Tragheim, Lecturer in Primary Education, London, England

When first learning about the importance of education research, I remember attending a university lecture featuring a demure and unassuming American educator. Her image and work has stayed with me. Jane Elliot, a school teacher based in Iowa, the USA, ran a thought-provoking experiment with her grade-three (Year 4) class. Filmed in 1970, and inspired by the assassination of Martin Luther King Jr, her classroom experiment gained national media attention for its portrayal and examination of racial inequality. One day, after the children arrived in class for the start of school, Elliot divided her class by eye colour (brown and blue) to show children how it felt to experience racial segregation. Initially, children in the minority blue-eyed group were resistant to the idea that brown-eyed children were superior. However, over time, they became increasingly subservient and passive. In her teacher position of power and authority, Elliot reinforced growing feelings of inferiority and inadequacy amongst the children by listing out unfounded 'scientific' reasons why blue-eyed children lacked intelligence, ability or aptitude. Although entirely untrue, she knowingly recounted these falsehoods to engender growing feelings of opposition and animosity. Over time, the majority (brown-eyed) group became increasingly arrogant, domineering and dismissive of their blue-eyed counterparts. Perhaps more unsettling, academic performance also changed whilst stress, anxiety and discriminating language increased. Brown-eyed children began to score higher in writing and maths

(Continued)

assessments, whilst the minority group started to underperform against their previous test scores. Elliot's experiment demonstrated how quickly the seeds of division, discrimination and prejudice can be sown; these discussion topics are just as pertinent for children today.

Although perhaps unintentional, Elliot had conducted participatory action research in her classroom. By triangulating qualitative and quantitative data from her behavioural experiment, Elliot could identify how, by changing certain parameters, she could deliberately influence and affect learning. Although Elliot's research is undoubtedly thought-provoking and valuable when viewed within the context of her time, it raises serious ethical questions. Using action research at a grass roots level is important for advancing our own knowledge as practitioners. It helps us to better understand the children we teach, the context we teach in and the way children learn. It also enables us to examine how learning processes, interactions and behaviours shape educational outcomes. However, children are highly impressionable and teachers assume a privileged position of authority and power. Contemporary educational researchers have suggested that the possible psychological and emotional impact of Elliot's experiment outweighs the potential benefits. When conducting education research in my own context, knowledge about Elliot's experiment has stayed with me. Not simply for what it attempted to articulate at the time, nor for its parallels to modern debate, but for the duty of care and ethical consideration that must always be undertaken when researching children.

Although the teacher is evaluating their own practice within action research, this normally involves activities requiring some form of pupil participant involvement. As such, this necessitates obtaining consent from a parent/guardian for children under 18, as well as from the participating children. Loco parentis approval, for example by the headteacher delegating consent, no longer qualifies as appropriate consent; individual participant consent must be actively given. Informed consent detail, provided by the researcher, enables the child (participant) and parent/guardian to consider what the research project entails and helps inform whether or not they consent to participation. It should also be acknowledged that even if a parent/guardian gives consent, the child (participant) can refuse to consent to participation. This can raise research challenges to consider; for example, what if a teacher wishes to explore a whole class intervention and a few parents/guardians or children do not provide consent? This means that the focus or reporting of the research cannot extend to these pupils, even if an intervention is provided to the whole class. If the intervention is part of everyday teaching practice, then presumably the activity itself will occur, but the data gathering and reporting of those children, where consent has not been given, cannot be undertaken.

Stutchbury (2008) presents an ethical framework based on moral theory to support educational researchers consider ethical issues proactively, prior to undertaking action research, from multiple perspectives to highlight difficulties which may affect the quality and impact of the research. The ethical dilemmas may be considered 'situated' – relevant to a specific context only, which is why the framework has much utility. It comprises four layers:

a   The external or ecological layer focused on the research context, the wishes of individuals who are external to the situation, the institutional culture and the relationship between the part of the setting in which the researcher works and the institutions as a whole.
b   The consequential or utilitarian layer focused on how much good is anticipated for those affected by the research, e.g. humanity, a specific group, individual or researcher such as a school, teachers, pupils or parents.
c   The deontological layer focused on the duties and motives underpinning the research and is about preventing doing wrong, e.g. avoiding harm, doing good, having integrity and being truthful, and keeping promises. This would entail considering how the research is undertaken, and informing relevant parties of research outcomes at relevant times and how sensitive information might be dealt with.
d   The individual layer/relational ethics focused on the needs of those individuals who are involved in the research and the underpinning relationships, for example in education this may be centred around trust.

Stutchbury (2008) attaches questions to consider against each of these themes which are presented in Table 13.2.

There may be overlap between questions in the different sections, not all questions may be relevant and the relevance may shift as the research project shifts from data collection to analysis and interpretation, so questions are likely to need revisiting.

Ethical considerations include confidentiality associated with qualitative data and anonymity associated with quantitative data, informed consent (Coffelt, 2018), data storage, selection of participants and when research activities might occur during the school day. Examples of questions guiding ethical considerations and informed consent are presented in Table 13.3 followed by examples of letters for informed consent in Tables 13.4 and 13.5. A copy of the consent forms, signed by the teacher researcher, should be returned to the relevant parent/guardian and pupil participant. The documentation has been adapted from ethical forms developed in consultation between the University of Greenwich and SCITT leads who deliver mini-action research projects to those training to be teachers as part of a PGCE.

Who owns the research?

Tensions may exist with who owns the research – the teacher researcher or the pupil participants? There needs to be acknowledgement and understanding about the power dynamics (Lambirth et al., 2021). It also links in with ethical considerations too as there is a 'corresponding change in the unspoken contract with the children in their care – from teacher and pupil to researcher and participant' (p. 826). This power imbalance is pertinent with pupils as participants, where coercion to participate, along with 'social desirability bias, and perfectionism to create a positive impression' (p. 826), may be present, often tacitly and under the surface. These issues can be avoided by promoting open dialogue with the children so

Table 13.2 Ethical questions

External/ecological	Questions
Cultural sensitivity	What are the values, norms and roles of my institution?
Institutional awareness	What is the relationship between who I work with and the setting as a whole?
Responsive communication – awareness of others' wishes	How might the research be considered by others within my setting?
Responsibilities to others	What are my obligations to those 'paying' for the research? NB. 'paying' could also involve paying for cover to enable a teacher to undertake the research.
BERA guidance/ BPS code of practice	Have I attended to the BERA guidance and/or BPS regulations?
The law	Is anyone at risk from my research? Have I complied with GDPR?
Consequential/utilitarian	Questions
Benefits for individuals – informed consent	Are participants and parents/guardians aware of what the research entails and why it is being undertaken? Has information about withdrawal been provided? How will confidentiality and anonymity be upheld?
Benefits for specific groups	What are the benefits of undertaking the research to my setting? How will I share my findings? Is the research compatible with the school development plan?
Most benefits to society	Is the research of interest to others working within education?
Benefits to researcher	Will the research benefit my professional development?

(Continued)

Table 13.2 Ethical questions (Continued)

Deontological	Questions
Avoidance of wrong	Have I been transparent and honest with those affected by the research?
Fairness	Have all those participating been treated fairly?
	How will participants be selected and why?
	Has GDPR opt in been adhered to?
Reciprocity	What if findings are unpopular to the participants or setting, and how will they be reported?

Relational/individual	Questions
Genuine collaboration and trust	How may constructive relationships be developed and nurtured?
Avoiding imposition/ respecting autonomy	Are unreasonable demands being made upon anyone? Is participation considered voluntary?
Confirmation of findings	How will I ensure valid and reliable findings?
Respect	How will respect be shown to participants? Is the same level of respect shown to pupils as teachers?

Source: Adapted from Stutchbury (2008).

Table 13.3 Questions guiding ethical consideration and informed consent

Name of researcher
1. What aspect of teaching and learning do you plan to research?
2. Why do you want to focus on this?
3. Who will be involved? (Which year group, pupils specifically and why?) How will you choose the pupils?
4. The chosen methodology is action research. Why does this methodology suit the research you are proposing?
5. What method(s) will you use? What actions will you be taking? Why have you chosen this/these method(s)? What are the limitations? What sort of questions will you be asking? What are the ethical issues and how will you address them?

Chosen method(s)	Quantitative and/or Qualitative results?	Reason for choosing this method? (e.g., Was it used in any of the literature you have read?)	Limitations of the method?

What are the ethical issues linked to the methods you will use and how will you address them? E.g. group interviews, timings, personal questions, sensitive questions…..what are the ethical considerations for any actions you will undertake?...

(Continued)

Table 13.3 Questions guiding ethical consideration and informed consent (*Continued*)

(If applicable) What questions will you be asking in an interview or in a survey? If you are doing an observation, then what will your observation schedule look like?
6. Consent of Parents - How do you plan to gain the consent of parents? (Parents need to opt in.)
7. Voluntary Participation of Pupils - how will you ensure that your pupils have voluntarily offered to participate and are not coerced? (N.B. If you are not providing a letter (e.g. if they are too young to read), how will you gain their consent? Even for very young children, a sheet with smiley faces can be used. Providing a script for you to read from with the relevant information as well as smiley faces for children to give consent would be a good idea.)
8. Data Protection - what strategies do you propose for storing, protecting and disposing of the information you collect in the course of this research? (NB Detail where your data will be stored. Will it be password protected?)
9. Anonymity - how will you ensure that the data you collect is not traceable to the pupils? (This means 'collecting data without obtaining any personal, identifying information' (Coffelt, 2018, p.2)).
10. Confidentiality - how will you ensure that you can adhere to confidentiality? ('separating or modifying any personal, identifying information provided by participants from the data' (Coffelt, 2018, p.2)).
11. How will you disseminate your findings with others? For example, will you share with the senior leadership team, or with colleagues you work with? Are there issues of adhering to confidentiality?
This research has been approved by the headteacher **Headteacher's signature** _____ **Date** _____

Source: Adapted from the University of Greenwich (no date a).

Table 13.4 Template for informed parental consent

Dear Parent/ Guardian,

I am undertaking some action research on **[write briefly what your research will be about and why you are doing it]**. I am writing to ask for your permission to allow your child to participate in my small-scale research, where they... **[explain what the participants will have to do as part of the research e.g., complete a 10-minute survey on a computer, be interviewed...]**. This research has been approved by **[provide details]**.

I will be undertaking my research on/between **[delete as appropriate] [give date(s)]**. Please note that even if you give consent for your child to participate, their involvement is completely optional and they themselves may choose to opt out. Upon return of your consent form, your child will also be given a similar consent letter about the research and they will also have a chance to give their consent by a return slip/I will be explaining the research to your child and giving them a chance to say whether or not they wish to take part **[delete as appropriate]. [Explain how you will choose from the pool of child participants you may have.]**

For data protection, data collected from your child will be stored securely in a password protected file **on the institutional cloud/ in a locked cupboard on school premises [delete as appropriate]**. The raw data will be destroyed by _____ **[give date]**. No raw data will be shared with anyone except **[and give details and explain why]**.

Please note that:
- Your child can decide to stop the research whilst data is being collected.
- If your child takes part, they can withdraw until **[give a date, e.g. a couple of weeks before the research is due to be published/shared**] and all their data will be withdrawn and deleted.
- Your child's name will be anonymised and it should not be possible to identify your child in any final report and/ or when findings are shared **[delete as appropriate]**.
- The raw data will only be shared with **[and give details]**.
- A report and/or the research findings **[delete as appropriate]** will be shared with **[and give details]**.

[Add anything else of relevance - use points which are relevant for your research e.g. your child need not answer questions they do not wish to in the survey/interview.]

If there are any further questions you wish to ask about the research, I will be happy for you to contact me **[give appropriate contact details]**.

Thank you in anticipation and please complete the attached form below and return to me, to give consent for your child to participate.

Yours faithfully

_____

(Continued)

Table 13.4 Template for informed parental consent (Continued)

Parent/Guardian Consent
• I have read the information sheet about this project
• I have had an opportunity to ask questions and discuss this project if needed
• I have received satisfactory answers to all my questions if asked
• I have received enough information about this project
• I understand that a report and/or the research findings might be shared with ... **[define who]**
• I understand that my child:
   o can stop taking part **[e.g. in the interview - be specific]** whilst data is being collected
   o is free to withdraw from this project at any time until **[give a date, e.g. a couple of weeks before the research is due to be published/shared]** and their data will be deleted and not used in the research.
   o does not have to give a reason to withdraw

I give consent for _____ [name of child] to take part.	
Signed [parent/guardian]	Date
Signed [teacher]	Date

Source: Adapted from the University of Greenwich (no date b).

Table 13.5 Template for informed participant consent

NB For very young children, a sheet with smiley faces can be used to give consent. So, if you are working with children in Reception, for example, providing a script below instead would be a good idea, with the relevant information which you can read from, as well as a sheet demarcated with smiley faces which the children can colour in to give consent.

Dear Pupil

I am doing some research about **[write briefly what your research will be about and why you are doing it]**.

I am writing to ask if you would like to take part in my research. If you do, you will... **[explain what the participants will have to do as part of the research, e.g., complete a 10 minute survey on a computer, be interviewed...].**

I will be undertaking my research on/between **[delete as appropriate] [give date(s)]**.

Information I collect about you or you give to help me with the research will be stored safely in a password protected file **on the institutional cloud/ in a locked cupboard on school premises [delete as appropriate]**. The raw data will be destroyed by _____ **[give date]**. No raw data will be shared with anyone except **[and give details and explain why]**.

If you do wish to take part:

- You can decide to stop taking part **[e.g. in the interview]** whilst I am doing the research.
- You can ask for any information collected about you or given by you to be deleted until **[give a date, e.g., a couple of weeks before the research is due to be published/shared]**.
- Your name will be anonymised **[or use child-friendly language]** and no-one else who hears about the research will be able to identify you.
- The raw data will only be shared with **[and give details]**.
- A report and/or the research findings **[delete as appropriate]** will be shared with **[and give details]**.

[Add anything else of relevance - use points which are relevant for your research, e.g., you do not need to answer questions you do not wish to in the survey/interview...]

If there are any further questions you wish to ask about taking part, please come and speak to me.

I hope you will want to take part. Please complete the form below to agree and return it to me.

Yours faithfully/sincerely (**delete as appropriate**)

(Continued)

Table 13.5 Template for informed participant consent (*Continued*)

Dear Pupil
Please return this to your teacher.

• I have read the information sheet about this project
• I have asked any questions and talked about the research, if needed
• I am happy with the answers to all my questions, if asked
• I know what the research project is about
• I understand that:
   ○ I can stop taking part **[e.g. in the interview – be specific]** whilst the research is being done
   ○ I can ask for any information collected about me or given by me to be deleted until **[give a date]** and it will not be used in the research project
   ○ I do not have to give a reason to stop taking part
   ○ I understand that a report and/or the research findings might be shared with … **[define who]**
• I agree to take part.

Signed [pupil]	Date
Pupil name in block letters	
Signed [teacher]	Date

Source: Adapted from the University of Greenwich (no date b).

their voices are central to any decisions made and actions undertaken by you, as the teacher researcher (Lambirth et al., 2021).

> Pupils … should feel empowered to use their right not to participate in the activities if they do not want to, feel comfortable to share their ideas without being afraid to go against what the teacher thinks… and be open about any fragilities or learning difficulties.
>
> Lambirth et al. (2021, p. 826).

Ethical integrity considerations around informed consent, pupil voice and ownership, and trust, transparency and negotiation are critical components for the teacher (practitioner) researcher and pupil participant activities. They need careful consideration as part of the research process.

Conclusion

This chapter has explored rationales for engaging with action research within your class. The benefits of transformative experiences for your own professional development and the autonomy which it may bring, as well as the central benefits for the children's learning, have been highlighted. The importance of ethical procedures has been spotlighted, especially in the context of GDPR. The sky literally is the limit, and you are encouraged to dip your toes in the water and explore something which is niggling you and you want to do something about. Perhaps your educational values are being compromised, or perhaps you have seen something within another school or from some training you have attended, which has ignited your passion to explore further within the context of your own class. Perhaps you want to start or join a professional learning community face-to-face or online. The impact might not change the whole world, but it could change your world and your pupils' world. You are wished successful and meaningful periods of research ahead.

References

Ahmed, L. (2021). 'What impact does tasks varying in demands of cognitive engagement have on the motivation of pupils?' In *ACAD1396: Professional Development One: Making an Impact on Teaching and Learning*. Mid Essex SCITT and University of Greenwich. Unpublished essay.

British Educational Research Association (BERA). (2018). *Ethical Guidelines for Educational Research*. 4th edn. London: British Educational Research Association. [Online]. Available at: https://www.bera.ac.uk/publication/ethical-guidelines-for-educational-research-2018 [Accessed 1 October 2022].

British Psychological Society (BPS). (2021). *British Psychological Society code of human research ethics*. [Online]. Available at: https://www.bps.org.uk/guideline/bps-code-human-research-ethics-0 [Accessed 1 October 2022].

Bruner, J.S. (1961). The act of discovery. *Harvard Educational Review*, 31, pp. 21-32.

Bubb, S. (2010). 'Engaging teachers in action research'. In P. Earley and V. Porritt (Eds.), *Effective Practices in Continuing Professional Development: Lessons from Schools*. London: Institute of Education Press.

Capel, S., Leask, M., and Younie, S. (2016). *Learning to Teach in the Secondary School*. Oxon: Routledge.

Carr, W., and Kemmis, S. (1986). *Becoming Critical: Education, Knowledge and Action Research*. London: Routledge.

Christie, M., Carey, M., Robertson, A., and Grainger, P. (2015). Putting transformative learning theory into practice. *Australian Journal of Adult Learning*, 55(1), pp. 9-30.

Coffelt, T. (2018). 'Confidentiality and Anonymity of Participants'. In M. Allen (Ed.) *The SAGE Encyclopedia of Communication Research Methods*. Thousand Oaks, CA: SAGE Publications, Inc.

Coughlan, P. and Coghlan, D. (2002), 'Action research for operations management', *International Journal of Operations & Production Management*, 22 (2), pp. 220-240.

Creswell, J. (2012). *Educational Research*. Boston, MA: Pearson Education.

Day, C., and Sachs, J. (2004). 'Professionalism, performativity and empowerment: Discourses in the politics, policies and purposes of continuing professional development'. In C. Day and J. Sachs (Eds.), *International Handbook on the Continuing Professional Development of Teachers* (pp. 3-32). Maidenhead: Open University Press.

Department for Education (DfE) (2019a). *Early career framework*. [Online]. Available at: https://assets.publishing.service.gov.uk/government/uploads/system/uploads/attachment_data/file/978358/Early-Career_Framework_April_2021.pdf [Accessed 1 October 2022].

DfE. (2019b). *ITT core content framework*. [Online]. Available at: https://assets.publishing.service.gov.uk/government/uploads/system/uploads/attachment_data/file/974307/ITT_core_content_framework_.pdf [Accessed 1 October 2022].

Dewey, J. (1910). *How We Think*. Chicago, IL: D. C Heath & Co Publishers.

Fisher, D., Frey, N., Quaglia, R.J., Smith, D., and Lande, L.L. (2018). *Engagement by Design: Creating Learning Environments Where Students Thrive*. Thousand Oaks, CA: Corwin Press.

Freire, P. (1970). *Pedagogy of the Oppressed*. New York, NY: Seabury.

Fullan, M. (2016). *The New Meaning of Educational Change*. 5th edn. London: Routledge.
Glenn, M. (2020a). 'Chapter 3: How can I develop a better understanding of my practice'. In C. McDonagh, M. Roche, B. Sullivan, and M. Glenn (Eds.), *Enhancing Practice Through Classroom Practice: A Teacher's Guide to Professional Development*. Oxon: Routledge.
Glenn, M. (2020b). 'Chapter 4: Thinking critically about educational practices'. In C. McDonagh, M. Roche, B. Sullivan, and M. Glenn (Eds.), *Enhancing Practice Through Classroom Practice: A Teacher's Guide to Professional Development*. Oxon: Routledge.
Glenn, M., Roche, M., McDonagh, C., and Sullivan, B. (2017). *Learning Communities in Educational Partnerships: Action Research as Transformation*. London: Bloomsbury.
Information Commissioner's Office (ICO). (no date). *Consent*. [Online]. Available at: https://ico.org.uk/for-organisations/guide-to-data-protection/guide-to-the-general-data-protection-regulation-gdpr/lawful-basis-for-processing/consent/ [Accessed 1 October 2022].
Kemmis, S., McTaggart, R., and Nixon, R. (2014). *The Action Research Planner: Doing Critical Participatory Action Research*. Singapore: Springer.
Kligyte, G. (2011). Transformation narratives in academic practice. *International Journal for Academic Development*, 16(3), pp. 201–213.
Kolb, D. (1984). *Experiential Learning*. Englewood Cliffs, NJ: Prentice-Hall.
Lambirth, A., and Cabral, A. (2017). Issues of agency, discipline and criticality: An interplay of challenges involved in teachers engaging in research in a performative school context. *Educational Action Research*, 25(4), pp. 650–666.
Lambirth, A., Cabral, A., McDonald, R., Philpott, C., Brett, A., and Magaji, A. (2021). Teacher-led professional development through a model of action research, collaboration and facilitation. *Professional Development in Education*, 47(5), pp. 815–833.
Lofthouse, R., Flanagan, J., and Wigley, B. (2016). A new model of collaborative action research: Theorising from inter-professional practice development. *Educational Action Research*, 24(4), pp. 519–534.
Louis, K.S. (2006). Changing the culture of schools: Professional community, organizational learning and trust. *Journal of School Leadership*, 16(4), pp. 477–489.
McCombs, B. (2011). Reducing the achievement GAP. *Society*, 37(5), pp. 29–36.
McDonagh, C. (2016). 'Chapter 5: Generating data'. In B. Sullivan, M. Glenn, M. Roche, and C. McDonagh (Eds.), *Introduction to Critical Reflection and Action for Teacher Researchers*. London: Routledge.
McNiff, J., and Whitehead, J. (2005). *Action Research for Teachers: A Practical Guide*. London: David Fulton Publishers.
Mezirow, J. (1990a). 'Preface'. In J. Mezirow and Associates (Eds.), *Fostering Critical Reflection in Adulthood: A Guide to Transformative and Emancipatory Learning*. San Francisco, CA: Jossey-Bass.
Mezirow, J. (1990b). 'How critical reflection triggers transformative learning'. In J. Mezirow and Associates (Eds.), *Fostering Critical Reflection in Adulthood: A Guide to Transformative and Emancipatory Learning*. San Francisco, CA: Jossey-Bass.
Mezirow, J. (1991). *Transformative Dimensions of Adult Learning*. San Francisco, CA: Jossey-Bass.
Nias, J., Southworth, G., and Campbell, P. (1992). *Whole School Curriculum Development in Primary Schools*. London: Falmer.
OFSTED. (2010). *Learning: Creative approaches that raise standards*. [Online]. Available at: https://dera.ioe.ac.uk/1093/1/Learning%20creative%20approaches%20that%20raise%20standards.pdf [Accessed 1 October 2022].
Roche, M. (2016). 'Chapter 2: What is action research?'. In B. Sullivan, M. Glenn, M. Roche, and C. McDonagh (Eds.), *Introduction to Critical Reflection and Action for Teacher Researchers*. London, UK: Taylor & Francis Group.
Roche, M. (2017). 'Initial teacher education and school-college partnerships: The potential role of self-study action research'. In M. Glenn, M. Roche, C. McDonagh, and B. Sullivan (Eds.), *Learning Communities in Educational Partnerships: Action Research as Transformation*. London: Bloomsbury.
Roche, M. (2020). 'Identifying an area of professional concern or interest'. In C. McDonagh, M. Roche, B. Sullivan, and M. Glenn (Eds.), *Enhancing Practice Through Classroom Practice: A Teacher's Guide to Professional Development*. Oxon: Routledge.
Schön, D.A. (1983). *The Reflective Practitioner: How Professionals Think in Action*. New York, NY: Basic Books.
Southworth, G. (2009). 'Learning-centred leadership'. In B. Davies (Ed.), *The Essentials of School Leadership*. London: Sage.

Stutchbury, K. (2008). 'Chapter 5: Ethics in educational research'. In E. Wilson (Ed.), *School-Based Research: A Guide for Education Students*. London: Sage.

Sullivan, B. (2017). 'A theoretical examination of the practical significance of learning communities'. In M. Glenn, M. Roche, C. McDonagh, and B. Sullivan (Eds.), *Learning Communities in Educational Partnerships: Action Research as Transformation*. London: Bloomsbury.

Taylor, E.W. (2007). 'An update of transformative learning theory: A critical review of the empirical research (1999-2005)'. *International Journal of Lifelong Education*, 26, pp. 173-191.

The University of Greenwich. (no date a). *Ethical Proposal Form for SCITT Action Research* (unpublished).

The University of Greenwich. (no date b). *Informed Consent and Permission Slip for Parents/Guardian and Participants for SCITT Action Research* (unpublished).

Thomson, P. (2010). *Whole School Change: A Literature Review*. Newcastle upon Tyne: Creativity, Culture and Education.

UK Data Service. (no date). *Data protection act, the general data protection regulation, and the UK GDPR*. [Online]. Available at: https://ukdataservice.ac.uk/learning-hub/research-data-management/data-protection/data-protection-legislation/data-protection-act-and-gdpr/ [Accessed 1 October 2022].

Wenger, E. (1998). *Communities of practice: Learning, meaning, and identity*. New York: Cambridge University Press.

Whitehead, J. (1989). Creating a living educational theory from questions of the kind, 'how do I improve my practice?. *Cambridge Journal of Education*, 19(1), pp. 41-52.

Whitehead, J. (2019). Creating a living-educational-theory from questions of the kind, 'how do I improve my practice?' 30 years on with living theory research. *Educational Journal of Living Theories*, 12(2), pp. 1-19.

Whitehead, J., and McNiff, J. (2006). *Action Research: Living Theory*. London: Sage.

Wilson, E. (2008). 'Chapter 7: How to do action research'. In E. Wilson (Ed.), *School-Based Research: A Guide for Education Students*. London: Sage.

Wilson, V. (2016). 'Chapter 4: The literature review: What is already out there?'. In R. Austin (Ed.), *Researching Primary Education*. London: Sage.

14 Teaching overseas

KEY WORDS
Teaching abroad, overseas, migration, overseas, international

Contributors within this chapter:

1. Sam Durrant
2. Kelly Austen
3. Sally Burns
4. Suzie Dick
5. Sven Carrington
6. Jess Gosling
7. Chris Barnes
8. Scott Read
9. Mark Cratchley
10. Nieky van Veggel
11. Thomas Godfrey-Faussett
12. Jasmine Kay-Moyle
13. Oksana Agamova
14. Joe Rose
15. Simone Hackett

Introduction

Critical question

What would teaching in another country be like?

Have you even wondered about teaching overseas or in a different country? Is there a particular country you have considered travelling to teach in, or are you open to suggestions? This fascinating chapter shares 15 contributor voices, reflecting upon their experiences of

DOI: 10.4324/9781003218098-14

teaching overseas and communicating and collaborating internationally. Covering a global span of places including Goa, Thailand and Ethiopia (and everywhere in between!), we are sure you will enjoy hearing about the educational challenges, joys and curricula curiosities that can be found in these alternate school settings.

Teaching Abroad: Goa Edition

By Sam Durrant, Online Private English Tutor, Chester, England

'If you want to seriously offer me a job, I promise I'll seriously consider it', I said.

'I want to seriously offer you a job', came the reply. And so began the most recent 7 years of my life; a brand new start, a new country, a new school and a whole new way of thinking about education.

I had been a head of year in big inner-city secondary comprehensives all my working life, a job I loved and loathed in equal measure. Loved because finally I had found something that I was really good at and was making a measurable difference to vulnerable children's lives, and loathed because I simply couldn't do it without giving every ounce of my heart and soul. And it was destroying me.

Then 'life' happened, as it is so often wont to do, and I took a sabbatical, bought a round-the-world ticket and set off to see what was out there. And 'what was out there' was a tiny community of international families with primary age children in the remote hills of South Goa, a community with whom I soon discovered I had a great deal in common!

There were no schools for international students in South Goa at the time, and education was a glorious, bare-foot affair, centred mainly on the beach and almost exclusively around 'learning through play'. Which was nice, but it wasn't really enough for many parents who had the vision to wonder what, exactly, their beautiful little hippy child might want to do, you know, post-16, as it were. So when I came along with my years of secondary experience, an actual teaching qualification, knowledge of exam boards, bank of good GCSE results and the like, 'I want to seriously offer you a job' was music to everybody's ears.

And so began an extraordinary journey. To cut a long story short, I am now the deputy headteacher and head of secondary of South Goa's only international school. We are an all-through school, from kindergarten all the way up to 16-year-olds in Year 11. We are growing year by year, and, having recently found the land that we needed, with the help of a South African architect parent, we have built our very own premises right here in the middle of our community.

You can see pictures of our beautiful school here www.riverhouseacademy.com

We have achieved one of our first ambitions, which was to have a class for every year group and a teacher for every class, and we are now massively over-subscribed. Our next step is to achieve Cambridge international accreditation so that our students can sit their IGCSEs with us as a recognised examinations centre. This is the dream; not yet achieved but we are very very close.

(Continued)

Life here is amazing. Amazing India they call it and with good reason. Goa, though, is India-Lite, not quite 'the real thing'. As the most prosperous of the 29 Indian states, life here is more comfortable than most people might imagine. For those of us who live here full time who are not of Indian origin, we don't miss out on much. The local people are incredibly fun and friendly, the food is fantastic, prices are unbelievably low (as are salaries mind you, mine included) and there is wildlife galore and, of course, the beaches. The beaches! I have more sun, sea and sand than I ever thought possible.

If I had only known all those years ago that all I needed in order to stay sane was to ride to work on a Royal Enfield, to swim in the sea every day and then enjoy a curry and a pint for less than a pound hindsight is a wonderful thing.

From Zimbabwe to the Isle of Sheppey

By Kelly Austen, Teacher, Isle of Sheppey, Scotland

My name is Kelly and I was born in Zimbabwe, where I was diagnosed with dyslexia as a child. When it was time for me to go to high school, the headteacher at the time told my mother, 'Kelly is too stupid to come to school. Better save your money and put her to work'. Thankfully this was not good enough for my mom, and I was able to repeat my last year of primary school and then I attended home school until I was 15 years old. When I was 15, I was able to do an apprenticeship at a nursery school. When I was 16, the head teacher asked me to teach her class as her husband had become sick. So when I was 16 I was in charge of 30 children aged five turning six, on my own. In Zimbabwe children have to pass an entry test before being allowed to attend primary school. I rose to the challenge, and the children in my care where able to go on and pass their entry test. Some things that are included in this test are as follows:

- Children have to know their home address and phone number by heart.
- Children have to be able to throw a bean bag through a hoop.
- Children have to be able to accurately draw a house, which means having the sky at the top and green grass at the bottom. The house is not allowed to be floating in the air.

This is just a snapshot of what children in Zimbabwe are expected to do. I think it is important to say that in Zimbabwean schools we do not have teaching assistants. This on-entry test is so that the children in the same cohort are of the same ability. Children with special educational needs went to a school that was locked away from society.

I left Zimbabwe when I was 17 due to the political situation and came to England with my family. When I arrived, I had no higher education and had to go to college, and I did a level 1 in childcare. I did this and was able to achieve a foundation degree in early childhood studies.

(Continued)

I started work in a one-form entry school. I was the nursery lead. The school became an apple school, which means every child has an iPad of their own; this included the two-year-olds. This was a major debate in our Early Years team.

I embraced the iPads as for me it meant a new way of engaging with the children, using different hooks for learning, which are so valuable. One of the best experiences I had was when I showed a child {3 year olds} how to use a drawing app. After I showed the child how to use the app, he then had his friends sitting around him as he taught his peers how to use the app. I also found that the iPads allowed me to share the children's learning in different ways. For example, I always had to take photos of the children as they are learning for evidence. So I would often display the pictures on the board and talk to the children about their learning. I role modelled the language, so I would ask, 'can you tell me what you were learning in this picture?' At first the children would say, 'I don't know'. I would then ask, what were you doing? And then I would say so you were learning; for example, if a child said, 'I was playing hide and seek', I would say, 'That is great way to learn how to count to ten'. Slowly the children were able to say 'I am learning to…'

I then moved to a bigger school, three-form entry, again in a very deprived area with a lot of difficulties, social difficulties and a lot more special educational need. Before I go any further I want you to know how much I love this school. They put the children at the heart of everything they do. When I first arrived at the school, it was like stepping back into time. The Early Years was bright and colourful with loads of hanging thing work. The environment was busy. I was at this time the reception teaching assistant. I was in charge of an area, and so I stripped it back and calmed it down using natural materials and calmed everything down. The children gravitated to the area which made the Early Years lead look at what I did, and she then implemented it in the setting. The difference was amazing, and the difference to the children was almost immediate; they came into the school a lot calmer. I explained to the Early Years lead that the hygge approach is something to look into. Two years later I was given the nursery lead position.

Teaching Overseas: Reflections

By Sally Burns, The Values and Visions Foundation, London, England

We stepped off the plane into a hairdryer on full blast. It was 33°C at 3.00 a.m. I didn't know that was possible. One of our group refused to leave the airport and asked to be put on the next plane back. It was 1982, and we had just landed in Khartoum, capital of Sudan.

The cockroaches in the shower of the dowdy hotel bathroom were the next shock. I am not sure I had ever encountered a cockroach before, and there I met many.

Two weeks of bureaucracy ensued in daytime temperatures of over 35°C, tramping around the mud-encrusted city or avoiding the torrential monsoon downpours. It

(Continued)

was tedious and wearing, but new and fascinating. It was during this process that we learned we were not going to the Red Sea province we had selected but were being posted up north to the desert. There was no arguing. They needed couples in the more remote villages.

We were eventually released to fly – yes fly! – up to Dongola, the capital of Shamaliya, Northern Province. It was there that the inevitable tummy bug hit, and we struggled for over a week in a tiny room with no air conditioning in temperatures of 42°C.

To get to our village, we had to take the overnight ferry up the Nile. This was not the Nile steamer of Agatha Christie's novels but an ancient boat trailing two side boats which took around twelve hours to do the eighty-kilometre trip. A man met us at the riverside where we docked, loaded our backpacks and trunk on to a camel and invited us to follow him through the date palm fringed village, across a stretch of desert to our new home: a shabby rectangular building with one room, a fair bit of verandah, a tiny 'bathroom' for washing (if you took in water, a cup and a bowl for the purpose), a mud-brick kitchen and a well; there was no running water and no electricity.

I cried when I arrived, and I cried when I left. That year was one of the best of my life. I learned to survive in the desert in temperatures of up to 50°C, to cook on a charcoal-burning converted biscuit tin and to speak Arabic thanks to the amazing women who taught me so much about their culture and their lives. I could write a book about it (I will one day).

What I learned from this experience stood me in good stead for other postings overseas. There are the challenges. These include the inevitable bureaucracy of visas, work permits, accommodation, furnishings and equipment. In addition to the usual stress of starting a new job, you face all the administrative process of moving to a new home in a new country. You may not get what you signed up for: a remote desert village in lieu of a seaside town. Your school may not have what you have been trained to expect as standard, especially in terms of technology: a blackboard, limited chalk, not enough desks, chairs or books and no way of sticking things to the walls; not a whiteboard or projector in sight. However, approached with an open mind and armed with my personal credo, the four Ps: Pleasantness, Politeness, Patience and Perseverance, the lessons learned are invaluable.

Then there are the benefits. You are in the privileged position of living in another environment, immersing yourself in a culture very different from (yet often surprisingly similar to) your own, and you have the chance to learn the language of the country. Your colleagues become your family, and, if you move around, you may find you meet up a few thousand miles away on another continent one day. From a professional point of view, you may be teaching an educational system you know in a new context or you may need to work with an unfamiliar curriculum. All this broadens your experience and, in a competitive job market, is proof of your initiative and resilience.

Still thinking about it! Take the plunge. You will not regret it.

Teaching Overseas – Sandford International School, Addis Ababa, Ethiopia

By Suzie Dick, Lecturer in Education at Queen Margaret University, Edinburgh, Scotland

There are many stories from Ethiopia, some 'African', some 'Ethiopian' and some just about pupils, as pupils are, wherever you are in the world. I have chosen three that will hopefully give you a flavour of some of the more interesting aspects of life abroad.

The day the locusts came

We knew they were coming – believe it or not, there is a Locust Watch, a 'weather' forecast if you like for locusts. It is run by the United Nations Food and Agricultural Organisation. Think of it as a wet play situation where instead of going out for playtime the pupils stay in. Unfortunately, no one told the locusts that, and to be fair to them, the school is open plan with courtyards and many different buildings. Think, 2- to 3-inch-long flying guzzling things whose sole purpose is to munch their way through any and every vegetation. Add to that a plague so thick you can't see your way through them from one building to another; hold your hand up and five locusts will be there; touch your hair and locusts will be entangled in it. They also like long hair, and little boys aged about ten, like locusts. Think the chaos when one measly wasp flies into your classroom. Imagine that? Now add in lots of children catching, hiding and then releasing locusts as a novel way to disrupt the lesson. I'll leave the rest to your imagination.

Camping anyone? Hyenas welcome too

It can be quite important to ensure that third culture children, those who are from one place but live in another and moving on every few years, have the opportunity to experience what could be considered normal school activities. This can be important in later life, when back home for school, work and university, that they have a language or experiences in common. So we had a school camp and hike for the older girls one weekend. Complete with tents, Trangias, bonfire and campfire songs and games. It was really lovely and brought back a sense of home and memories to many, including those just moved to begin to form new friendships in another new place. The hyenas on the hill behind us particularly enjoyed the singing and joined in with their laughs.

English as an additional language x 52

In my day-to-day job as a lecturer, and previously as a teacher, I am always intrigued by teachers that worry about the 4-5 English as an additional language (EAL) children in their class, differentiation and attainment. In some of the international schools

(Continued)

the majority are non-English speaking with various degrees of understanding and fluency. It certainly had its challenges, but less concern or, dare I say it, the overthinking went into it. There was a curriculum to teach, and that was that. Lots of words, signs and pictures were used, but the expectation was full immersion and getting on with it regardless of what age they started. No extraction, but every class had a classroom assistant to help out. No one had time, or ability, to translate into 52 languages, but as almost everyone was learning in that second (or third or fourth) language, the children helped each other to learn and make progress. There were occasional issues, but in the secondary school there was a 100% pass rate at the International Baccalaureate, read and written in English. It changed my mindset from 'it's a problem, what shall we do' to a very much ok let's do this together.

Becoming a Headteacher in Saudi Arabia

By Sven Carrington, Head Teacher at BISR Tabuk Campus, Tabuk, Saudi Arabia

I began my teaching career in a beautiful and well-run inner London school. The experience of teaching in a challenging UK school gave me a superb base and model for my practice. When recruiting in my current role as head of school, I am always on the lookout for candidates who have worked in the UK within diverse communities.

I decided to move to Saudi Arabia to broaden my horizons and gain valuable cultural experiences. Teaching at a British international school on a small compound in Tabuk (northwest Saudi Arabia) has been wonderful. The community are supportive and caring, and the staff have been inspirational. Their dedication and understanding that we, as a school, are the centre of the community is of great importance. Again, when recruiting, I am looking for those candidates who have gone above and beyond to engage their wider communities and parent bodies.

Continuing professional development (CPD) has been second to none, with many links to schools across Saudi, Dubai and Bahrain. One of the core principles of the school I work at is a strong emphasis on evidence-based teaching and learning. Weekly CPD sessions on a Thursday afternoon have seen big names from the world of education give talks and workshops for all staff development.

As a head, my life/work balance is something I am always conscious of. International school teaching is certainly not for the workshy, and there are high expectations put upon teachers as parents demand standards for their fees. However, the pay-off for me has been incredible travel opportunities, immersion in different cultures and experiences such as diving and desert camps.

Big Fish: The Amazing World of International Teaching

By Jess Gosling, International Early Years Teacher, Warsaw, Poland

Jess Gosling can be reached via Twitter @JessGosling2 or via her website, jessgosling-earlyyearsteacher.com.

> 'Big Fish' is an early 90s film, whereby the lead actor would go to a different world at different times of his life, then return to his own. Others were unsure if this world was true, or a figment of the lead's imagination.

Leaving the UK and becoming an international teacher led me to feel that when I returned home, my life abroad was that of 'Big Fish'. The fact that I was living in a foreign place, where I was happy and thriving, amazed me. I lived life to the full, enjoying every opportunity with the increased work/life balance, as well as the long school breaks. Every summer I would return to the UK and tell my stories of safaris, dune hiking and snorkelling in the red sea, to notice the eyes of the listener glaze over. I soon realised that people didn't want to hear about this alternative lifestyle, but preferred to talk about their norm. So, I kept my stories to myself.

After graduating from the UK, I set out to teach abroad. The thrill of seeking a new school, new country and new adventures still spurs me on, even after more than 13 years abroad. There is something so exciting about the unknown, and I find comfort that these moves need not be permanent, as each placement begins as a temporary two-year contract.

I left to teach in Cairo for my first placement, and in hindsight, I realise I was incredibly naÔve. Living in Egypt was challenging, as the culture didn't suit my own. One memory that sticks in my mind was approaching the driveway of a majestic-looking building, my new school. It took my breath away. The facilities included a dedicated Early Years Unit and an Olympic-sized pool. I loved the children I taught; they were respectful, articulate and bright. However, the decision of whether to renew our contract was easily made due to the Revolution in 2011. It was a frightening time to witness, and upon return to school, it was obvious that our safety was compromised. I recognised the place was changing fast.

We decided to move next to Vietnam. Asia had always been a place we loved, we had taught as English teachers in Japan and I had spent my teens backpacking in SE Asia. Vietnam was beautiful and liberal and the people warm. I spent two years teaching and another five raising my daughter in a lovely suburb outside of Ho Chi Minh City. I thrived as a mum in the small community and contributed to its growth. Soon I was organising playdates and gatherings for parents. In the evenings I would study for a Masters and later I set up my own Early Years business. Having the opportunity to have a go at being a boss was liberating.

Yet, as my daughter grew up, I understood that both the school and country no longer fit us as a family. The weather was incredibly hot, and playgrounds didn't exist

(Continued)

as grass was viewed as ornamental. The pollution was high, and our daughter forever suffered from a chesty cough.

Taking this into consideration, we decided to relocate to Taiwan. Friends had highly recommended this little-known country. First, we visited the country, which appeared to offer so much more than Vietnam: mountains and beaches all within an hour of the school. Our move was a successful one. We enjoyed travel once again; however, in 2020, we received news that COVID had begun to spread around the world. We were protected from the intense pressure as Taiwan maintained very low infection rates for more than two years.

Even in this time, Taiwan has offered further opportunities, although perhaps initially hidden. Travel restrictions were strict, but instead of travel planning, I wrote. I authored a book, articles and blogs and created a website, Twitter following and Facebook group for international teachers. Then I began to reach out to my community, by establishing WomenEd Taiwan. I was surrounded by highly skilled professionals and was offered high-quality professional development. My research and writing were noticed by a consultant, and now I contract for her consultancy, training and advising on EAL in Early Years.

As I face my next move this year, I am again excited for a scene change. I wonder what the change will entail. I have already had discussions with my new school about leading staff development and helping support the expansion of Early Years. This new chapter I am sure will be one in which I am challenged and grow.

Independent or International Schools?

By Chris Barnes, Prep school teacher, Manchester, England

I read my undergraduate degree and then went straight into a PGCE at the end of the last century/millennium. It almost frightens me to write that because it really doesn't seem like yesterday (and amazingly, my university top still fits me!). In terms of careers advice, our admissions tutor gave us an excellent maxim that is still relevant 22 years later: don't just take the first job that's offered to you. Be sure that you are right for the school. Better to be sure than sorry. It remains great advice; although with the changes to university funding and pressure to secure a teaching position, a more circumspect approach is understandable.

In the year that I qualified, the statutory induction year was introduced, and everyone was being ushered in the direction of maintained schools 'to ensure that we were properly qualified'. Little, if any, mention was given to other options. As I have been given the opportunity to do so, I remind the reader of the importance of looking to both independent and international schools as further possibilities.

(Continued)

UK independent schools

Around 7-8% of pupils are educated at independent/private schools in the UK. 'Preparatory' (prep) schools were to get children ready to join the larger senior schools, traditionally at 13 but increasingly now at 11. Disregard the stereotyped photographs of top hats and tails: uniforms are smart, but most are much more prosaic. Some prep schools are run by charitable trusts; others by large educational groups. The age ranges vary but all finish at either 11 or 13, at which point the children take entrance exams for senior school: a mixture of 11+ (English, maths, science and reasoning), ISEB Common Entrance at 13+ or the Pre-Senior Baccalaureate. The focus is not solely on academia: arts, music, drama, sport, debating and residential activities are all seen as important and forming part of the experience of being at prep school.

If not independent, how about going international?

There are few jobs in the world where you can combine a love of travel and an opportunity to work. Teaching is one of them. The world is reopening post-pandemic and with QTS – even if you have not yet undertaken induction, which is only required to teach within the UK itself – you have options to gain experience elsewhere.

If the idea of going overseas appeals to you, a few questions to consider:

1. **How would I feel being away from my family/friends?** Could I deal with 'not being there' if there was an emergency, or being parted from those whom I know best? Similarly, how easy would it be for others to come and visit me?
2. (If travelling overseas by yourself) **How comfortable would I feel about going alone?** Could I get a friend to apply with me? Even though the international schools community is very welcoming, having someone with whom to take that initial step helps it seem less daunting.
3. **Where in the world would best suit me?** As a couple of examples: the Middle East has no taxes but high living costs. In Southeast Asia, salaries are less but there is a lower cost of living. Most international schools do not contribute towards pension arrangements, so you may wish to set up a savings scheme to put money away.
4. **What are my tax liabilities?** In some countries you are taxed at a higher rate for the first part of your first year – usually 183 days – until you can be classed as a 'resident', at which point you pay the local rate of tax. Look up the country's taxation relationship with your own country to see if you are liable to pay any kind of tax whilst overseas (in most cases the answer will be none, unless you are, for example, receiving income such as rental for a property).
5. **How will diet and/or allergies be catered for?** You do need to research this carefully. Western countries' allergy levels are quite different from those in Asia, the Middle East and Africa. Nuts and seeds form part of the everyday diet, and it is less common to find information about allergens.

(Continued)

6. **What about medication?** This depends on the healthcare package offered by your prospective school. If you have a pre-existing condition, you should check if the same medication is available and, if so, who would be paying for it.
7. **LGBTQ?** Tolerance, diversity and inclusion are not the same across the world – if you identify as anything other than your biological sex, use different pronouns, or if you are in a homosexual relationship, choose your country carefully. A prison sentence or (in some cases) the death penalty is still in place for anything perceived to be outside of heterosexual, male-female relationships.
8. **But that's not my religion!** In some parts of the world, religion can very much influence daily life, in terms of dress, behavioural norms, food and drink, etc. This is a norm for those that live in that country. To anyone moving there, don't expect to be treated differently because you are a temporary worker – the same expectations, fines and punishments apply.

International teaching is an adventure, and many who start with the idea of doing it for a few years end up spending their lives and careers outside of their passport country. It is now very much a positive choice made by teachers, either straight out of university or soon after qualifying.

Thailand

By Scott Read, Year 1 Specialist Teacher, PSHE/Wellbeing Curriculum Leader – Foundation at Amnuay Silpa School, Bangkok, Thailand

For as long as I can remember Asia has always had a special place in my heart. I was taken by the collectivist cultures, the history and the warmth of the people I'd met. Ever since watching the 'King and I' with my grandmother at a young age, Thailand (formerly Siam) has always sparked my interest. I first travelled to Thailand in 2018, and I fell in love with both the country and its people. I quickly found that Thailand is not called the 'land of smiles' for no reason.

I began my training to become a teacher at the University of Greenwich – first completing my BA and then progressing onto my PGCE. The training was not easy, and I can assure there was a lot of blood, sweat and tears. However, I always had my end goal in sight to teach overseas in Thailand. Unfortunately, I did not know a lot about how I could teach overseas, so I began by watching YouTube videos and looking at the council of British international schools (COBIS) website. Towards the end of my teacher training, a friend of mine had seen a job advertised on TES and said I should apply. I applied without thinking I would get an interview, but I was mistaken. I was invited to attend an online interview with the principal and was asked to record a 10-minute demonstration teaching video. At that time, I hadn't had much teaching experience, but I submitted my demo video and attended the interview.

(Continued)

Two weeks passed, and I thought I had not been successful. I prayed I would hear a response, and that same day I received an email from the school informing me that they would like to offer me a position as a Year 1 specialist teacher. Words cannot express how happy and excited I was. I booked my flight and applied to the Thai Embassy for my visa and certificate of entry into the kingdom of Thailand. When I arrived in Thailand I was welcomed with open arms by my school, and an amazing team of staff who are so supportive and made me feel part of the team right away. Every day I thank the Buddha for this amazing opportunity that has come into my life.

I am very fortunate to have been blessed to work at the first and only accredited bilingual thinking school in Thailand as my first official teaching job. Moving 6000 miles away from the UK can be a struggle, and I do get days where I miss home, but seeing my students' faces and smiles reminds me just how much I am making a difference to their lives. Thai children highly respect their teachers and are all willing to learn and really push themselves to try. I commend them as learning a new language has its ups and downs and being EAL students the commitment and proactiveness they put into each, and every lesson is a joy. Learning is a journey, and I am truly glad I get to share my learning and teaching journey with my students.

It all Started with Backpacking...

By Mark Cratchley, English Teacher at Cheltenham Bournside School, Cheltenham, England

Halfway through a backpacking trip around Southeast Asia, I stumbled on the idea of how I could live that kind of life more permanently; TEFL teaching. Fifteen months later, I was back in Thailand with a rucksack and guitar, a CELTA under my belt, and a vague plan to work either there, Singapore or Japan.

Whilst I was making my mind up, I ended up teaching the manager of the beach bungalows I was staying at on Ko Pha Ngan, and her nephew. Every afternoon, I would head off to teach in my first classroom; a pagoda on the beach. The boy's mother had contacts in Bangkok and told me about an available teaching position there, and within a few days I was teaching at a kindergarten off the Samsen Road.

I had my own classroom, and the classes would come to me throughout the day for their weekly 30-minute lessons. As part of the contract, I also taught elementary and junior high school students on weekend mornings, with a day off on Monday. This seemed to be the norm for many agencies, and unless you work in a regular school or an international school, you can expect to work six days a week. Many teachers also work the weekend classes for extra cash. My guitar came in handy for me, and I had a nightly gig in a local bar, away from the beaten track of the Khao San Road, with a regular clientele of Uni students, expats and Bangkok musos. I was also lucky enough to have the unique experience of delivering a week-long course to a group of Thai teachers from all over the

(Continued)

country at a remote tamarind farm for the Dept. of Education. The old phrase of no two days in teaching ever being the same is amplified when working abroad!

Then a call came from Japan.

I'd made many great friends in Thailand and loved living there, but the time was right to move on, and if I hadn't taken up the job offer, I know I would have regretted it. So, within a few days, I found myself (eventually) navigating Ueno train station and heading to Saitama to meet my friends from back home who were living in a 'Gaijin House' in a small town near Omiya.

In all, I was there for 11 years and, as you can imagine, had a plethora of experiences in that time. In the smaller private language schools I taught every age range, from children as young as two to octogenarians. I taught in immersive kindergartens, worked for the local council visiting schools as part of a cultural exchange programme and briefly dabbled with one of the big corporate English schools – being recently married and a new parent, I wanted a more secure job, but the battery-farm style of teaching was not my cup of tea.

So what could I do to ensure stability for my new family? Start my own school. That may sound counterintuitive, but we were offered the opportunity to build a house from scratch, so that's we did. We designed the house with the classroom downstairs and the living area upstairs. We worked hard to advertise the school locally and quickly built up a solid base of students, running an immersive kindergarten class in the morning, cram classes in the afternoons and adult classes for stay-at-home parents, business people and doctors from the local hospital. We ran special events for Easter, Halloween and Christmas, and summer camping trips. As you can imagine, there are pros and cons to running your own school, but ultimately it is worth every effort, and if you are planning to live abroad for the long term, a wonderful way to be able to do it.

So, what are my main takeaways from teaching abroad? Be prepared for some culture shock but know that it does become easier, and you will very quickly learn to appreciate and celebrate the differences. Find the job that's right for you – there are many different types of school and jobs within those schools – you will find your feet and make it work for you. Seize opportunities when they are presented to you, you will open yourself up to some unique and life-changing experiences.

How Teaching Abroad has Made me a Better Teacher

By Nieky van Veggel, Senior Lecturer in Animal Health, Writtle University College, Chelmsford, England

Nieky can be contacted via *nv@writtle.ac.uk* or alternatively via @NiekyWUC on Twitter.

Throughout my career as an educator I have been fortunate enough to teach abroad on multiple occasions. I have been fortunate enough to teach in Belgium, the Netherlands, Germany, Ukraine and Armenia. This was done through informal personal links, as well as part of formal international exchange projects.

(Continued)

To me, the most interesting aspect of teaching abroad is that it has really opened my eyes to different ways of doing things. I found that irrespective of where I was teaching, everyone involved has a common goal, which is getting their students to achieve to the best of their ability. However, the means of getting there, through the various education systems of different countries, is infinitely fascinating.

On a more personal level, I have found teaching abroad incredibly rewarding. Despite what the media portray, the UK has a good reputation for producing high-quality teaching staff. It was humbling to be treated as an expert educator by fellow university teachers simply because I came from a better resourced institution in a Western country. Equally, it was fascinating to have discussions with students abroad, who are not only interested in what I have to say, but also endlessly fascinated by what student life is like for my students.

I guess my concluding message is this: If you get the chance to teach abroad, even if it is only for a short time, do it. It will make you a better educator, guaranteed!

Zambia

By Thomas Godfrey-Faussett, Research Assistant and DPhil Candidate at the University of Oxford, Oxford, England

Onora O'Neill, initially in her 2002 Reith Lectures and since in other talks and articles (2004, 2013a, 2013b), has explored the role of trust and relationships in systems of accountability. In essence, my understanding of her argument is that systems of accountability do not replace trust between individuals; they merely redirect it. In education, accountability systems mean that rather than trusting the teacher of your children to provide a quality education, you can place your trust in an external regulator, such as Ofsted, who will hold them to account on your behalf. When asked to reflect on my time teaching in a parent-owned community school in Zambia, I immediately thought back to O'Neill's discussion and the role of teacher-parent relationships in education.

Before moving to Zambia, I had trained and worked in London at a 2500-pupil secondary comprehensive school. Moving to a parent-owned community school was a revelation. The entire secondary school catered for just under 200 pupils. I taught 70 pupils. I could reflect generally about working in a smaller school, but specifically what I want to think about here is the impact that the school being parent owned had on teacher-parent relationships. In particular how this impacted both the ways in which we, as teachers, were held accountable and the meaning of accountability in the first place. In this school, parents were deeply involved. There were the usual parent's evenings, which happened every term, but because parents had been involved in the initial design of the school, systems were in place to ensure their involvement in many

(Continued)

different aspects of the running of the school. This meant, as teachers, we were held to account much more directly by teachers. At the extreme end, ultimately it was their decision whether or not contracts were renewed at the end of each two-year period! A dictionary definition of 'accountability' throws up four synonyms which, to me, highlight this shift (Merriam-Webster, 2022):

1. Liability or culpability
2. Answerability or responsibility

In my time teaching in London, accountability came to mean liability or culpability. My response to systems which were designed to hold me to account was to produce data or evidence which I could point to in the instance that I was blamed for the poor outcomes of a pupil or a class. In Zambia, accountability was a much broader term, whose meaning was closer to answerability or responsibility. Parents wanted me to be able to explain why I had chosen to make certain decisions. It was all very well if their child was on target to get an A, but were they happy? What excited them in class? And the flip side was I could ask parents to support their child outside of school or find out what they were interested in at home. The Home-School Knowledge Exchange project is an example of an attempt, in England, to similarly blur the boundary between the home and the classroom (Feiler et al., 2008). Could state-run schools learn from the approach of this parent-owned school to explicitly design for greater parental involvement, particularly in the systems of accountability? At the very least, it feels to me that as a classroom teacher, making strong and collaborative parent-teacher a priority feels like a good way of being accountable beyond the performative data production mechanisms of accountability which seem to be threatening our current system.

Teaching Refugees Abroad which Led to Setting up the First 'School of Sanctuary' in Suffolk

By Jasmine Kay-Moyle, Assistant Headteacher and School of Sanctuary Leader for Suffolk, Suffolk, England

In 2016, I was laying newspaper on my classroom tables in preparation for a painting lesson with my Year 6 class. A headline caught my eye: 'Swarms of Migrants Heading for Europe'. The terminology alone made me internally curse. The derogatory language used to compare refugees to loathsome insects was repulsive, and similar quotations were rife within the mainstream media at that time. I scrunched the newspaper up in frustration. In my classroom, I promoted empathy and an anti-racist curriculum, but it felt like the outside world was becoming more hostile every day.

At this time, there were 10,000 refugees in Calais, France, just a few hours from my home. I was hesitant to visit initially. Whilst at university, I had visited The Gambia on an alternative teaching placement. The intention was to support unqualified teachers

(Continued)

by regurgitating our lecturers' recently taught pedagogy. When our team of inexperienced trainees arrived, 100 children greeted us in one class. Our limited experience of teaching in England had not provided us with transferable knowledge, and we spent the week singing nursery rhymes and relaxing in the hotel pool. We naively snapped pictures of children who clung to our waists and made us feel like celebrities. I feel ashamed that we had not applied our safeguarding training to our new environment. It wouldn't be appropriate to post a selfie on social media with a photo containing one of our students in England, and later this would be one of the biggest reflections from my trip 'teaching' abroad: even if the overseas organisation deems this an acceptable move, you should never do something abroad that wouldn't be acceptable in the UK. Thankfully, over the last decade or so on my travels, I've seen a decline in cultural experiences which exploit local people and animals.

Not wanting to repeat previous voluntourism mistakes, I signed up to complete purposeful work in a warehouse on the outskirts of Calais near to the refugee camp. I spent weeks helping to prepare Afghan bolani, cardamom chai and Sudanese peanut stew. I had been tasked with checking retro 1970s tents (without instructions) to check that they were complete before distribution. I organised collections of sleeping bags, toiletries and clothing back home and would drive them over before completing long shifts in the warehouse. It wasn't glamorous work: it was exhausting, but I was part of something that felt exciting. Being around like-minded people was refreshing. A bouncy American solider whose jokes were a gift during those bleak winter months kept my spirits up during those physically demanding tasks. He felt conflicted about his role serving on a base in the UK and wanted to engage with the refugee crisis. He would lie about his real job on distribution in fear of repercussions from refugees who may have worked for the American army and felt as though they were left behind. It wasn't the refugees who he needed to fear though, for he would be run over by French national on one of our trips. Hate crimes were common and were aimed at both refugees and volunteers. For the first time in my teaching career, I was in danger due to the work that I was completing – many Europeans disagree with people helping refugees, and some will go to extreme lengths to prevent charitable acts from taking place.

When I later became a teacher in the camp, it wasn't uncommon for students to enter the classroom needing medical attention after being attacked. When people ask me about the camp, I usually focus on how intrinsically kind the residents were and rarely go into detail about the unsanitary conditions that the men, women and children lived in. I heard stories in that settlement that will haunt me for the rest of my life and saw things that regularly keep me up at night. It is clear that no one chooses to live in such conditions in the age of the budget airline.

Many of the residents in the camp started to recognise me. On one occasion, I spotted Will I Am playing Connect Four with a group of refugees. Like a true fan girl, I started to sing 'Where is the Love' to some of the refugees who were asking me why I was so intrigued by this man.

(Continued)

'You're lewanaii', they remarked. 'Lewanaii' means 'crazy' in Pashto. 'He's not famous here. No one knows him but we all know you. You're the crazy English girl who drives her car here every week to help us'. I was building connections with people, and I knew that I could not walk away. I taught English, maths and basic French. It was common for journalists to walk into my lessons and start snapping away without permission or to be tear gassed mid grammar lesson. People were hungry, cold and frustrated. Lessons were a welcome distraction from rat-infested tents, distribution lines and dangerous border crossings. Residents often died trying to swim to family members in the UK; they suffocated in lorries and fell from the bottom of vehicles. Some of the unaccompanied minors had French IDs, but there was a lack of practical information for them to improve their situations. I always remembered that I was a teacher and never pretended to be a medic, councillor or lawyer. As their teacher, they put their trust in me, and at times, I was able to connect them with appropriate services. Sadly, I have also spent time in A&E with students who have attempted suicide.

Continuing to work and volunteer with reputable charities allowed me to access training on psychological support, cultural appropriation and unconscious bias: all of which provided me with a fantastic foundation for the work that I have continued to do supporting refugees over the years. I came to realise that teaching abroad could have long-lasting impacts on those you are supporting under the right conditions. It is important to be mindful of your impact when thinking about such professions:

- As a teacher abroad, are you potentially taking a job from a local person?
- Are you qualified for the role?
- Are you able to commit time to ensure your students make progress?
- Why are you volunteering? Do your actions benefit you more than those you are seeking to help?

By the time I was invited to become a project lead in a camp for Yazidis in Greece, I felt that I had transferrable skills for the role. I wanted to encourage some of the residents to teach alongside me. I was thrilled when I found out some had been teachers in Iraq. However, I had underestimated the trauma that these people had experienced during the very recent genocide. My vision of taking a step back was not going to work: they wanted me to support their children within our safe space so they could prioritise on accessing psychological and legal support also available within the camp. I had learnt another important lesson here: allowing refugees to have a say in the type of support that you are offering is paramount.

As we develop into a more culturally diverse society in Europe, blame can grow and people in positions of power have been known to point fingers at refugees for our country's problems. In reality, the UK hosts 0.26% of the world's refugees (UNHCR, 2016) and the majority of refugees are in countries that surround conflict zones. When my local Afghan bridging hotel began to house holidaymakers again, one of my students was saddened that the staff started to place tablecloths on the tables

(Continued)

at mealtimes. Her husband was also continuously rejected for cleaning jobs despite being overqualified with a first class degree. She felt dehumanised – it is this systemic racism that needs addressing too. Our children in UK classrooms often believe racism is a thing of the past, occasionally presenting itself as a slur at a football match or a bar fight. Contrary to this, racism is so entrenched within our society and teachers have the responsibility to have challenging conversations with colleagues, parents and children to ensure that our society does not limit somebody due to their cultural heritage.

In 2022, my community primary school in Suffolk was awarded the 'School of Sanctuary' award. We were the first to achieve this within our county, and we hope that other schools will follow the steps that we have taken to address misinformation surrounding migration. A School of Sanctuary is a school that is committed to being a safe and welcoming place for all children including migrants and refugees. As staff, we teach the pupils about the difficulties that people experience around the world, which builds empathy and understanding. We encourage visitors to the school to ensure the pupils have a broad understanding of the wider world as well as their own culture and identity. Since the launch of the award, many parents from diverse backgrounds have offered their skills to enhance our curriculum including multicultural cooking workshops and language exchange sessions. We have amplified our message of solidarity through art exhibitions, sent welcome cards and gifts to new arrivals and provided information to our pupils to allow them to make informed opinions about migrants and refugees. Our children know that diversity is a strength. As teachers, we have an incredible gift to allow empathy, equality and love to win within our classrooms. In turn, our lessons may contribute towards a fairer society for all.

My Experience of Teaching in Russia

By Oksana Agamova, PhD Student, Norfolk, England

I am a Russian PhD student, currently living in the UK. The topic of my PhD is exploring the formation of moral values in medical students, within an educational environment. I have extensive experience of teaching college students in Moscow. I have taught the English language in several colleges across Russia, in addition to the basics of Latin with medical terminology to students aged 14 to 16. In contrast to the educational pathway in the UK, the students I taught were already studying towards a medical degree, such as medicine, nursing and midwifery.

School education in Russia is free and divided into three main stages: primary, basic general and secondary. Primary education starts at age six or seven and lasts for four years, basic general education continues for the next four years and secondary education for the last two years. Russian school education lasts for 11 years

(Continued)

in total; however, each pupil can decide whether they want to leave after this time or continue. There are also examinations throughout schooling that the children must pass. At the end of basic general education, each pupil must pass a compulsory examination called the Basic State Exam (BSE). The children can then decide whether to continue their education in college or to stay in school for two more years and then sit the Unified State Exam. If a pupil unfortunately fails their BSE, they are not allowed to continue their education in secondary school and have to decide whether to find employment or try to pass placement exams in different colleges.

There are schools in Russia that specialise just in primary education, where upon completion of which, a child's parents or carers have to decide on further education. They will choose the school for their child so they can receive basic general and if needed secondary education. Separate primary education schools are gaining popularity due to the fact that by the end of the 4th year the pupil is showing interest towards this or that subject, making it easier for parents or carers to understand in which area their child is likely to succeed. Some parents or carers prefer private schooling or home education to the state schooling. They believe that private schooling or home education is of good quality as their children are taught by highly qualified professionals, whereas state schools are lacking good specialists. However, state schools are very careful in choosing their teachers and every teacher must be highly qualified in order to be successful.

An important role of primary school teachers in Russia is to help develop a portfolio of and for each pupil concerning their academic performance in different subjects, grades they have received, certificates they have gained and extracurricular activities such as crafts. This portfolio is open for parents to view and forms an important role in the pupil's future. This portfolio is seen as a reflection of the pupil and will be examined by the headteacher at any future schools the pupil may attend. Each school has a different focus and intensively teaches a particular subject such as English, physics, mathematics and so on.

Moving to Russia to teach

If you are thinking about teaching in Russia, there are various routes. Initially you will have to prove your qualification and appropriate degree, as well as passing DBS checks. You will then need to undergo a health check alongside psychiatric and substance abuse examinations, a yearly requirement for teachers in Russia. Then, you will have to demonstrate your Russian language skills as all classes, except for the English subject, are taught in Russian within the colleges. If you wish to teach English in Russia, you should have a TEFL/CELTA or equivalent qualification. Depending upon your teaching specialisation, you have to upgrade your skills at least every five years and gain certification by the state organisation. It is also a necessity to provide classes teaching morality and ethics to the students.

Vietnam

By Joe Rose, Further Education Curriculum Team Leader, Lead IQA and Lecturer at The Sheffield College, Sheffield, England

Being 6,000 miles away from home, in 45°C heat (with 100% humidity) in the middle of nowhere playing 'talk for a minute' with 48 overly excited teenagers screaming and cheering on their peers, was probably the most enriching moment in my teaching career to date.

The phrase 'You weren't there man' or if that wasn't as obvious as I thought maybe 'Good Morning Vietnam' sheds light on where my overseas teaching experience blossomed. How did I end up teaching nearly 6,000 miles away? In short, a childhood of British holidays (brilliant I may add) and a rather progressive yet 'traditional' professional career that had created an itch that simply moving to another city/role wouldn't scratch. My ambition to 'see the world' but use my passion for education saw endless 3 am Skype interviews until a gifted high school and primary state school in Halong Bay, Vietnam, offered me a position.

Vietnamese culture is vibrant, beautiful and exciting and exquisitely emphases the images you might see on TV or in travel brochures. Teachers are highly regarded in society, and the manner in which they are respected is evident. However, the stark differences from what you would experience in a traditional classroom back home can at first take you back. As you enter the sense of an authoritarian style of classroom management is overwhelming. Students sit in rows, quietly in rows; they raise their hand, stand up, answer and bow after each interaction. All classrooms have very strict (even physically punishable) rules when it comes to participation, desk tidiness, student conduct and even the neatness of their handwriting. Students at this age attended school Monday to Friday 8 am–5 pm and Saturdays 8 am–1 pm with a massive emphasis on grades and national targets. The entire opposite to what I imagined my teaching environment to be. However, I had a motivation 'environments create environments'.

In Vietnam, students at primary age were not required to attend preschool and primary school isn't entirely free. Many from lower income families do opt out and prioritise work and in turn sadly encourage gender inequalities. I saw this as an opportunity to create an environment where equality was the focus: a small plenary where answers were anonymously screwed up and read out by different students. At first I was blissfully unaware of the impact, but my teaching assistant noticed the smiles and look of pride from several of the more reserved girls in the class. Simple yet effective, with limited resources you had to think on your feet.

My inspirational idea wasn't as such an innovative method of pedagogy, nor a world-changing teaching activity. My idea was simple and stemmed from Maslow's Hierarchy of Needs. Create an environment that clearly shows students that they're respected and loved and their participation and involvement is valued and sought

(Continued)

after. Stripping it back to basics enabled me to see the students in their rawest form, over time challenging their ideas and allowing them to develop and articulate an opinion, collaborate, problem solve and even some begin to self-actualise. It can be easy as an educator to fall into the trap of trying to use the most innovative methods all the time but don't forget the basics. I highly recommend any aspiring or new teacher to take the plunge and use your gift to teach to see the world. In my opinion it's the greatest opportunity to learn more about yourself as a teacher and as a human.

Developing Student Teachers' Intercultural Competence through Collaborative Online International Learning (COIL)

By Simone Hackett, Department of Physical Education Teacher Training at The Hague University of Applied Sciences, The Netherlands

As migration patterns change and the world and our classrooms become more multicultural, there is an urgent need for student teachers to be prepared for this by being culturally responsive in their teaching to meet the learning needs of their students. However, research has indicated that teachers feel they are ill prepared and need more training for teaching children of diverse backgrounds (Lin and Bates, 2014; OECD, 2014; UNESCO 2020).

What is Collaborative Online International Learning (COIL)?

Collaborative Online International Learning (COIL) is an online pedagogy that facilitates students' intercultural competence development. COIL falls under Virtual Exchange, which is a term used to describe activity which involves online intercultural interaction and collaboration with students from other cultures or geographical locations as an integrated part of course work, under the guidance of educators (O'Dowd, 2018). COIL is seen as a more inclusive and efficient way to internationalise the classroom and promote intercultural learning compared to approaches such as studying abroad, as it offers students an international experience at their home institution. The essence of COIL is in 'developing team taught learning environments where teachers from two different cultures work together to develop a shared syllabus, emphasising experiential and collaborative student learning' (Rubin, 2017). This includes educators from different countries connecting and co-designing collaborative online group assignments for their students with intercultural learning in mind. During a COIL course, which can be anywhere between 4 and 20 weeks long, students work on collaborative assignments in multicultural teams online and through this process develop intercultural competence (see Figure 14.1).

(Continued)

The COIL Educational Model

Figure 14.1 COIL model

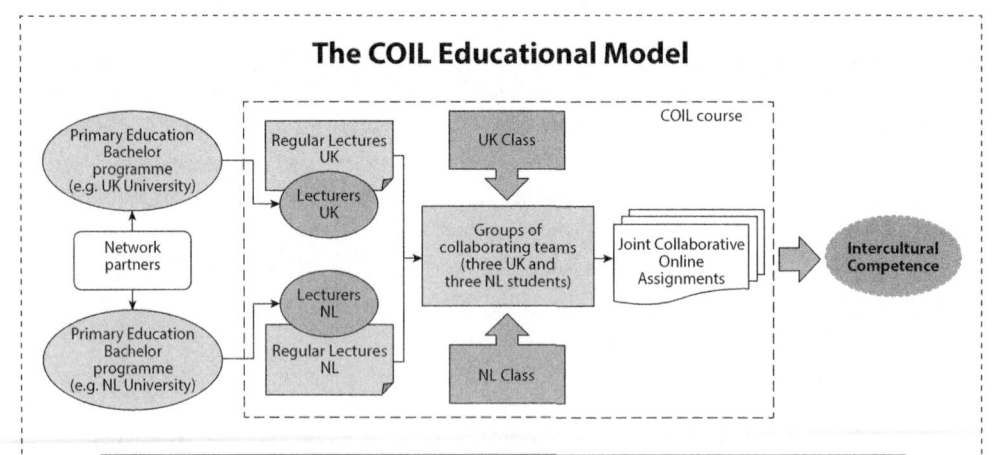

Goal: to enhance the intercultural competencies of students who might not have the opportunity to study abroad.

Theoretical foundations of COIL

COIL is based on two educational learning concepts. First, COIL's essence is based on the collaborative learning educational approach, which involves pairs or teams of students working together to solve a problem, complete a task or create a product either in a face-to-face or online setting (Dillenbourg, 1999; Janssen 2014). Collaborative learning is rooted in social constructivism and Vygotsky's (1978) ideas about a zone of proximal development, in which the focus is on learning and building on knowledge through social interaction. The second is contact hypothesis theory (Allport, 1954; Pettigrew, 1998) which holds the view that exposure to diversity will lead to increased intercultural competence

Implementing COIL with teacher training programmes

Developing a COIL course includes several steps. First, educators need to find a partner to co-design the COIL assignment with. Once educators find a suitable partner, it is important to ensure that both parties are equally committed to developing a COIL course, their institutions support this initiative and the educational visions and curriculums align and match. Important elements to consider are as follows:

- Course schedules: Course schedules should be checked to ensure that they are offered during the same term and that the timelines of both courses match (i.e. start/end dates, holidays and exam periods).
- Class size/student numbers: The class size should be equal on both sides so that there is a balance when forming collaborating teams.
- Duration: Although students can meet asynchronously, students collaborate best when they can meet during class time. Therefore, ensure there is enough time

(Continued)

during class time for students to meet online and collaborate regularly during the course. A minimum of four meetings for a least 45 minutes to an hour is recommended to create team cohesion and ensure intercultural learning occurs.
- World time zones: It is important to check what time zone each partnering COIL institution is in. It is also important to check whether daylight saving changes will occur during the course which could interfere with scheduled collaborative asynchronous sessions.
- Credits: Ensure credits that are awarded for each course are equivalent as this could interfere with how much effort and commitment students have to the course and assignments.
- Team formation: Collaborating teams should consist of two or more students from both partnering universities. Although teams of two (pairs) can work, they are vulnerable due to the chance of one student dropping out of the course and leaving the remaining student alone to complete the tasks.
- Online platforms: Decide on what online platforms are available and will be used for collaboration, and ensure all students will be easily able to access these.
- Data protection and sharing: Is there a data sharing and protection agreement in place between the two institutions to protect students' personal data?
- Formal partnership or Memorandum of Agreement: Although not necessary to initiate and develop a COIL course, a formal agreement is advisable to ensure commitment from both partnering institutions.

Given this, COIL is a valuable tool for developing student teachers' intercultural competence and therefore would be a beneficial approach to embed in teacher training programmes to better prepare student teachers for their future careers and deal with the increasing cultural diversity within their classrooms.

Conclusions

- Teaching abroad offers opportunities for different pedagogical and cultural experiences.
- Teacher requirements may vary from country to country.
- School systems and educational curriculums are widely diverse.

References

Allport, G.W. (1954). *The Nature of Prejudice*. Reading, MA: Addison-Wesley.
Dillenbourg, P. (1999). 'What do you mean by collaborative learning?'. In P. Dillenbourg (Ed.), *Collaborative-Learning: Cognitive and Computational Approaches* (pp. 1-19). Oxford: Elsevier.
Feiler, A., Andrews, J., Greenhough, P., Hughes, M., Johnson, D., Scanlan, M., and Yee, W.C. (2008). The home school knowledge exchange project: Linking home and school to improve children's literacy. *Support for Learning*, 23(1), pp. 12-18. doi:10.1111/j.1467-9604.2008.00363.x
Janssen, J. (2014). *Opening the black box of collaborative learning: A meta-analysis investigating the antecedents and consequences of collaborative interaction* (Report No. 411-11-632). Commissioned by NWO-PROO and NRO. Utrecht: University of Utrecht.

Lin, M., and Bates, A. (2014). Who is in my classroom? Teachers preparing to work with culturally diverse students. *International Research in Early Childhood Education*, 5(1), pp. 27-42.
Merriam-Webster. (2022). 'Accountability'. In *Thesaurus*. Available at: https://www.merriam-webster.com/thesaurus/accountability
O'Dowd, R. (2018). From telecollaboration to virtual exchange: State-of-the-art and the role of UNICollaboration in moving forward. *Journal of Virtual Exchange*, 1, pp. 1-23. doi:10.14705/rpnet.2018.jve.1
OECD. (2014). *Education at a Glance 2014: OECD Indicators*. Paris: OECD.
O'Neill, O. (2004). Accountability, trust and informed consent in medical practice and research. *Clinical Medicine*, 4(3), pp. 269-276. doi:10.7861/clinmedicine.4-3-269
O'Neill, O. (2013a). Intelligent accountability in education. *Oxford Review of Education*, 39(1), pp. 4-16. doi:10.1080/03054985.2013.764761
O'Neill, O. (2013b). *What we don't understand about trust*. TEDx, Houses of Parliament. Available at: https://www.ted.com/talks/onora_o_neill_what_we_don_t_understand_about_trust
Pettigrew, T.F. (1998). Intergroup contact theory. *Annual Review of Psychology*, 49, pp. 65-85.
Rubin, J. (2017). *Embedding Collaborative Online International Learning (COIL) at higher education institutions an evolutionary overview with exemplars*. Available at: https://studyabroad.uic.edu/wp-content/uploads/sites/256/2020/08/Rubin-Embedding-Collaborative-Online-International-Learning-at-Higher-Education-Institutions.pdf
UNESCO. (2020). *Inclusive teaching: Preparing all teachers to teach all students in International Taskforce on Teachers for Education 2030 UNESCO Global Education Monitoring Report*. Available at: https://unesdoc.unesco.org/ark:/48223/pf0000374447
UNHCR. (2016). *Global trends: forced displacement in 2016*. Available at https://www.unhcr.org/5943e8a34.pdf
Vygotsky, L. S. (1978). *Mind in society*. Cambridge: Harvard University Press.

15 Developing parent partnerships after COVID-19 lockdowns

Giving a positive spin to the effects of the pandemic

KEY WORDS

Parents, collaboration, partnership, relationship, home learning, COVID-19

Contributors within this chapter:

1. Kate Davies
2. Marc Smale
3. John Parkin and Sara Spear
4. Matthew Tragheim

(With thanks to Rachel Wolfendale, Janet Morris and Debbie Wallace)

Introduction

Critical question

What positive steps may be undertaken to promote enhanced home-school collaboration for children's learning?

(For the purpose of this chapter, the term parent(s) will be used for whoever looks after the child.)

This chapter proposes that developing partnerships between parents and school environments could be enhanced by capitalising on experiences of home learning. This is based on exploring how schools could learn from opportunities or missed opportunities afforded by experiences of home learning during the lockdown periods of the COVID-19 pandemic. This reflection may enhance our methods of understanding and valuing children's experiences of learning in the home (including a developed understanding of home-school relationships) and the school's vital role in supporting this process. It may support us to identify what has been learnt and what strategies might be used in the future to strengthen effective collaborations between the educational setting and home to enhance children's learning and education.

DOI: 10.4324/9781003218098-15

This chapter does not seek to answer all questions posed, but to present them to readers for them to question their own practice and what might stay the same and what might change – what an opportunity to research your practice! (Also see Chapter 13 about action research.)

The chapter begins with considering the relevance of a focus around parent partnerships linked to COVID-19 and home learning and then progresses to exploring why parent partnerships are valued within the education system to benefit children. Parental involvement and engagement are explained as important factors, but an argument is made that this can go beyond mere homework to valuing home learning experiences. Next, an argument is made that types of learning and experiences from home learning can be considered to extend beyond the immediate home environment. This leads to the suggestion for schools to explore what discussions and explorations they may have with parents about how home learning experiences parents provide could be valued to enhance their child's education. Some questions are posed, which might form the basis of school-based research. A reflection from Kate Davies (headteacher) around home learning, during the COVID-19 lockdown period, notes some important implications around technology. This acts as a stepping stone to considering the importance for us, as educators, to skill ourselves up with our prowess for using technology. This is so that our digital interactions with parents may strengthen our relationships with them, particularly if we want to use technology to help promote opportunities to celebrate what is going on outside of school. A contribution by Marc Smale, a programme lead for a PGCE in primary education, provides us with an opportunity to reflect on our technological competencies and to note implications and take appropriate next-steps' actions. Next, lecturers John Parkin and Sara Spear provide a contribution about how participating in primary learning networks can develop our confidence with technology; this is pertinent because through enhancing our proficiency with technology, we can enhance the way in which we interact with parents to benefit home-school partnerships. The chapter concludes with a contribution from Matthew Tragheim who helps us to reflect on key learning points discussed.

Why a focus on the COVID-19 pandemic linked to parent partnerships?

The COVID-19 pandemic created unprecedented challenges for schools and educational institutions as well as for families. Expecting schools and parents to educate/support online or remote learning made huge demands on both families and teachers at a time when many adults were juggling dual roles as keyworkers, as parents and as carers. Adults (teachers and parents) were expected to manage new technologies in order to educate children. Parents were expected to support their children's learning (Waite et al., 2022), and teachers were expected to communicate with parents and children at home via unfamiliar technology or through other means such as the production of hard copy learning packs. Two key themes emanated from a research project into the impact of COVID-19 on education and children's services (International Literacy Centre, 2020). This was around 'lessons learnt for education going forward' (p. 1) and responses 'rooted in the local landscape' (p. 7). In particular, the idea of schools sharing ideas to 'locally-responsive plans that are attuned to their community's needs' (Moss et al., 2020) may be seen as still having relevance against consideration of home-school collaboration. In other words, how might our home-school collaboration develop, to enhance our children's learning, based on our localised knowledge of our parents' needs? Do we know any more about our parents, than we did before the pandemic in March 2020 when most school-based provision was terminated for periods of time to prevent the spread of COVID-19? How might this knowledge impact upon how we may develop future collaborative partnerships going forward? And, if we do not have this knowledge, then how might we develop this knowledge and what might we consider to establish or develop (more) effective collaborative practice, depending upon the current status quo?

The periods of lockdown and self-isolation if one contracted the virus meant that children's learning was transferred largely to outside the school, mainly at home, unless you were a child of a key worker, a vulnerable child or a child in a preschool setting (Department for Education [DfE, 2020]). However, for those children attending a formal educational setting in person, was any knowledge gained by your school about the parents during this period, which could enhance collaboration in the future? Furthermore, what opportunities for learning at home, experienced by (the majority of) children not attending a setting during lockdown, could be valued by schools to strengthen their future parent-school partnerships to enhance children's learning?

Valuing parent partnerships – a brief overview

Critical question

Why is parental partnership valued within education, and how is its growth developing?

Hornby and Blackwell (2018) spotlight the benefits of parental involvement on 'improved parent-teacher relationships, teacher morale and school climate; improved school attendance, as well as attitudes, behaviour and mental health of children; and increased parental confidence, satisfaction and interest in their own education' (p. 109). Further benefits are highlighted by Wilson (2018) that teachers' well-being is also improved through establishing positive partnerships with parents, which can then translate into benefitting children's attitudes, behaviour and mental health.

The value of establishing relationships with parents and the role of parents are considered important assets within education. For example, improved academic achievement for children is acknowledged as being facilitated by parental involvement (Epstein, 2002; EEF, 2018, 2021). The impact of parents' home-based involvement in their child's learning is relevant because the frequency is likely to be higher than school-based interactions (Pomerantz et al., 2007). Parental expectations and aspirations can also be regarded as more significant than home skill supervision to help support their children's motivation and reinforce the value of education (Fan and Chen, 2001; Jeynes, 2005; Pomerantz et al., 2007). That is not to say that parents supporting skill development is not important or discounted. However, it could be argued that schools could acknowledge and value parental involvement in more holistic learning opportunities which can occur in a home (i.e. those that could happen within the COVID period) or other forms beyond school boundaries. This could make parents feel valued and enhance their relationships with schools and their children, to benefit their children's learning.

Hornby and Blackwell (2018) acknowledge that although barriers and challenges exist, engagement with parents to support children's learning and well-being is developing. This is because teachers acknowledge that learning transcends the school boundaries to that of home and community and parental involvement is seen as central to a school's ethos. This centrality within the school's ethos is underpinned by a whole-school approach discussed with parents and the wider community and shared within policies, plans and informs planning of events and teachers' professional development; schools are better at 'implementing a wider range of needs-based interventions to engage with parents, using a mix of approaches in school, at home, in the community with partners and through digital technology' (Hornby and Blackwell, 2018, p. 118).

Hornby and Blackwell (2018, p. 118) astutely highlight that 'declining support for families from external agencies and services has meant that schools now see [parental involvement] PI as being of central importance to their job of educating children and are therefore developing broader roles in supporting parents'. With this greater value of parental partnership as a key factor to support children's education, let us explore the theme in a bit more detail and make links to the importance of home learning.

More about relationships and partnerships with parents – relationships during and moving beyond lockdown

Collaboration and communication between schools and families are considered vital to partnerships which support child development (Kambouri et al., 2022). Kambouri et al. (2022) acknowledge the importance of these relationships during the COVID-19 pandemic and the increased dependence upon parents which educational settings relied upon to 'continue the education of their children' (p. 640). Montacute and Cullinane (2021) comment that during the January 2021 period of lockdown 'Parents may also feel increased pressure to help their children, given the longer periods of schooling pupils have now missed, making doing so adequately feel more difficult'. However, their commentary relates to the more academic side of learning.

> **Critical question**
>
> How may we value relationships beyond COVID-19 lockdowns?

This chapter is concerned with a holistic view of the role of parents, post-lockdown, and how we can acknowledge and develop our understanding of learning in the home and support this process to enhance our children's experiences of learning going forward. Our acknowledgement, as educators, could extend to embrace and capitalise upon the diverse opportunities afforded by learning experiences encountered by children at home; an educational position to see opportunities for learning at home and school as being complimentary, rather than positions of formal schooling being classed as superior to that of the home. It should also be acknowledged that social and cultural capital and economic and economic affluence and deprivation can also impact on levels of parental engagement.

Discussions need to recognise 'families' challenging circumstances and a more constructive approach to parental engagement is needed, to ensure that parents affected by disadvantage feel valued and enabled to take an active role in their children's education' (Sime and Sheridan, 2014, p. 341)

Parental involvement and engagement

> **Critical question**
>
> What is the difference between parental involvement and engagement, and why do both matter?

There is debate around the distinction between the terms 'parental involvement' and 'parental engagement' in supporting children (Kambouri et al., 2022), though both terms can be deemed to relate to the theme of partnership (Goodall and Montgomery, 2014). Goodall and Montgomery (2014) refer to involvement and engagement being on a continuum and propose a shift 'from parental involvement with school to parental engagement with children's learning' (p. 399).

Goodall and Montgomery (2014) distinguish the involvement as the act of participating, from the engagement as a feeling of involvement of action and autonomy with greater commitment. However, they acknowledge that parental engagement with the school should not be equated with engagement with their children's learning. They refer to an example of ethnic minority families or parents facing economic challenges who might find engagement with school difficult, e.g. because of times of meetings, but have strong inclinations for involvement in their child's learning. This could echo some of the possible challenges faced by parents during the school lockdown periods during the COVID-19 pandemic, such as online meetings, lack of access to technology or feelings of isolation from the school community. But going forward, we can reflect upon and support the learning opportunities which may be present at home and which can enrich children's learning experiences, and to which we might not have previously paid so much attention. These opportunities can enhance school-parent partnerships to 'increase [pupil] motivation and engagement with learning' (Goodall and Montgomery, 2014, p. 401).

Partnerships can be viewed as inequitable, and issues of roles and power can detract from working together to support the child (Kambouri et al., 2022). Therefore, we may align with the term of *collaborative partnerships with mutual respect* and embrace the notion of effective parent-practitioner partnerships involving 'time and space to reflect, exchange knowledge, and share experiences and ideas ... to support the children' (Kambouri et al., 2022, p. 649). This perspective gets to the heart of developing an understanding of how we can acknowledge and develop our understanding of learning in the home, and support this process, to enhance our children's experiences of learning going forward.

One challenge for establishing relationships and enhancing engagement with parents is that they can harbour emotional experiences of their own schooling and education (Goodall and Montgomery, 2014). But by respecting diversity of home learning experiences (beyond homework), we may create stronger relationships, help to counteract negative emotions from parents' conceptualisations of education and in so doing support their children's education. A central idea of emphasising the benefits of establishing partnerships between parents and schools is to help children succeed in school, and with mutual respect established, a caring community (involving parents, the school and others within that community) can develop around the children (Epstein, 2002). Moreover, reiteration of common messages within this community may be facilitated about the value of school, working hard, creative thinking and supporting each other (Epstein, 2002). If children feel valued and are exposed to encouragement to work hard in their learner role, they are increasingly likely to succeed in their education (Epstein, 2002). Epstein (2002) indicates that one of the components within the partnership is learning at home and incorporates provision of information and ideas to the family about supporting their child with 'homework and other curriculum-related activities, decisions, and planning' (p. 14). Within the practical suggestions of what this might look like, Epstein proposes information on 'how to monitor and discuss schoolwork at home', a homework schedule requiring children to 'discuss and interact with families on what they are learning in class' (ibid.) and scheduled activities for children and parents to do at home (as well as within the community), involving the family in setting targets. The homework component is conceived as being interactive and encourages children to take responsibility to talk about the things they are learning, helping families to be aware of the classwork. But, 'homework' extends beyond work done alone to interactive activities shared with others in the home or community and can establish links between work done at home and real life.

Types of learning/experiences from home learning

This chapter wants to extend the idea of learning which goes beyond mere homework and proposes that Epstein's ideas could also be considered in terms of drawing on families and what educational experiences they think they can bring to the table – whatever those experiences may be. Goodall and Montgomery (2014), discussing their continuum from parental involvement to engagement with their children's learning and activities, note that locations of interaction can shift from school to eventually an appropriate location. This location, they acknowledge, could be at school but increasingly likely to be 'other locations such as the home, or during recreational activities or even in supermarkets or cars' (p. 407) where it can have the most benefit.

The periods of lockdown during the early stages of the COVID pandemic seemed to be accompanied by a variety of phrases associated with parents' education of their children not occurring at school, such as home schooling, home learning, parents becoming teachers, facilitating school work and remote learning. Whilst Montacute and Cullinane (2021) refer to home learning linked to the situation of the pandemic (which obviously was pertinent during the stages of enforced lockdown), we may wish to extend home learning beyond this immediate environment akin to Goodall and Montgomery. Therefore, the concept of learning within the home environment could be extended to not just the home but beyond, involving any learning experience which families may bring, and to value those experiences to enhance the children's learning experiences. By valuing these experiences and acknowledging them, we may enhance the strength of the relationships between parents and schools.

An exploration for your school community

> **Critical question**
> How might you explore and take steps to value home learning experiences?

What do you know about your families in your class and the contributions they make outside of school to their children's learning (phrased 'home learning' here)? Maybe your awareness grew during the lockdown periods of the pandemic. One valuable question around developing an understanding and valuing a contribution of home learning to children's learning may be phrased as follows: what discussions may we have with parents about how home learning experiences, which they provide as part of everyday life, could be valued within and enhance their child's education?

To unpick this, you may wish to explore the following sub-questions (or adapt them) in your settings:

- What positive experiences of home learning did children have during enforced lockdown due to the COVID-19 pandemic?
- How have experiences of home learning (from lockdown) influenced home-school partnerships to support children's learning in the future?
- What perceptions about parent-child-school relationships are there; how would participants like to see things develop?
- What strategies are used by the school and parents to facilitate relationships and communication around the children's education?
- What perceptions exist about the children's learning (e.g. what is learning – think holistically and beyond (though do not neglect) the curriculum), what is the school community's values about education beyond the immediate school environment and how does that mesh together with the values currently held at school?
- What experiences related to learning beyond school, whatever those experiences, are explicitly valued and acknowledged by the school?
- What strategies (including online) to support learning are adopted by the school and home, why are they used and how effective are they?
- What ideas for the future about collaboration between home and school do the school community have?
- What is being done to make parents feel properly valued about what they contribute to their child's learning, via out-of-school learning?
- How might teachers and schools valuing contributions which parents make to their children's learning be used as tools in the armoury to foster parent-school relationships?

Answers to the previous questions posed, explored in parallel with parents, teachers, senior leaders and governors, may help you to consider whether there is a connection or disconnection between home and school and then to consider does anything need to shift in the way that things are done. If your school belongs to a trust, can you learn anything by exploring themes together, or perhaps schools within a particular area might come together to learn from one another and share effective practices and steps of change?

Technology

> **Critical question**
>
> How can technology help school communication with parents?

Kate Davies reflects on the home-school learning processes that occurred during the lockdown periods of the pandemic and some implications noted for moving forward, including the use of technology. Kate's contribution acts as a stepping stone for us to then consider the relevance of enhancing teachers' digital competency to strengthen home-school relationships.

Our Experiences During the COVID-19 Pandemic and the use of Computer Technology

By Kate Davies, Headteacher at The Pines School, Bracknell, England

In my current school, prior to COVID-19, we reduced homework or home learning to prioritise reading at home, times tables and a project. The project-based learning was more open ended and enabled success for all. The engagement with the projects has increased over time. We got rid of the weekly spelling tests as we did not see any impact on improving spellings within writing and replaced it with alternative provision.

During the first lockdown, starting in March 2020, we quickly realised that our children were significantly lacking in technology. For at least half of our families, there was either only one device in the household or just a tablet. Before the government started distributing laptops, we could offer our families devices, as both the school and PTA had purchased equipment and we had also received some donations. However, we were all massively underprepared and not skilled enough to manage home learning.

During the points of lockdown, interspersed with periods back at school, research went into which platforms would be best to facilitate home learning. We looked into a variety of platforms and opted for ClassDojo. The logistics of setting this up and distributing logins and instructions was a challenge. What we found was that a lot of our parents needed support in setting these platforms up for their children. Once up and running it ran relatively smoothly and most children took part in submitting work, although all teachers have said that the standard of work was not as good as it would have been if the children had been in school. As a primary school, it was important

(Continued)

> to understand the different stages of learning for our children and therefore manage the expectations for both staff and parents. Our Early Years Foundation Stage (EYFS) and Key Stage 1 children were provided with more physical resources as we knew they would find online learning more challenging.
>
> Since the general return to school, in March 2021, we have reflected upon the situation we were in, and have now chosen Microsoft Teams as a platform to support home school learning when children have been at home. Microsoft Teams has enabled more feedback from the class teacher. This is not something that we will use yet for enhancing children's learning at home in the 'normal' school term and have only used this for children who have been isolating for COVID-19. What we have learnt in this process is that parents in our community need a lot more support to understand the processes of teaching. From this, we will be delivering more face-to-face sessions in how to teach phonics, early reading, maths and writing. We have also recorded teaching sessions on how to use Teams for parents.

Enhancing our use of technology to support relationships and celebrate home learning

> **Critical question**
>
> How might we align our confidence with our use of technology, as teachers, to value home learning experiences and in doing so enhance our relationships with parents?

Whilst good-quality teaching is undeniably critical, as opposed to the medium or method employed, it is acknowledged that the role of technology during the pandemic has come to take on a greater role with promoting greater/different forms of connection (Montacute and Cullinane, 2021; SMART Technologies, 2022). Part of our development as educators during the pandemic, commencing particularly through the periods of lockdown, has been in forging connections with parents through technology, as well as developing our digital literacy. If we feel confident with our use of technology, then we may enhance any communications, and hence relationships, with parents. This chapter acknowledges that there is a digital divide, with some families lacking adequate technology and digital confidence, and some parents may not wish to engage with technology as a preferred form of communication; indeed, face-to-face contact is critical between teachers and parents. But as a tool to complement communication, technology certainly has its benefits, and if we want to celebrate learning opportunities occurring outside of school, then technology may help capture these episodes and meetings around this. The COVID-19 pandemic has highlighted the need for us, as educators, to be aware of our professional development within this sphere (Knight, 2022) and to be able to support families and enhance relationships (SMART Technologies, 2022. NB This source has effective home-school communication ideas).

During lockdown, many schools delivered online learning with some teachers and trainee teachers feeling more confident than others. Parents, and of course their children, received different forms of online learning experiences accordingly. It may be argued that if we develop confidence with our digital interactions with parents, when appropriate, then it may enhance our relationships with them, particularly if we want to use technology to help promote opportunities to celebrate what is going on outside of school. Marc Smale helps us to reflect on our professional development in the form of implications and advice for practitioners around digital competence.

Digital Competence for Teachers – Implications for Teachers Post-Lockdown

By Marc Smale, Programme Leader for PGCE Primary Education at University of Wolverhampton, Wolverhampton, England

Currently, no digital framework exists specifically for England and Wales ITE provision. Neither is digital teaching and learning referenced in the ITT Core Content Framework (DfE, 2019) – the curriculum for teaching training, nor the Teachers' Standards (DfE, 2011) which a trainee teacher is assessed against towards the end of their training to award Qualified Teacher Status (QTS). The Teachers' Standards also is the reference framework for qualified teachers' professional development. This could suggest that without a framework of standards, digital competence is varied amongst teachers at the beginning of their teaching careers, as well as for those teachers currently practising.

Only assumptions exist that technology is integrated into a teacher's practice. This was explicitly emphasised when teachers overnight, during the early stages of the COVID-19 pandemic, had to respond and engage in a very different teaching paradigm: online teaching and learning in March 2020 and during the two further lockdowns.

Practical tools to measure digital competence

To support their professional development, teachers can engage in the following online digital competence assessment instruments, free of charge.

A **Personal digital competence assessment: This measures an individual's personal digital competence.**
Two tools I have spotlighted align to the DigComp 2.1 Framework for Citizens (Carretero et al., 2017). Both, in effect, do the same job and take approximately 20 minutes to complete. Upon completion, the participant receives a report identifying particular strengths and areas of development to address minimising the digital divide within their personal life.

1 *The Digital Competence Wheel: An interactive online testing tool that maps digital competences* (Digital Dannelse, no date) – see https://digital-competence.eu/ (see also Skov (2016) *What is digital competence?* https://digital-competence.eu/dc/front/what-is-digital-competence/)
2 MyDigSkills (Clifford et al., 2020, p. 10) – see https://mydigiskills.eu/index.php

(Continued)

B ***Professional digital competence assessment:*** **This measures a teacher's digital implementation.**

The European Framework for the Digital Competence of Educators (DigCompEdu) is a framework designed and aimed to capture and describe educator-specific digital competencies (Punie and Redecker, 2017). The Framework outlines descriptor competencies detailing how to make efficient and innovative use of digital technologies when an educator plans for teaching, learning and assessment of their learners' progress. The core digital pedagogic competencies of the Framework are complemented with proficiency statements relating to an educator's professional engagement and how an educator facilitates, in the capacity of a role model, their learners' digital competence (Punie and Redecker, 2017).

SELFIEforTeachers (European Commission, no date) is a self-evaluation tool that aligns to the DigCompEdu Framework (see https://educators-go-digital.jrc.ec.europa.eu/).

Upon completion of engaging in the SELFIEforTEACHERS self-assessment tool, the participant receives individual results and a feedback report which outlines an overall summative digital competence percentage grading along with specific percentage measures against six categories. To support continued professional development, clear guidance is provided as to how the respondent can further improve their digital practice.

John Parkin and Sara Spear reflect on how primary learning networks may benefit teachers' confidence with technology post-lockdown going forward. This contribution can be used to support the argument that teachers' confidence with technology can help develop an environment in which we may present ourselves to parents in a positive way, which will then enhance our relationships with parents in how they perceive us.

The COVID-19 School Closures: How Teachers Learnt to Teach Remotely

By John Parkin, School of Education and Social Care, Anglia Ruskin University, Chelmsford, UK

Sara Spear, School of Management, Anglia Ruskin University, Chelmsford, UK

The school closures during the COVID-19 pandemic created an unprecedented challenge for primary teachers, as remote learning suddenly replaced classroom teaching. In the light of these new educational demands, we sought to investigate how primary teachers learnt to teach remotely during the first lockdown period in England from March to June 2020. We were particularly interested in how teachers used professional learning networks (PLNs) to develop their practice, and the implications that this could have for teachers' continuing professional development beyond the pandemic.

(Continued)

We conducted an online survey in June 2020 and gathered responses from over 270 teachers in primary schools across England. We then interviewed 24 of these teachers to gain further insights into their experiences of remote teaching. The results showed minimal formal training for remote teaching – only 17.7% of participants had received training on how to use remote teaching technologies before the pandemic started, and although another 18.5% had received training since then, the majority of teachers had still not received any training. One interview participant summarised the experience of many in saying, 'The learning experience for me about doing the online stuff has been pretty steep'.

In some schools, existing pockets of technology use for remote learning were adapted and shared across the school, or senior leaders used their PLNs to research materials and technologies available for remote learning and then disseminated good practice to be used across the school. Alongside these top-down approaches to continuing professional development (CPD), many primary teachers utilised connections with colleagues in the school to develop their skills in remote teaching. For example, some teachers used Whatsapp groups as informal communities of practice, where colleagues would share ideas and resources, and support each other in developing new skills. Some primary teachers also used PLNs beyond their immediate colleagues, particularly facilitated by social media such as Twitter and Facebook. These networks helped teachers develop their subject knowledge and remote teaching skills, for example by finding new materials and accessing training courses, and also provided a valuable sense of community for teachers working at home during the pandemic. As one teacher said, 'Twitter has really made me feel like I'm part of something when I felt very isolated'.

This study showed that PLNs enabled primary teachers to share knowledge, develop skills and connect with teachers in their own schools and from further afield, in a rapidly changing context. PLNs also offer benefits beyond the pandemic, by providing teachers with the flexibility to engage in CPD at home, at times that suit them, and in the areas they wish to develop. Providing teachers with guidance and time to develop and utilise their PLNs, and to share insights with colleagues, is therefore a potentially important way for schools to support both individual staff CPD and encourage whole school learning.

This chapter concludes with Matthew Tragheim's contribution, which brings us around full circle to considering a positive spin on education in the light of the pandemic: a fluidity in learning and a consideration of the value of digital technology.

Positive Spins on Education During the Pandemic

By Matthew Tragheim, London, England

In the UK, children spend 190 days in school annually. With an average 6.5 hours of formal schooling on each of these days, it would be fair to say that school actually occupies a relatively small amount of children's learning time. Although COVID-19 brought the

(Continued)

highest risk children into even greater focus, the much-peddled idea of 'lost learning' is a pervasive and recurrent theme that neglects the nuance of the pandemic. I saw firsthand the spectrum of 'leveraged learning' that took place with children, parents and families. Families and communities came together to construct new home-school practices with the skills, personal experience and tools they had available. Cooking, crafting and creativity were rife, and, although curriculum content needed to become more fluid, learning was not simply lost. Unexpected avenues of possibility were explored in ways unfathomable before lockdown. For example, I had children taking on home projects ranging from rocking chair building, bird-box carpentry with observation camera, shoebox doll houses, scarecrow stuffing, seed sowing on allotments, COVID-19 diaries, stop-animation river forming with scattered cushions, pot plants and blue bed sheets, papier-m,chÈ solar systems and rocky road comet cakes. Moreover, children, teachers and grown-ups all developed resilience, adaptability and digital skills. However, perhaps the most pertinent and enduring theme was the importance of community, collaboration and connection. Schools and/or communities, brought individual families together through shared experiences, support and opportunities. They are important hubs for nurturing aspiration, bridging social inequality and reducing education inequity.

In other sectors and industries outside of education, the emergence of COVID-19 has not been considered a disruptor in the traditional sense. Rather, it has been viewed as a mobiliser that significantly accelerated already emerging technologies, practices and behaviours. By not entering the four physical walls of a classroom, teachers were given unparalleled freedom to create learning spaces without borders or boundaries. Teachers were given greater freedom to challenge established conventions, thinking and assessment processes as well as demonstrate the impact of changing the status quo. The series of successive lockdowns also demonstrated that learning in the digital age is truly continuous and it reminded me that formal learning is but one element of educating the whole child. In my view, as the digital age evolves, children and families will continue to experience wider access to content, increasing visibility of children's progress, a growing transparency of processes, ownership of curriculum choices and control over blended learning. However, caution is advised and continued reflection required. Children will also need to be taught new skills and behaviours for learning, to enable them to navigate, regulate and curate this easily overwhelming flow of new realms of learning.

Conclusion

This chapter has explored the benefits of parent partnerships. It has argued that, after the periods of COVID-19 lockdown, schools can benefit from strengthening their relationships with parents by valuing more of their home (out of school) learning experiences they provide for their children and, in so doing, benefit their children's learning. It is important to acknowledge that this is not necessarily a silver bullet, but a tool in an armoury of strategies which can support the partnership. For some parents, perhaps, by schools valuing the home learning experiences they can bring to the table, whatever the experiences are, they will be encouraged to participate more, involve themselves more and engage more with the school community as a whole. The value of acknowledging learning opportunities, afforded by parents for their children, is there for the taking – let us embrace them, because parents do an amazing job and can provide holistic opportunities to complement formal schooling. This chapter has also suggested that if teachers develop their use of technology, it can yield benefits for nurturing additional, interactive partnerships with parents and promote what goes on beyond formal schooling.

References

Carretero, S., Vuorikari, R., and Punie, Y. (2017). *DigComp 2.1: The digital competence framework for citizens: With eight proficiency levels and examples of use*. EU Science Hub. [Online]. Available at: https://publications.jrc.ec.europa.eu/repository/handle/JRC106281 [Accessed 1 October 2022].

Clifford, I., Kluzer, S., Troia, S., Jakobsone, M., and Zandbergs, U. (2020). *DigCompSAT: A self-reflection tool for the European digital competence framework for citizens*. EU Science Hub. [Online]. Available at: https://publications.jrc.ec.europa.eu/repository/handle/JRC123226 [Accessed 1 October 2022].

Department for Education (DfE). (2011). *Teachers' standards*. [Online]. Available at: https://www.gov.uk/government/publications/teachers-standards [Accessed 1 October 2022].

DfE. (2019). *ITT core content framework*. [Online]. Available at: https://assets.publishing.service.gov.uk/government/uploads/system/uploads/attachment_data/file/974307/ITT_core_content_framework_.pdf [Accessed 1 October 2022].

DfE. (2020). *Actions for schools during the coronavirus outbreak*. [Online]. Available at: https://www.gov.uk/government/publications/actions-for-schools-during-the-coronavirus-outbreak [Accessed 1 October 2022].

Digital Dannelse. (no date). *The digital competence wheel: An interactive online testing tool that maps digital competences*. Center for Dannelse. [Online]. Available at: https://digital-competence.eu/ [Accessed 1 October 2022].

Education Endowment Foundation (EEF). (2018). *Working with parents to support children's learning: Four recommendations on working with parents to support their child's learning*. [Online]. Available at: https://educationendowmentfoundation.org.uk/education-evidence/guidance-reports/supporting-parents [Accessed 1 October 2022].

Education Endowment Foundation (EEF). (2021). *Parental engagement*. [Online]. Available at: https://educationendowmentfoundation.org.uk/education-evidence/teaching-learning-toolkit/parental-engagement [Accessed 1 October 2022].

Epstein, J. (2002). 'School, family, and community partnerships: Caring for the children we share'. In J.L. Epstein, M.G. Sanders, B.S. Simon, K.C. Salinas, N.R. Jansorn, and F.L. Van Voorhis (Eds.), *School, Family and Community Partnership: Your Handbook for Action. Preparing Educators and Improving Schools*. California: Corwin Press Inc.

European Commission. (no date). *SELFIEforTeachers – Discover your digital potential*. [Online]. Available at: https://educators-go-digital.jrc.ec.europa.eu/ [Accessed 1 October 2022].

Fan, X., and Chen, M. (2001). 'Parent involvement and students' academic achievement: A meta-analysis. *Educational Psychology Review*, 13(1), pp. 1–22.

Goodall, J., and Montgomery, C. (2014). Parental involvement to parental engagement: A continuum. *Educational Review*, 66 (4), pp. 399–410.

Hornby, G., and Blackwell, I. (2018). Barriers to parental involvement in education: An update. *Educational Review*, 70(1), pp. 109–119.

International Literacy Centre. (2020). *Written evidence submitted by the International Literacy Centre, UCL, Institute of Education to the Education Select Committee Inquiry into the impact of COVID-19 on education and children's services, July 2020*. [Online]. Available at: https://committees.parliament.uk/writtenevidence/9081/pdf/ [Accessed 1 October 2022].

Jeynes, W. (2005). A meta-analysis of the relation of parental involvement to urban elementary school student academic achievement. *Urban Education*, 40(3), pp. 237–269.

Kambouri, M., Wilson, T., Pieridou, M., Quinn, S.F., and Liu, J. (2022). Making partnerships work: Proposing a model to support parent-practitioner partnerships in the early years. *Early Childhood Education Journal*, 50, pp. 639–661.

Knight, J. (2022). 'Opening: Planning and prioritising for success'. *SMART Technologies (2022) Assessment Report Capabilities for Success: What's Working in EdTech Today*. [Online]. Available at: https://go.smarttech.com/hubfs/0222_Edtech%20Assessment%20Tool_web_en-gb_singles.pdf [Accessed 1 October 2022].

Montacute, R., and Cullinane, C. (2021). *Learning in lockdown*. [Online]. Available at: https://www.suttontrust.com/wp-content/uploads/2021/01/Learning-in-Lockdown.pdf [Accessed 1 October 2022].

Moss, G., Allen, R., Bradbury, A., Duncan, S., Harmey, S., and Levy, R. (2020). *Briefing Note 2. Learning after lockdown*. [Online]. Available at: https://www.ucl.ac.uk/ioe/research-projects/2021/jan/learning-after-lockdown [Accessed 1 October 2022].

Pomerantz, E., Moorman, E., and Litwack, S. (2007). The how, whom and why of parents' involvement in children's academic lives: More is not always better. *Review of Educational Research*, 77(3), pp. 373–410.

Punie, Y., and Redecker, C. (2017). *European framework for the digital competence of educators: DigCompEdu*. JRC Publications Repository, European Commission. [Online]. Available at: https://publications.jrc.ec.europa.eu/repository/handle/JRC107466 [Accessed 1 October 2022].

Sime, D., and Sheridan, M. (2014). You want the best for your kids: Improving educational outcomes for children living in poverty through parental engagement. *Educational Research*, 56(3), pp. 327–342.

Skov, A. (2016). *What is digital competence?* Center for Digital Dannelse. [Online]. Available at: https://digital-competence.eu/dc/front/what-is-digital-competence/ [Accessed 1 October 2022].

SMART Technologies. (2022). *Assessment report capabilities for success: What's working in EdTech today*. [Online]. Available at: https://go.smarttech.com/hubfs/0222_Edtech%20Assessment%20Tool_web_en-gb_singles.pdf [Accessed 1 October 2022].

Waite, P., Shum, A., Burgess, L.C.H., Pearcey, S., Lawrence, P.J., Klampe, M., and Cattel, C. (2022). *Parenting in a pandemic: A qualitative exploration of parents' experiences ofsSupporting their children during the Covid-19 pandemic*. [Online]. Available at: https://psyarxiv.com/tnasg/ [Accessed 1 October 2022].

Wilson, T. (2018) *How to develop partnerships with parents: A practical guide for the early years*. London: Routledge.

16 Supporting pupils' well-being

KEY WORDS
Self-care, well-being, pupils, inclusion, nurture, development

Contributors in this chapter:

1. Evo Hannan
2. Kate Williams
3. Georgeanne Lamont
4. Rhiannon Rigby
5. Olly Cakebread
6. Terri Gibson-License
7. Ashley Morgan
8. Amy Burrows
9. Vidya Bellur
10. Graham Dickie

Introduction

This chapter and the next focus on well-being; this first chapter of the two considers how we can support pupils' well-being through the guidance and nurture we give in our schools, whilst the next chapter moves on to consider how we can protect and maintain our own levels of well-being as busy educators who are giving out so much energy and emotion on a daily basis. In this chapter, ten contributors share their views on ways we can support pupils' well-being, through helping them understand their behaviours and identities and ensuring that our classrooms are safe spaces for big conversations to take place.

Well-being

Critical question

What is well-being, and how can we help to support children's well-being?

DOI: 10.4324/9781003218098-16

Supporting pupils' well-being 261

It is worth starting by talking about the term 'wellbeing'. There are many different types of well-being, or, in effect, areas of our lives which may feel balanced or unbalanced and thus affect our overall emotions and general levels of happiness.

For children, the three key areas of well-being are the following:

- Emotional well-being
- Physical well-being
- Social well-being

In the next chapter we will add two more to the adults' list, that of

- Workplace well-being
- Societal well-being

For children, who do not yet have a workplace, or an observable role in society, it is perhaps the school environment that offers this similar space, away from home, where well-being may be majorly affected through the relationships, interactions and activities that are encountered in this setting. When children are spending so many hours of their weekdays in the school institution, it is of paramount importance that we make the most of opportunities to help not only support well-being but also educate young people on how to take control of their own well-being in order to prepare themselves for a happy future in modern Britain.

Supporting our mental well-being is similar in some ways to caring for our physical health; if you started eating healthily for a month, cutting out excess sugar and junk food, and making sure you were properly hydrated, you would likely feel much better. But if you then switched back to a poor diet, you would feel less well. Caring for our well-being is similar, and the best way we can maintain levels of feeling positive is through continuing to engage in well-being activities to maintain our skills and focus. Of course it is possible to eat unhealthily and still feel well, or vice versa, but the point being made is that making small daily practices can help sustain our well-being better than solitary actions that do not last.

Aim to help your children develop well-being toolkits that they can carry with them throughout their lifetimes. Aim to be the role model they need to see.

Emotional well-being

Emotional well-being requires us to have skills to build our positive emotions and to help acknowledge and manage our negative feelings. Being mindful is a core part of emotional well-being, as it is important to understand that it is normal and healthy to feel a range of powerful emotions, even just in the course of one day. We must speak to children about this and also consider being a healthy role model for emotions in our classrooms. Yes, teachers need to be mostly positive to engage the class, but it does not hurt to show your emotional side and vulnerabilities in age-appropriate ways, such as sharing if something happened like your car breaking down that make you worried or scared, or losing a pet that made you feel sad. Talk to children about these feelings and share how you helped to make yourself feel better.

If we are emotionally aware, we can better cope with our levels of stress; this applies to children too. Make space in the school day to share how they are feeling, maybe through a simple vote of hands or a 10-second talk with their partner at registration time.

Physical well-being

Keeping on top of our physical well-being is easier as adults, but for children who have less autonomy over their diet and home activities, perhaps the most useful thing we can do is facilitate conversations in school about how to be physically well. There is an inherent link between physical well-being and emotional well-being, and small practices at school can help transfer to a child's happiness both in and out of school.

Some simple techniques that schools use are the following:

- Walking the 'daily mile', a mile track or loop that children take time to complete each day to ensure that children are taking part in at least a mile of exercise each day
- Dancing between lessons: some schools buy schemes such as '5-a-day Fitness', but there are many short dance videos on YouTube that you could play throughout the day and get involved in.
- Encourage 'walk to school' or 'scoot to school' initiatives, often which are run locally or nationally, rewarding with house points or stickers for those that engage.

Social well-being

Social well-being relies upon the development of social skills, such as kindness, gratitude and the power of communication. Having stronger social skills is more likely to allow us to engage better with others and thus may help to combat loneliness, isolation or anger. Feeling socially well is about feeling connected to those around us, and school is thus a great location for building these feelings of community and togetherness. Davis (2019) stresses that building social well-being is one of the most successful ways to develop our emotional well-being, and when we feel socially connected, we are often more able to deal with challenges (Davis, 2019).

Ensure you have group work as a comfortable part of your teaching, and allow for opportunities for pupils to work with a variety of peers and groups to strengthen their relationships in their wider network, rather than always working with the same table groups.

Encourage your class to engage in simple practices like at the end of each day sharing what they are grateful for, or keeping a gratitude journal.

Future Ready Students

By Evo Hannan, Founder of Innovation X, London, England

The world is changing so quickly. It wasn't so long ago that we had to dial into the internet, mobile phones were the new things to have and social media was just starting to make an appearance.

Fast-forward two decades, and we now live in a world where we learn and work from home, electric cars are becoming more commonplace on our roads and we are

(Continued)

discussing ways we can use digital currency and digital art in exciting ways in the new realm of the metaverse. We have also seen an exponential rise of young entrepreneurs – a new breed of digital creatives as young as 12 years old who push boundaries and use their voice to create and sell products and services.

As a school, how can we promote, develop and nurture such talent? How can we help students become founders of their own agency, making decisions on ways they can be creative and enjoy the journey along the way? There are more and more students who have ambitions to become the next big YouTuber, podcaster or digital influencer. This new generation of entrepreneurs are adaptable, nimble and prepared to forge their own path.

My five tips on how your students could be future ready would be as follows:

Nurture relationships – By putting energy into your relationships, developing communication skills and understanding that discussing ideas and having conversations is mutually beneficial. Be a good person, and empathising with others will help build your connection and trust with people. Human connection will become even more important as we transition into the digital space.

Fail first and fail fast – The world is changing quickly, and as we try to develop new ideas, we will often face failure early in our journey. This can be hard to accept, but if you're aware that failing is part of the path to your goals, it becomes a learning experience as you move forward. Learn to accept and own the small failures.

Persevere – If you read any backstory of YouTubers or influencers, most will talk about how difficult it was to start, but believing in themselves and staying true to their cause helped them towards a path of success. This consistency, even when you don't see results immediately, will help you stay motivated. Keep striving and never give up.

Manage your space – Being mindful of your own space and your own limits is key to maintaining a good level of well-being. Sometimes we can push too far with our expectations, and you may end up distancing yourself from everybody around you. This also connects to the first point. Keep your energy in a positive space so you can keep building.

Take care of your health – Another part of your well-being is your health. Develop a strong routine that allows you to fit in school, your hobbies and any additional activities. The most successful people in the world manage their own schedules extremely well. Sleep well, eat well and exercise. You will always have more to bring to the table when this is balanced. Remember that your mental health is just as important as your physical health.

Here's to the new generation of creatives on making a positive impact on the future.

(Continued)

Well-Being and Social Work

By Kate Williams, Social Work Apprentice at Anglia Ruskin University, Essex, England

Social workers support some of the most marginalised and vulnerable adults and children in society (Parker and Crabtree, 2018). Practitioners promote and uphold the well-being of those they support, with the term reflected in Social Work England's professional standards and the British Association for Social Worker's professional capability framework (British Association of Social Workers, 2021; Social Work England, 2022). However, the well-being term has no universally agreed definition and cannot be applied into ethical social work practice without deeper understanding of the word (British Association of Social Workers, 2018).

The United Nations Convention on the Rights of the Child (1989) states that a child's well-being is met by having access to an 'acceptable standard of living; quality of family life; coordinated care; health; food; sleep; being safe; and having equal opportunities' (United Nations, 1989). However, this definition of quality of life does not consider the subjective nature of well-being nor the evolvement alongside UK societal attitudes (Lister, 2021). Furthermore, what is considered acceptable quality of life standard is influenced by political agendas and government policies (Karisto, 2018). The revised Children Act 1989 mentions well-being, but does not stipulate how the scarce resources will meet and maintain the well-being of children). Therefore, the concept can be a distraction and does not acknowledge the intersectional and structural factors impacting vulnerable families (Payne, 2021).

A social worker's role is to assess for interventions to safeguard and meet a child's needs. One theory which a social worker can use to inform an assessment is Bronfenbrenner's ecological systems theory (Bronfenbrenner, 1979 cited in Teater, 2020). Systems theory assesses the relationships between the individual and others on distinct levels; 'the microsystem, the mesosystem, the exosystem, and the macrosystem' (Healy, 2014, p.125). By mapping an individual's system, it can identify where there are strengths, issues and additional stressors (Payne, 2021) whilst considering the interrelation between resources and a child's social network and environment. Thus, social workers can consider the strengths of a child's education system in the microsystem-level context, and how this is impacting the other parts of the child's network (Bronfenbrenner, 1979 cited in Teater, 2020). However, whilst systems theory identifies problems, it does not describe how to challenge the identified issues (Healy, 2014).

Social workers using ecological systems theory can also consider the influences of government policies and legislations when focusing on the macrosystem. The current cost of living crisis is having an increasing impact on families, with 830,000 emergency food parcels being provided for children between April 2021 and March 2022 (Trussell Trust, 2022). Thus, social workers and professionals need to be mindful of the context of situations to not to pathologise and point blame at families who are financially struggling to maintain the well-being of their children (Spray and Jowett, 2012).

Self-Care for Children – Empowering and Equipping Young People with Habits for Self-Care

By Georgeanne Lamont, The Values and Visions Foundation, London, England

Children need to feel that they belong, they are safe, seen, heard, valued, respected, and accepted for who they are. And, in turn, they delight in giving to others, helping others feel safe, seen, heard, valued, respected, and accepted for who they are. It is a dynamic flow of positive care – receiving and giving. As children enter this flow, they feel part of a community that holds them, and it is this that gives them a sense of safety, a sense of their own worth and the implicit ability to care for themselves by staying connected to their self-respect and to others.

The volatile, uncertain, chaotic and ambiguous nature of our world engenders anxiety, stress, self-doubt and unease. Below are six antidotes for children to practise habits of self-care.

1. **The self:** Focus on activities to gradually and consistently understand the self as it unfolds. What is this self, and what does it mean to be a human being? This sense of self is the foundation on which all the rest of our experience is built. We are shaped by four aspects of what it is to be a human being. Firstly, we are unique; no other person on the planet is quite like us, so appreciate this uniqueness. Secondly, being human, we have unlimited potential for good, creativity, learning and growth, so help the child believe in that potential, experiment with that creativity and monitor for themselves that growth. Thirdly, as a human we have unlimited potential for messing up, for hurting and harming ourselves, others and the planet. So, a child needs to be aware of this and have a tool to explore the difficult emotions, the knee-jerk reactions, to reflect and learn from the uncomfortable experiences. Fourthly, we have choice; moment by moment we can choose to move forward into positivity or slip back into or get stuck in negativity. Equip the child to learn to be self-aware and make choices for themselves to continuously move forward. This daily choosing to grow into their highest potential is like giving a plant space to thrive. It is the first step of self-care.

2. **Our values**: These are a vast inner resource to help us successfully navigate uncertainty. They provide the anchor. Equip children to understand what matters to them, what makes them tick and what lights them up. What are their values? Give them opportunities to recognise, name, apply and develop the use of those values, for example respect. When a child is aware of their values and able to make a daily practice of using them to transform situations, they are taking good care of themselves.

3. **Stillness**: Practising stillness or mindfulness helps a child to self-regulate and keep themselves safe from reactivity. Our mind, left to itself, is like a wild horse, or a 'supersonic' car with no brakes. By teaching a child how to press the pause button – to become still – you empower them to move from reacting to responding. This gives the child the power to choose their response to the situations they face and the

(Continued)

emotions within them. Start a lesson with a minute of quiet. Take some deep breaths and become aware of the breath coming into the body and out of the body. Teach them a very simple meditation to bring them fully into the present moment:

In...... Out
Deep.... Slow
Calm .... Ease
Smile .... Release
Present.... Moment
Wonderful Moment

4. **Celebration**: Show children how to counter the negative bias of their mind, how to shift from negative to positive using appreciation and gratitude. Start the day with celebrating three things that went well the day before. Teach the children to challenge their own negative thinking about others and the self – 'Oh she's mean'. 'He's a big-head'. 'I'm useless'. Practise looking for the positive qualities in others and especially in oneself. Children can practise acknowledging their own and others' strengths each day. This counters the tendency to be too self-critical and discontented with oneself. Encourage children to reframe situations and to find the benefit in any situation. Make a habit of an attitude of gratitude. A gratitude journal is a powerful way to care for oneself.
5. **Grieving**: Again, using a journal, a child can recognise, name and share the pains and sorrows they experience. Make a habit of journaling tough times. Encourage a child to talk and share the sad emotions; this is vital for self-healing.
6. **Vision**: Regularly write a positive vision, be it for the day, week, month, year or lifetime, for yourself and for your community; set yourself a clear aim. Holding a distinct and confident vision of one's future releases the child's sense of hope

Together these six habits help to build the child's inner strength and their capacity to handle situations and sustain a sense of meaning and purpose. They equip a child with tools of self-care that will empower their whole being to grow and give through tough times.

Full instructions for activities for all these six antidotes, and more, can be found in Burns and Lamont (2019).

Supporting the Mental Health of Gender-Diverse Pupils

By Rhiannon Rigby, MA, Staffordshire University, Stoke on Trent, England

Teachers are often at the front line of supporting pupils with their mental health and well-being; they are a vital part of pupils' support systems. Gender diversity is arguably a daunting and often divisive subject, leaving teachers unsure of the best way to support pupils. Pupils who are gender diverse may face gender identity difficulties that can negatively impact their mental health and well-being. The Department for

(Continued)

Education (DfE) has published guidance for schools stating that teachers should never tell a child they have the 'wrong' body or use physical characteristics to tell a child what their gender is. Whilst this is sound advice teachers are often the people pupils will turn to with concerns or worries, teachers need to be empathetic and understanding to manage these sensitive situations. Training for teachers in gender diversity is not mandatory, and therefore understandably teachers can face difficulties in feeling confident in supporting pupils who are gender diverse.

Gendered language is inherent throughout society; the use of gendered pronouns and gendered language such as endearments, i.e. sweetheart, mate, buddy and darling, may be distressing for gender-diverse pupils. Imagine spending a large portion of your days being referred to as a gender that you do not feel aligned to. Over time pupils report this can have a detrimental effect on their mental health and well-being. This is not to suggest that teachers will never use gendered language. Being mindful of how such language impacts pupils may be a small change to teachers that could positively impact gender-diverse pupils' everyday lives.

In addition, the resources teachers use can also have an impact on pupils' ideas of gender. Teachers can challenge gender stereotypes using texts and literature and other resources which do not reinforce gender stereotypes. This may result in a reduction of unconscious gender bias and stereotyping and can help promote gender equality for all pupils. Inclusive language benefits all pupils not just those who may be gender diverse. Teachers also should avoid segregation of pupils into boy/girl groups and boys vs. girls teams as this may force pupils to align themselves with a gender which may not be a comfortable experience for them.

Supporting diversity and providing a sense of belonging for gender-diverse pupils does not detriment any pupils but may improve the educational experience for all.

Mental Health and Well-Being of Children

By Olly Cakebread, Primary Teacher, Bexleyheath, England

One of my proudest moments when teaching was when one of my classes was doing a workshop and they were asked who in their life loved them. Obviously, the workshop leader was met with the usual answers of Mummy, Daddy, and the family dog Sebastian; however, to my surprise every single member of the class said, 'Mr Cakebread' (a funny teacher name, I know!) I knew that I always tried my hardest to show them my love for them, but to know they actually felt it and recognised it was just the greatest feeling. It really was the moment that I realised the key to keeping children mentally healthy and well in a primary school. It was not mindfulness colouring sheets or PSHE lessons on feelings; it was just simply, love.

(Continued)

As educators, we are a constant in our children's lives, with them sometimes seeing us for more hours a day than their own families. They look up to us and see us as effectively their 'second parents', so they look to us to model all of the emotions that they would hopefully be receiving from other family members at home, and it is our duty to reciprocate these to allow them to form solid emotional responses to people and events around them. Take a very low ability Year 6 SATs cohort, for example. This is the first time they will probably ever be experiencing true educational stress as they are having pressure from both their families and their school to succeed. It is a very overwhelming time, and we need to use this first opportunity to model resilience and coping strategies to help them continue to deal with many situations like this in the future. Whilst all the anxiety-reducing mechanisms we are taught to teach do help and there is place for them, I believe most importantly, we should be encouraging children to talk about their feelings to a safe person, discussing their worries with their peers and creating a safe and open forum for them to just release all of their worries, and in turn, they should receive nothing but love back. As Winnie the Pooh put it wonderfully, 'Sometimes the smallest things take up the biggest room in your heart' – if we ensure our actions show this, imagine the number of lives we could be changing just by simply showing we care.

Self-Care for Pupils

By Terri Gibson-License, Primary Education studies graduate at Anglia Ruskin University, Essex, England

During my time at school, I cannot remember a focus on self-care nor well-being, but I am also aware that the demands I felt then are contrastingly different to the demands on today's children. As adults, we have the ability to understand our needs, desires and what keeps us balanced when things get too much. But do children have this ability yet? Is it something that develops as we learn more about ourselves? And does this only develop with age? Children require explicit teaching and direction regarding their well-being and the methods they can use to care for themselves as they grow older. Ensuring that pupils are aware of their mental, emotional and physical well-being helps to develop their introspective thinking, a skill which they will depend on throughout their lives. I believe that apart from explicit teaching of self-care and well-being techniques, the most effective way of demonstrating the skills needed is through active modelling from both parents at home and teachers within schools. However, as adults, we must remember that our understanding of self-care is vastly different to that of a child's understanding which is constantly developing. This modelling can include 'mindfulness' sessions during the school day and curating opportunities for active and creative self-exploration using music or art activities.

(Continued)

At home, the use of the outdoors provides valuable opportunities to explore emotions, ensuring they are connected to nature. Everyday tasks within the home can be used to instruct children about self-care such as the importance of eating a healthy and nutritious diet, which can be achieved through involving children in the cooking process (again, a skill which is vital throughout life). As adults, and as difficult as this can be, it is vital that we take a step back during these moments, breaking activities down into manageable steps and ensuring children have the opportunity to try for themselves.

Thinking about Gender and Stereotypes for Primary Teachers and Trainees

By Ashley Morgan, Masculinities Scholar at Cardiff Metropolitan University, Cardiff, Wales

Most small children have very little understanding of what gender is and, more importantly, how it 'works' until they start primary school. Yet primary school becomes the place where stereotypes of gender become entrenched and reproduced, and girls and boys learn the latent rules by which society is constructed.

As primary teachers or trainee teachers, you will doubtlessly have witnessed and experienced for yourselves how gender works. Many boys are more boisterous than girls: perhaps it's more difficult to make them sit down and listen. Girls might be more cautious and reticent and might be more likely to put their hands up to ask a question or wait their turn more quietly than the boys.

Gender presents through obvious stereotypes, such as in appearance, discourse and affect.

Appearance: Often boys will have short hair and girls long. Names often refer to specific genders. But some might be interchangeable (like my name!). School uniforms work hard to impose gender stereotypes on children; girls wear skirts and boys wear trousers.

Discourse: People 'gender' babies from a young age, and many studies have shown that if people believe a baby is a boy or a girl, they will both treat and speak to them differently. This is why people dress their babies in colours which refer to gender, such as pink for girls, because babies tend to look like babies rather than obviously girls and boys. If a baby is believed to be a boy, and he cries, many people will think this is a positive thing and that he has strong lungs. If a baby is believed to be a girl who cries, people tend to think there is something 'wrong'.

Affect: The ways in which emotions are produced, appear and are assigned to different genders. Boys are discouraged from showing negative emotions.

(Continued)

But teachers and trainee teachers have an opportunity to help young people navigate through this situation in which boys dominate girls and to be agents for change. You can do this by

- Using the same language with boys as you do with girls. If you are praising a child, for example, try not to say 'good boy/girl' but say 'good job'. Words like 'silly' or 'fussy' tend to be applied to girls; either apply to both genders or think of others.
- Help boys talk about their emotions. Many boys tend to laugh at others who display sadness or who cry as they are taught that sadness is negative and that boys don't cry.
- Encourage girls to speak up and out.

Three Recommendations for Supporting Children's Mental Health and Well-Being

By Amy Burrows, Primary Education studies graduate at Anglia Ruskin University, Essex, England

It is clear that remote lockdown and social isolation have had catastrophic effects on children's well-being, resulting in long-term effects; now children are back in the classroom (Glasper, 2021). Evidence provides reasoning to believe that there has been a clear decline in children's mental health since the start of the COVID-19 pandemic in March 2020 (NSPCC, 2021).

Recommendation 1: Increased Funding for Child and Adolescent Mental Health Support Workers

Mental health conditions, whether that be as a result of the pandemic or other contributing factors in children and adolescents, are rising (NHS, 2022). The Association of Child Psychotherapists (2022) stress that although there is an increased demand for child mental health therapists, CAHMS have reported that their service is downsizing due to a lack of government funding (NHS, 2022). The proof of the devastating effects this is having is indisputable, as Glennon (2021) analyses current survey findings that underline the crucial need for increased funding for mental health services, in order to support the ascending number of children and young people suffering from progressively poor mental health. Child and adolescent mental health services have been historically underfunded. Hefferon et al. (2022) highlights that the pandemic needs to be a turning point for increased funding in this area. Only 30% of children with mental health needs are currently receiving access to mental health services (Mind, 2021). Additional funding will allow for each child, regardless of their family's economic status, access to receive the treatment needed to flourish (Rethink Mental Illness, 2022). Hefferon et al. (2022) also suggests that the work force for child and adolescent support services needs to increase, in order to address the demand for child mental health cases.

(Continued)

A 72% increase in child mental health nurses and psychologists is required to meet the demands for the existing backlog evidencing the importance for funding in this field.

Recommendation 2: Statutory Mental Health Training for all Teachers

Although Theresa May outlined in the Green Paper legislation (DfE, 2017) that every school will be offered mental health first aid training by 2020, only 46% of schools have reported receiving this training to support their pupils' needs (Kim and Asbury, 2020). Making mental health training statutory for teachers will provide explicit guidance on identifying needs, as well as statutory guidelines for addressing next steps (Born, 2021). The Green Paper does not outline the importance of teachers understanding a holistic multidisciplinary approach to children's mental health (RCPCH, 2019). The focus of the Green Paper is to provide greater access to services such as CAMHS, not the identification process of needs for concern (RCPCH, 2019). Making accredited mental health training compulsory for teachers will tackle the first hurdle in what the NHS (2021) report as vital early intervention.

Recommendation 3: Introduction of Mental Health and Well-Being within the National Curriculum

Whilst the government outlined the implementation of Relationships and Sex Education (RSE) in 2019 (DfE, 2019) with the intention to incorporate mindfulness and well-being, there is no statutory curriculum for mental health and well-being within the UK education system. If children were able to identify their own emotional state through understanding what mental health means at school, professionals would be able to intervene much sooner (Radez et al., 2020). Emotional regulation is a fundamental part of child development. The question needs to be asked, why is this not a statutory requirement throughout the national curriculum (Desautels, 2019)? Whilst teachers promote and track children's social and emotional development throughout the Early Years Foundation Stage (EYFS), there is no further need to observe and track development in this area when pupils go into Year 1.

Supporting Highly Sensitive Pupils

By Vidya Bellur, Dip Hyp, GQHP, CNHC; Therapeutic Coach and Mentor; Anxiety and Stress Expert: Vivid Outcomes, Redhill/Reigate, England

The subject of 'sensory processing sensitivity' was first researched closely in the nineties, by Psychologist, Dr Elaine Aron. She coined the phrase 'Highly Sensitive Person' (HSP) to describe a person who is likely to have a central nervous system that is deeply sensitive to stimuli, be it emotional, social or physical. It is thought that 15-20% of the population are highly sensitive, potentially meaning that in a class of 30 children, roughly 4-5 of them may be considered to be a HSP. As a practitioner, for many of the children that attend my clinic who present with 'anxiety', I would say that lots of them could well be thought of as being a HSP.

(Continued)

They are as follows:

- Highly empathetic, caring individuals and typically have high emotional intelligence
- Deep thinkers with a rich inner world that they may/may not share conversationally with others, but are more often than not driven creatively to express themselves
- Wanting to build strong and lasting bonds with others where their needs for being caring and sensitive to others are served
- Deeply moved by a sense of 'beauty', but can also express a similar response when they see or hear something that is distressing or sad to them

Oftentimes, in school environments, these children are thought of as being

- 'Overly sensitive' – unable to 'regulate' their emotions
- Highly anxious in certain situations, which may be accompanied by a physical manifestation, such as the feeling of sickness in their 'tummy', or needing to vomit
- 'A bit of a worrier' and sometimes involve themselves in situations that require appeasing or resolution
- Overwhelmed in certain environments for the sensory stimuli
- Open to experiencing 'separation anxiety' when leaving their primary caregiver/s to attend school

Being a HSP is considered more to be an evolutionary personality trait, where environment, genes and early childhood experiences all play a part in its development and expression. At times some of the behaviours can potentially be confused with other personality traits or mental health conditions, such as introversion, sensory processing disorder, ASC or ADHD.

For example, a child who is finding it difficult to leave their caregiver in the mornings: 'I imagine it's really hard to leave them behind in the morning, and you feel a sense of responsibility towards them. Perhaps you're wondering if they will be ok without you there, to make sure that they are alright. What would help you to feel easier about that situation?'

Only by such engagements will we nurture and grow the very people needed in our society to help heal and lighten the load on the growing issues we are having with mental illness. Pathologising them, labelling them with 'anxiety' and 'over-treating' them will mean these sensitive children grow up believing something is wrong with them to feel so intensely. They will be added to the growing scale of the mental health crisis, when in actual fact, they are the evolutionary eyes and ears that keep our society safe from harm and growing – be it the doctors, nurses, therapists and educators of our tomorrow. They are actually the 'solution' that stares at us. It's up to us to nurture and tend to them so that they fulfil the very reason that they feel and experience so deeply.

Taking Children's Needs Seriously

By Graham Dickie, Headteacher at Kilchrenan Primary School, Taynuilt, Scotland

Strange to say, but it's easy to lose sight of the child in education: pressures, expectations, rules, data and time can deflect us from taking children's needs seriously. These are my seven hard-learned lessons.

1. **Question, Question, Then Question**
   You have to keep curious about children. Why do they not listen, understand or progress? Why do they fight, bite or answer back? Why do they hide or walk in circles? Behaviours, like failures in learning, are the result of something. They are the symptoms, not the problem.
   'What is getting in the way of this child or young person's wellbeing?'
   You might find it's your teaching or the school's behaviour policy, a wrong grouping or the way instructions are given, or hunger, depression or anger. These are barriers a child may have to climb before they can access 'the curriculum'. To know the barriers, we need people professional enough to ask, 'why?'

2. **Observe Properly**
   What is the child doing? Look, listen and resist the urge to rationalise (she does that because…) It took me 2 months to realise that a child did walk in circles, even though I'd 'seen' it many times!

3. **Listen to the Child**
   There are lots of good ways to help children express themselves, and for us to hear their voice, but to listen, *we* need to be quiet!
   It doesn't take time to hear, but it does to listen. And sometimes we must 'bite our tongues'. Remember, the child has the right to be heard and have those views taken seriously.

4. **Recognise That Not Every One 'Gets It'**
   This can be hard. You think you understand a child's needs, but others can't see it or, worse, interpret everything in an opposite way. 'You care so much' might not be praise, but an accusation of oversensitivity and of an impractical approach. Hard-pressed senior leaders are not always understanding. Experienced teachers might have developed poor and uninformed practice in their classes.
   We need to seek others with a like mind. Problem-solving with another colleague works. It can also save you from getting it wrong. You may have to arrange it for yourself, but a colleague for a sounding board and a coach for perspective are sanity savers.

5. **Log It!**
   Keeping dated notes helps build case histories, gives clear examples to parents and partner agencies (psychology, health, speech and language, and social work) and helps leadership make informed decisions when you raise a concern.

(Continued)

> Also, keeping notes of meeting decisions, informal referrals, phone calls, emails, parental comments and advice given can keep you safe. Time spent in sending a quick, brief, formal, copy summary of a key parental conversation can guard against later confusions.
>
> Keep the evidence; have the proof.
>
> 6. **Know Your Role**
>
>   You cannot save the world. You cannot sort all parents. You cannot fix every broken school. You might not be able to help that child. You can make a difference, just not every time.
>
>   You have to stop, switch off, look after yourself and live. This is your job, not your family. You have to let others do their bit, even if you don't agree.
>
>   You are a professional; be professional in your development and practice, but learn when it's the professional time to pass it on or walk away.
>
> Finally, don't stop learning. I'm still embarrassed by some of my teaching!
> When faced with children in need, you can rely on what you've got, or you can learn.

Conclusion

- Get to know your pupils so you can recognise when they are acting differently.
- Ask them what is wrong.
- Communicate and cooperate with others in the child's network.

References

Born, J. (2021). *Five ways to wellbeing for children*. [Online]. Sanctuarymentalhealth.org. Available at: https://www.sanctuarymentalhealth.org/2020/10/06/five-ways-to-wellbeing-for-children/?gclid=CjwKCAjwxOCRBhA8EiwAOX8hi3oaOX4JQ4dH3-b5F6qg4VTHI-zKNtAs6ZJMqowCrEy849Ug8iZVpxoC-nIcQAvD_BwE [Accessed 21 March 2022].

British Association of Social Workers, 2018. *Professional capabilities framework*. [Online] Available at: https://www.basw.co.uk/professional-development/professional-capabilities-framework-pcf/the-pcf [Accessed: 22 May 2022].

British Association of Social Workers, 2021. *Code of ethics*. [Online] Available at: https://www.basw.co.uk/about-basw/code-ethics [Accessed: 22 May 2022].

Burns, S., and Lamont, G. (2019). *Values and Visions: Energising Students, Refreshing Teachers*. London: The Values and Visions Foundation.

Davis, T. (2019). What is well-being? Definition, types, and well-being skills. *Psychology Today*. Available at: https://www.psychologytoday.com/us/blog/click-here-happiness/201901/what-is-well-being-definition-types-and-well-being-skills [Accessed 1 October 2022].

Department for Education (DfE). (2017). *Transforming children and young people's mental health provision: A green paper*. [Online]. Available at: https://www.gov.uk/government/consultations/transforming-children-and-young-peoples-mental-health-provision-a-green-paper [Accessed 28 February 2022].

Desautels, L. (2019). *The role of emotion co-regulation in discipline*. [Online]. Edutopia. Available at: https://www.edutopia.org/article/role-emotion-co-regulation-discipline [Accessed 21 March 2022].

DfE (2019). Relationships Education, Relationships and Sex Education (RSE) and Health Education Statutory guidance for governing bodies, proprietors, head teachers, principals, senior leadership teams, teachers. Available at Relationships Education, Relationships and Sex Education and Health Education guidance (publishing.service.gov.uk) [Accessed 9 March 2023].

Glasper, E. (2021). Protecting the mental health of children and young people during the Covid-19 pandemic. *Comprehensive Child and Adolescent Nursing*, 44(1), pp. 1–5.

Glennon, N. (2021). *Barnardos: 'Children have lost their sparkle'*. [Online]. Barnardos.org.uk. Available at: https://www.irishexaminer.com/news/arid-40240274.html [Accessed 6 March 2022].

Healy, K., 2014. *Social Work Theories in Context: Creating Frameworks for Practice*. 2nd ed. London: Red Globe Press.

Hefferon, C., Taylor, C., Bennett, D., Falconer, C., Campbell, M., Williams, J., Schwartz, D., Kipping, R., and Taylor-Robinson, D. (2022). Priorities for the child public health response to the COVID-19 pandemic recovery in England. *Archives of Disease in Childhood*, 106(6), pp. 533–538.

Karisto, A., 2018. Reciprocity and well-being. In: M. Törrönen, C. Munn-Giddings and L. Tarkiainen, eds. 2018. *Reciprocal Relationships and Well-Being: Implications for Social Work and Social Policy*. Abingdon: Routledge. Chapter 1. pp. 11–25.

Kim, L., and Asbury, K. (2020). 'Like a rug had been pulled from under you': The impact of COVID-19 on teachers in England during the first six weeks of the UK lockdown. *British Journal of Educational Psychology*, 90(4), pp. 1062–1083.

Lister, R., 2021. *Poverty*. 2nd ed. Cambridge: Polity Press.

Mind. (2021). Coronavirus mental health response fund. *Mind*. [Online]. Available at: https://www.mind.org.uk/news-campaigns/campaigns/coronavirus-mental-health-response-fund/ [Accessed 21 March 2022].

NHS. (2022). Children and young people's mental health services (CYPMHS). [Online]. Available at: https://www.nhs.uk/nhs-services/mental-health-services/mental-health-services-for-young-people/children-young-people-mental-health-services-cypmhs/ [Accessed 1 March 2022].

NSPCC. (2021). *Childline raise concerns about mental health as counselling sessions delivered to children passes 50,000*. [Online]. Available at: https://www.nspcc.org.uk/about-us/news-opinion/2021/childline-press-release/ [Accessed 28 March 2021].

Parker, J., & Crabtree, S. (2018). *Social work with disadvantaged and marginalised people*. SAGE | Learning Matters, https://doi.org/10.4135/9781526416667

Payne, M., 2021. *Modern Social Work Theory*. 5th ed. London: Red Globe Press.

Radez, J., Reardon, T., Creswell, C., Lawrence, P., Evdoka-Burton, G., and Waite, P. (2020). Why do children and adolescents (not) seek and access professional help for their mental health problems? A systematic review of quantitative and qualitative studies. *European Child & Adolescent Psychiatry*, 30(2), pp. 183–211.

RCPCH. (2019). *Clinical guidelines and evidence reviews*. RCPCH. [Online]. Available at: https://www.rcpch.ac.uk/resources/clinical-guidelines-evidence-reviews [Accessed 18 March 2022].

Rethink Mental Illness. (2022). *Funding for mental health social care*. [Online] Available at: https://www.rethink.org/get-involved/campaign-with-us/right-treatment-right-time/funding-for-mental-health-social-care/ [Accessed 21 March 2022].

Social Work England. (2022). *Professional Standards*. [online] Available at: https://www.socialworkengland.org.uk/standards/professional-standards/ [Accessed: 22 May 2022].

Spray, C. and Jowett, B. (2012). *Social Work Practice with Children and Families*. 1st ed. London: SAGE Publications Ltd.

Teater, B., 2020. Systems theory. In: B. Teater, ed. 2020. *An Introduction to Applying Social Work Theories and Methods*. 3rd ed. London: Open University Press. Chapter: 2. pp. 16-37.

The Association of Child Psychotherapists. (2022). Association of Child Psychotherapists. [Online]. Childpsychotherapy.org.uk. Available at: https://childpsychotherapy.org.uk/ [Accessed 18 March 2022].

Trussell Trust, 2022. *Food banks provide more than 2.1 million food parcels to people across the UK in past year, according to new figures released by the Trussell Trust*. [On-line] Available at: https://www.trusselltrust.org/2022/04/27/food-banks-provide-more-than-2-1-million-food-parcels-to-people-across-the-uk-in-past-year-according-to-new-figures-released-by-the-trussell-trust/ [Accessed: 22 May 2022].

United Nations, 1989. *Convention on the Rights of the Child*. [Online]. United Nations Human Rights Office of the High Commissioner. Available at: https://www.ohchr.org/en/instruments-mechanisms/instruments/convention-rights-child [Accessed 22 May 2022].

17 Self-care and well-being for staff

KEY WORDS
Self-care, well-being, staff, retention, burnout, stress

Contributors in this chapter:

1. Paul Hamilton
2. Annelies Paris
3. Michael Redmond
4. Georgeanne Lamont
5. Joanne Bowser-Angermann
6. Mark Carter-Tufnell
7. Andrew Lloyd
8. Lou Mycroft
9. Amber Browne
10. 'Miss May'
11. Stefanie Tinsley
12. Stephanie Martin
13. Henry Aylett

Introduction

This chapter builds upon the conversations in the previous chapter around how to incorporate simple practices into the classroom on a daily basis to support and improve our well-being. This chapter, however, focuses on the needs of busy educators and encourages you to reflect upon your own levels of well-being. As the famous quote says, you cannot pour from an empty cup. You are in a profession where you spend your days caring for others, but it is essential you do not forget to care for yourself.

In the previous chapter, we discussed that there are five major areas of well-being:

- Emotional well-being
- Physical well-being
- Social well-being
- Workplace well-being
- Societal well-being

DOI: 10.4324/9781003218098-17

The first three were defined in the previous chapter, but the final two deserve further explanation here.

Workplace well-being

As a teacher or educational leader, ensuring our workplace well-being means developing skills that help us to pursue what really matters to us (Davis, 2019). In earlier chapters of this book, Chapters 12 and 13, the roles of continuing professional development (CPD) and further study, as well as becoming an educational researcher, were discussed. Having career goals can help us to stay focused and motivated. Having higher levels of motivation and workplace well-being can help each day to feel full of purpose and meaning, leading to generally higher levels of satisfaction. This is especially important in teaching, as we spend so many hours of our week at school.

Societal well-being

The fifth major category of well-being to discuss is that of societal well-being. This is an extension of previously mentioned 'social wellbeing', as in addition to the local connections and networks we make, societal well-being occurs when we feel part of a wider community, something bigger than just ourselves (Davis, 2019). Being part of a community, be it the school community or the bigger community in the country, means we feel connected to people, places and things around us and can both offer support and be supported. Alone, we are each an island, but together we make up our society; in order to be part of a happy society, we need to bring the skills of kindness, justice and empathy and extend these to others.

But caring for others on top of the daily job of teaching can be exhausting.

> **Critical question**
>
> How can teachers avoid burnout?

Earlier in this book in Chapter 2, we explored classroom organisation and considered how to be organised with your physical teaching and learning space and help reduce workload in some areas. But avoiding burnout is part of a much bigger well-being picture.

As you read through the following 12 contributions, reflect upon not only how you can support those staff around you, but how you can perhaps make some small changes to better support your well-being as you continue through another busy term!

Teachers, Adapt!

By Paul Hamilton, Teaching Fellow in History Education at Edinburgh University, Glasgow, Scotland

No one will forget 2020 in a hurry, that's for sure! All of us, we adapted – changed our approach to daily life, and now, maybe just maybe, recovery is actually happening! But, as teachers, let's not be too hasty to condemn what we all experienced to the annals of history just yet. Instead, let's see what can be learned.

(Continued)

We began working from home (not because we wanted to, but because we had to). Thus giving rise to the baptism of fire that was online learning. Across the world, an army of teachers took to Microsoft Teams, Google Classroom and Zoom in an attempt to provide a learning experience that would act as a substitute for the standard classroom environment. It was not easy, and it was not a level playing field either. Despite what society might think, not all teachers are tech whizzes. Yes, they can answer emails, create PowerPoints and knock together booklets on Microsoft Word, but this new reality required an entirely different level of technical wizardry!

Yet, it happened! As long as access to technology was not an issue, young people continued to learn through the medium that was online home learning, attending live-streamed classes, watching pre-recorded lessons and engaging with materials posted electronically by their teachers. This was a sharpening of teachers' IT skills, something that for the most part was approached with enthusiasm and curiosity by teachers. Also, equally positive, were the ways that online learning made it easier for teachers to more effectively engage with parents and carers who in many instances were themselves active participants in the digital learning experience. For some, in teaching, it felt as if a barrier was removed; the gap between home and school now felt like much less of a distance. Yet, all of this was, of course, dependent upon a young person and their family having access to the internet. Without it, they were effectively excluded. And this was something teachers were (and continue to be) incredibly concerned about!

So, what was learned from the COVID era? If nothing else, it confirmed that teaching is an adaptable profession, one that despite the challenges of COVID and the criticism that is sometimes so wilfully directed at teachers, they managed to endure! Teachers should stand tall in this period of recovery (provided they have the energy left to do so) and reflect upon the many positive differences they made to the lives of so many young people during an exceptionally difficult time. We should be thankful to every teacher, in every school, in every country – a new era is on the horizon, and teachers have most certainly made it!

Our Well-Being

By Annelies Paris, Primary Teacher and YouTube Content Creator as 'PetitePrimary', Dorset, England

Well-being is a term that is often thrown around in a society and frequently intertwined with the notion of self-care. Defining well-being can consequently be tricky, with people potentially associating this with materialistic objects, such as bath bombs, candles or taking holidays. Well-being, however, is more of a state. It's a state of being healthy, happy and comfortable. Although there exist many different dimensions of well-being, such as physical, spiritual, intellectual and social well-being, today I will be focusing on emotional well-being.

(Continued)

Teaching is one of those professions where no day is the same. This can be both a blessing and a curse. It can be a blessing because your days are varied: you see, hear and learn new things and you experience spontaneous moments that cannot be planned or taken for granted. It can also have its negative aspects too. Days can be tiring and unpredictable; factors out of your control can dictate the course of your day, how successful and effective your lessons are. Things might come up from either the children or staff around you that add to your workload unexpectedly, that make you stressed or get your hear pacing.

As a trainee or early career teacher, the desire to impress, show that you deserve to be there and show that you care (because somehow, we feel that this is quantified by how much work we take on) can result in us saying 'yes' all the time. Saying no when we have too much going on, when we don't feel like we're suited to do a task or saying no just because we don't want to do something is not a crime. Not only is there the workload result of saying yes, all the time, but then it almost becomes an unwritten expectation. 'Oh, I'll ask X because they always say yes'. Saying no reinforces your boundaries and your work-life balance. It gives you autonomy and allows you to evaluate your situation by checking in on yourself. Have I got the time to do this? How am I feeling right now? Could I take this on?

My last point that I would like to raise to you before it becomes too much information to take in is that of sleep. When I was a trainee, I would work until I went to bed, and then I would proceed to play through the running of every single lesson, particularly observations. I'd think about which child needs what sheet, how the transitions would go and the timings I'd give to each component of a lesson, and then I'd rehearse my inputs in my head to try to keep to them. I found that once I was qualified (like I said, nobody told me any of this before; it's all been down to growing and making the realisations myself) and prioritising my well-being, I found that I slept better. Why? One could suggest multiple hypotheses, but I believe it is because I stopped trying to do it all. I stopped trying to be perfect because there's no such thing. If I thought of something last minute, I'd jot it down in the notepad by my bed or ask my boyfriend to text it to me, so I'd see it again in the morning. Done. No more thoughts given to it. My nightmares decreased, my sleep increased and mornings became that *slight* bit easier. Once I focused on myself and made that switch to cutting off work at a certain point/at the school's exit, my stress levels decreased and everything else that was worrying me followed suit.

Training is stressful, and there's no doubt that sometimes you will break your habits, you will work longer and you will become overwhelmed. That is ok and that is normal. You're not the first, nor the last to experience this. Not everyone, though, has had the heads-up nor the reminder that it's ok to focus on yourself. It's ok and better to not spend your whole life working. You are not saying you don't care. You are not any worse of a teacher because of it. You are in a competition with nobody, but yourself and when you're the only one in your race, you want to go as far as you possibly can. Look after yourself, keep yourself healthy and happy in your career journey and you will do just fine!

Attitude, Achievement, Advantage and Amity

By Michael Redmond, Deputy Headteacher (Pastoral) at Bedford Modern Junior School, Bedfordshire, England

Well-being and attainment are the two inextricably linked?

The Department for Education's 2018 report on teacher retention found 66% of teachers asked felt the amount of marking, planning and data tracking led to a feeling of unsustainability within the profession. (Department for Education, 2018). If two-thirds of a workforce consider their role to be 'unsustainable' and if there is a correlation between student outcomes and well-being, surely some consideration as to the mindset of those within the profession and the direction that the profession is moving in should be of paramount importance. The problem, it would seem, is that the data is there, and the data is telling an important story, but the story is not being suitably and effectively acknowledged: leading to teachers leaving their jobs. Whilst Hausman argues 'We don't have a satisfactory theory of wellbeing' (Hausman, 2016). Martin Seligman (2011) would counter that with the PERMA model. This approach encourages the individual to take control and ownership of their well-being with a view of having a positive impact on those around them – they need to drive the change.

P – Positive emotions
E – Engagement
R – Relationships (+)
M – Meaning
A – Achievement/accomplishments

Next steps...

It is evident that there is teacher dissatisfaction, and this is having an impact on teacher well-being. Categorising the reasons behind the discontent and measuring impact within each field would lead to more distinct conclusions.

Who is really accountable for a person's well-being? Is it solely down to the individual or are there several actors at play?

Organisational theory could be considered to guide the application of Individualism and Collectivism.

How much autonomy does a teacher actually have? Can they lead any required changes?

Self-Care for Teachers: Values First, an Inside-Out Approach

By Georgeanne Lamont, The Values and Visions Foundation, London, England

This is the story of a teacher finding her way through overwhelming change, demands and criticism.

Over the past three decades, we have seen how many educators have been faced with huge change. Some get through it safely and grow in the process, and others get wearied, even crushed and leave the profession.

What makes the difference? It is a small thing that requires very little time: a shift in focus. We have consistently discovered that work becomes soul-destroying when we *react* to external circumstances and are not able to hold to our core values, but work becomes life-enhancing when we discover a response within ourselves that *aligns with what we hold dear*. This means that the first step in taking care of yourself is to press the pause button and make space to go inside, reflect and *choose how to respond, using your values as a guide*.

An experienced Yr. 6 Trafford teacher was struggling as she tried to cope with an enormous number of demands. In a recent inspection she had been harshly criticised for her maths provision. Moreover, she needed to undertake a business enterprise project, implement design and technology and do a project on money – all this whilst preparing her pupils for a high-stakes exam, including English. She felt overwhelmed by the pressures placed on her and was hurting from the criticism. She felt like throwing in the towel. Instead, she chose to turn inside and reflect on her values. She decided that rather than focus on the demands, she would take as her personal starting point the values she lived by and her vision for the children. One of her values was integrity – having a sense of the whole – and her vision was for the children be aware of the wider world in which they lived and to explore for themselves their ability to respond and contribute meaningfully to it. She decided to focus the term's work on developing a sense of giving, and she used the parable of the talents as a starting point.

The children were surprised one day to come into the classroom to find a 'gold' coin (a £1 piece), for each of them on the desk. She read them the Bible story of the talents and then challenged them to use their *inner* talents to raise money. The students used their geography/humanities work to help them decide where in the world they wanted to focus on. They opted for street children, their own age, in Peru. They were completely absorbed in the project, expanding their skills of cooperation and communication, their creativity and energy, to set up mini-businesses with their 'gold'. Some were making notebooks, others food and small gifts to sell. Needless to say, their maths was tackled with fresh vigour as bar charts and pie charts tracked their progress in managing costs and income, weighing and measuring materials. Design and technology and the other curricular requirements took care of themselves, as the students engaged, with full enthusiasm, in developing their businesses and understanding the impact they

(Continued)

could make. The teacher had used her values and her vision to transform a mountain of burdens into a meaningful and energising little project which everyone – including herself – could enjoy. She stayed in the job!

The clarity of the vision – of helping a group of children in Peru – gave a dynamic focus and energy to the work. The anchor of the values of integrity and generosity gave it coherence. What could have felt like a burden that had to be delivered was transformed into an exploration that drew on the choices and efforts of the children.

'To thine own self be true.' William Shakespeare

Five steps to develop self-care habits

Press the pause button; practise regularly taking a moment to turn within and check what is right for you, and choose the response which is true for you – use a daily journal.

Energise yourself and your pupils by holding a clear agreed vision – it is this that pulls us forward.

Appreciate yourself and your specialities; appreciate others; appreciate the amazing path you are on; record the things you appreciate every day in a journal morning and evening.

Compare yourself to no one; compete with no one; you are unique – your strength is being you.

Enjoy exploring the rich laboratory of your inner world – your thoughts, feelings, values and vision; they are valuable because it is these that shape your choices, actions and your life.

Do these five things and you will have a vibrant PEACE filled classroom, and that is fundamental to a teacher's well-being.

Full instructions for practising this inside-out approach to self-care outlined here can be found in Burns and Lamont (2019).

Teachers' Pet

By Joanne Bowser-Angermann, Associate Professor of Applied Teaching and Learning at Anglia Ruskin University, Chelmsford, England

My own childhood was blessed by the love and understanding of a companion dog, called Charlie. We grew up together; he was a constant source of comfort and made me happy every single day. There is now considerable research about the positive impact a dog can have on children, from improving children's motivation (Noble and Holt, 2018) to improving academic attainment in reading (Hall et al., 2016). Research and evidence like this have helped to get more dogs working in UK schools than ever before. But what about the positive impact a dog can have on the teacher?

(Continued)

For me, the positive impact of having a companion dog has never wavered. Whilst I taught in primary school, I was supported by Mimsy my Labrador cross; my own therapy dog who looked after my mental well-being. This view is supported by research that shows adults with companion dogs have increased mental well-being than those without a dog (Carr et al., 2020).

Teaching is an incredibly stressful but of course a rewarding job. But it is the only job I have ever had where I have had to work before work to ensure the work for that day works, whilst being too busy at work to do all my other work, so I have had to work after work to make sure all my work gets done! Mimsy was a marvellous friend and assistant for me as a teacher, even inspiring me to write my own children's book about a little black dog! Over the years there has been a gradual but undeniable dripped increase of pressure placed on teachers, which has slowly eroded staff morale and mindset. But this can be damaging as the mindset of the teacher and that of the children are intrinsically linked.

A teacher's mindset influences the children that they teach; their engagement, motivation and belief are reflected in each other's behaviour. Therefore, if a teacher's morale is low because they are tired, stressed and anxious, it is not just them that suffers or their family at home, but the children they teach as well. With a new focus on improving the mental health and well-being of teachers and increasing evidence of dogs in the workplace improving staff morale, I wonder if dogs could be the perfect teaching assistant and colleague. A new head of happiness needed in every school?

If you haven't thought about a teacher's pet for your school before, I urge you to find a way to get one into your classroom. You will soon see that anything is paw-sible when you have a dog!

Markisms

By Mark Carter-Tufnell, Headteacher at St Osyth CoE Primary School and Mistley Norman CoE Primary School, Manningtree, England

The colleagues I work with are wonderful. They have to be to put up with me leading them! Like all teachers and leaders I have my own 'style' and approach – both of which are far from perfect! But they do include the importance of the words we use – words have such immense power; we should use them wisely to help ourselves and to help others. Some colleagues have remarked that I have 'Markisms' – words and phrases that reflect my values, beliefs and approach to teaching and to leadership. Whilst they are not original, I share a few 'Markisms' in the hope that they prompt thought and reflection and inspire you to your own ideas about words you will use as a teacher and a school leader. Children need teachers and schools need leaders that are inspiring. Our words can have an amazing impact, for good or for ill. After all, President John F.

(Continued)

Kennedy said of Churchill: 'He mobilized the English language and sent it into battle'. (The president was quoting Edward R. Murrow of CBS News.)

Children first and everything else second.

Obvious I know, yes? But as teachers we have so many demands on our time – assessments, marking, planning displays, meetings, parents and so. Whatever the demands on us and whatever decisions we make, it must always be children first and everything else second. Whatever is going to have the biggest impact on children, focus on that. Is spending ten hours making a display worthy of the Turner Prize going to have more or less impact than spending an hour producing a good display and nine hours on other things such as working directly with children? When considering a budget issue, what's going to help children have the best outcomes for children?

It's Ofsted not oncology.

Teachers stress about Ofsted. Leaders stress about Ofsted. Often, those that have had much bigger issues to face, such as oncology, results keep Ofsted in perspective. Ofsted is Ofsted. They are not the be all and end all of schools and teaching. Does that we can afford to ignore Ofsted? No, of course not. But nor can we afford to let any fear of Ofsted dominate our working lives. It is, after all, 'Children first and everything else second'.

Never write a child off.

We have no idea what a child, a young person, may achieve. We do know that if we make the right choices and they make the right choices there will be the right result, excellent progress. One of my primary teachers once said that I would never amount to anything. These are the only words I remember them saying. What will your pupils and your colleagues remember you saying? What will the impact be of your words?

Good Mental Health

By Andrew Lloyd, Copywriter at Liverpool John Moores University, Manchester, England

Ever heard the one about the guy it took eight years to complete a three-year degree? I have because it was me. You see, from my late teens to my late thirties, I suffered with poor mental health. Studying whilst I suffered with severe OCD was a bit like having a fight but with one hand tied behind my back. It was like building a house without any foundations.

Fifteen years on, however, and I am pleased to report that my mental health has never been as good as it is now. I have had cognitive behavioural therapy, I take medication for my OCD and I practice daily self-care. Now, I want to share with you all some of my tips for maintaining good mental health.

Top of the list must be exercise. It is no coincidence that I always feel amazing after coming back from the gym. I get this amazing rush of endorphins. Many times, I have

(Continued)

gone into the gym with worries on my mind, only then to have completely forgot about them upon leaving. If I could make up a term for this, then I would call it 'gym magic'.

Mind occupation, mind occupation, mind occupation, so crucial a thing for good mental health that it needed writing down three times. It diverts and pushes me away from ruminating about my anxieties. I have fallen in love with writing because the creative process forces me to push my 'Mr Irrational' to one side.

In 2017, in Teen Vogue (https://www.teenvogue.com/story/psychologists-say-fandoms-are-amazing-for-your-mental-health), writer Brianna West stated, 'Fandoms are big and they are important'. I completely concur with this view because it is the sense of belonging and togetherness that they provide that makes following sports teams or your favourite pop group say, such a special thing.

An example of the last point is how I struggled during the first lockdown due to professional football being stopped. I guess it felt like I momentarily lost a certain part of my identity. I was no longer actively Andy, the avid Manchester United fan. I missed the comradeship on social media with my fellow fans.

It is only through life experience that I have learnt about the art of self-forgiveness. Allow yourself to forgive yourself about the past. Fretting about the past is wasted energy; focus instead on the here and now. It has taken me over 30 years for me to finally like who I am. I am at one with myself, I am at peace and this feels lovely.

My final tip for good mental health beautifully encapsulates all that has been written here. It is to try and become your very own therapist. Show yourself kindness and compassion. Try and take a step back at times and advise yourself, like you would do to others.

Remember, maintaining good mental health is forever an ongoing process. I never thought I would become one of these people who genuinely replies now, 'not too bad thanks', when asked, how I am? After reading these words that I have written, I hope you can be too.

The Power of Microjoys

By Lou Mycroft, Nomad, Yorkshire, England

Sometimes the world seems too much to deal with. From global events to toxic workplace cultures and not forgetting the noisy overwhelm of balancing work and family life, we may long for change yet feel powerless to make it happen.

At the start of the COVID lockdown in 2020, a group of educators gathered online to form the collective movement #JoyFE – joy for education. We wanted to 'do something' in that terrifying time, and our starting point was an ethics of joy. Not simply good intentions, or meta-plans we could talk about then not see through, but small, regular and consistent acts of joyful practice. Things we could do. We called these 'microjoys'. Ways of countering the macro-aggressions of life, by creating cultures of appreciation and practices of care.

(Continued)

Our inspiration came from an unexpected place: the work of seventeenth century Dutch Jewish philosopher, Baruch Spinoza. Spinoza lived in troubling times too, and he was interested in developing a personal ethics which connected human beings, guiding small acts of affirmative joy. Writing in Latin, he had two words for 'power' at his disposal: potestas (which is power as we generally understand it in English) and potentia (a joyful, activist energy; a life force which we all share).

Observing the impact of microjoys on home and workplace cultures, we came to understand that they were an expression of potentia. Microjoys are not about the 'everything is awesome' positivity that we see everywhere on social media. Everything is not awesome. But we can be critical about it, without being cynical. We're not pitching for being happy all the time, because we all experience pain, sorrow and fear. Happiness is a fleeting commodity. Spinoza's 'joy' takes those dark feelings and puts them to work.

Our most compelling microjoy is asking people how they are – and then listening to their response. We don't have to do anything about it, but we have welcomed each other into the space by being reciprocal about this. We take time to recognise the work and appreciate the person, which helps people feel valued. We don't shirk difficult conversations, but we approach them with radical candour (clear is kind) and a practice of care. And we always practise equality, no matter what our respective places in the hierarchy. We are equal as thinkers.

A joyful practice is an act of resistance in a world where – often – we feel we have no power or don't know what to do with it. Our persistent, affirmative practice means we are activists in a very different way. Or, as Karen Walrond (2021) puts it in her excellent and very practical book, we are lightmakers.

For more about #JoyFE, see www.linktr.ee/joyfe

Preventing Stress and Burnout in Educational Professionals

By Amber Browne, Mental Health Crisis Practitioner, Norfolk, England

Being a teacher can be one of the most rewarding careers; inspiring, supporting and enabling a future generation to reach their full potential. However, the role also comes with many stressors, both mentally and physically. Burnout is very common with those in the education sector; in fact 50% of teachers reported suffering at least one symptom of burnout at all times, since the beginning of the school year (Education Support, 2021). This is a very worrying figure and suggests more needs to be done to protect the welfare of those in the teaching profession. Burnout is as a result of stress that does not abate and results in physical and mental exhaustion.

Signs of burnout include the following:

- Feeling tired or drained most of the time
- Feeling helpless, trapped and/or defeated

(Continued)

- Feeling detached and/or alone in the world
- Having a cynical/negative outlook
- Self-doubt
- Procrastinating and taking longer to get things done

(Mental Health UK, 2022)

Significant long-term stressors can negatively impact mental and physical health over time. Job burnout can cause headaches, prolonged fatigue and depression, to name just a few (Salvagioni et al., 2017). It is important to prioritise your own health and well-being; after all, you cannot pour from an empty cup and prevention is better than cure. Below are some suggested ways of managing stress and preventing burnout.

Positive self-talk

When you are experiencing stress, it is more important than ever to talk to yourself in a kind and positive way, just like you would a close friend. At the end of each school day, make a list of what you have done well and the highlights and achievements of your day.

To-do lists

To-do lists are a great way of getting the busyness of your mind onto paper. If you feel yourself stressing about things you have to do over the next few days or weeks, make a list and organise items according to their priority. This tip is especially helpful if you feel overwhelmed when trying to sleep or focus on other tasks.

Journaling

Following on from the previous suggestion, journaling is a great way of getting thoughts and feelings onto paper. Positive expressive writing can help to reduce anxiety and enhance job satisfaction (Round et al., 2022).

Self-care

Set aside some time each day for self-care; even the most seemingly small actions can make a big difference. Mind-body therapies such as yoga, mindful walking, deep breathing and meditation can have a profound effect on mental health and well-being (Gibson and Bale, 2021).

Talk to others

Remember the saying a 'problem shared is a problem halved?' This couldn't be truer when it comes to reducing stress. Whether it be colleagues, close friends or families, talk to others if you feel yourself getting overwhelmed. Colleagues may be able to give tips from their own experience or offer help to reduce your workload.

Taking Control of my Self-Care

By Miss May, An Anonymous Primary Teacher, England

In September 2020, I was working as a class teacher and a member of the senior management team as a well-being ambassador. Supporting the mental health of staff and pupils was the school's mission, and as a team, we collaborated on several projects including an Emotional Literacy programme for students and well-being initiatives for teachers including team-building sessions and various sports and fitness activities. I believed we were making small steps in the right direction to support the mental health of our school community, but there was a long way to go, particularly for staff, especially given the impact of numerous lockdowns and the upheaval juggling 'hybrid teaching' (a combination of teaching in person and virtually). Teachers are notorious for complaining of work-life imbalance; the pandemic has only exacerbated this disproportion. Quite frankly, staff yoga after school and other niche add-ons like a croissant on a Tuesday break time are not going to relieve staff of the pressures put upon them.

In June 2021, I contracted COVID-19 and then pneumonia as a complication. After a week in bed, paramedics were called to my bedside, and after revealing that I was only saturating 85% oxygen, I was put straight onto oxygen and admitted to an intensive care unit. Since my stay in hospital, I was diagnosed with post-COVID syndrome with severe fatigue and I am yet to return to school. A year on since my illness, I have recuperated well; however, I have also resigned from my role. Personally, although I was willing to sacrifice much of my social life and weekends to the profession, the past year has taught me that my physical and mental health are worth much more than the job I love. On top of living with long COVID, I have endured questions over the severity and existence of my symptoms, and whilst I have come to terms with adjusting to my 'new normal', I have reflected on the toll the profession has on our mental well-being.

Teacher retention in the UK has remained low, particularly for newly qualified teachers – in 2010, only 72% of early career teachers remained in the profession, whereas by 2019 this figure reached a new low of 67% (Fullard and Zuccollo, 2021). The duty of care, or rather lack of, to teachers was certainly the straw that broke my back.

I came to the realisation that the responsibility lies within me to care better for myself, and leaving my role was the start taking ownership of my mental health. However, whilst the solution for teacher well-being is yet to be found, those who lead schools should set the example for others to follow. 'Well-being' has actually got to be valued and modelled by school leaders in order for meaningful change to take place.

Be your Own Well-Being Champion

By Stefanie Tinsley, Quality Improvement and Well-being Specialist at Culture of Excellence Ltd, Cheshire, England

If you haven't worked it out by now, then spoiler alert.... Working in education is not always easy. In fact, it's often overwhelming, relentless and exhausting. It takes a lot of energy every day; we don't get to switch off much from the minute we wake to the moment we go to sleep. Lesson planning, marking, behaviour management, motivating, encouraging, innovating and trying to make a difference to our students or our teams; it's go go go.

The to-do list does not get smaller.
The wheels do not stop turning.
If we are not mindful, then we can get to every half-term and experience exhaustion or illness.
The pay-off is high, but the investment is too.

So, what have I come to realise about how we can be, enjoy and even flourish in education? That well-being is a collective responsibility; however, you have to commit first and foremost to your own well-being as an educator. No one is going to do it for you. No one is going to ever tell you that you've done everything you need to do and so we can have a chilled week or month. It's not happening. So it means that we have to be our own well-being champion and learn what this means for us personally very quickly.

Write down all the things that you thoroughly enjoy doing. Even better if it's a list of things that when you do them, you feel refreshed, recharged, or energised. This might include a certain sport, walking on a beach, a specific place, talking with friends, going out for lunch or spending time with animals. Whatever they are, have the list and commit to doing something on the list once a week. If your list isn't very long, then get out there and try new things to add to the list.

Try to set up systems and processes that help you do manage your workload. Where possible set yourself time slots for the things you need to do so you can switch off from the to-do list of work every day. Commit to your own time.

Have hobbies, especially ones where you would feel bad if you let other people down if you didn't go. Or get an accountability buddy for your daily walks/exercise so that you can't talk yourself out of it. Remember 15 minutes (or even 5) of movement every day is better than trying to commit to hours in the gym.

Have time where you have no technology/screen time to help slow the brain whirring down. I sometimes use social media as my down time rather than watch TV, but I also recognise that sometimes I just need to have time with no screens.

(Continued)

The bottom line is that we get to choose. We get to choose everything. What we do, when we do it and how we approach things; we even get to choose whether we let our brains run on autopilot and spin us an unuseful narrative, or whether we catch it and instruct it to give us something better to think. It's not easy; we have to show up for ourselves, which can be hard when we are always told to or have a nature which wants to make a difference to others. But we can't always be the givers. Our batteries run out. I had to experience a significant health issue before I 'got it'. So take the steps, tiny as they may be, just one at a time, to champion your own well-being and make for a healthy supercharged educator, who can do more good when they have gas in the tank.

Champions of the Classroom

By Stephanie Martin, University of Derby, Lincoln, England

I struggled to concentrate and talked too much at school; my report would read 'Could do better', year in year out. I hoped it might be different in secondary school. I had visions of being exposed to many new subjects and teachers who would be desperate to inspire me, but I continued to scrape through. There was not a subject I particularly excelled in, and my motivation to do well was non-existent. I found science particularly overwhelming but would never admit that as a child.

Fast forward 20 years, I am now a trainee teacher. During my School Centred Initial Teacher Training, I have listened to many expert educators talk about different subjects and pedagogy, but one particular day has stuck with me. Dr. Craig Early led a day on science. He had boundless, positive energy, and his love for the subject poured out of him. It was truly inspiring. I can remember talking to Dr. Early, saying that I was worried about teaching science, that it was my worst subject at school. So he looked at me and said, 'Really?' with the biggest smile. During the day, we experimented, laughed a lot, and had many discussions about how educators should be teaching science. The most important thing I took away from that day was that science lessons should be for children to do science, not write about it - so that children fall in love with science through the practical side; getting messy, investigating, and doing!

In terms 4 and 5 of my training, I taught science to my class; it was a pleasure. I had two hours each week and worked hard to instil a love of this subject in the hearts of these children. I ensured the children spent their lessons making pulleys and gears, hunting for bugs and that dichotomous keys were made using natural items rather than reams of printed pictures. Nothing fancy, nothing more than many other primary teachers had done in the past. But these lessons helped me connect with a child, someone who struggled to concentrate or produce work in nearly every subject. Something in this child lit up, their hand was waving at me during discussions, and the work they were creating was just incredible! I talked to this child about their work and found out

(Continued)

they were passionate about wildlife, especially bees. Teaching this subject helped me become a champion for this child. I found something that made them tick - part of this child came to life. It made my heart sing and break at the exact moment - this is what I missed during my education.

I have learnt so much from the children in my class and have been lucky enough to see the results of being a champion for all of them. Spending time getting to know them and making sure they feel the power of your connection. It is essential that all children feel seen and heard; by discovering their passions, you can allow them to show their talents and superpowers. Once you find them, rejoice and use this knowledge to draw out the magic.

Relationships

By Henry Aylett, Key Stage 2 Leader, Worcester Park, England

To begin, I will go out on a limb and say that almost all other advice you will receive about teaching can be enhanced in some way by spending time focusing on what I believe is the most fundamental aspect of the educational world: relationships.

On a daily basis, you will interact with children with the most wonderfully different personalities and stories, with staff fulfilling a huge range of roles, fellow teachers with a wide variety of expertise and experience, parents and carers from many walks of life, outside agencies and organisations offering services to schools and many more besides. Approaching each one of these hundreds of daily interactions with positivity, kindness and a reflective attitude has been for me the single biggest thing which has helped me contribute effectively over the last decade to the lives of those around me, especially the pupils.

How do you do it? Find out about people: take an interest in their lives; lift them up through encouragement and celebration of success; help and support them when you have the capacity to do so. If they are going through a tough time, then make capacity to help them a priority. Notice the quieter people: get to know them and appreciate them because they are often overlooked. Listen to people actively, and they will know you care. Share some of yourself and your life as and when you are comfortable to do so, particularly if it makes people smile or shows you can laugh at yourself. Cultivate relationships and you sow seeds which will grow over days, weeks, years and sometimes lifetimes.

None of this is possible without a positive relationship with yourself. The old adage that you should put your own gas mask on before helping others could not be more true in teaching. I have learned to be 'selectively selfish' (mainly by proactively seeking a good work/life balance), and this, generally, has led to me being able to give my best, most energetic and positive self to this who I encounter in the school community.

All the best to you in your career and remember to work on your relationships!

Conclusions

- You matter.
- Start with a positive relationship with yourself.
- Develop a range of self-care strategies to nurture your well-being and avoid burnout.

References

Burns, S., and Lamont, G. (2019). *Values and Visions: Energising Students, Refreshing Teachers*. London: The Values and Visions Foundation.

Carr, D.C., Taylor, M.G., Gee, N.R., and Sachs-Ericsson, N. (2020). Psychological health benefits of companion animals following a social loss. *The Gerontologist*, 60(3), pp. 428–438.

Davis, T. (2019). What is well-being? Definition, types, and well-being skills. *Psychology Today*. Available at: https://www.psychologytoday.com/us/blog/click-here-happiness/201901/what-is-well-being-definition-types-and-well-being-skills [Accessed 1 October 2022].

Department for Education. (2018). *Factors affecting teacher retention: Qualitative investigation*. Available at: https://assets.publishing.service.gov.uk/government/uploads/system/uploads/attachment_data/file/686947/Factors_affecting_teacher_retention_-_qualitative_investigation.pdf [Accessed 30 October 2018].

Education Support. (2021). *Significant signs of burnout amongst teachers*. [Online]. Available at: https://www.educationsupport.org.uk/news-and-events/news/significant-signs-of-burnout-amongst-teachers/ [Accessed 17 June 2022].

Fullard, J., and Zuccollo, J. (2021). *Local Pay and Teacher Retention in England*. Education Policy Institute. London: Gatsby Foundation.

Gibson, B., and Bale, A. (2021). Teaching in a pandemic: Using body healing to support your wellbeing. *Compass: Journal of Teaching and Learning*. 14(2), pp. 1–4.

Hall, S.S., Gee, N.R., and Mills, D.S. (2016). Children reading to dogs: A systematic review of the literature. *PLoS ONE*, 11(2), p. e0149759.

Hausman, D. (2016). *Theories of wellbeing*. Available at: http://serious-science.org/theories-of-well-being-6188 [Accessed 27 October 2018].

Mental Health UK. (2022). *Burnout*. [Online]. Available at: https://mentalhealth-uk.org/burnout/ [Accessed 17 June 2022].

Noble, O., and Holt, N. (2018). A study into the impact of the reading education assistance dogs scheme on reading engagement and motivation to read among early years foundation-stage children. *Education 3-13*, 46(3), pp. 277–290.

Round, E., Wetherll, M., Elsey, V., and Smith, V. (2022). Positive expressive writing as a tool for alleviating burnout and enhancing wellbeing in teachers and other full-time workers. *Cogent Psychology*. 9(1), p. 2060628. doi:10.1080/23311908.2022.2060628

Salvagioni, D., Melanda, F.N., Mesas, A.E., Gonz·lez, A.D., Gabani, F.L., and Andrade, S.M. (2017). Physical, psychological and occupational consequences of job burnout: A systematic review of prospective studies. *PLoS ONE*, 12(10), p. e0185781. doi:10.1371/journal.pone.0185781

Seligman, M. (2011). *Flourish: A Visionary New Understanding of Happiness and Wellbeing*. New York, NY: Free Press.

Walrond, K. (2021). *The Lightmaker's Manifesto: How to Work for Change Without Losing Your Joy*. Minneapolis, MN: Broadleaf Books.

18 Homework

KEY WORDS
Homework, projects, home learning, topic work

Contributors within this chapter:

1. Amanda Araceli Alejandre
2. Andrew Flowerdew
3. Nathan Burns
4. Andrew Hartshorn
5. Susan Strachan
6. David Goodwin
7. Philip Van Mellaerts
8. Mike McGrother

Introduction

This chapter deals with the often prickly issue of homework. Whilst some educators rave about the potential for home learning and homework tasks, others wish homework did not exist. Many teachers agree that reading, spelling and times tables practice are useful home learning tasks, but what other forms may homework take (if at all)? These are some of the debates unpicked in this final chapter. Eight contributors share their views on the role of homework in the contemporary classroom.

Critical question

What are the benefits and purposes of homework and the best approach to take?

Homework is a part of education that arguably every pupil remembers from their own school days, usually negatively, yet has no legal bearing and has not been part of DfE guidance since 2012. The discretion is down to headteachers about whether to issue homework at all or the amount of time children should take to do it. The previous guidance from 1998

DOI: 10.4324/9781003218098-18

specified that homework was for primary school children to spend no more than the following: Years 1 and 2: one hour per week; Years 3 and 4: 1.5 hours per week, and Years 5 and 6: 30 minutes per day (HM Government, 1998). This chapter suggests that the setting of homework will follow a specific requirement within pedagogy, will need to be inclusive and is not an add-on to a lesson but rather a core component that increases the value of learning. It also suggests that some children will always benefit from homework whether that is set by the teacher or whether it forms part of an extra home-based activity. The contributors in this Homework chapter share their views and experiences with you to hopefully inspire your own practice.

What is homework?

Homework has been defined by Cooper (2007, p. 4) as 'tasks assigned to students by school teachers that are intended to be carried out during non-school hours' which may seem obvious until you ask yourself the questions, 'what is homework for my children and why do I set it?' Do you set homework because the school advocates it, or do you see its worth as complementing what you teach? Homework sits within the 'Planning - Teaching - Assessment' cycle, so you have an immediate choice if the school has no forthright policy on setting homework that if you want to set it that it has an obvious place in that cycle and a purpose.

What is homework for, and is it productive?

Cooper (2007) and Porter (2014) provided reasons that explored the positive purposes of homework that have been synthesised in Table 18.1.

In terms of the negative aspects of setting homework and requiring children to complete it, the noticeable feature is the emotional stress concerned with it, the not knowing what to do, fear of the grade outcome or the imposition on non-school time. Parents either enforced the completion of homework, by a differing set of standards or teaching methods, did the homework themselves (which teachers usually spotted) or expected homework to be set.

Table 18.1 Positive purposes of homework

Cooper (2007, pp. 8-9)	Porter (2014, p. 257)
Immediate academic effects (Retention of facts, increased understanding and critical thinking, and curriculum enrichment)	**Academic purposes** (Practice and opportunity to consolidate taught content, to prompt elaboration of ideas covered in class, transfer knowledge and prepare for tests)
Long-term academic effects (Encouraging learning during leisure time, improved attitude to school and better study habits)	
Non-academic effects (Improved self-direction and self-discipline, organisation, more inquisitiveness and independent problem-solving)	**Self-regulation goals** (Self-discipline, motivation and personal responsibility)
Parental involvement effects	**Parental involvement** (Parents expect homework; keep them informed and involved)

The logical question is, therefore, does setting homework achieve anything? The IMPACT project from the 1980s and 1990s, as a vehicle for increased parental participation that went nationwide, was successful because it sustained parental cooperation that was planned by the teacher. It led to enhanced children's learning (Merttens and Newland, 1996). There is evidence that homework does have an effect but not enough to have an overwhelming effect for all children. Porter (2014) found that conscientious students are more likely to perform better with their homework only because they are also conscientiousness in class, that there is a slight improvement in grades but not achievement (also found by Cooper, 2007) and that, overall, it brings 'limited academic benefits'.

The most useful analysis by both authors was that teachers should spend their time and energy in targeting homework to support those who would benefit from it, notably those who were with learning needs. This is echoed by the Education Endowment Fund (EEF, 2021) who advised that if teachers were to set homework for materially disadvantaged children, then research found that they 'are less likely to have access to a device suitable for learning or a stable internet connection and may receive less parental support to complete homework and develop effective learning habits. These difficulties may increase the gap in attainment...'. Homework is not a straight-forward part of teaching and learning, but the following section will attempt to give some ideas should you wish to set homework that is based on making it practical, efficient and purposeful.

Setting homework

Your starting point is whether to set homework for the class and, should you need its need, to use the 'planning-teaching-assessment' format. Homework requires a purpose; what do you want it to achieve? If this cannot be adequately answered, then the children will be able to provide you an answer that you may not favour; certainly the parents might also be of the same opinion.

Chapter 4's focus on planning made the point that all learning had to be centred on the learning objective and requested that homework followed likewise. The homework activity is of your design; it can require the children to write, perform, design, philosophise, or construct, but it needs to reflect the learning objective of the subject (either discrete or cross-curricular) that was planned and taught. The activity, of whatever duration you decide, either must prepare for the learning objective of the following lesson or complement the existing taught lesson (so that it consolidates or develops it). That will root the homework in a meaningful context.

Who will the homework be set for? Unless your school policy dictates that it should be for everyone, you have a choice. Homework is a time-consuming activity for you as a teacher to plan for and assess, so consider who would get the most benefit from completing it. This would enable you to shy away from a deficit model of thinking. It is not always necessary to set a homework task for those deemed 'less able', so that they are always in a 'catch-up' scenario; it could be to stretch the 'more able' (unless you do not subscribe to such broad demarcations of ability, and you set homework purely for exploratory reasons to find out either what the children are good at and then how to encourage that skill). The assessment records and your daily ongoing tacit knowledge of who has learnt what will determine who could be set homework; it could be a democratic model with a group rota system, or for those who have returned from absence, or any choice that can be easily justified. Plan to take time within a lesson that you choose to set homework from, explaining it, distributing the necessary materials and to discuss the submission. Would you insist on homework being returned, or would it be an option? This is something that will be discussed below.

After planning, you will need to consider the assessing of the homework. This will likely determine the amount and frequency of homework being set because you will need to think about your own well-being. When will you assess (mark) the homework, at home? In the school before going home? How much time will you devote to each piece, on top of the usual amount of assessment of the children's learning? Or will you incorporate homework into this whole assessment system and reduce content elsewhere?

The homework must be assessed just as effectively as any other assessed learning as detailed in the school's assessment policy; otherwise, children and parents will be demotivated in a paucity of attention. Give consideration as to how the homework will be returned, whether that be physically returned during morning registration or by electronic means. When it is retuned and assessed, the next steps are to incorporate it into future learning (which is where planning is necessary) and to build time into that learning time by devoting up to ten minutes to discuss the homework. Point out the key features that are positive (make a note of what needs to be developed or even re-taught should you discover misconceptions) and blend them into the lesson. This will enable the children to see that homework that you plan and set has a purposeful integration into their learning. A final point is to create an audit of the homework you set across the whole curriculum. Do this and gauge whether you focus more on English and mathematics rather than the foundation subjects – do you set homework as a consolidation of the main subjects or should you see it as an opportunity to engage the children more holistically?

Points to consider

This section aims to explore wider thoughts about the concept of setting homework that could influence your approach to it. It can be framed as the 'Teacher-Child-Parent' cycle because these will be the three groups of people affected by the setting of homework. The perspective of the teacher, notably in examining pedagogy, and well-being have been covered earlier in the chapter.

Some children will enjoy completing their homework, some will do it grudgingly, and some will detest it. Those who enjoy homework will probably be the same children that enjoy school and perform well there; how might you encourage children to complete homework? Might this be in the design of the homework, the type of learning desired, the rewards given or even the option of not choosing to do it? You will know your children and how to offer forms of encouragement to different children.

Not all parents have the same attitude to homework, which you may already know. It is not that some parents do not care whether homework is set or completed by their child; some parents actively encourage not only the homework to be done but are also engaging in extra-curricular activities that are designed to educate their child far more than can be achieved in school. By this I mean the enriching of the cultural capital, often assumed to be the more middle-class way of giving children experiences. These can include private tuition, visits to museums, galleries, selective sporting occasions, theatre, holidays abroad and, for older children, experience of the workplace. The EEF (2021) reminds teachers of the opposite side of some children's experiences, 'teachers should seek to understand any barriers to completing homework – for example, a lack of access to a quiet space or learning materials – and aim to avoid approaches that use homework as a penalty for poor performance'.

How can you as a teacher ensure that homework is an enriching experience for all children in your class?

Some parents may not feel capable of supporting their child with homework because of English not being their first language, or because mathematics, for example, was taught to them differently, or because they work shift patterns such as afternoons or nights when they cannot be at home to help. This does not mean they do not want to help, just they are unable to. Give some thought to this situation. Other parents may not want homework because it affects the family leisure time; some parents actively encourage it and see it as a sign of productive learning and how a 'good school' should be operating (a tip is to ensure that whatever you write on the children's homework, do get it proofread before it is distributed to avoid being embarrassed). Do you think setting homework teaches the children that the learning that cannot be finished in school is sent home to be considered as a form of unpaid (learning) overtime? Do you have a response for that?

Summary

You may not have a choice in whether homework is set, either because the school or parents expect it to be, but you do have a choice in its design. You will be aware of how it should support existing learning or be in preparation for future learning. You may have an ongoing homework system that is to enjoy reading at home or learning weekly spellings and is supplemented by carefully selected tasks.

Homework needs to be seen by all those involved as something that is productive and enjoyable, in that it has a meaning that is integral to children's academic development and that observers such as parents can appreciate. If children learn about their attitudes to learning and that learning is not always centred on the school but can be self-directed, at a place and time when they are comfortable with, then perhaps that can be the added stimulus for them to be confident with the skill of being a lifelong learner.

Homework

By Amanda Araceli Alejandre M.Ed. 8th Grade Science Teacher at Morris Middle School, Texas, USA

Homework has always been a concerning topic. Some educators love it and find it extremely useful; others are not huge advocates for the practice. I believe homework can be very useful given its intention. As a science teacher, much of our content is vocabulary rich; therefore, weekly homework assignments are highly encouraged to ensure pupils do not contribute to the curve of forgetting. I find that creating a system of different types of homework opportunities increases pupils' participation and gives choice. Consequently,

(Continued)

pupils too discover what type of 'studying' techniques work for them and are more invested in the curriculum. My homework assignments typically take 10-15 minutes and can range from flashcards to Cornell notes' summaries to online game play. Once my pupils get the feel for all given types of homework, I then allow them to choose one of the forms for homework twice a week. I have taught full academic school years where homework was not integrated versus others where it was, and I have deduced that pupil concept attainment was at the higher end when implemented appropriately and strategically. If you believe in the practice, then you will see the fruit of it. If you are opposed to the practice, do not poison the experience in pupils for other educators.

Pupils learn through repetitive practice. If they are granted the opportunity to practise a skill outside the classroom, it is more likely that they will retain the information. It gives them a chance to practise independently. When pupils take part in extracurricular activities, such as band, choir, orchestra or sports, they are repeatedly completing the same task over and over again. This is to ensure that mistakes are caught and 'perfected' before a performance or game. I commonly use this comparison with my pupils, so they understand the value of homework and the background behind repetitive exercise.

It is truly all part of a developmental plan. As pupils climb the educational ladder moving from grade level to grade level, they are expected to know certain concepts. If we do not support their education by providing them with a multitude of learning strategies, such as homework, we are depriving them of the education they deserve. This brings me to post-secondary readiness. Once a student enters college or the workforce, they will be required to complete tasks independently to then turn in for a grade or present to an organisation. If students were never given that experience or held accountable for the completion of independent activities, the transition might be more than challenging.

At the end of the day, being an educator is not just about teaching content, it is about preparing pupils for their futures. If I can contribute to helping them learn life skills through assigning homework to support their education and development of responsibility, I am all for it.

Homework

By Andrew Flowerdew, Technology Strategist at L.E.A.D IT Services, Derby, England

Homework has been found to have a positive impact on learning (Homework | EEF educationendowmentfoundation.org.uk); however, there are a number of factors that should be considered when using homework to support classroom learning, some of which are outlined below.

How useful is the homework? Does the homework move learning forward or help reinforce learning that was carried out within the classroom. Especially for younger learners there may need to be an explicit connection to something that they have

(Continued)

experienced that day or that they are going to experience the next day for the homework to be really useful. Also, how useful is it to the teacher? Giving out lots of homework that requires marking but does not inform future learning activities and gives little or no feedback to the learner may just add workload without being truly useful.

Does it engage and excite the learners? At the end of the day, we are all a little tired and frazzled, and this is even more the case with our learners. So effective homework should, perhaps, involve giving learners activities that engage their interest and, in some cases, excite and bring them fun. Of course, not all homework can be fun and exciting but there needs to be a good mix throughout the week. This is often where digital tools can help. Tools such as Microsoft Flip, where young people can use video and/or audio to give a presentation to their peers about a topic or Google Classroom where homework activities can be integrated with software such as Google Maps or Google Expeditions. Many of these tools work well even on a mobile phone and help bridge the potential digital divide that some schools face.

When, where and how much? Not all learners have home environments that are conducive to completing homework effectively. Some learners may not spend much time at home before they need to go to bed, especially if they have activities after school or their family circumstances mean that they do not arrive home until late. Some learners may have medical conditions that mean it is hard to complete homework after school. Schools should be sensitive to these and other factors that may impact a young person's ability to complete homework and look at differentiating homework in the same way that they address different learning needs in the classroom. This includes addressing the ways in which homework is supported. Systems such as homework and breakfast clubs, where learners can work on their homework in school, perhaps with adult support, can be highly effective.

Experience suggests that homework can be very effective where it is integrated effectively into the learning activities experienced by the learner in ways that address their individual needs and support their understanding of their own learning journey. Developing creative homework activities, especially those making use of digital tools, is fun for both the teacher and the learner and potentially more effective in terms of learning outcomes.

Homework

By Nathan Burns, Head of Maths in a Derbyshire Secondary School, Derby, England

It's not all that long ago since I was in school (7 years actually, if you count A-Levels as in school), yet I can't really remember ever doing homework. I can remember revising dates for the WW2 content of my History A-Level, and I can remember doing some A-Level Statistics revision in the library, but besides that, nothing. I know I did every piece of homework too, because my only detention at school was a break detention for

(Continued)

only half completing a French homework (I wrote the answers in French, but I hadn't copied the mathematical sums out in French).

When I began teaching, I was hugely in favour of homework. I did every single piece when I was at school, and I couldn't even remember doing it, so it couldn't be that bad, could it? So therefore, all of my students could do it too. Research said it was beneficial, and I wanted my students to do well. Hence, I set weekly 30 minute homework tasks. I was so pro homework that I even supported a homework review group in school, bringing research to the table on why it was so important.

Within those first couple of years, I certainly dealt with a lot of students who hadn't completed their homework. I never actually got any memorable reasons, but a lot of 'I didn't have time' or 'I couldn't be bothered'. Is this really a surprise, though? If homework lacks meaning and obvious benefit, why would a student do it (especially the very hard-solving quadratics tasks I may have set them as a secondary maths teacher)? Additionally, let's consider all of the societal expectations we put on students and families. Make sure they do some exercise. Have a wholesome meal sat down with the family. Play an instrument. Got to clubs. Don't go to bed late. And so on. When are we actually expecting students to do homework? Moreover, if we as teachers don't want to be working outside school hours, then why are we expecting students to?

I think I've now reached the happy medium in my teaching career. I do set a weekly homework for all of my groups, but it is short. Many can be done in 15 minutes, and no more. Every task I set has a clear learning outcome. If I'm expecting students to complete a task, then there needs to be a really significant benefit to that, which students need to understand as well. If students know that completing that 10- or 15-minute task will make their next week of lessons easier or will reduce the preparation required for a future assessment, they're more likely to do it. Equally, if they can see the value in a task, they won't begrudge giving up time doing something else to actually do it. This strategy also makes me feel better. If I wouldn't ever complete a pointless task or one where the time taken on the tasks significantly outweighs the benefit, then I shouldn't make students do it. Short sharp homework tasks with a focus ensure that students have a high-quality learning task, where they can see the value and are more motivated to get it done. This also allows me to exude the benefits of homework to students, rather than put them in a lunchtime detention for not doing it (and really, does this even work).

Reduced time, low stakes and high value. That's the way to go with homework!

Homework

By Andrew Hartshorn, Head of Food Preparation & Nutrition, Product Design and Engineering, Finham Park 2, Coventry, England

As Edwin Starr mused … Homework huh what is it good for … ABSOLUTELY NOTHING, or so I have thought for a long long time.

I teach Food and Nutrition, a subject that has had many names: food tech, cooking and home economics. Although the name has changed, the one thing for me that

(Continued)

has not is the issue around homework. Early in my career I can recall spending hours labouring over structured homework tasks to develop my young cooks. Then I would spend a hugely disproportionate time chasing missing homework, contacting home, setting detentions and souring great working relationships forged in a hot, exciting, fast-paced kitchen where they would experience success to then get my hands on the homework. By then it was totally irrelevant, and it had no impact on their learning, which surely is the point of homework, isn't it? Surely the point is doing work outside the classroom helps students learn more. Or is it just to follow school policy?

The homework I did receive was somewhat perfunctory. The majority was folded sheets of paper, some of which was clearly hurriedly copied from a friend. Teaching huge numbers of students would often mean a whole-year group's homework would require marking and hours and hours of my time that then was not spent planning lessons as well as they could have been. This left me asking, is the juice worth the squeeze? Was this 'homework' affecting my future chefs?

Time to think out of the box, so this is what I do now.

Feedback and targets; I know what you are thinking, as you are reading this and you are probably rolling your eyes as I have done so many times during INSET and CPD but hear me out. As we are finishing the 'clean down', I record on my phone a short 1-2-minute video going over what went well (WWWs) and Even better ifs (EBIs). This is uploaded from my phone to that class's Google classroom, and I ask them to respond with a specific area they will focus on next time in the kitchen.

Pre 'reading'. If we are about to cover a theoretical area then I will set an article to read, or video to watch, and ask them to come armed with an idea, a question and a potential disagreement. This can be checked using mini white boards at the beginning of the lesson. This has been invaluable when tackling subjects such as food security/poverty, animal rights and issues around fad diets/food trends.

There are, of course, some caveats to these 'ideas'. First, I do not chase or sanction those students who have not done these homework tasks. I encourage independence and taking pride in their work in the kitchen, and by giving work at home that will help them succeed, I have found homework completion far surpasses the levels other colleagues and I have experienced prior to making these changes. Both these ideas also negate the need for a homework 'extension' and further time and logistical energy being expended chasing homework; the task is relevant to next lesson.

As with all great ideas there are exceptions and flaws, what I think is no exception. For pupils especially at KS4 who are completing work that will contribute to their actual GCSE or revision tasks then this work will require a follow up, contact home. However, by this stage those who have opted for the subject have already bought into the culture established in KS3. Sorry, core subject teachers and primary colleagues, you get them all, but having said that, I will not pretend that all my KS4 students are diligently waiting for a Google classroom announcement.

Sell the sizzle not the sausage: I never refer to it as homework, I ask the students to complete some tasks so they either consolidate or reflect on learning or I ask them to

(Continued)

have a read and a watch of something so we can really get into next lesson. The flipside of the coin is as the teacher you must make sure that the lesson they are coming into was worth preparing for, but since you are no longer chasing homework and calling home you have more time to plan.

Praise: 'catch them being good' used to make me want to fetch up my breakfast; I found it so twee, but it works. The praise is lavished on those who have completed the work even those who have just about made the effort. It is not unusual for me to get extra and exciting ingredients for those who have gone the extra mile.

For example, the type of conversation I have several times a day in many lessons is based on the idea of 'praise loudly, chastise quietly'.

'Declan, Jasleen, Henry, Nathan come to my prep area. I loved your ideas around food security and over fishing, were making pasta today ready to go with the salmon and I was wondering if you wanted to use some of this saffron powder, more expensive than gold per gram... well done again chefs'

'Charlotte, such a shame you didn't look at the video on emulsification I think it would have helped today and made all those new terms seem a little less overwhelming, is everything alright? next time if you any issues with anything I set come knock on the kitchen door I'm sure we can get it sorted'

I realise I present an oversimplified view and I have ignored concepts and research that would undoubtedly poo poo what works for me, but that is the point it works; for me it might work; for you, got to be worth a punt?

Home Learning

By Susan Strachan, Leader of English at St Bernadette Catholic Secondary School, Bristol, England

How did we go from no home learning to a 96% success rate in English?

Five years ago, I was appointed Head of English and Drama at my school. One of the first things I undertook was a SWOT analysis, and one of the biggest concerns that came out from every member of the team was the lack of homework. Nothing so far had stuck! Show my homework didn't work, and Bedrock vocabulary didn't work. Essentially, students didn't buy into doing home learning. They couldn't see the purpose of it and didn't value it.

As a team we set about with a mission to change this.

What were the logistics?

We set up through Google Classrooms the sharing of home learning; we gave every student an orange home learning book; we gave students a plastic wallet to keep the home learning book clean and valued; we tracked and recorded every piece of home learning completed or not completed individually as teachers. I set up and ran detentions on a Thursday for non-completion, as head of department, so that no individual

(Continued)

teacher had to use their own time to set these detentions. They were recorded on a Google sheet in advance of the detention. We contacted home via text message and let home know that we follow up on the non-completion of home learning. As a team, we were relentlessly consistent in our high expectations of what the students do at home. We rebranded homework to home learning and we explicitly explained the reasons for this. We reiterated that learning doesn't stop when you leave the school building. We set out to change the non-completion culture.

What did we expect from the students for home learning?

We focused on a three-tiered approach: consolidation, reading and writing all of which was linked to current or prior learning in the class. We set up tasks that would support students in improving these skills.

Over the five years that we have been setting home learning, we have streamlined this approach and now have a slightly different three-tiered approach:

Week 1: Reading with a Google Quiz. This is self-marking which eases workload as it collects the email address of the student so we can track them having completed this. We can also quickly address misconceptions in lessons.

Week 2: Writing task with a WWW and EBI marking criteria that we feedback with in Key Stage 3. This means that students know we have read their work and the WWW and EBI are linked to the writing assessment foci.

Week 3: Carousel learning quiz that directly links to knowledge organisers and knowledge tests set as part of the school assessment policy.

We have systematically and rigorously focused on students understanding why we set home learning, why we value home learning and why we want them to be successful independently.

Why 96% completion?

The tracking I have completed consistently shows that we have a 96% success rate. That wasn't me. That was the strength of our whole team approach.

Homework

By David Goodwin, Assistant Principal, Author and Illustrator of Educational Ideas, Grimsby, England

To many students and teachers, homework is Marmite; you either recognise its worth or don't. Surveys about home learning indicate students and teachers don't think the time and energy invested are worth the pay-out. But there is overwhelming evidence pointing to the many advantages of homework. Regular homework has been shown to improve students' performance in exams, and the EEF says home learning can add over five months to students' attainment with low-cost implications. Schools' policies and how they implement homework might explain these conflicting findings. With this in

(Continued)

mind, here are some practical strategies to support teachers and leaders in effectively implementing home learning.

The first step is to consider the means of participation. If the homework requires students to use the internet or software they don't have access to, it will be ineffective. If students live in a home with multiple siblings and only have access to one computer, it is unfair to expect them to complete computer-based homework. So whilst websites like Seneca and Carousel are powerful home learning resources, it pays to check your students can access them. You will need to provide them with printed resources if they don't.

Your next consideration should be the level of challenge. Tasks which require students to engage in new and unfamiliar content are likely to be too challenging and cause students to give up. I am not suggesting you should lower your standards or expectations. But homework that connects with what your students are learning in your classroom, and the curriculum, is likely to yield better results. Therefore, resist setting homework that covers unfamiliar content. Without you there to explain, model and check for understanding, students will become overwhelmed and give up.

When setting homework, consider what you want your students to achieve and communicate this to them. Invest time in modelling how to complete the work and provide students with exemplar material. Resist the temptation to use gimmicks to make homework more engaging. Students are likely to enjoy making a rainforest model, but the chances are students will recall more the construction of the model and not what you intended for them to learn.

It seems reasonable to suggest that to overcome the barriers to homework, the solution is to keep it simple. Setting knowledge retrieval activities will reduce teacher workload, help students consolidate their learning and connect with what is happening in the classroom. Also, many retrieval activities are easily self- and peer assessed, reducing teacher marking and boosting student independence.

Many schools now use knowledge organisers and quizzing to support retrieval practice. Using these as homework activities and resources will give students an extra dose of knowledge retrieval. Such activities are low stakes and don't require students to spend hours trying to complete confusing homework, giving them more time to enjoy their hobbies and family life.

PHIL - Homework

By Philip Van Mellaerts, PGCE student, Chelmsford, England

As a parent to two young sons, homework from a primary school is an unnecessary addition to their day. Even discounting the inherent upheaval in their lives caused by the ongoing pandemic, the idea of giving children as young as four additional work to complete at home is anathema to me. Children spend a large amount of their waking hours in an educational setting, being taught and assessed, so to then impress further

(Continued)

work on them when they get home seems excessive. When in their day are they allowed to be children? When do they get to play for the sake of playing? When are they encouraged to develop interests that will round out their personalities? I am sure that I am not the only parent that sees the value in extracurricular activities, such as sports and the arts, and for me those additional endeavours are far more likely to benefit them as young people growing up than projects or tasks that extend their school day into their own homes. Further to this is the stress and conflict that can be caused by enforcing repetitive educational tasks on young children in an environment that is often time-poor without the resources and expertise encompassed within a primary classroom.

That is not to say that there is no place at all for children to continue their learning outside of school. There will inevitably be cases where further interventions are required with pupils to further scaffold their learning and deepen their understanding, especially if they are struggling in class. This can be supported by engaged parents either within the home or through extracurricular activities and clubs. However, should a child be identified as SEND, then there will inevitably be specific challenges that are more likely to create stress and conflict which could lead to damaging health or self-esteem owing to either inappropriate homework or an approach at home inconsistent with that taken at school.

I believe that a school's philosophy can help drive the difference in this area. A school that instils an attitude of inquisitiveness and encouragement necessarily dictates that learning does not begin or end at the classroom door. My own children love reading for pleasure – indeed, they have each set themselves targets on how many books they will read throughout this year – thereby developing their learning, through increased vocabulary, for example, and constantly test each other on their times tables whilst eating dinner. This attitude has been impressed upon them by their teachers (and parents, obviously) who have instilled a sense of curiosity and desire to learn, rather than setting rote tasks or worksheets to extend their school day. A joined-up approach between a school and parents that is collaborative and supportive and that identifies any specific needs is, I think, far more important than setting homework for a whole class beyond an expectation that children read and engage with their home and extracurricular environments.

Homework – Where the Heart Takes Over

By Mike McGrother, Teacher and Community Engineer, Stockton on Tees, England

I am a firm believer in ensuring that I can win over hearts and minds when setting homework. I work within the independent sector, and, as an associate tutor, I am often 'counselling' younger pupils who struggle to cope with the demands of a heavy homework timetable coupled with extracurricular sports and arts activities as well as, for many, not a short travelling burden to get to and from school.

(Continued)

> I always try to ensure that homework is linked to that 'place' of home in that it can be an opportunity for the learner to apply a concept, a skill or a process within a different context to that of the classroom. It could be that I ask the pupil to carry out an activity with their siblings, parents or guardians. Equally, it could be that I directly request the input of others in the household. At times, I ask the pupil to become the teacher – testing their confidence in a subject in order to be able to communicate it to others. In all cases, the change in dynamic, context and connection with the learning will undoubtedly change the process and reinforce or, perhaps better, *challenge* the understanding of the core pupil. It can have the advantage of removing peer pressures and everyday classroom dynamics standing in the way of the learner being feeling confident and contributes to my assertion that learning happens everywhere – if we allow it to.
>
> As a recent example – in order to reinforce and realise concepts of musical diversity and history, I have recently asked my 1st year senior school pupils to talk to parents and grandparents and attempt to chart their family ancestry. The topic – 'Our Musical Inheritance' – began in the classroom as we explored our individual and collective diversity across six groups. The homework task will enable them to continue to reflect on their 'musical inheritance' as pupils map the lives of their family or community and note and research consequent musical influences that will have been experienced.
>
> Taking the notion that we inherit physical attributes and personality traits into the realm of musicality, the pupils can then consider how their own musical tastes or abilities may have been inherited by the nurturing environment of their own family and that of previous generations. They will return their work in the format they want to – with credit given to creative presentation techniques. I have already had suggestions of edited video clips, board games, Tik Tok-style musical edits and song recordings.
>
> The process ensures that 'concepts' of musical diversity and history – often delivered in dry and textual formats – can become real and relevant for all, even the most reluctant musician. Music is within the heartbeat of all of us, and home is where that heartbeat can often be heard the clearest and loudest!

Conclusion

- Teachers are key in helping to engage parents and carers in a child's learning journey.
- Homework needs to have purpose, be relevant and be assessed to make it worthwhile.

References

Cooper, H. (2007). *The Battle Over Homework*. Thousand Oaks, CA: Sage.
EEF (Education Endowment Fund). (2021). *Homework*. [Online]. Available at: https://educationendowmentfoundation.org.uk/education-evidence/teaching-learning-toolkit/homework
HM Government. (1998). *Homework: what parents need to know*. [Online]. Available at: https://webarchive.nationalarchives.gov.uk/ukgwa/20121003010131/http://www.direct.gov.uk/en/Parents/Schoolslearninganddevelopment/SchoolLife/DG_179508
Merttens, R., and Newland, A. (1996). 'Home works: Shared maths and shared writing'. In J. Bastiani and S. Wolfendale (Eds.), *Home-School Work in Britain* (pp. 106-117). London: David Fulton Publishers.
Porter, L. (2014). *Behaviour in Schools*. 3rd edn. Maidenhead: Open University Press.

Index

ABC of behaviour intervention (Skinner) 17
ability grouping 5
action research 90, 95, 192-209, 214, 218
assessment for learning 92-93
Atkinson, Dennis 126
'Attuned school' approach to behaviour management 24, 246
Autism and sensory profiles 24-26
autonomy 192, 193, 197

Bastide, Derek 55
Behaviour management 13-14, 17-18, 21
Bell Foundation 63-64
Blaylock, Lat 55
book corner 7
Bourdieu, Pierre 124
Britzman, Deborah 126

career progression 174-177
career-long professional learning 173
carpet time 15
Clarke, Shirley 103-104
coaching 177-178
collaboration 193, 202, 246-247, 251
continuing professional development (CPD) 152, 173, 256, 301
COVID-19 245-258
creativity 153

Danielewicz, Jane 126
decolonisation of the curriculum 141
Dewey, John 136, 193
digital competence 255
discipline 14, 16, 19; (self) discipline 194

displays 3, 5, 8, 11
doctoral studies/doctorate 123, 185-185
dog 282, 283
Dweck, Carol 95

EAL (English as Additional Language) 64
early career teacher 174-175, 177-178
educational psychologist 184-185
ethical considerations (action research) 192-193, 201, 206-207
European Convention on Human Rights 135

feedback 101-102; peer feedback 103, 106-107, 253, 255
fluency in reading 64-65
formative assessment 89-109
Fundamental British Values 134-138
further study 169-189

GTCE (General Teaching Council for England) 60
Grouping 4, 5-6

handover 4-5
Hass, Glen 60
History curriculum and representation 144-145, 156
HLTA (Higher Level Teaching Assistant) 119, 123, 175
Hobbes, Thomas 138
home learning 112, 246, 249
home-school partnerships 112, 245, 246, 252, 253
hooks, bell 58

inclusion 10-11, 81, 231, 261

Kohn, Alfie 23

Index

leadership 273, 283
lecturing 186-187

Macpherson Report 144
Manent, Pierre 135
marking 99-101, 175, 280, 284, 289, 299, 301, 303-304
Masters 168, 180-182, 183-184
maths anxiety 81-87
mentoring 188
Montessori, Maria 62-63
motivation 181, 183, 186-187, 189
Moyles, Janet 16
multicultural Britain and diversity 144, 238, 241

NALDIC 64
National Literacy Strategy (1998) 122
National Numeracy Strategy (1999) 123
National Professional Qualifications (NPQs) 169, 178
National Workload Agreement (2003) 123

Ofsted 115, 118, 234, 284
open questioning 97

parent partnership/relationship 49-52, 111-121, 245-258
parent view (maths anxiety) 85-86
parental engagement 49-52, 111-121, 294-297
parental involvement 49-52, 111-121, 208-209, 213-215, 294-297
passion 4, 38-39, 48, 155-156, 160, 169-171, 175, 189, 291
pedagogical content knowledge 54-80, 122-129, 132
pedagogical identity 17, 126-127
pedagogy informed planning 29-53
peer assessment/evaluation 102-103, 106
peer talk 96
PGCert (SENCo) 182
planning 29-53
planning and adaptive teaching 31, 34, 44
planning and assessment and data 31-32, 36, 43
planning and resources 31, 34, 43-44
planning and the plenary 34-36
planning and the teaching of writing 33-35, 42-43, 46-47
planning and time spent doing so 32
planning for bilingual learners 42-43

planning for children with SEND 44, 52
planning for neurodiversity 47-48
planning for transitions 49
planning for a Welsh curriculum 44-45
planning through play 46, 50-51
play, importance of 46, 50-51
Plowden Report (CACE 1967) 123
Pollard, Andrew 19, 54-55, 58-59, 129
possible (possibility) thinking 6
postgraduate diplomas/certificates 181
power dynamics in behaviour management 14-16
practical action research 192-218
PRESSED acronym for behaviour management 17-21
primary religious education resources 57
primary science resources 71-72
professional development/training 168-190
professional learning community 195-196, 204-205
pupil conferencing 106-107
pupil involvement (in assessment) 92-93, 97-98, 102-103, 106-107
pupil mentor scheme 148
pupil voice 145-148

questioning (in assessment) 94-99

reading 7, 9, 65-67
reading fluency 65-66
reflection 173-174
resources 3-6, 8-9
Rosen, Michael 61-62
Rosenshine, Barak 58
Royal Borough of Greenwich Agreed Syllabus for religious education 57
Rumsfeld, Donald 57

SACRE (Standing Advisory Council on Religious Education) 57
Schiller, Christian 139
Schön, Donald 129
school councils 137, 145-146
Schwab, Joseph 55
SCITT action research 204-206
seating 5
self-assessment 92-94, 99, 102-103, 106
self-knowledge 77-78
self-study action research 193, 200, 206
SEND Code of Practice 64

Sendak, Maurice 65
Shulman, Lee 57-59
Smart, Ninian 55
SMSC (Spiritual, Moral, Social and Cultural development) 134
spectrum of behaviour management 14
Spielman, Amanda 136
stories 7
student view (maths anxiety) 86
subject knowledge and computing 73-76
subject knowledge and English as an additional language 63-64
subject knowledge and mathematics 69-70
subject knowledge and pedagogy 58, 61-63
subject knowledge and religious education 55-59
subject knowledge and science 70-73
subject knowledge and technology 73-75
subject knowledge and vocabulary 66-69
subject lead 39, 58, 180
success criteria 103-105, 107
summative assessment 108
Sweller, John 58

Tanner, Daniel 60
Tanner, Laurel 60
teacher feedback 89-97, 99-102, 107
Teachers' Standards 254
teaching assistants and audit of skills 127-128
teaching assistants and autonomy 129, 131
teaching assistants and behaviour management 124-125, 130

teaching assistants and communication 126-127, 130, 132
teaching assistants and constructing a relationship 123-126, 129
teaching assistants and deployment of 124-127, 129
teaching assistants and hierarchy 124-125
teaching assistants and identity of teachers 126
teaching assistants and 'issues' with teachers 128-129
Teaching Assistants and HMI (2002) Report 123
teaching assistants and pedagogy 123-124, 126-129, 132-133
teaching fellow 187
technical action research 196
technology 6, 73-75, 116, 161-162, 171, 180, 252-256
training teachers (lecturing, mentoring) 186-189
transformative/transformational learning 195
Turing, Alan 137

UNICEF 145

verbal feedback 90, 100-101
Vincent, James 56
Vygotsky, Lev 58, 162, 242

Wellcome: State of the nation' report of UK primary science education 70
'with-it-ness' and behaviour management (Kounin) 19
working memory (maths anxiety) 83
written feedback 99-101